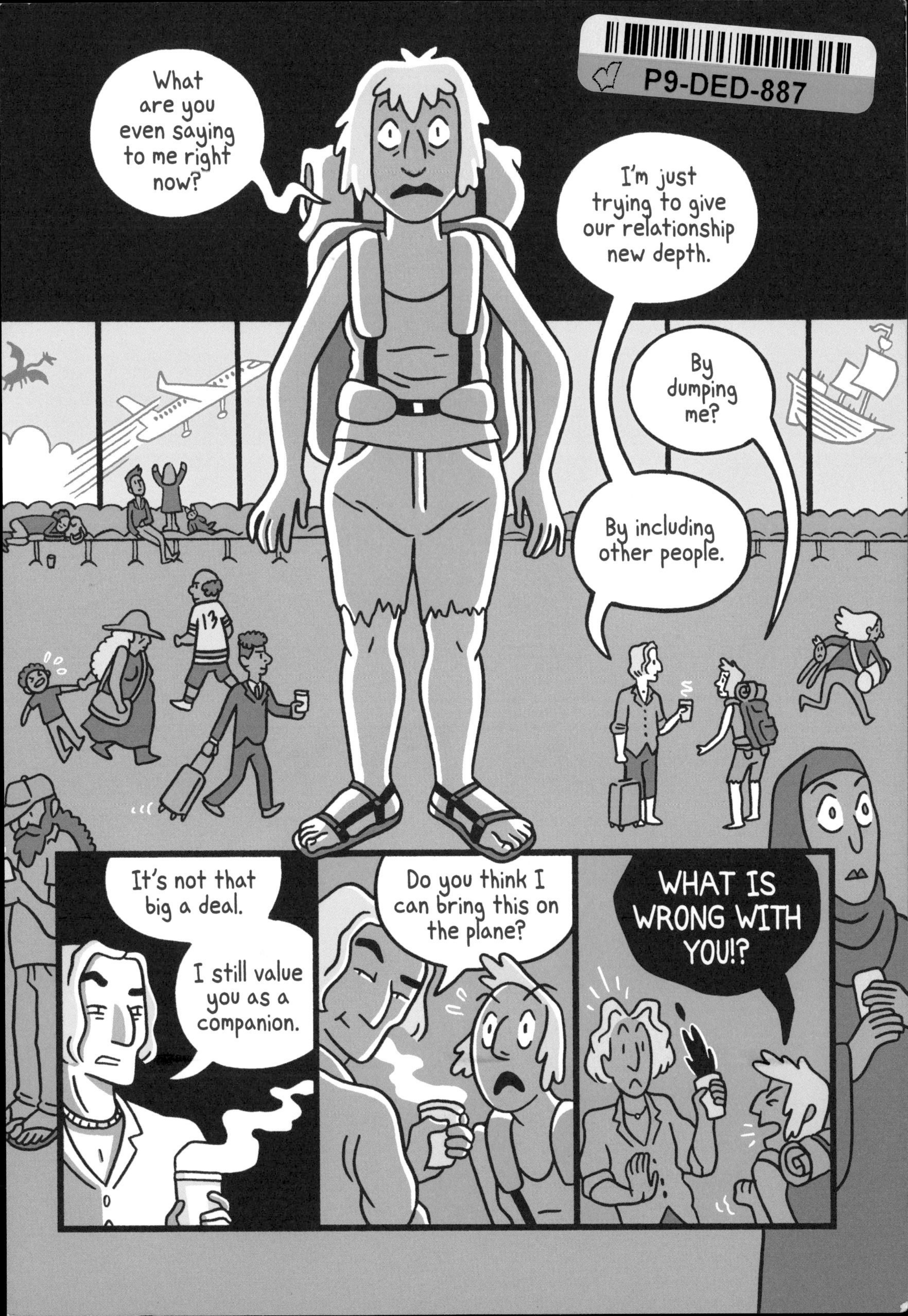
What are you even saying to me right now?
I'm just trying to give our relationship new depth.
By dumping me?
By including other people.
13
It's not that big a deal.
I still value you as a companion.
Do you think I can bring this on the plane?
WHAT IS WRONG WITH YOU!?

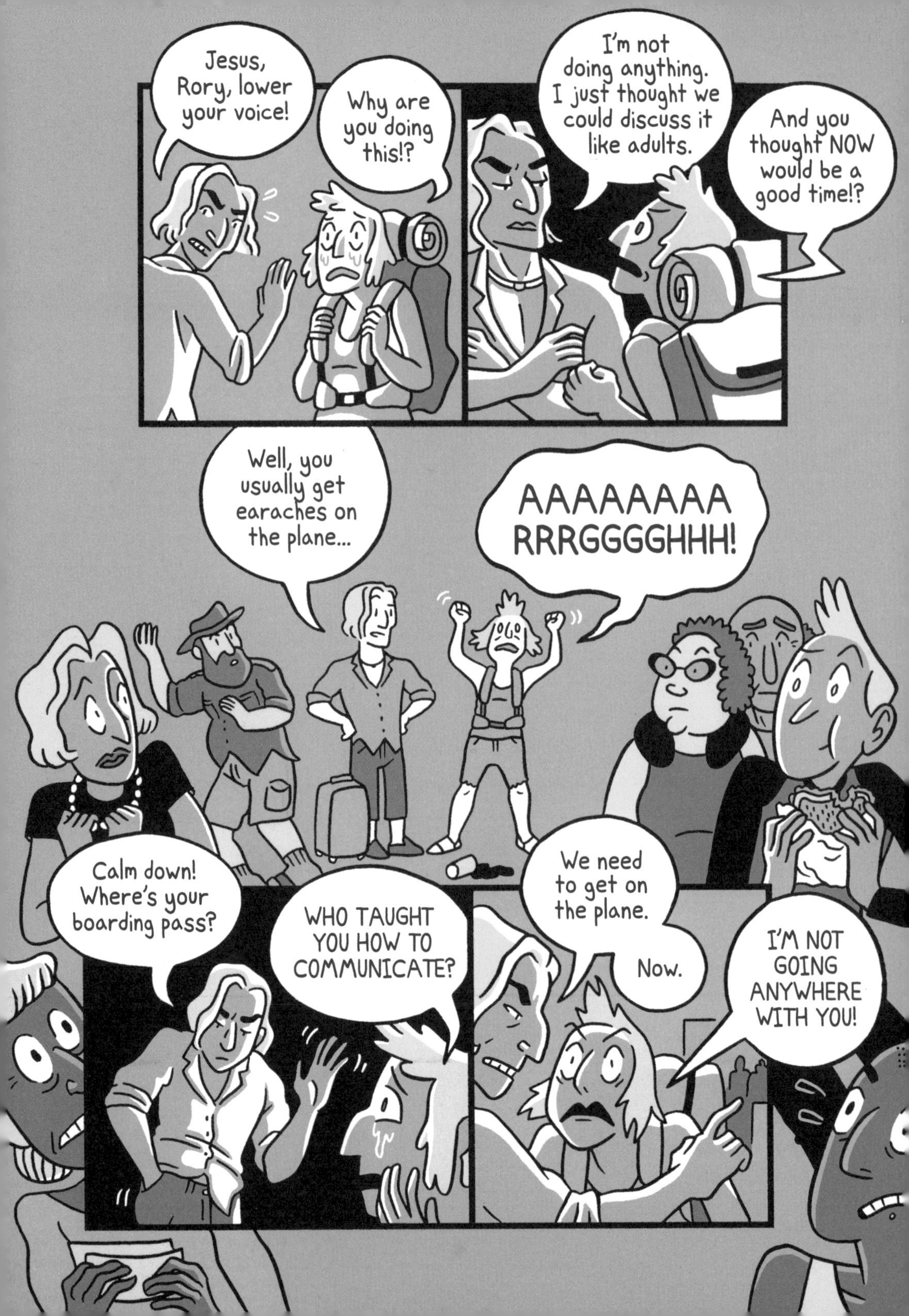
Jesus, Rory, lower your voice!
Why are you doing this!?
I'm not doing anything. I just thought we could discuss it like adults.
And you thought NOW would be a good time!?
Well, you usually get earaches on the plane...
AAAAAAAA RRRGGGGHHH!
Calm down! Where's your boarding pass?
WHO TAUGHT YOU HOW TO COMMUNICATE?
We need to get on the plane.
Now.
I'M NOT GOING ANYWHERE WITH YOU!

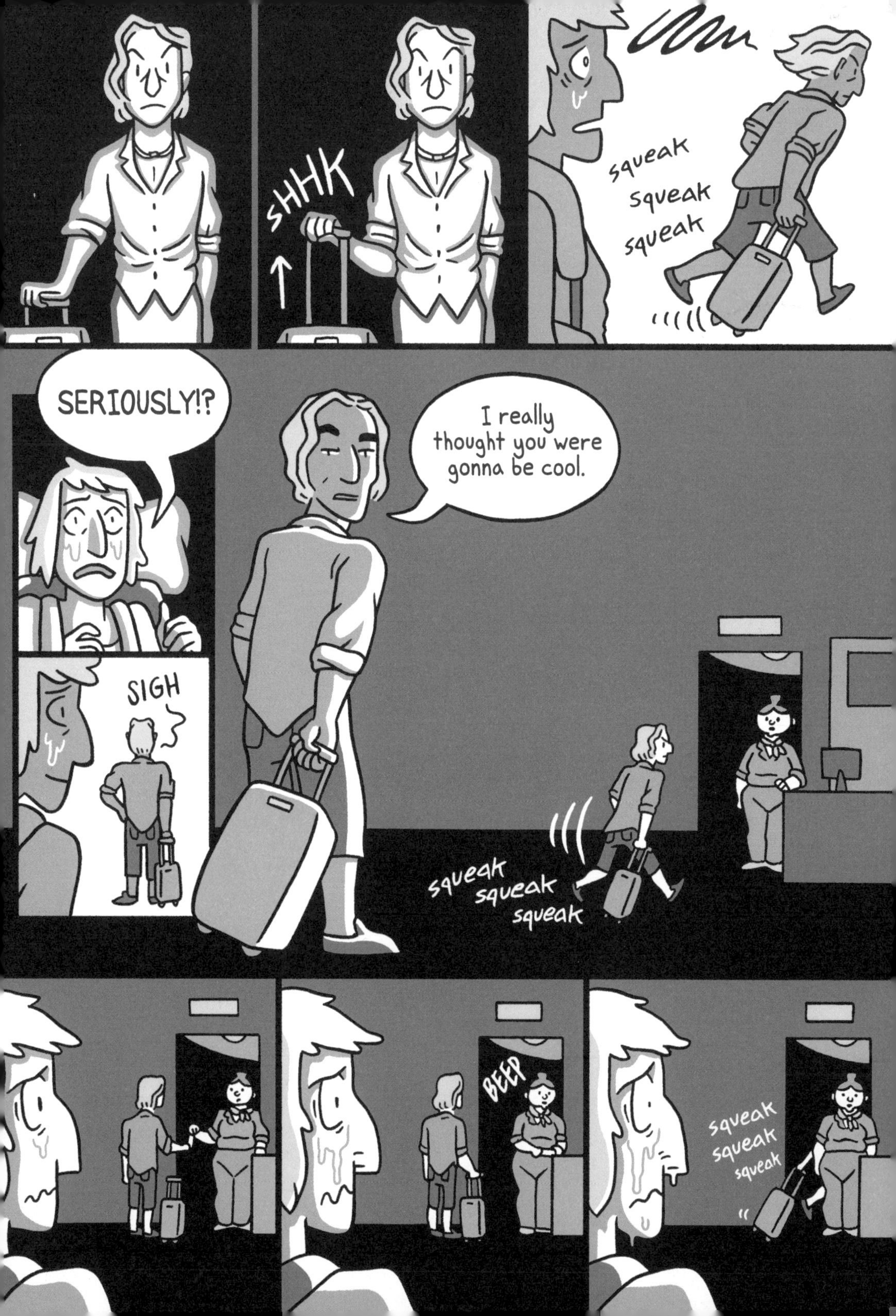

SHHK
squeak
squeak
squeak
SERIOUSLY!?
I really thought you were gonna be cool.
SIGH
squeak
squeak
squeak
BEEP
squeak
squeak
squeak

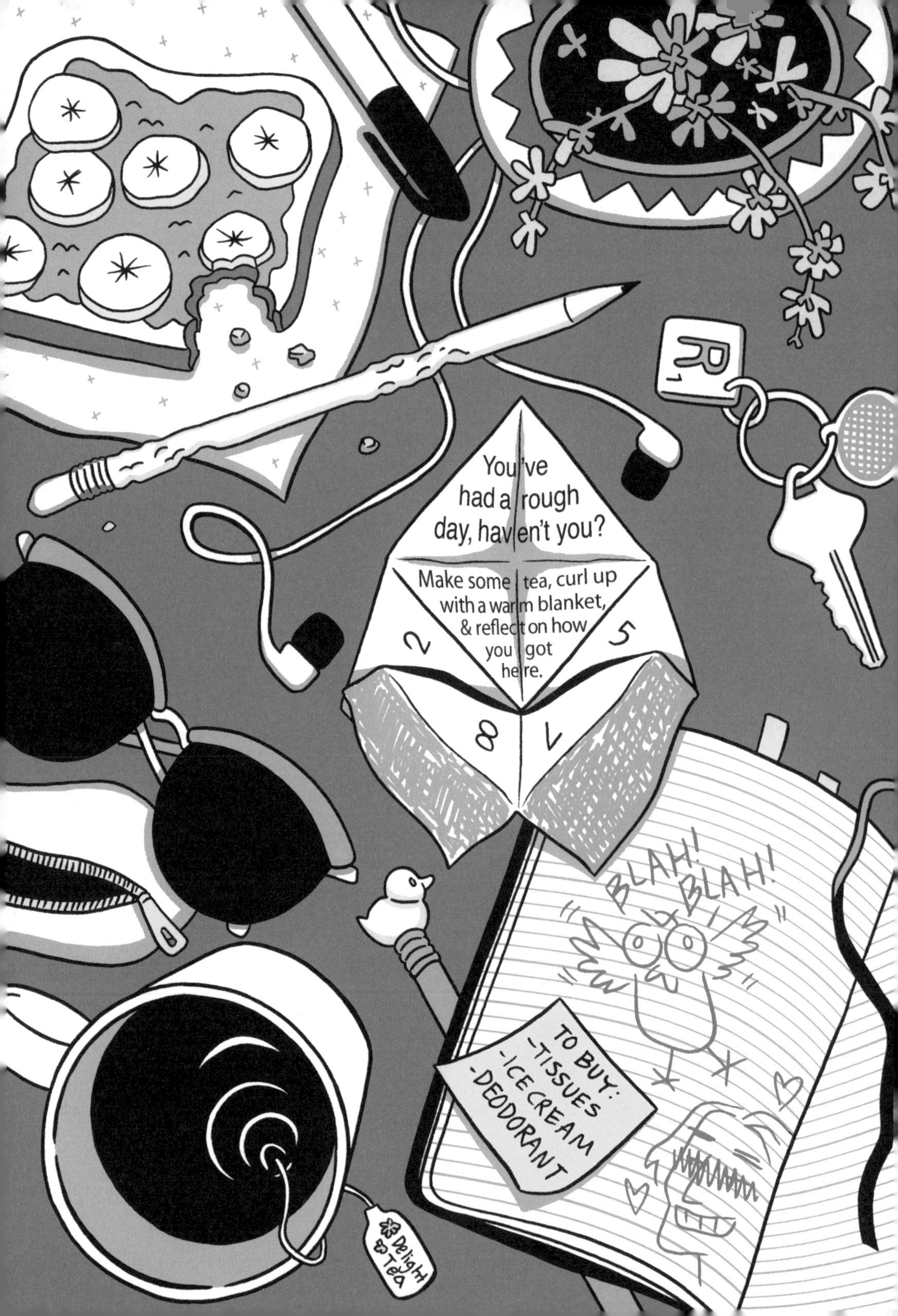

You've had a rough day, haven't you?
Make some tea, curl up with a warm blanket, & reflect on how you got here.
2
5
8
7
R
BLAH! BLAH!
TO BUY:
-TISSUES
-ICE CREAM
-DEODORANT
Delight Tea

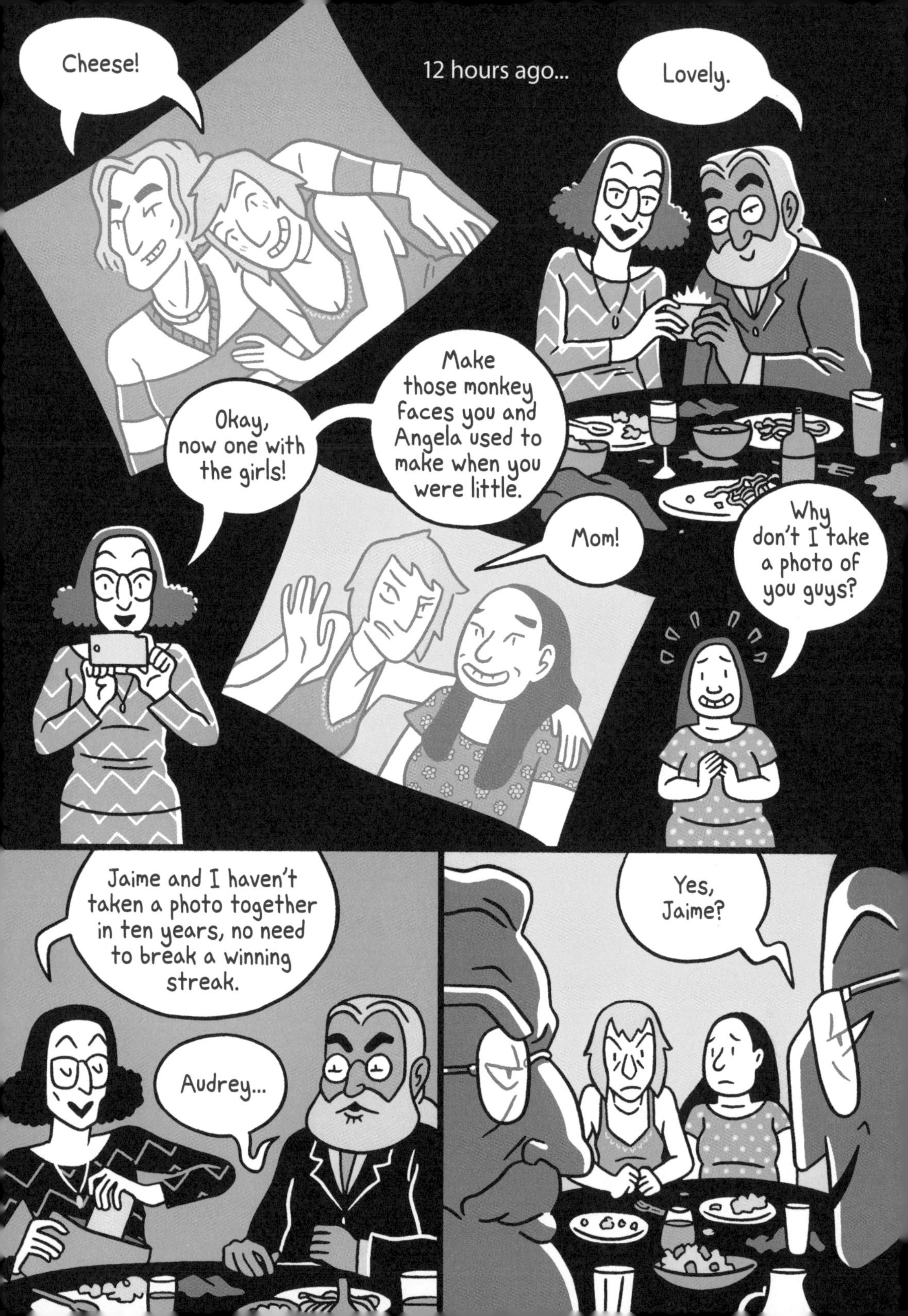
Cheese!
12 hours ago...
Lovely.
Okay, now one with the girls!
Make those monkey faces you and Angela used to make when you were little.
Mom!
Why don't I take a photo of you guys?
Jaime and I haven't taken a photo together in ten years, no need to break a winning streak.
Audrey...
Yes, Jaime?

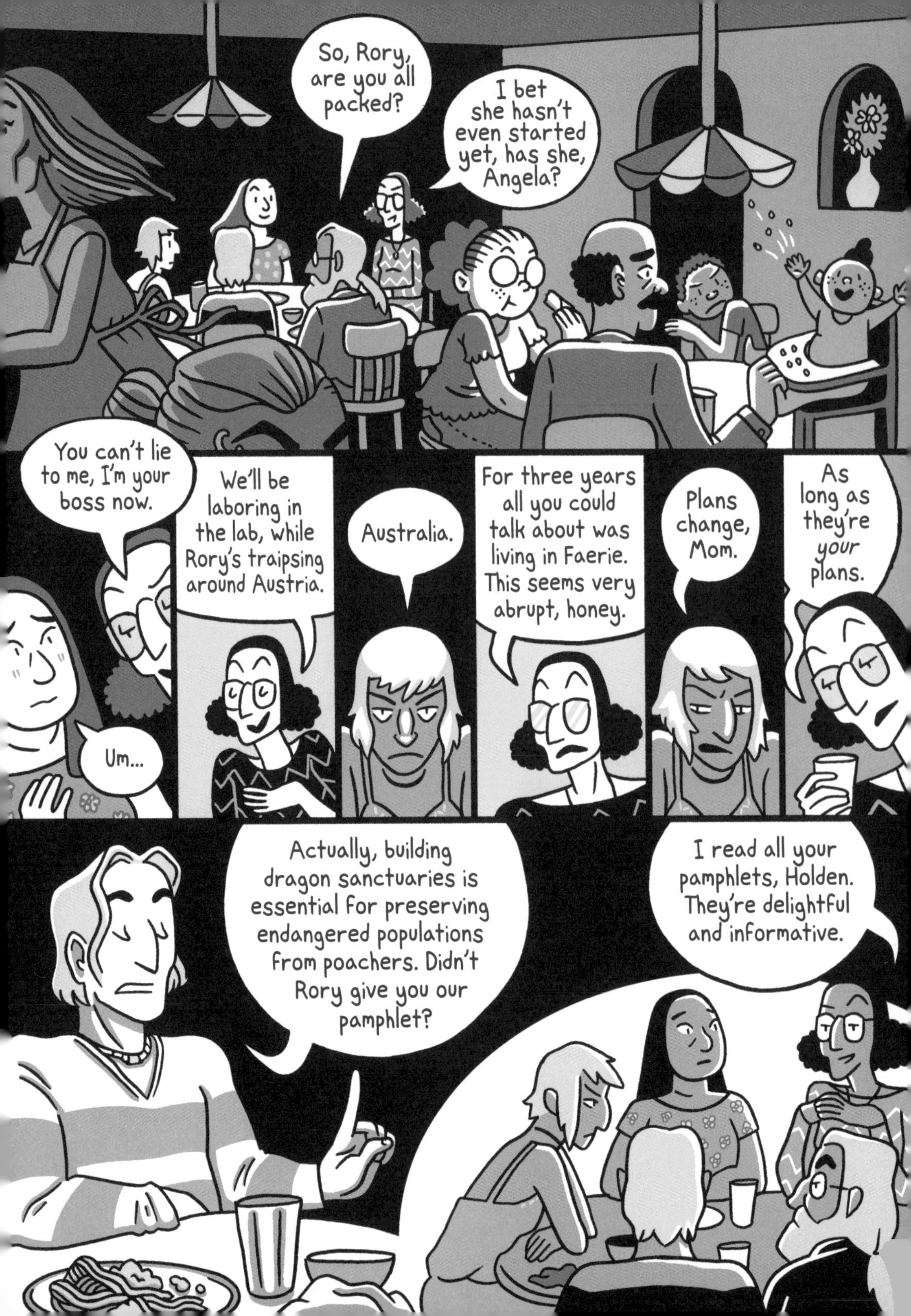
So, Rory, are you all packed?
I bet she hasn't even started yet, has she, Angela?
You can't lie to me, I'm your boss now.
Um...
We'll be laboring in the lab, while Rory's traipsing around Austria.
Australia.
For three years all you could talk about was living in Faerie. This seems very abrupt, honey.
Plans change, Mom.
As long as they're *your* plans.
Actually, building dragon sanctuaries is essential for preserving endangered populations from poachers. Didn't Rory give you our pamphlet?
I read all your pamphlets, Holden. They're delightful and informative.

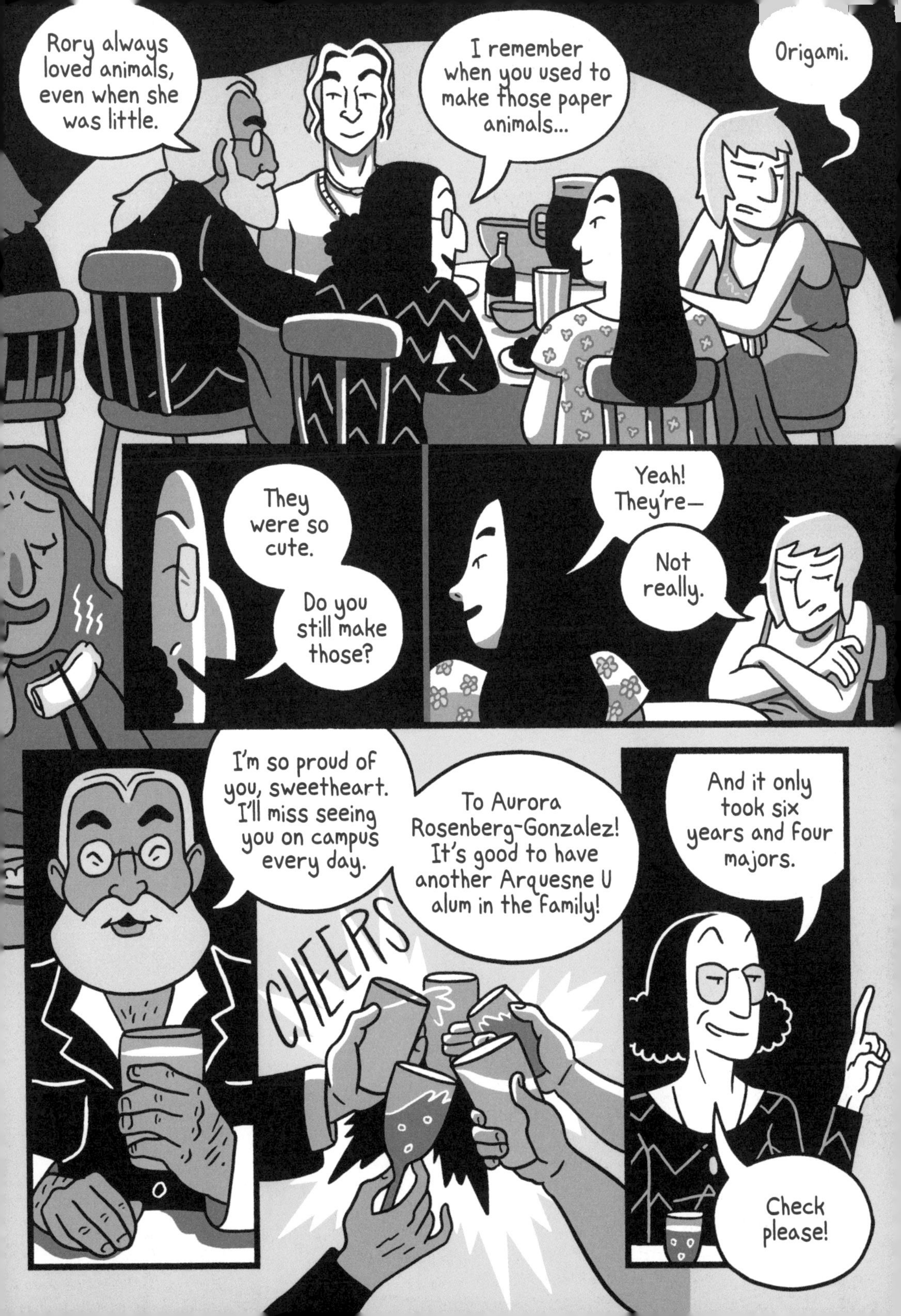

Rory always loved animals, even when she was little.
I remember when you used to make those paper animals...
Origami.
They were so cute.
Do you still make those?
Yeah! They're—
Not really.
I'm so proud of you, sweetheart. I'll miss seeing you on campus every day.
To Aurora Rosenberg-Gonzalez! It's good to have another Arquesne U alum in the family!
CHEERS
And it only took six years and four majors.
Check please!

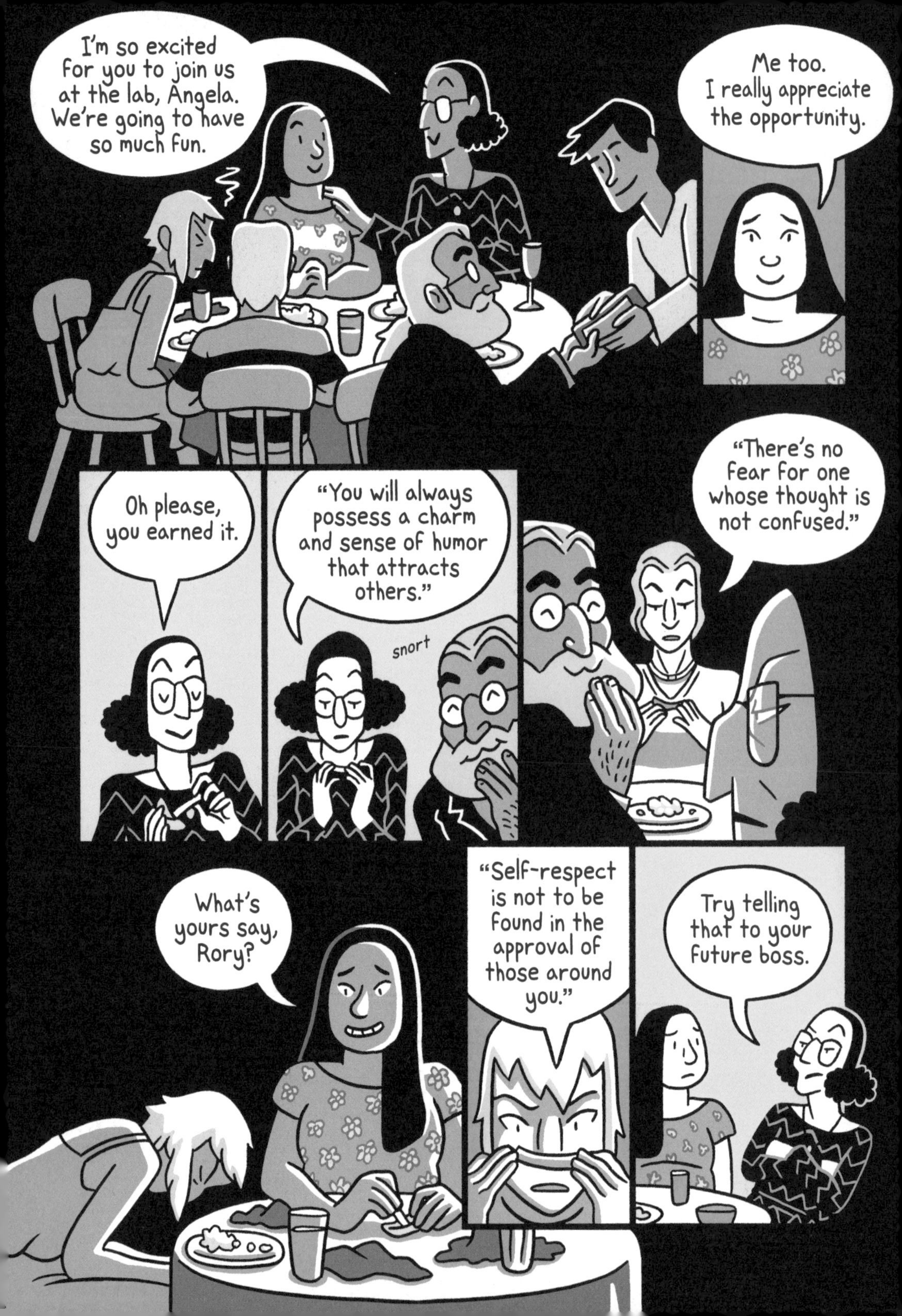
I'm so excited for you to join us at the lab, Angela. We're going to have so much fun.
Me too. I really appreciate the opportunity.
Oh please, you earned it.
"You will always possess a charm and sense of humor that attracts others."
snort
"There's no fear for one whose thought is not confused."
What's yours say, Rory?
"Self-respect is not to be found in the approval of those around you."
Try telling that to your future boss.

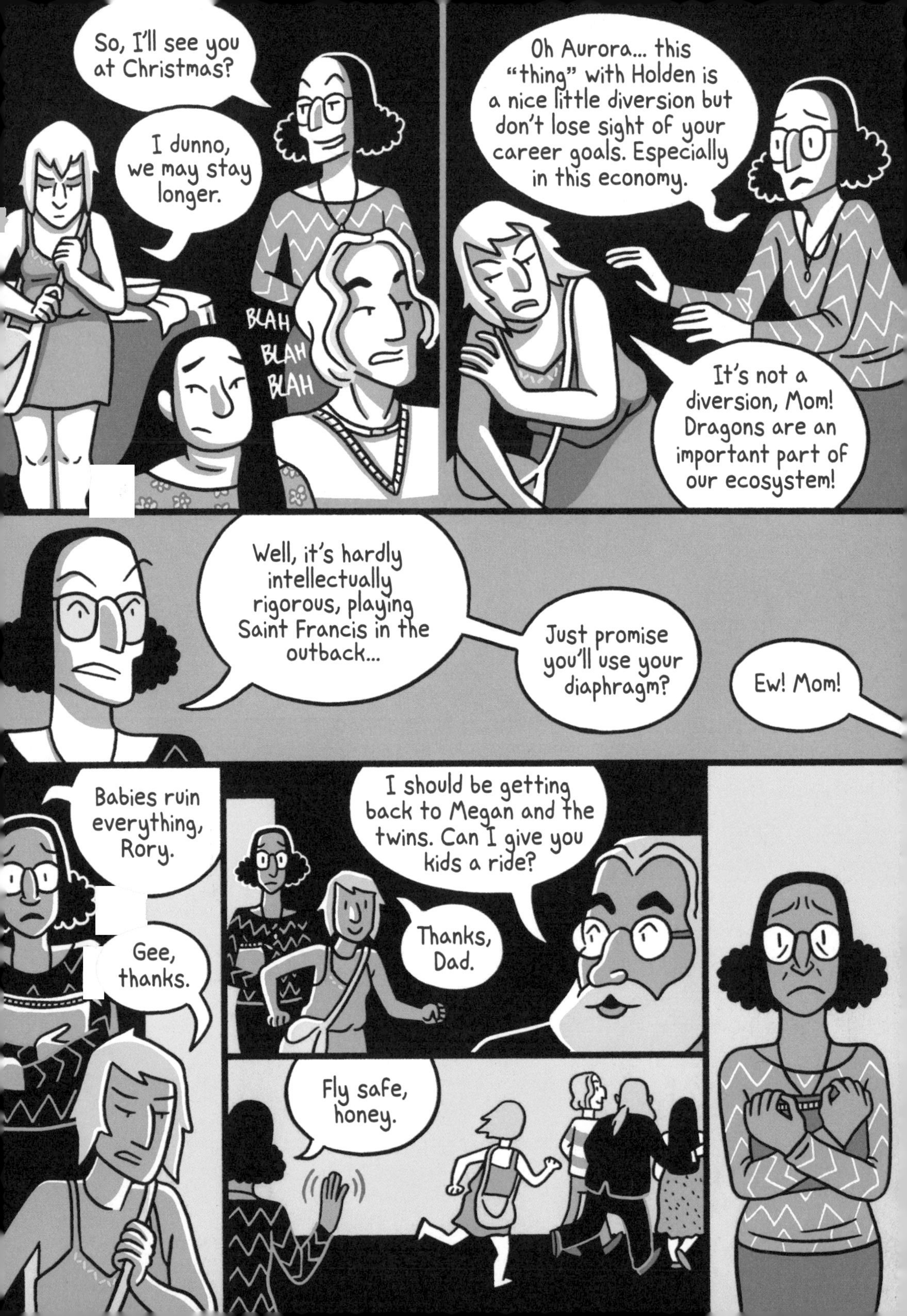
So, I'll see you at Christmas?
I dunno, we may stay longer.
BLAH BLAH BLAH
Oh Aurora... this "thing" with Holden is a nice little diversion but don't lose sight of your career goals. Especially in this economy.
It's not a diversion, Mom! Dragons are an important part of our ecosystem!
Well, it's hardly intellectually rigorous, playing Saint Francis in the outback...
Just promise you'll use your diaphragm?
Ew! Mom!
Babies ruin everything, Rory.
Gee, thanks.
I should be getting back to Megan and the twins. Can I give you kids a ride?
Thanks, Dad.
Fly safe, honey.

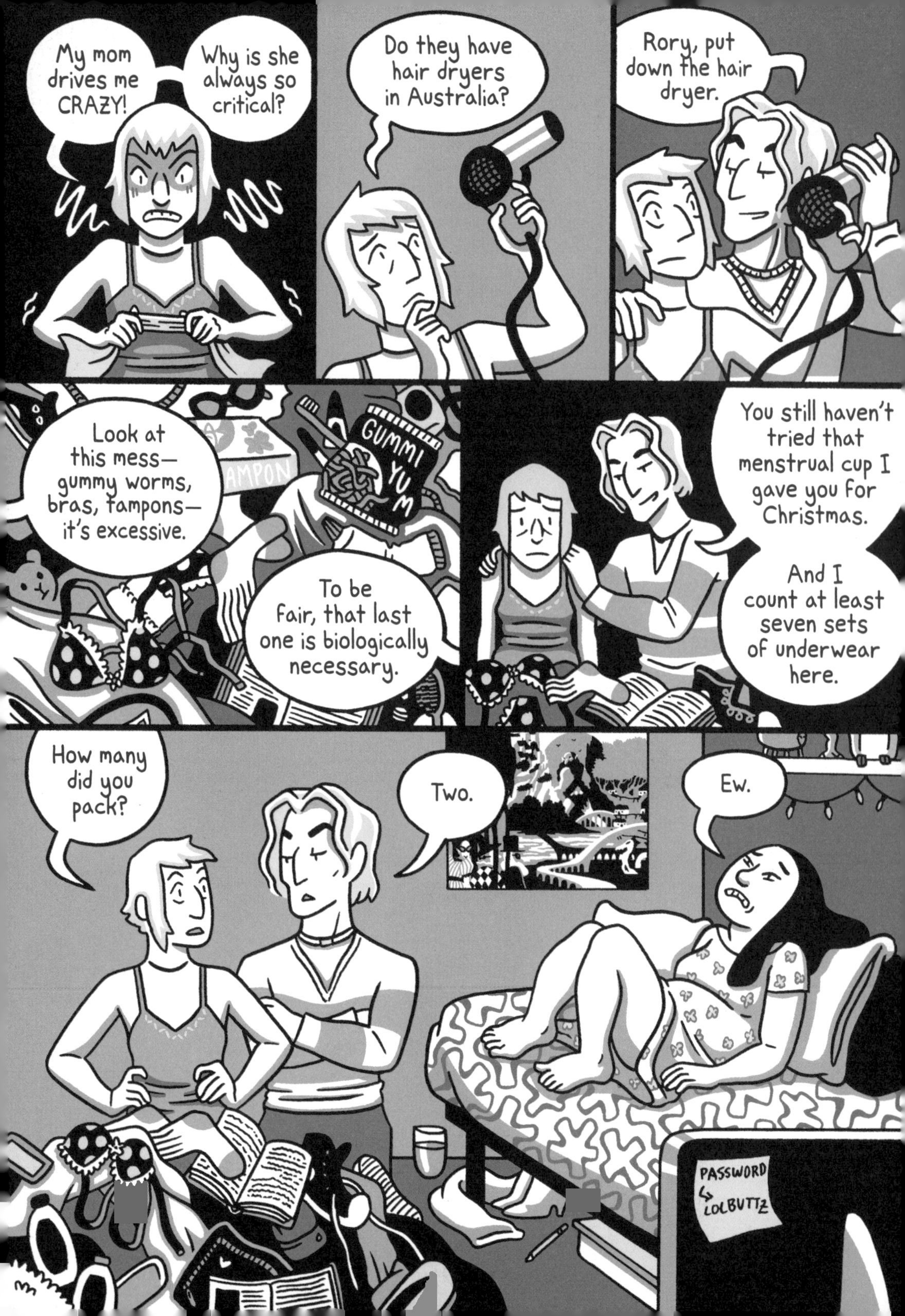

My mom drives me CRAZY!
Why is she always so critical?
Do they have hair dryers in Australia?
Rory, put down the hair dryer.
GUMMI YUM
AMPON
Look at this mess— gummy worms, bras, tampons— it's excessive.
To be fair, that last one is biologically necessary.
You still haven't tried that menstrual cup I gave you for Christmas.
And I count at least seven sets of underwear here.
How many did you pack?
Two.
Ew.
PASSWORD ↳ LOLBUTTZ

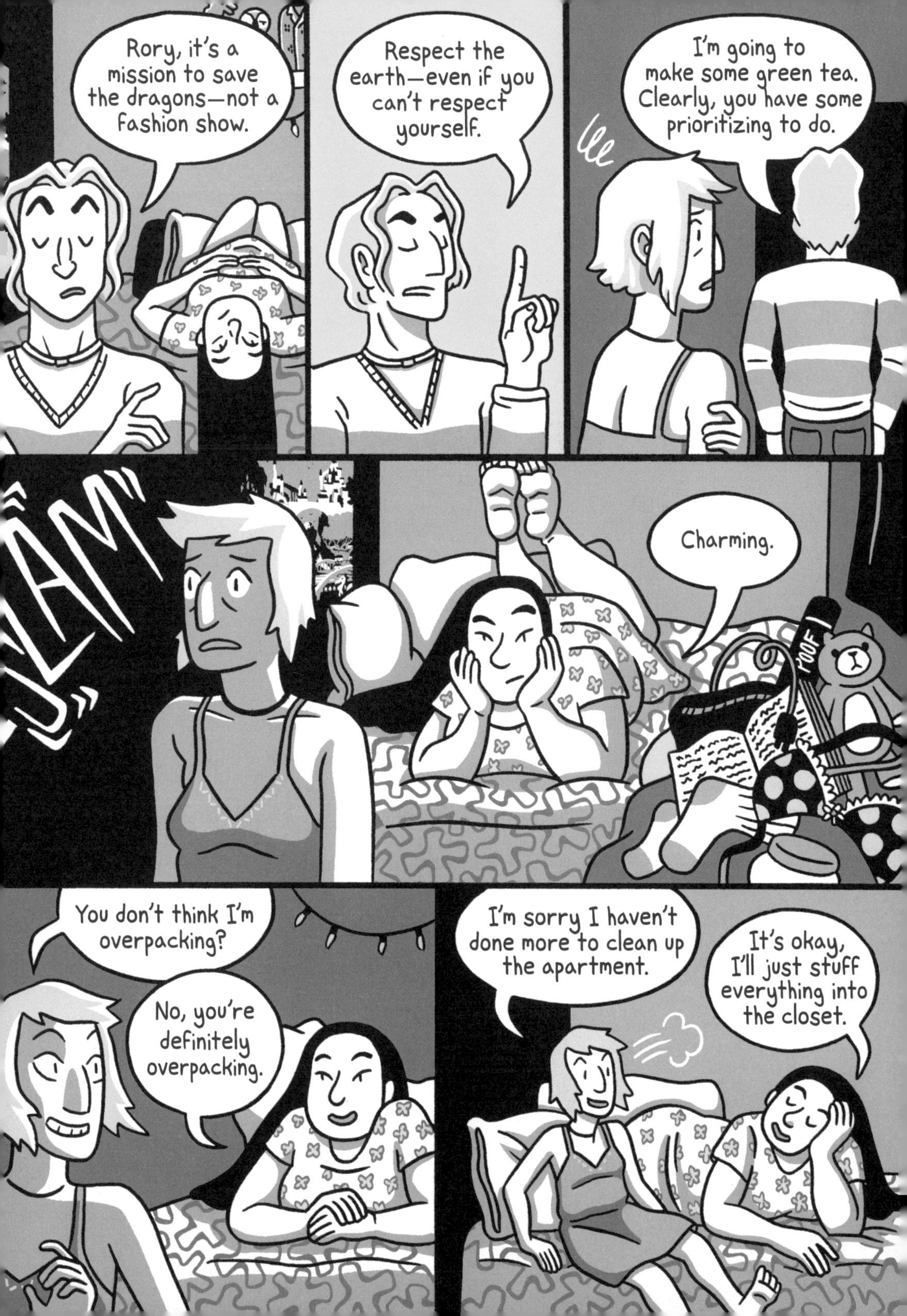
Rory, it's a mission to save the dragons—not a fashion show.
Respect the earth—even if you can't respect yourself.
I'm going to make some green tea. Clearly, you have some prioritizing to do.
SLAM
Charming.
POOF
You don't think I'm overpacking?
No, you're definitely overpacking.
I'm sorry I haven't done more to clean up the apartment.
It's okay, I'll just stuff everything into the closet.

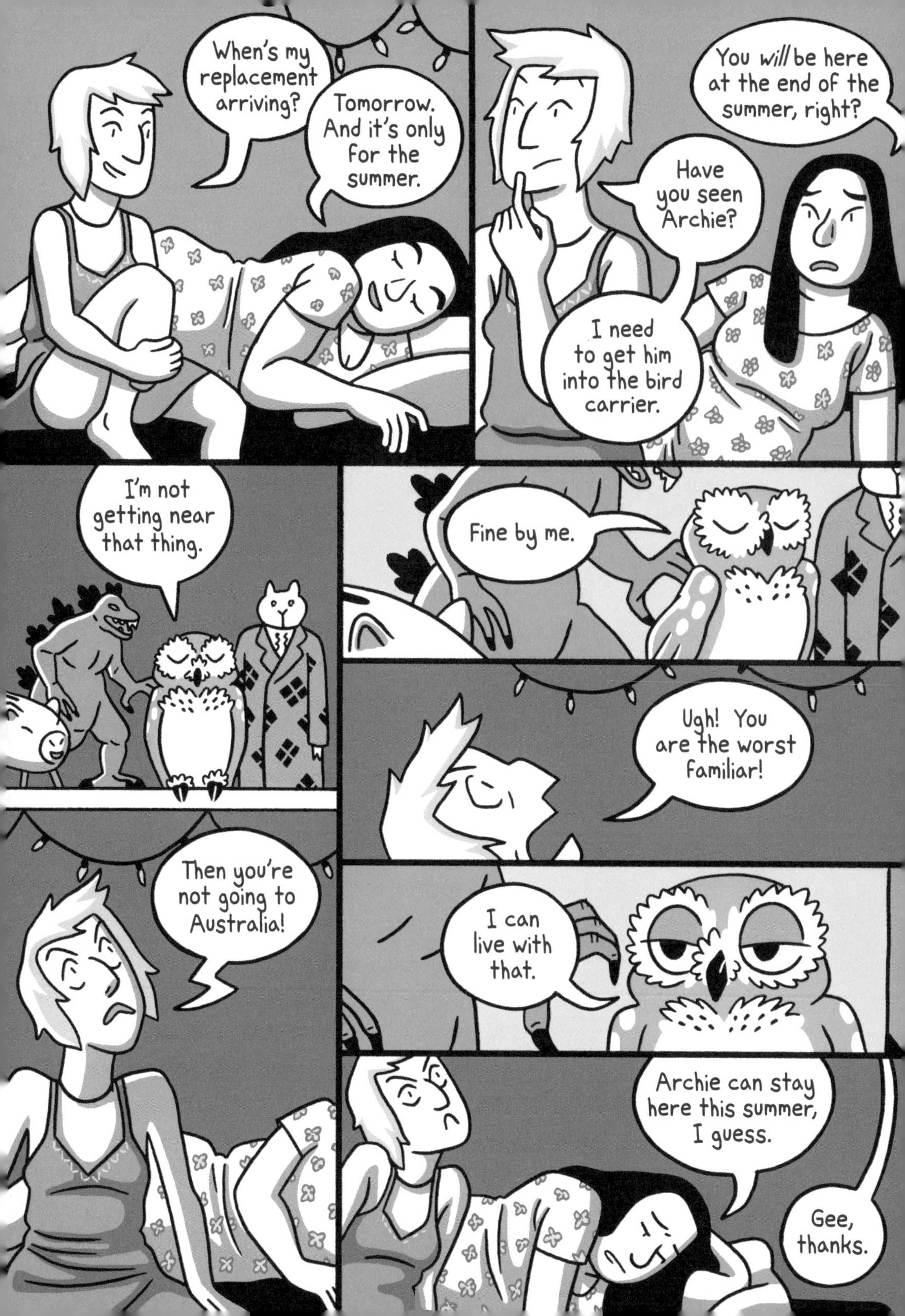
When's my replacement arriving?
Tomorrow. And it's only for the summer.
You *will* be here at the end of the summer, right?
Have you seen Archie?
I need to get him into the bird carrier.
I'm not getting near that thing.
Fine by me.
Ugh! You are the worst familiar!
Then you're not going to Australia!
I can live with that.
Archie can stay here this summer, I guess.
Gee, thanks.

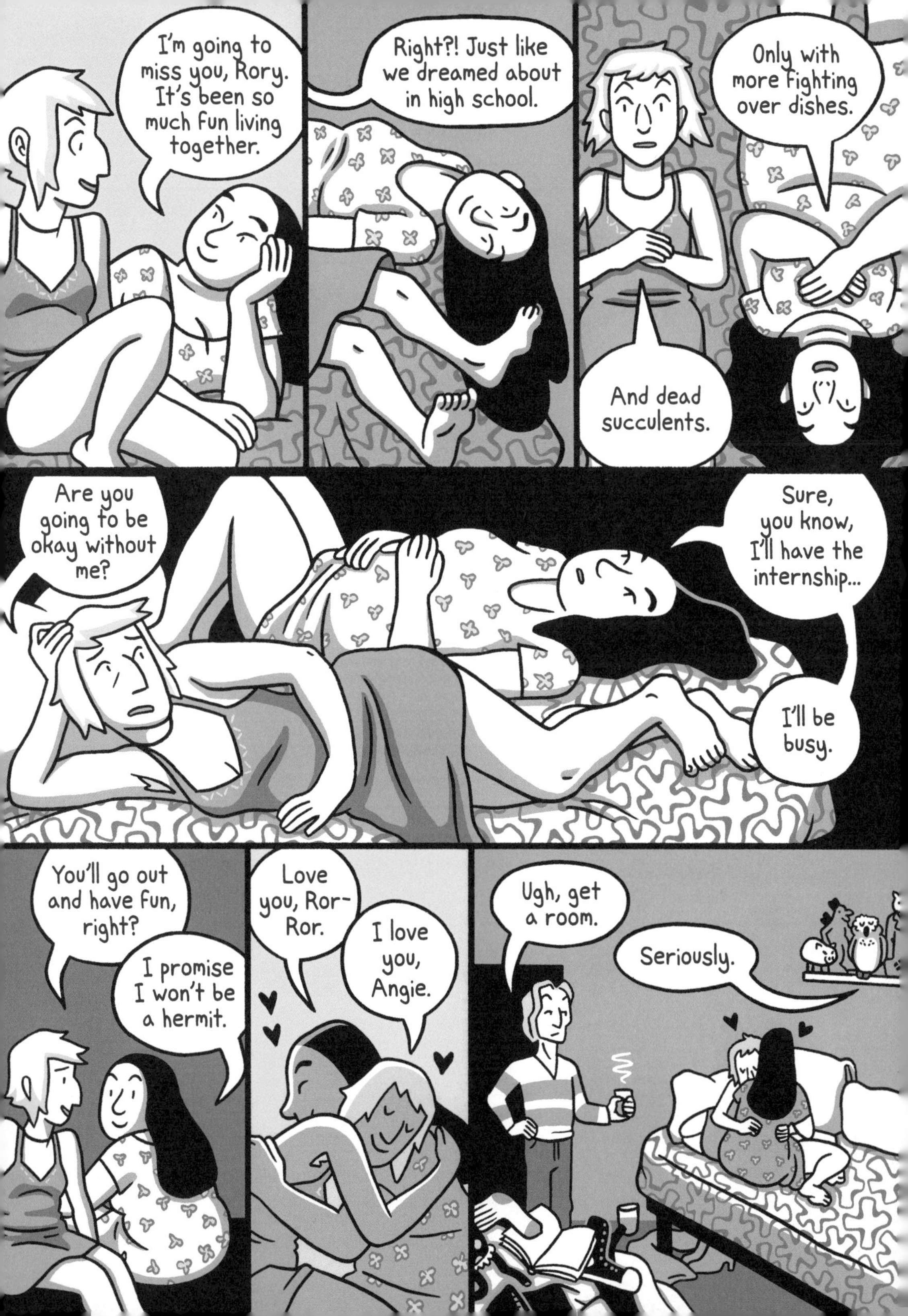
I'm going to miss you, Rory. It's been so much fun living together.
Right?! Just like we dreamed about in high school.
Only with more fighting over dishes.
And dead succulents.
Are you going to be okay without me?
Sure, you know, I'll have the internship...
I'll be busy.
You'll go out and have fun, right?
I promise I won't be a hermit.
Love you, Ror-Ror.
I love you, Angie.
Ugh, get a room.
Seriously.

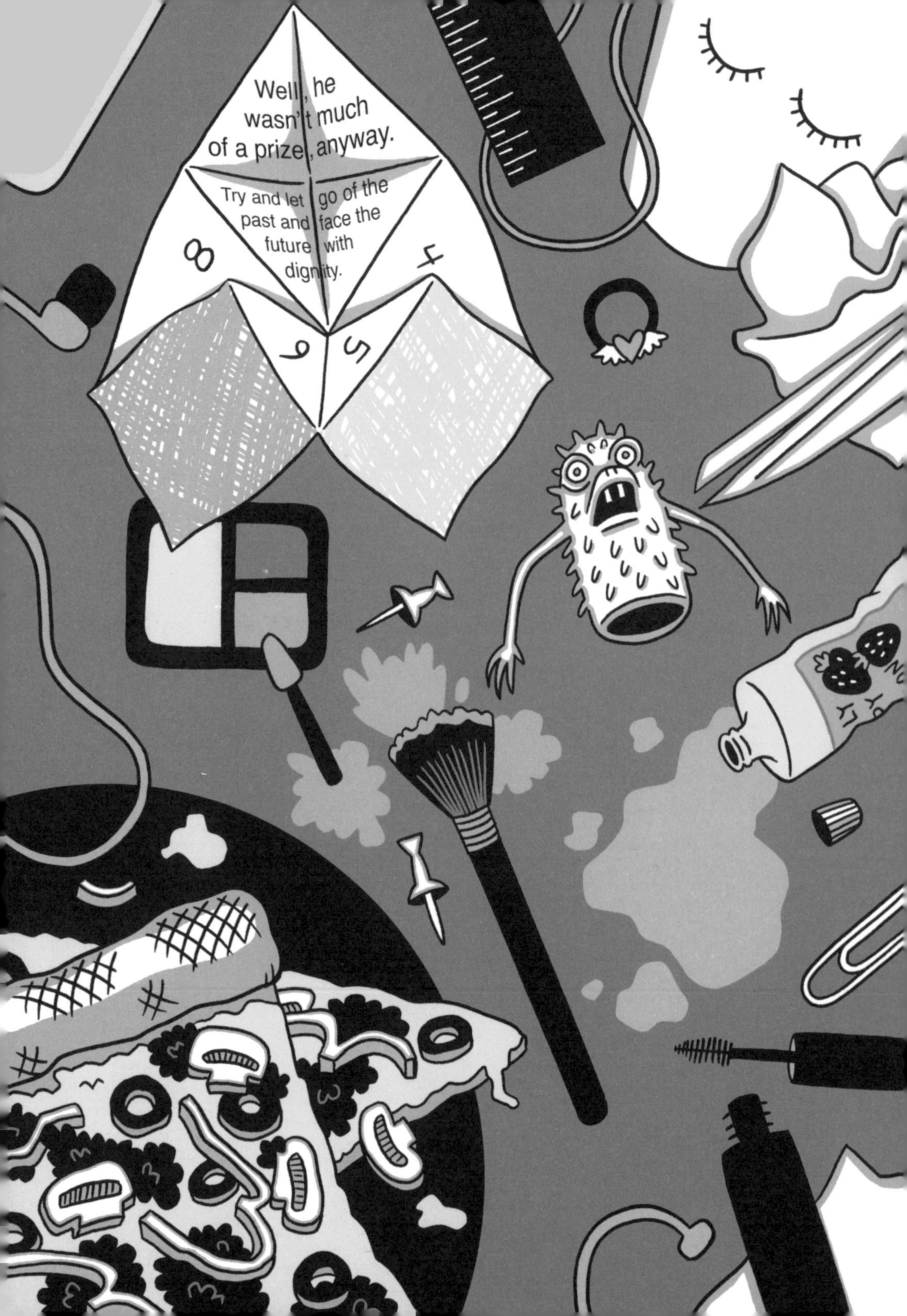
Well, he wasn't much of a prize, anyway.
Try and let go of the past and face the future with dignity.
8
4
6
5

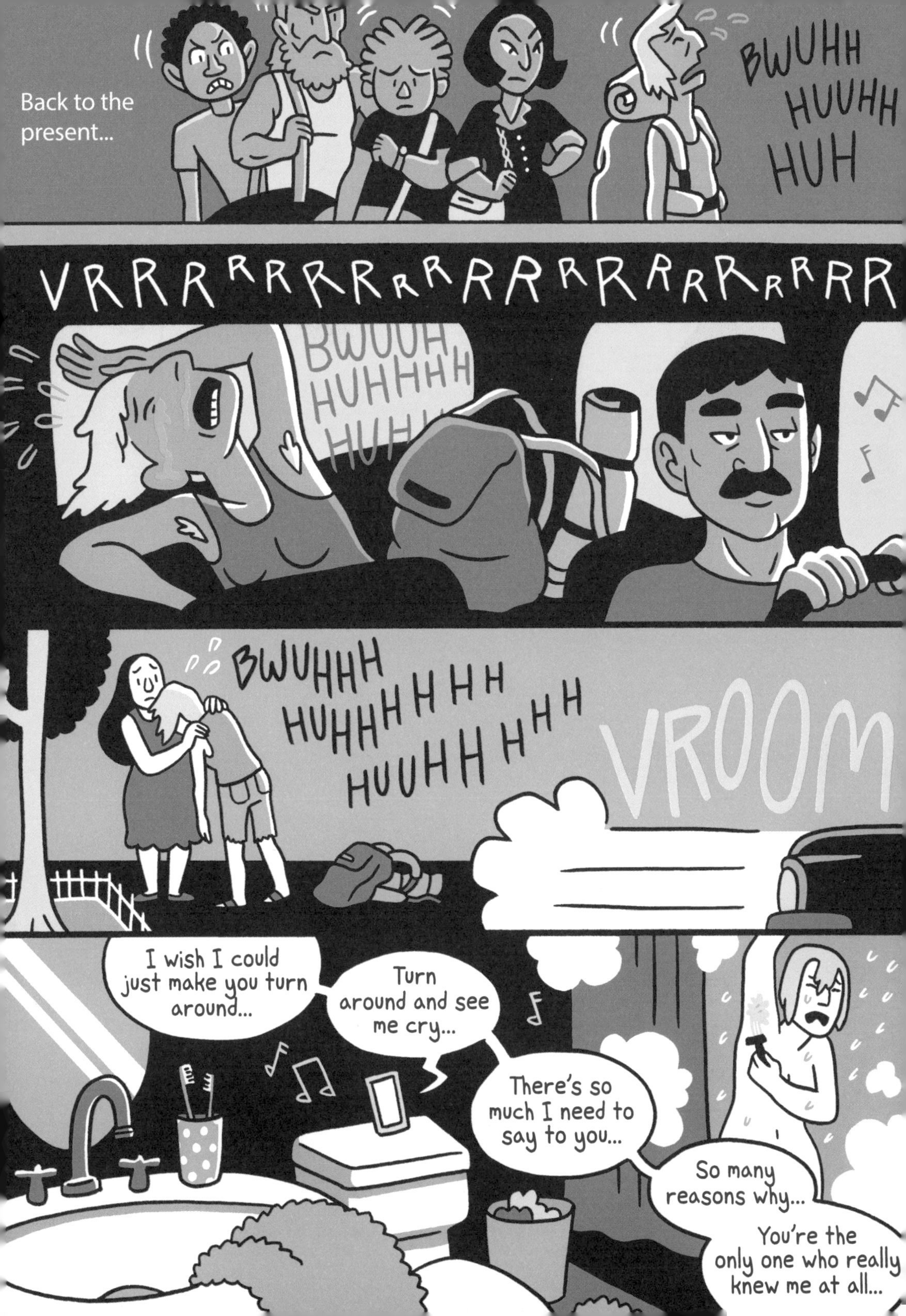
Back to the present...
BWUHH HUUHH HUH
VRRRRRRRRRRRRRRRRRRRR
BWUUH HUHHHH HUH
BWUHHH HUHHHHHH HUUHHHHH
VROOM
I wish I could just make you turn around...
Turn around and see me cry...
There's so much I need to say to you...
So many reasons why...
You're the only one who really knew me at all...

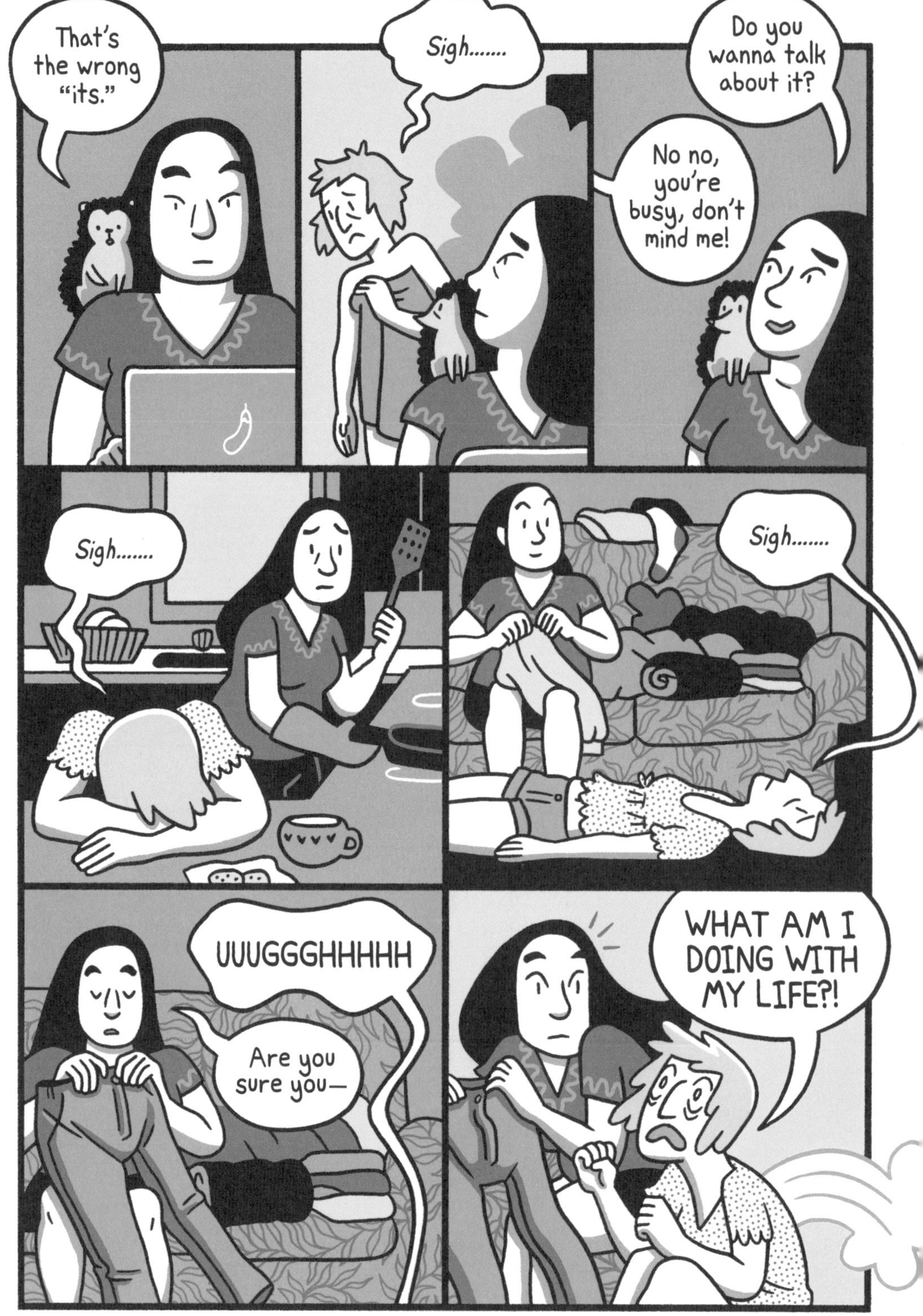
That's the wrong "its."
Sigh.......
Do you wanna talk about it?
No no, you're busy, don't mind me!
Sigh.......
Sigh.......
UUUGGGHHHHH
Are you sure you—
WHAT AM I DOING WITH MY LIFE?!

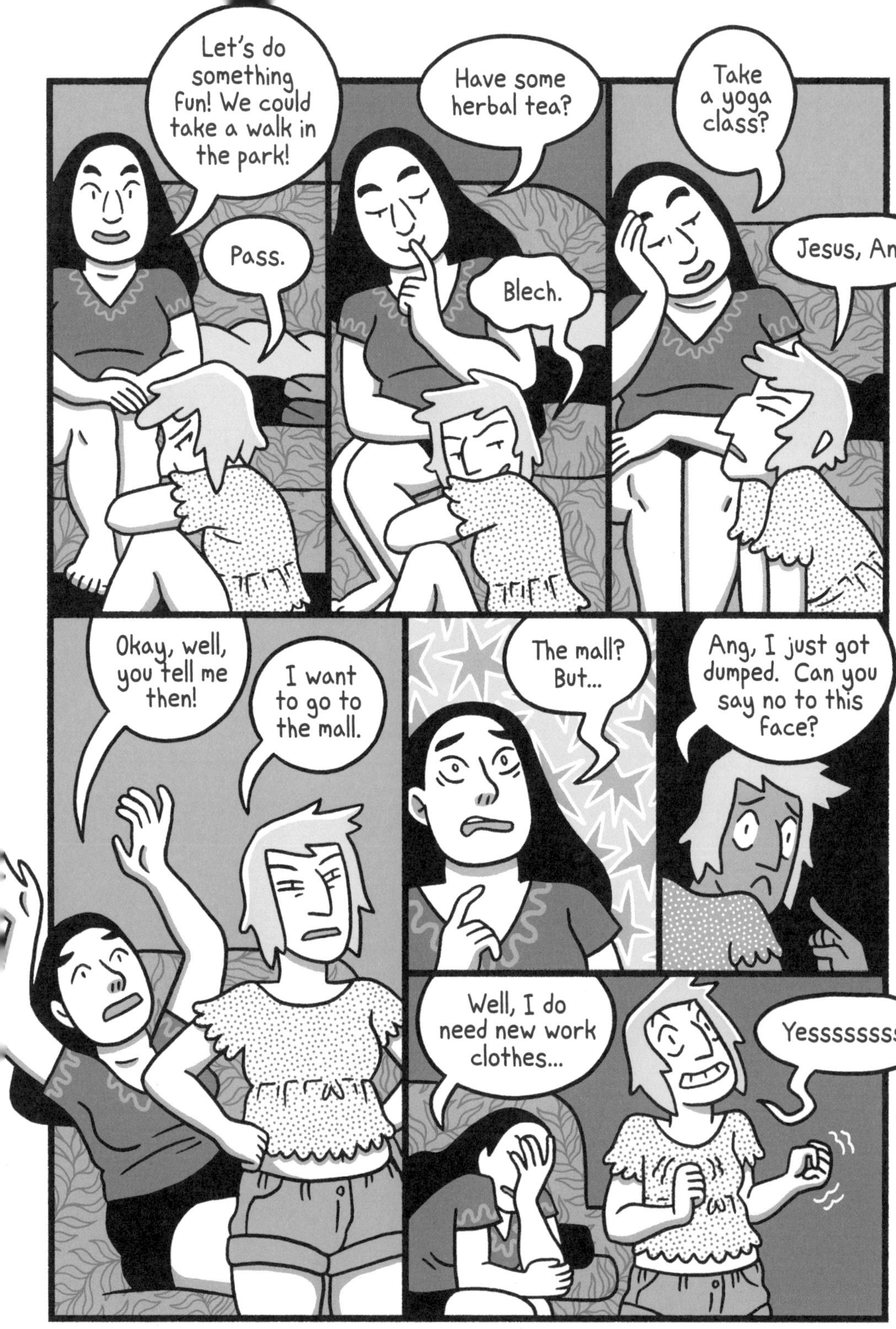
Let's do something fun! We could take a walk in the park!
Pass.
Have some herbal tea?
Blech.
Take a yoga class?
Jesus, Ang.
Okay, well, you tell me then!
I want to go to the mall.
The mall? But...
Ang, I just got dumped. Can you say no to this face?
Well, I do need new work clothes...
Yesssssss.

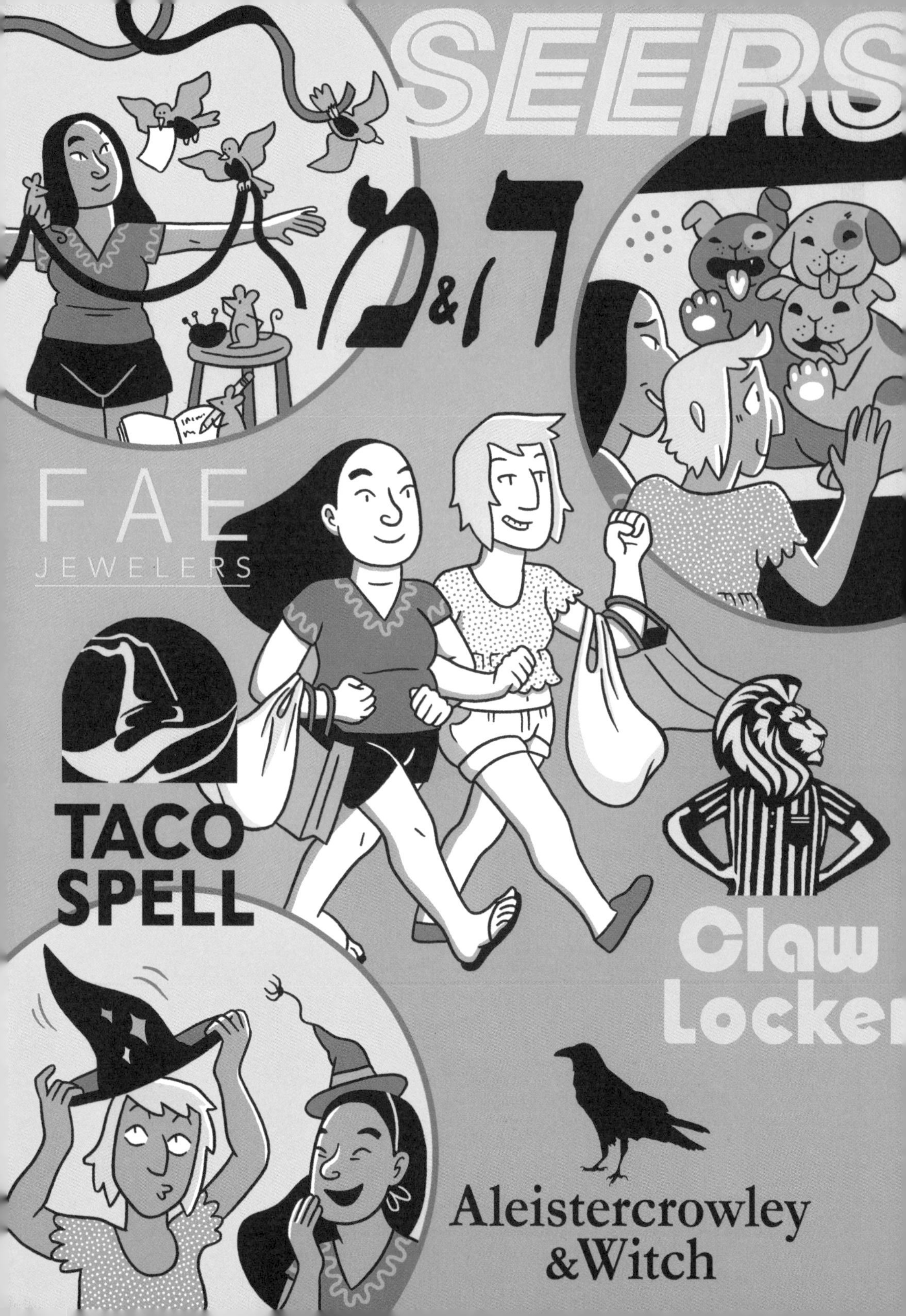
SEERS
&
FAE
JEWELERS
TACO
SPELL
Claw
Locker
Aleistercrowley
&Witch

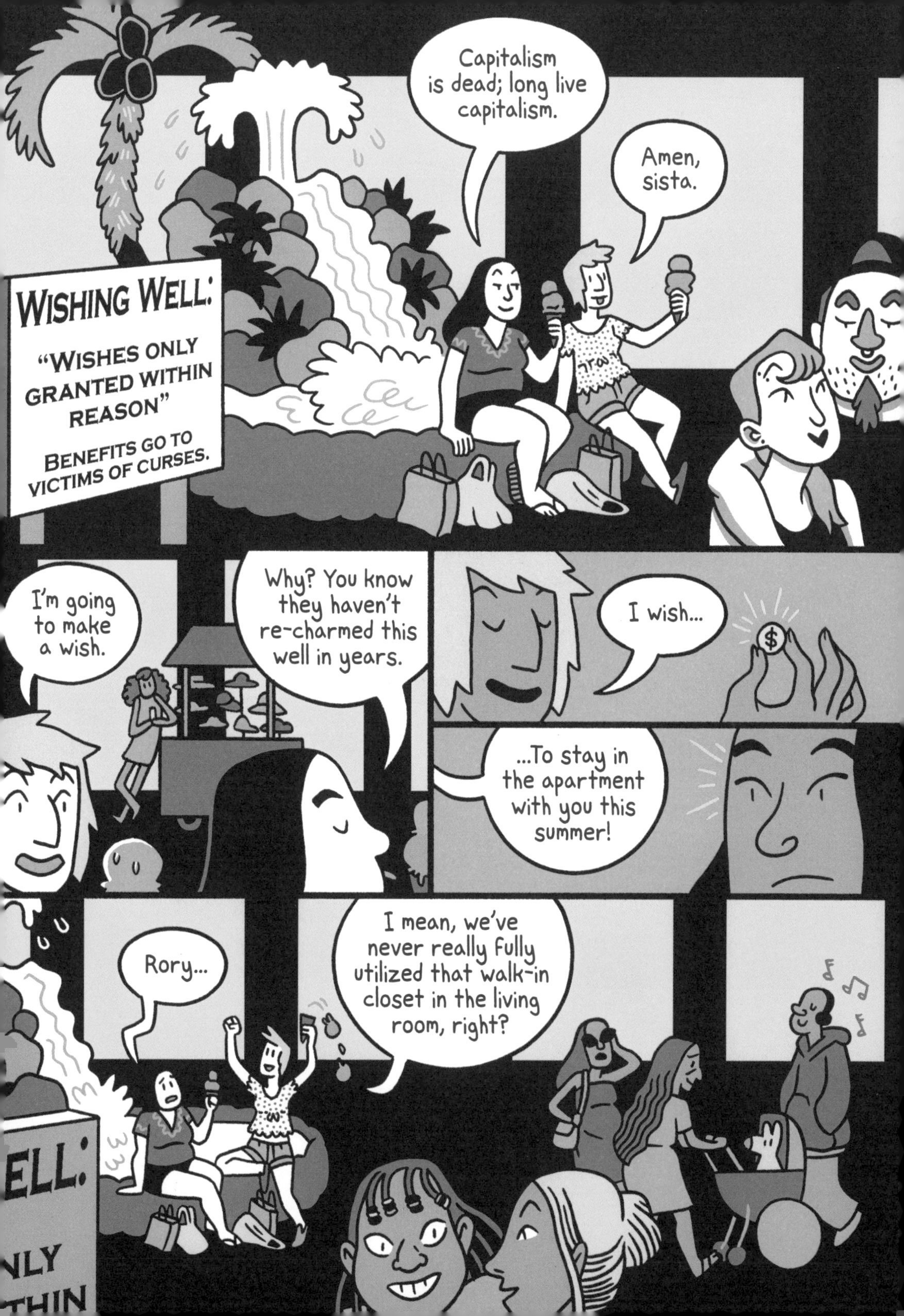
Capitalism is dead; long live capitalism.
Amen, sista.
WISHING WELL:
"WISHES ONLY GRANTED WITHIN REASON"
BENEFITS GO TO VICTIMS OF CURSES.
I'm going to make a wish.
Why? You know they haven't re-charmed this well in years.
I wish...
...To stay in the apartment with you this summer!
Rory...
I mean, we've never really fully utilized that walk-in closet in the living room, right?

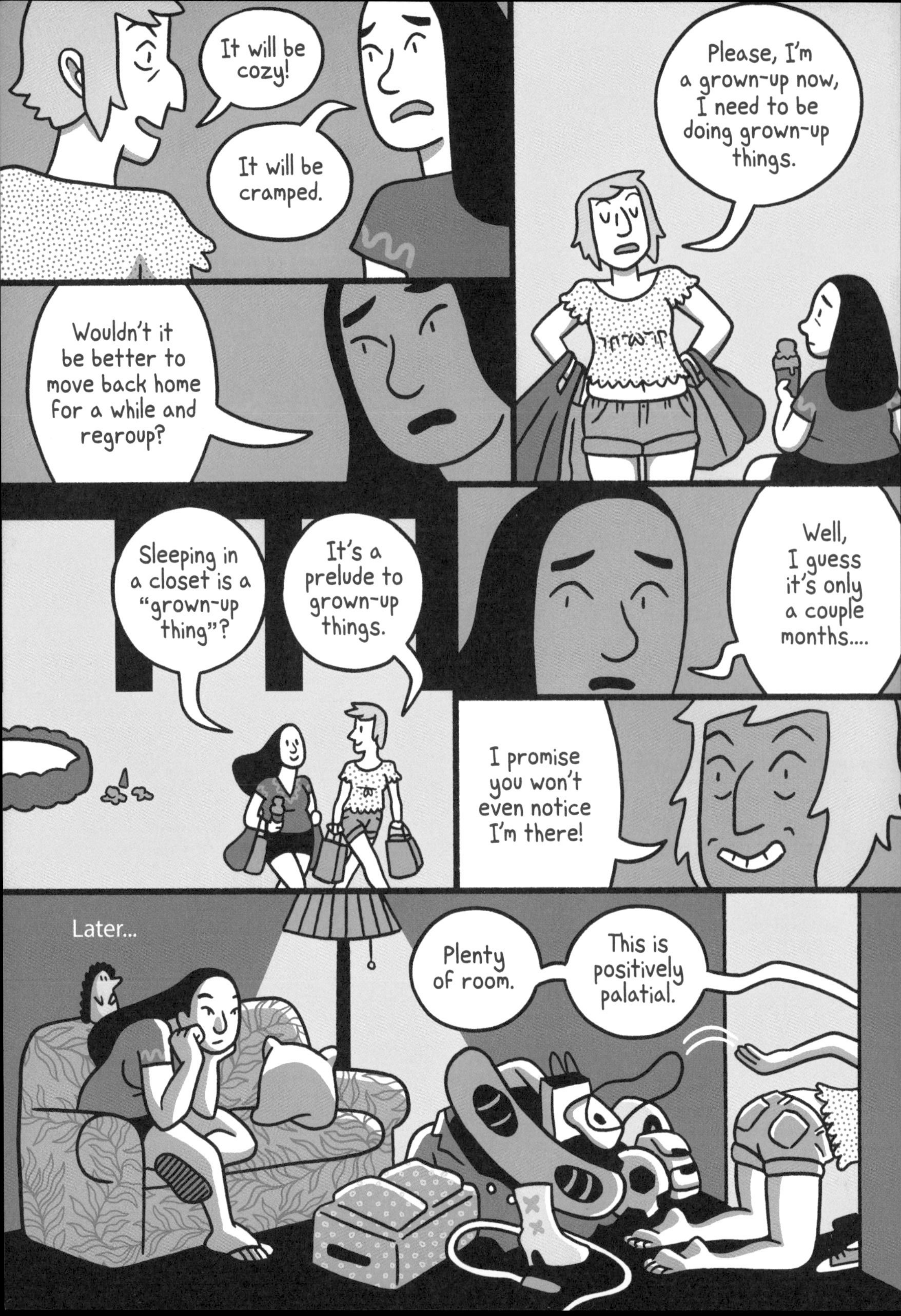
It will be cozy!
It will be cramped.
Please, I'm a grown-up now, I need to be doing grown-up things.
Wouldn't it be better to move back home for a while and regroup?
Sleeping in a closet is a "grown-up thing"?
It's a prelude to grown-up things.
Well, I guess it's only a couple months....
I promise you won't even notice I'm there!
Later...
Plenty of room.
This is positively palatial.

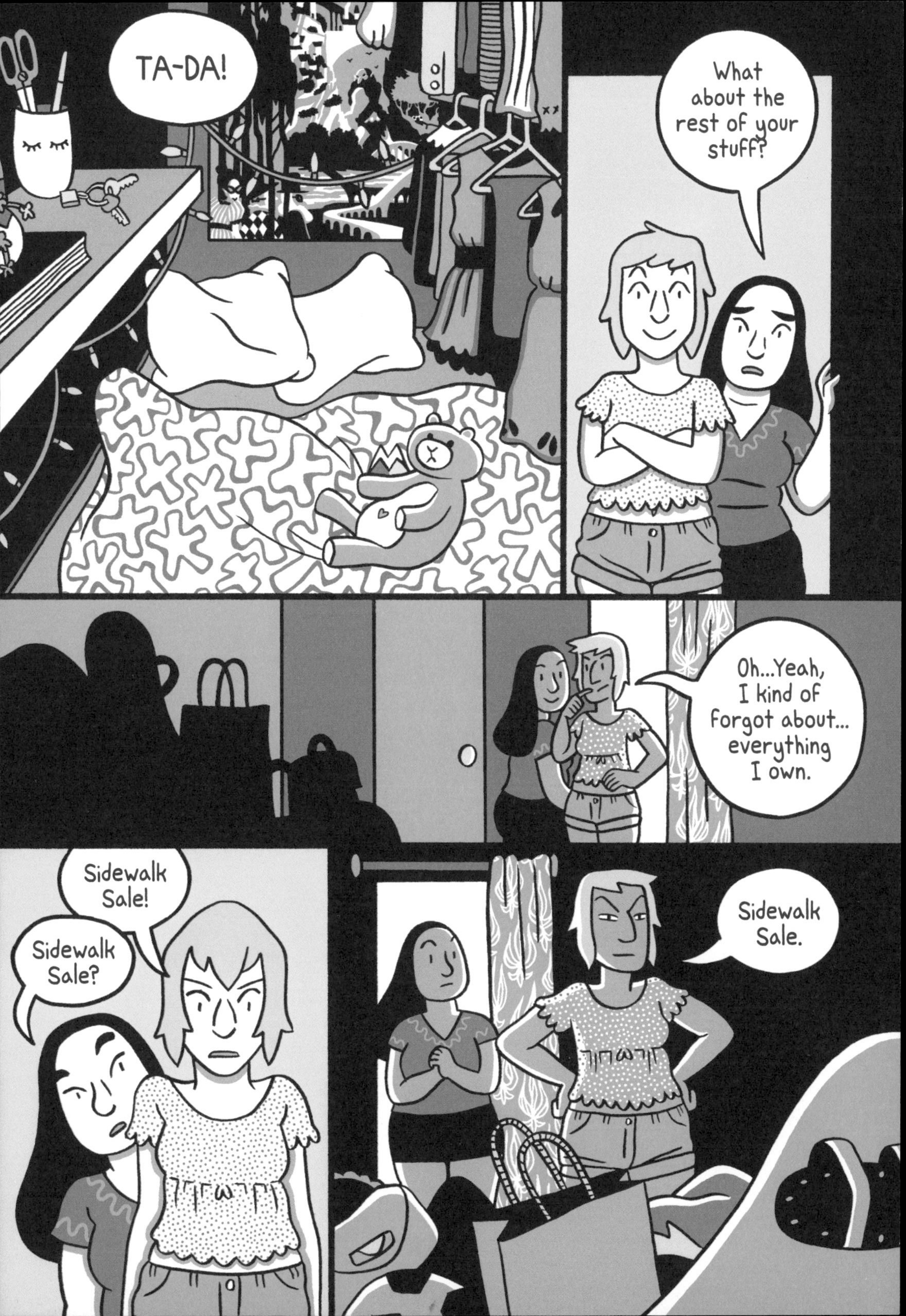
TA-DA!
What about the rest of your stuff?
Oh...Yeah, I kind of forgot about... everything I own.
Sidewalk Sale!
Sidewalk Sale?
Sidewalk Sale.

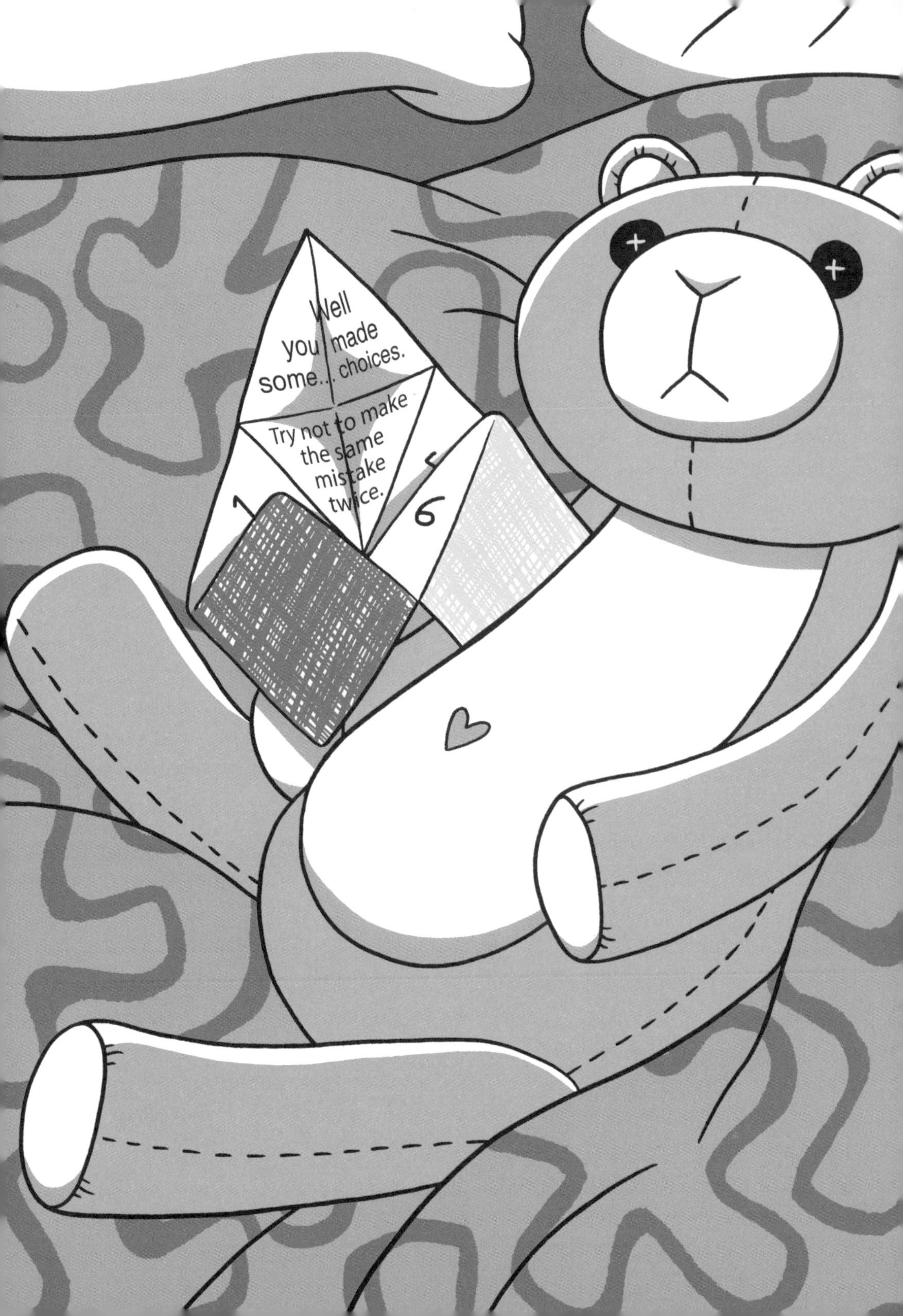
Well you made some... choices.
Try not to make the same mistake twice.
1
5
6

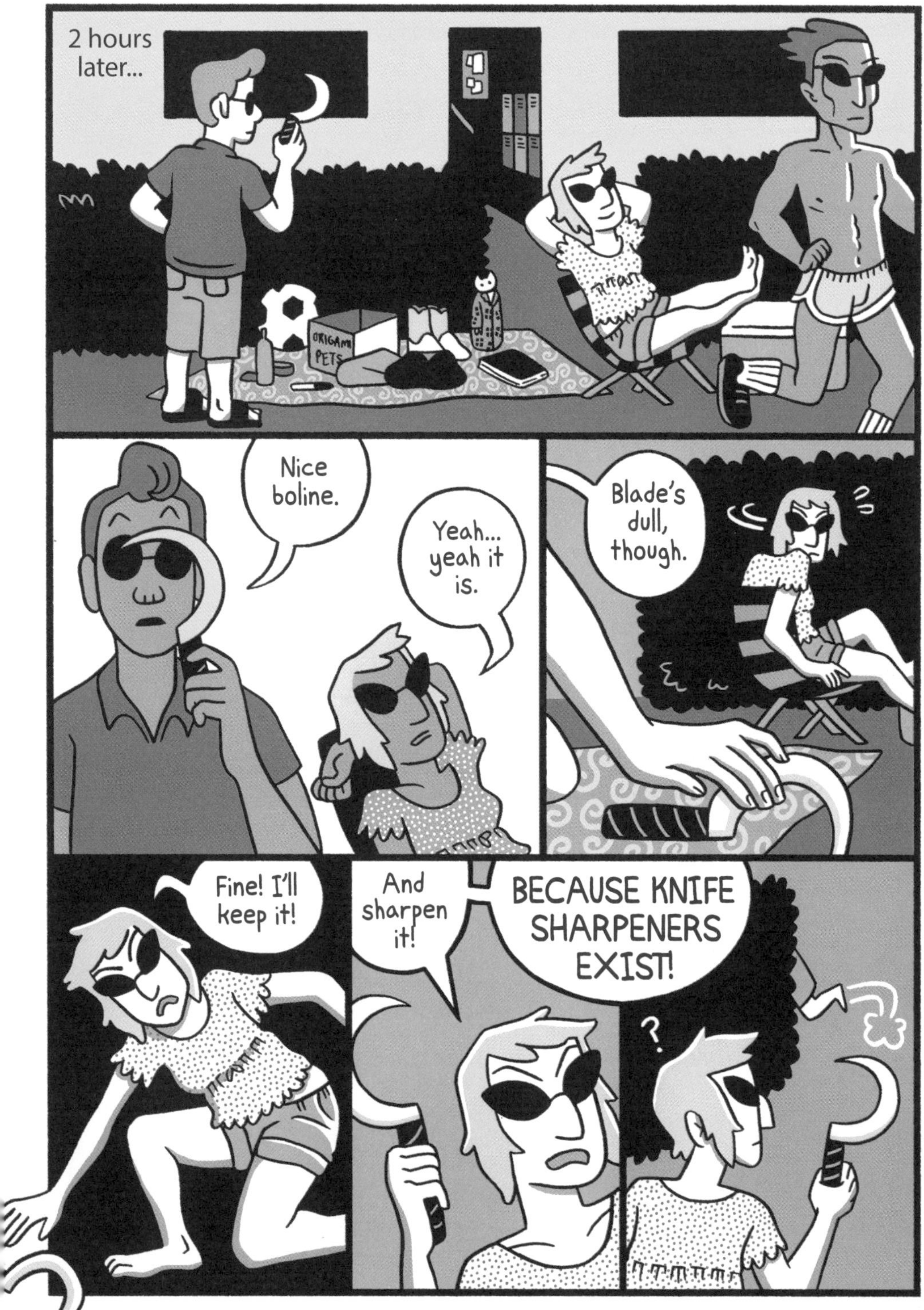
2 hours later...
ORIGAMI PETS
Nice boline.
Yeah... yeah it is.
Blade's dull, though.
Fine! I'll keep it!
And sharpen it!
BECAUSE KNIFE SHARPENERS EXIST!
?

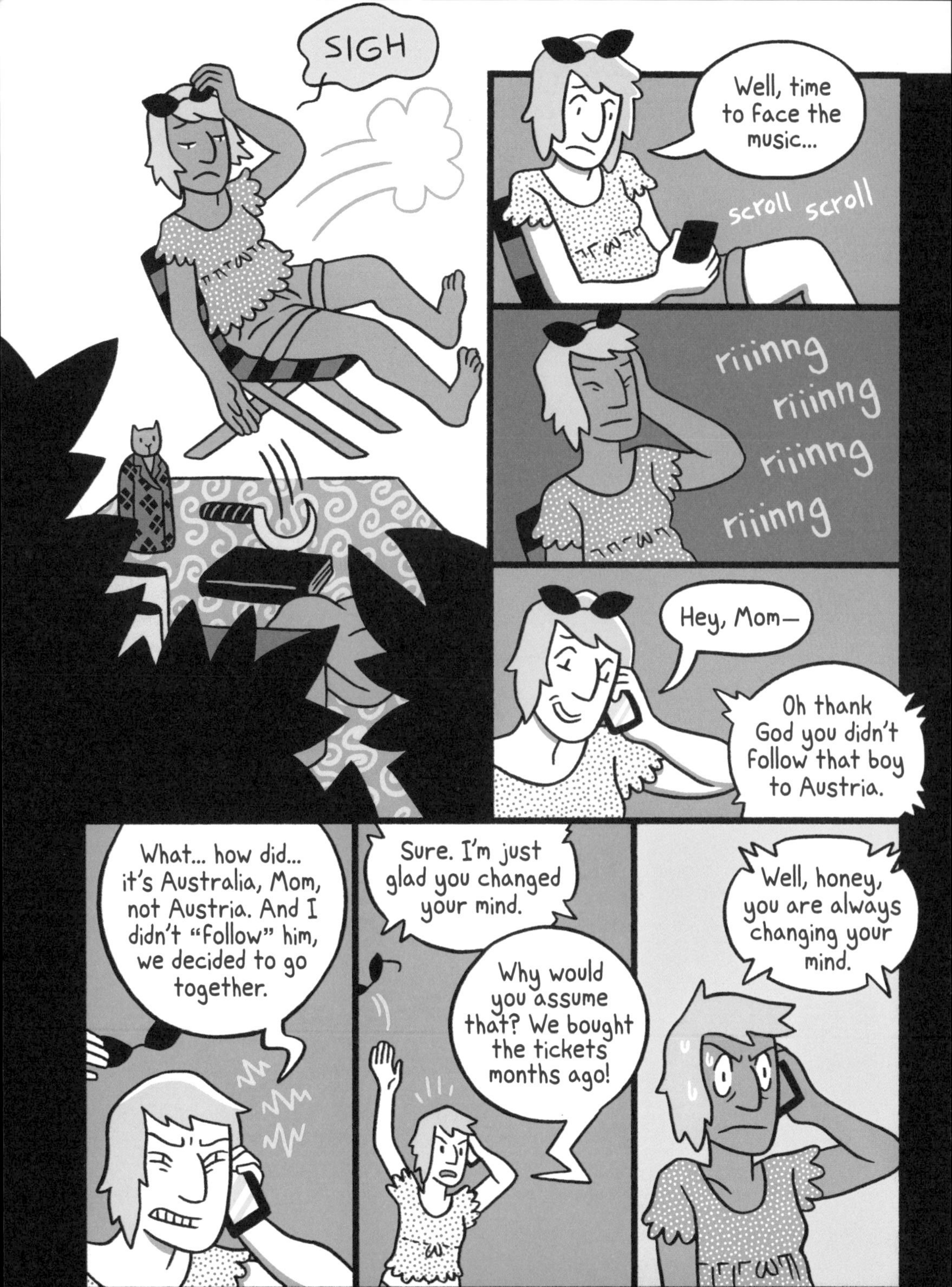
SIGH
Well, time to face the music...
scroll scroll
riiinng riiinng riiinng riiinng
Hey, Mom—
Oh thank God you didn't follow that boy to Austria.
What... how did... it's Australia, Mom, not Austria. And I didn't "follow" him, we decided to go together.
Sure. I'm just glad you changed your mind.
Why would you assume that? We bought the tickets months ago!
Well, honey, you are always changing your mind.

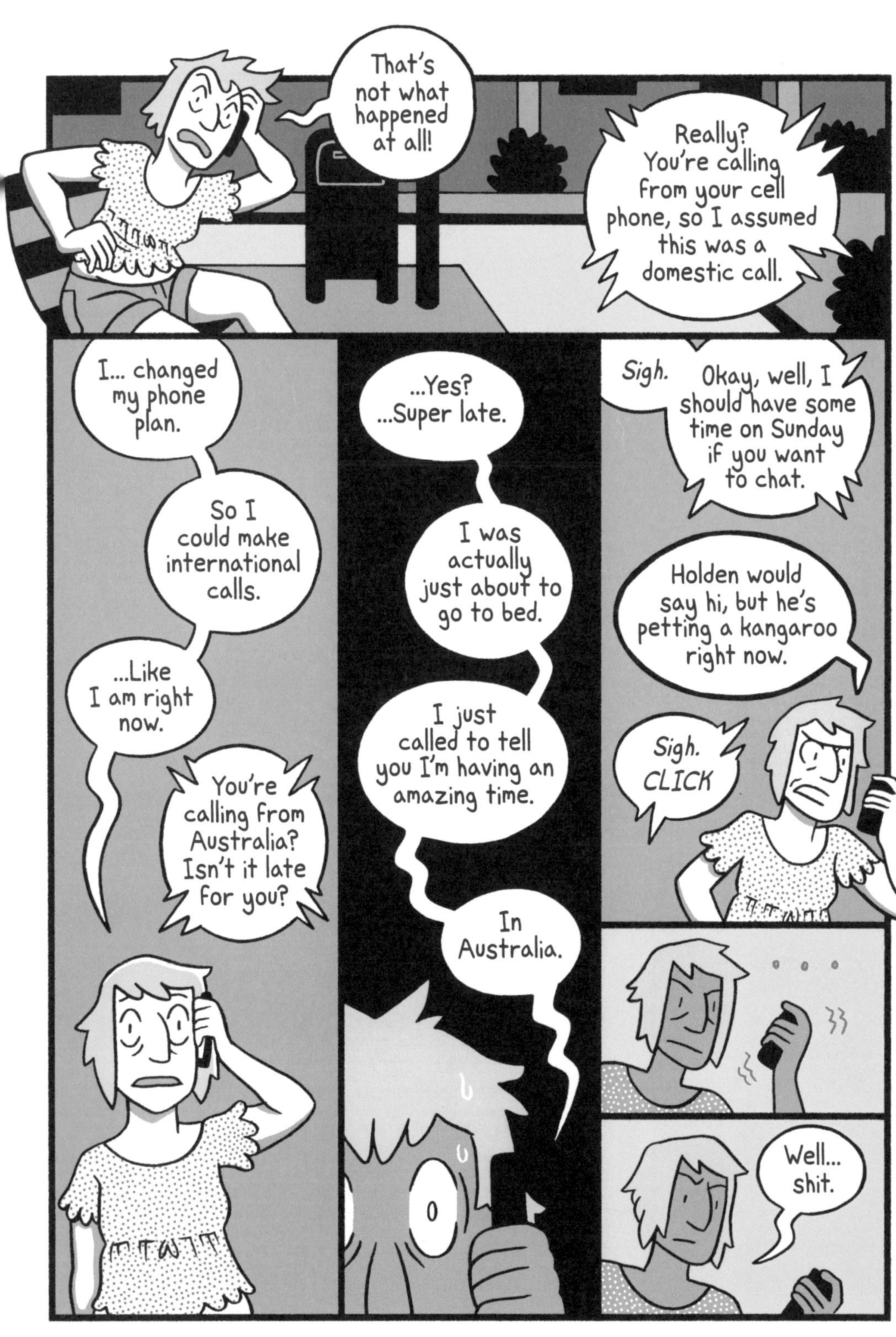
That's not what happened at all!
Really? You're calling from your cell phone, so I assumed this was a domestic call.
I... changed my phone plan.
So I could make international calls.
...Like I am right now.
You're calling from Australia? Isn't it late for you?
...Yes? ...Super late.
I was actually just about to go to bed.
I just called to tell you I'm having an amazing time.
In Australia.
Sigh.
Okay, well, I should have some time on Sunday if you want to chat.
Holden would say hi, but he's petting a kangaroo right now.
Sigh. CLICK
Well... shit.

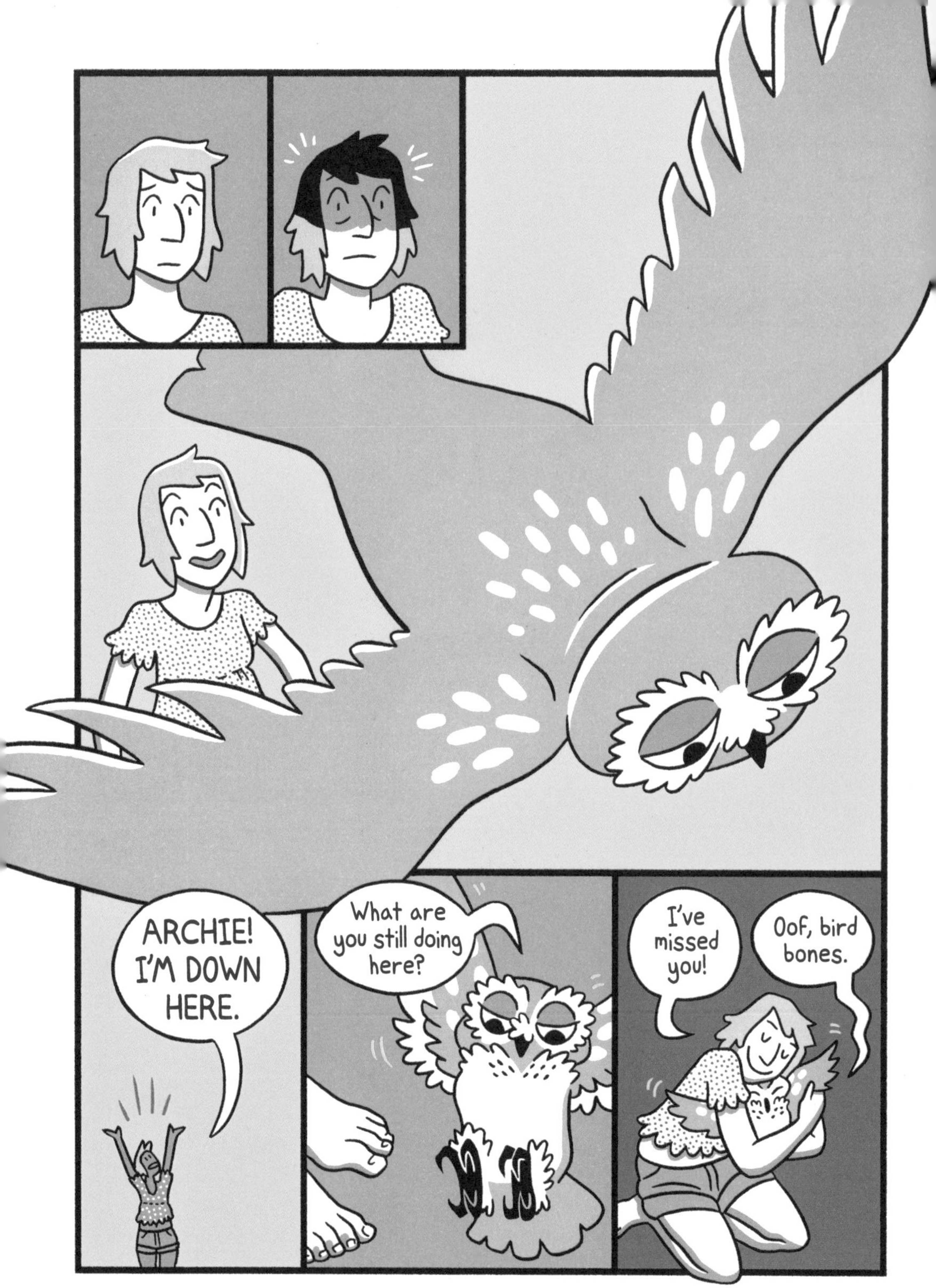
ARCHIE! I'M DOWN HERE.
What are you still doing here?
I've missed you!
Oof, bird bones.

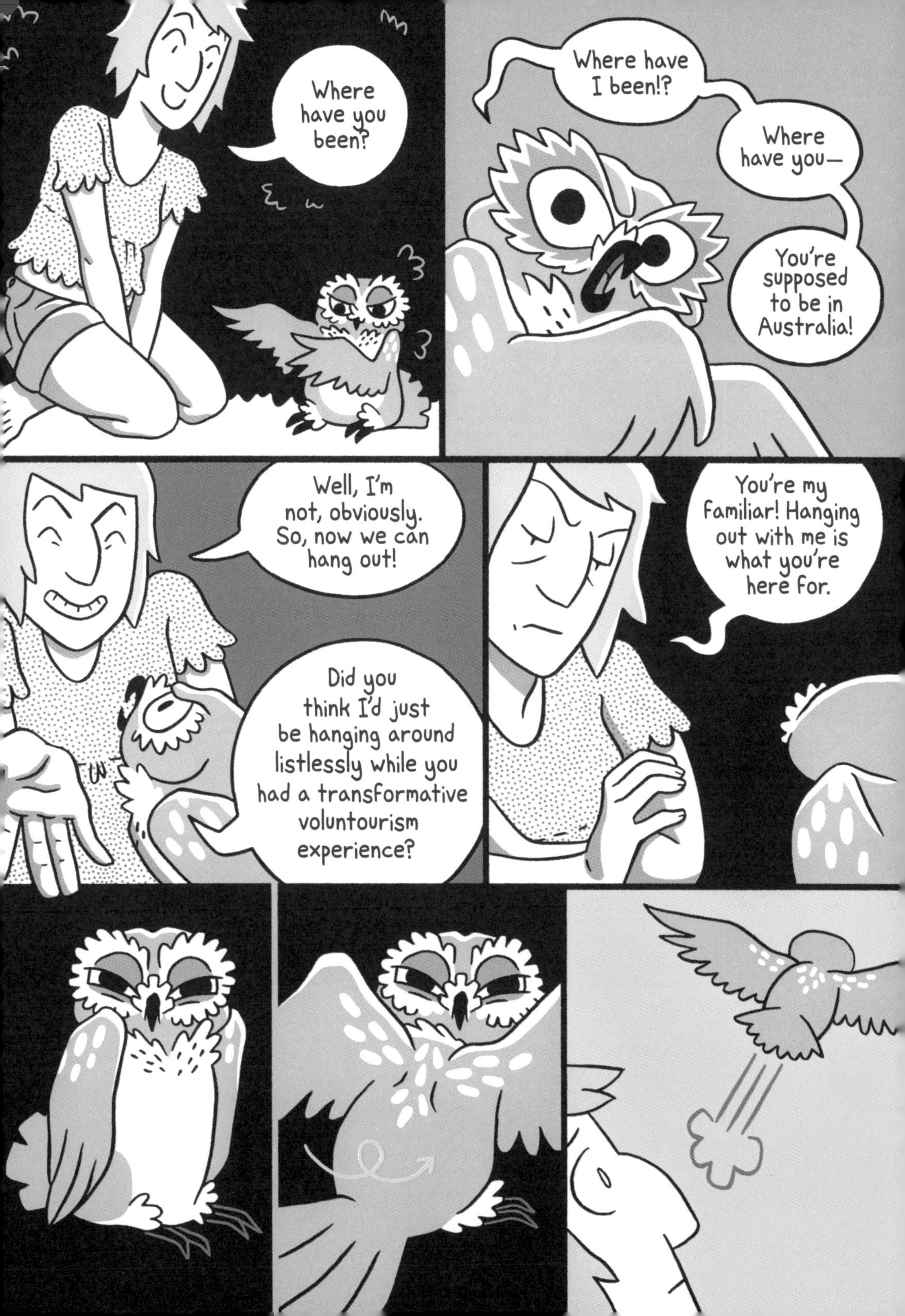

Where have you been?
Where have I been!?
Where have you—
You're supposed to be in Australia!
Well, I'm not, obviously. So, now we can hang out!
Did you think I'd just be hanging around listlessly while you had a transformative voluntourism experience?
You're my familiar! Hanging out with me is what you're here for.

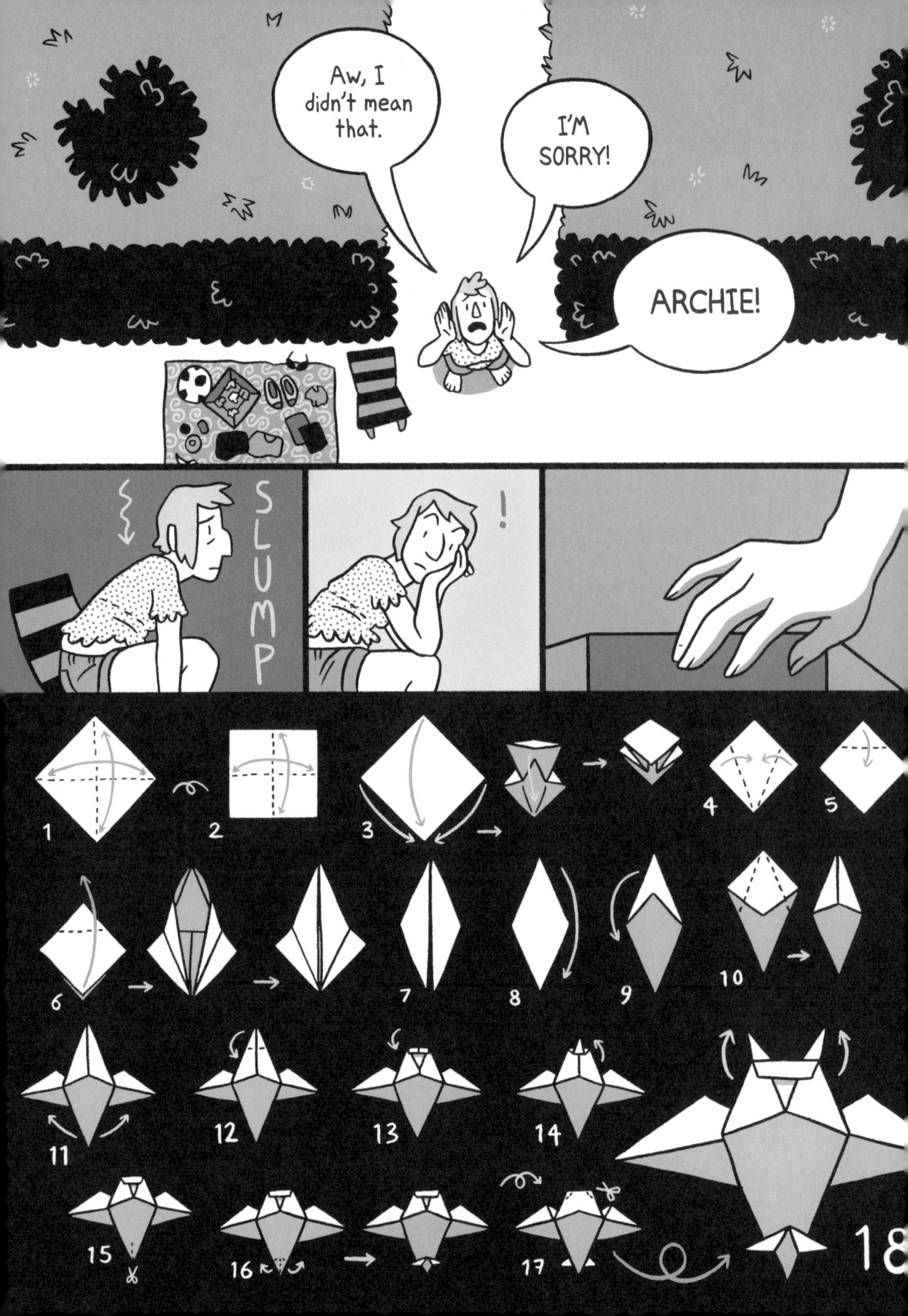
Aw, I didn't mean that.
I'M SORRY!
ARCHIE!
SLUMP
!
1
2
3
4
5
6
7
8
9
10
11
12
13
14
15
16
17
18

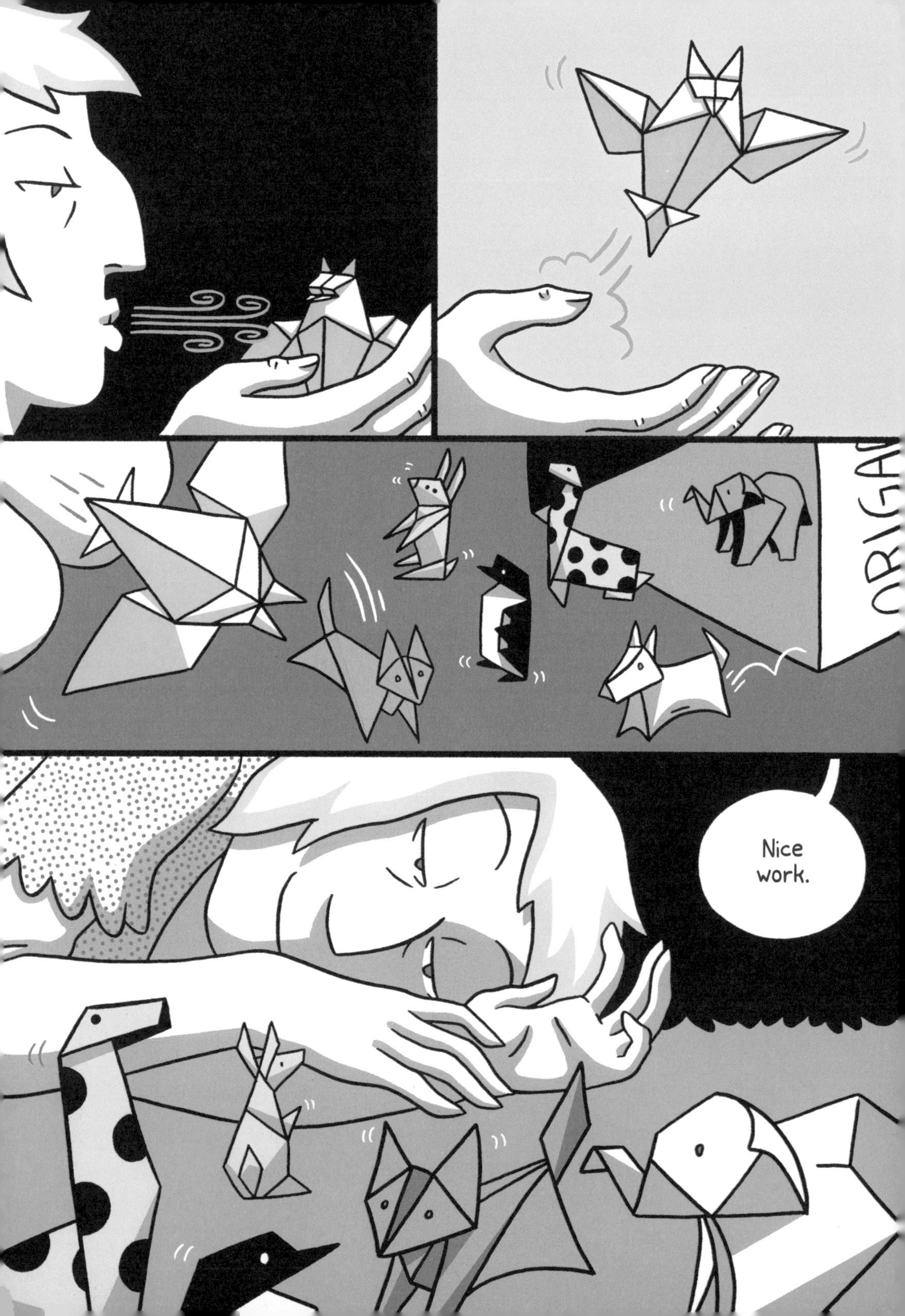
Nice work.

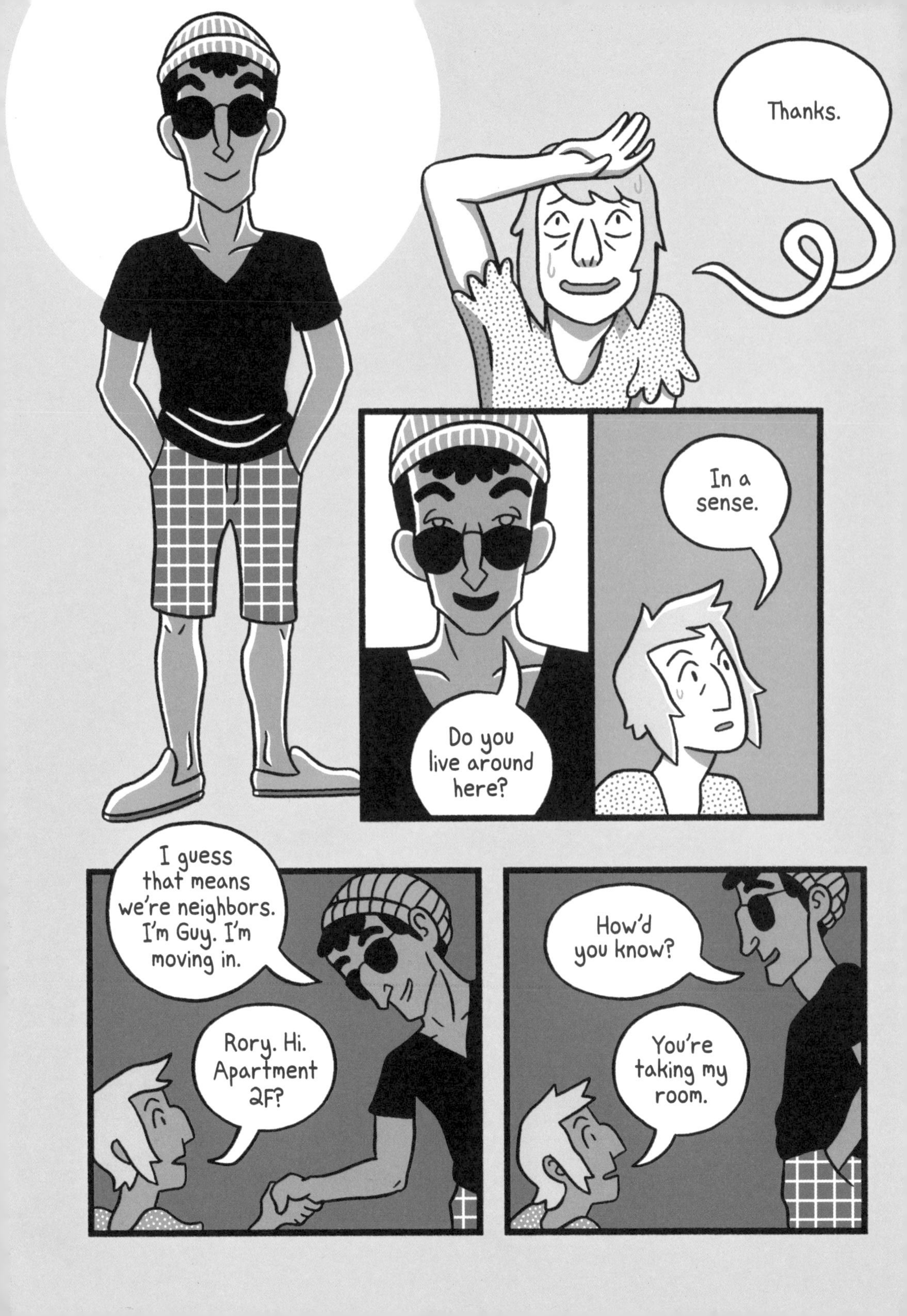
Thanks.
Do you live around here?
In a sense.
I guess that means we're neighbors. I'm Guy. I'm moving in.
Rory. Hi. Apartment 2F?
How'd you know?
You're taking my room.

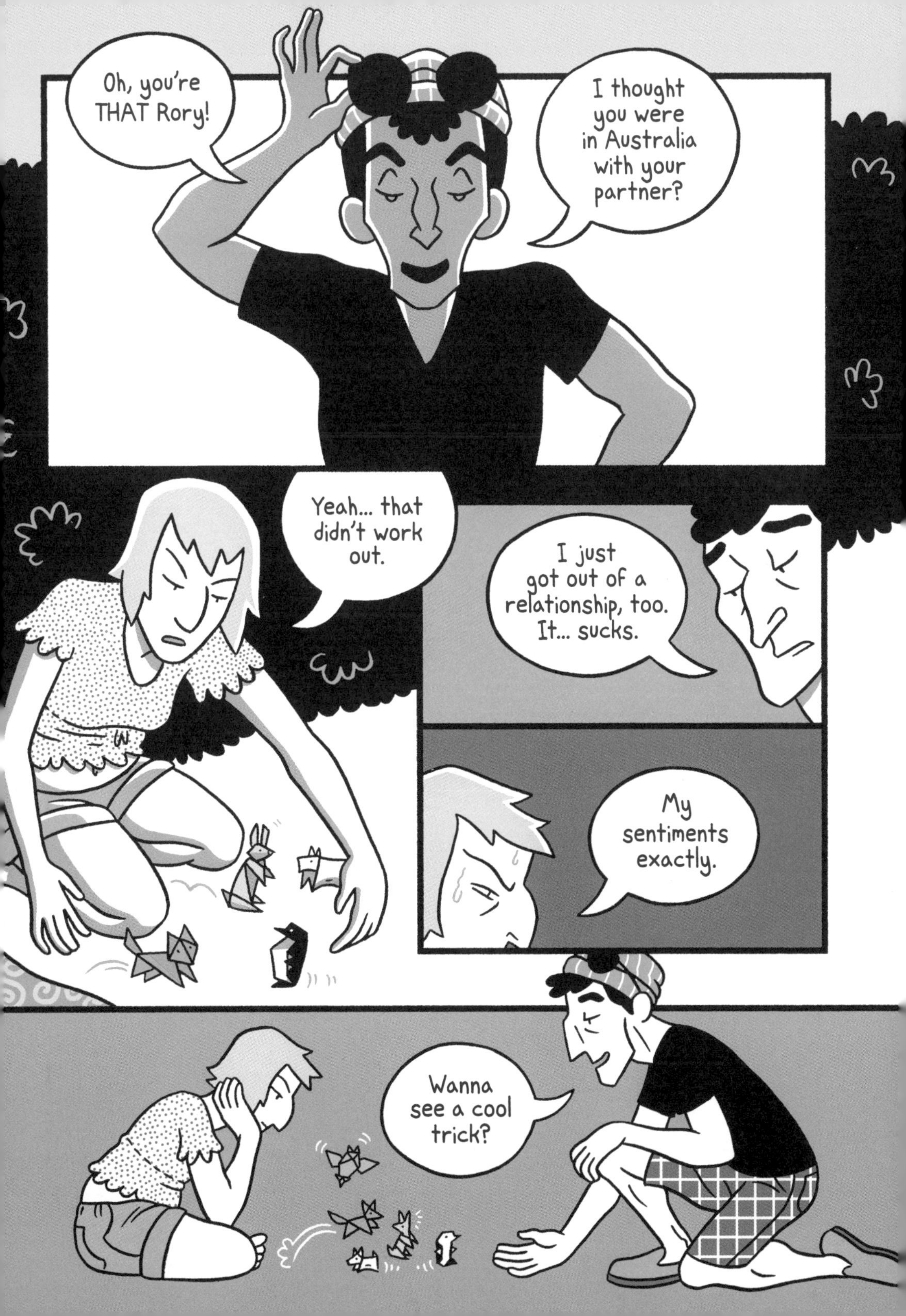
Oh, you're THAT Rory!
I thought you were in Australia with your partner?
Yeah... that didn't work out.
I just got out of a relationship, too. It... sucks.
My sentiments exactly.
Wanna see a cool trick?

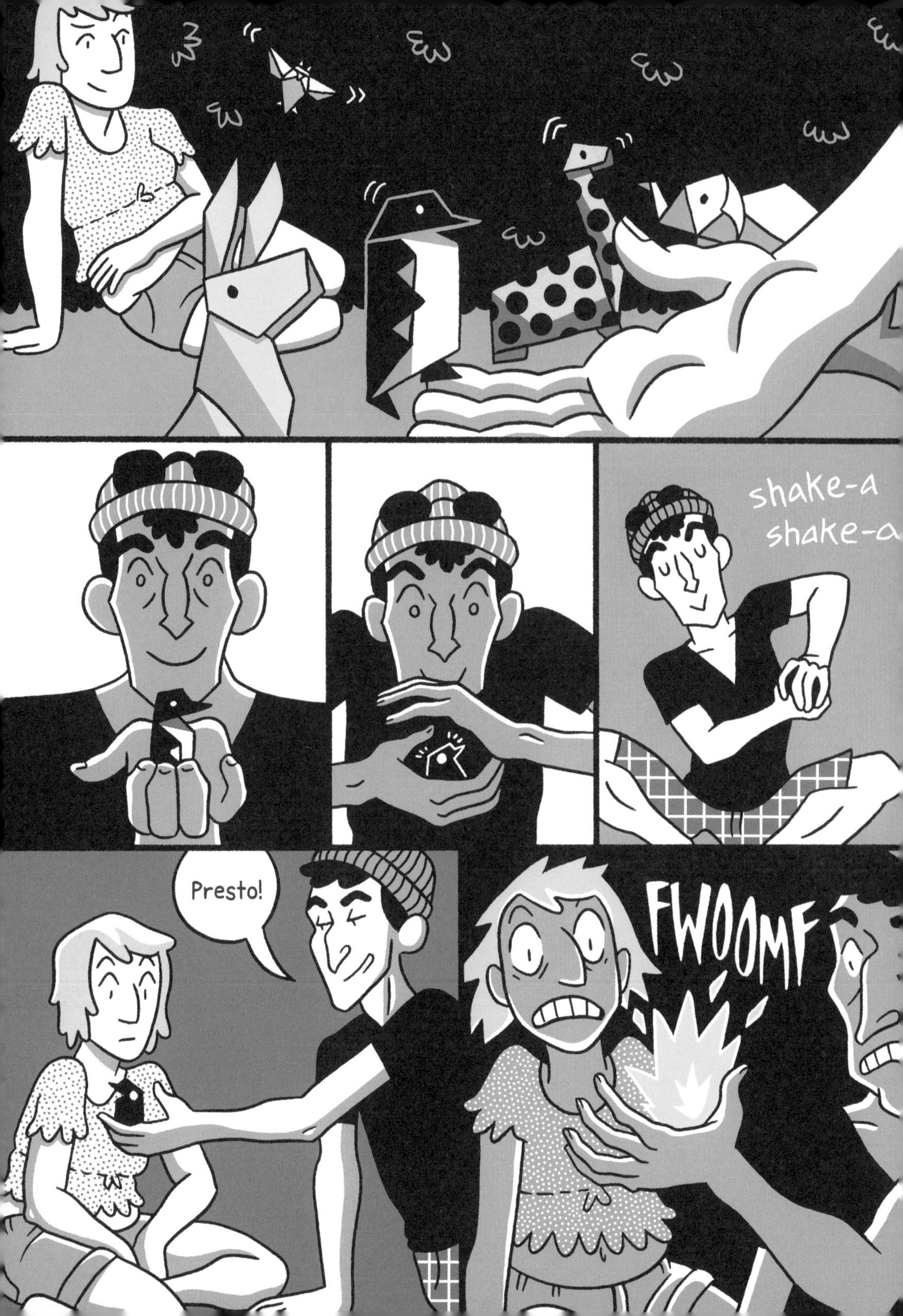
shake-a
shake-a
Presto!
FWOOMF

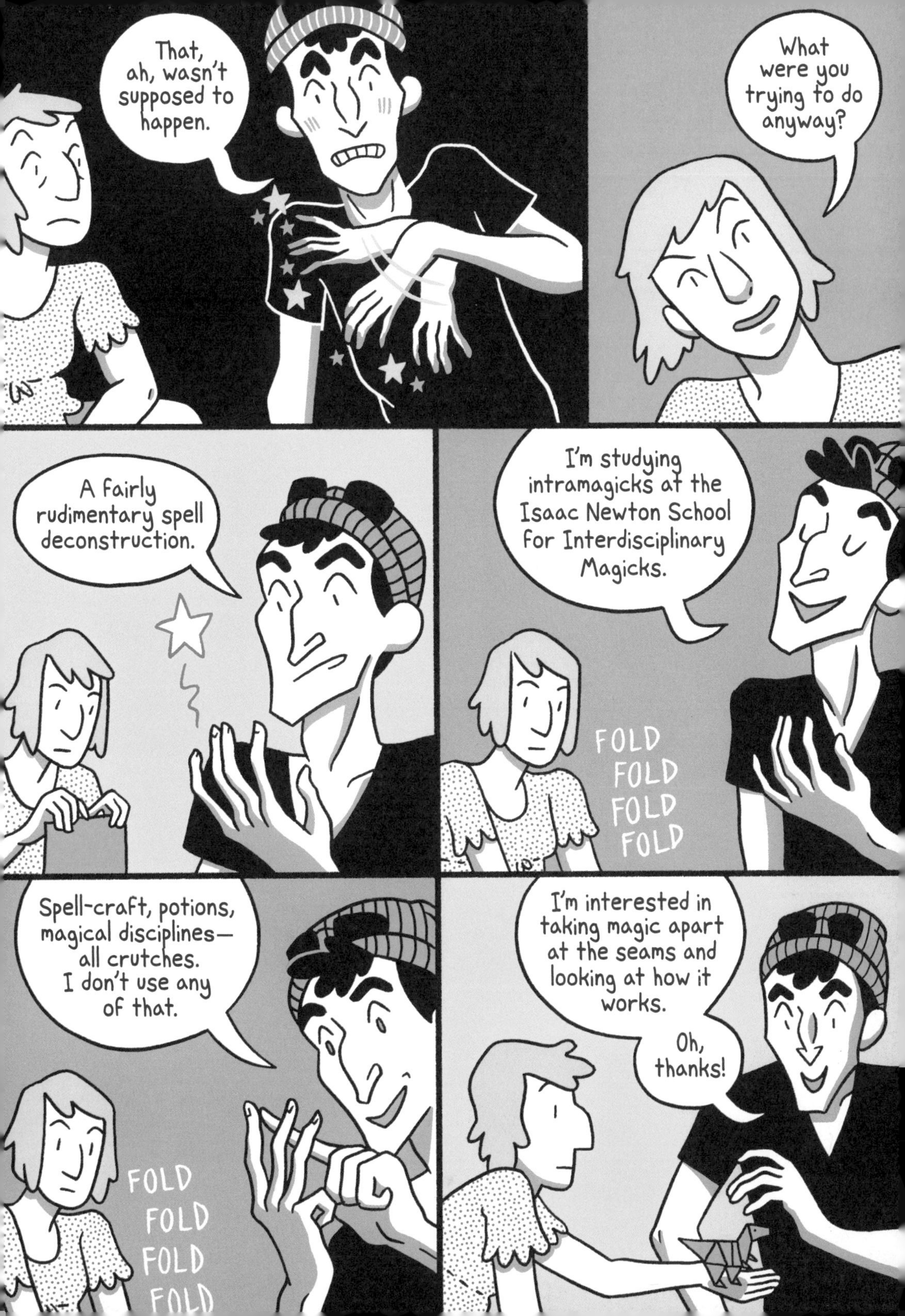
That, ah, wasn't supposed to happen.
What were you trying to do anyway?
A fairly rudimentary spell deconstruction.
I'm studying intramagicks at the Isaac Newton School for Interdisciplinary Magicks.
FOLD FOLD FOLD FOLD
Spell-craft, potions, magical disciplines—all crutches. I don't use any of that.
FOLD FOLD FOLD FOLD
I'm interested in taking magic apart at the seams and looking at how it works.
Oh, thanks!

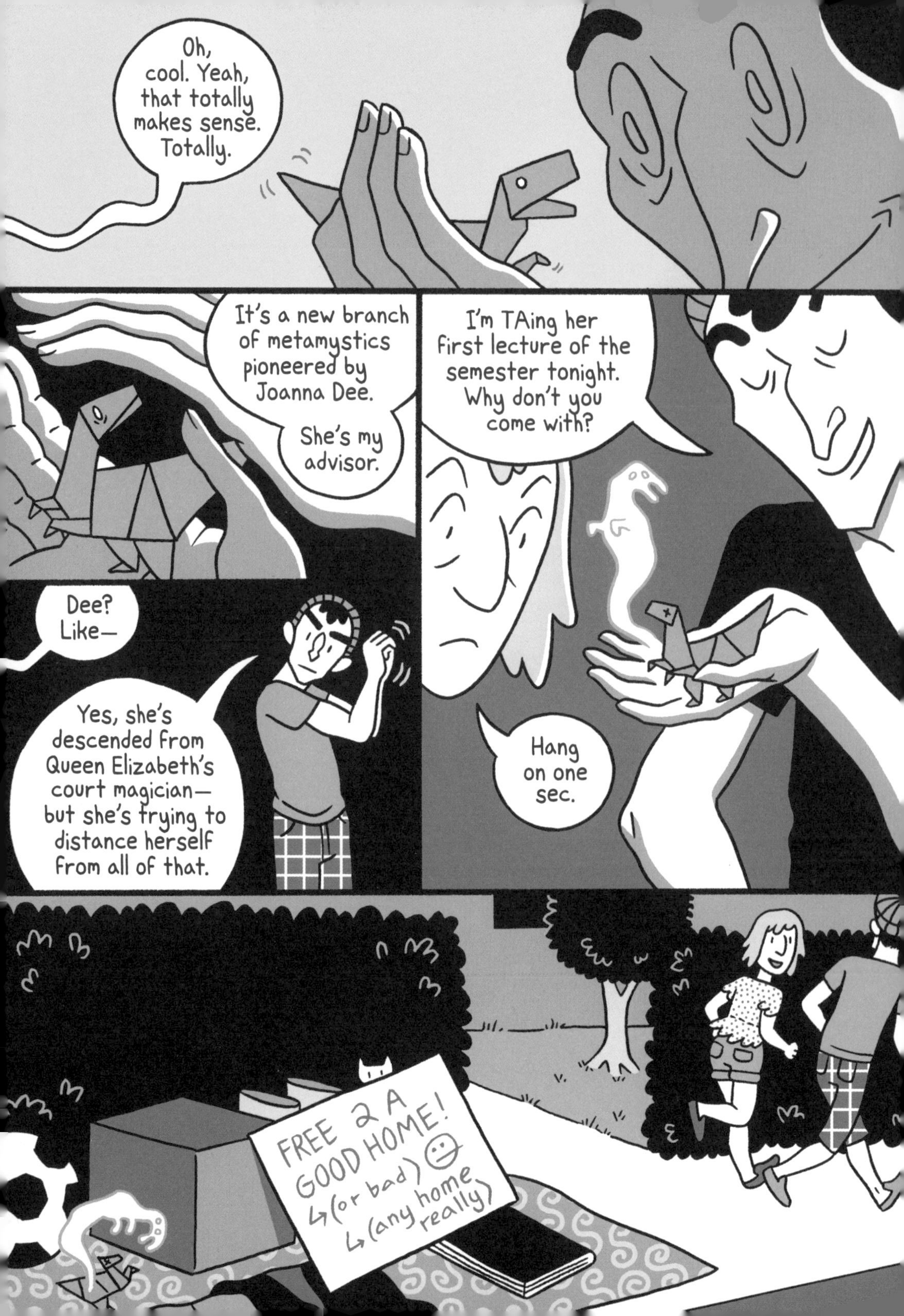

Oh, cool. Yeah, that totally makes sense. Totally.
It's a new branch of metamystics pioneered by Joanna Dee.
She's my advisor.
I'm TAing her first lecture of the semester tonight. Why don't you come with?
Dee? Like—
Yes, she's descended from Queen Elizabeth's court magician— but she's trying to distance herself from all of that.
Hang on one sec.
FREE 2 A GOOD HOME!
↳(or bad)
↳(any home really)

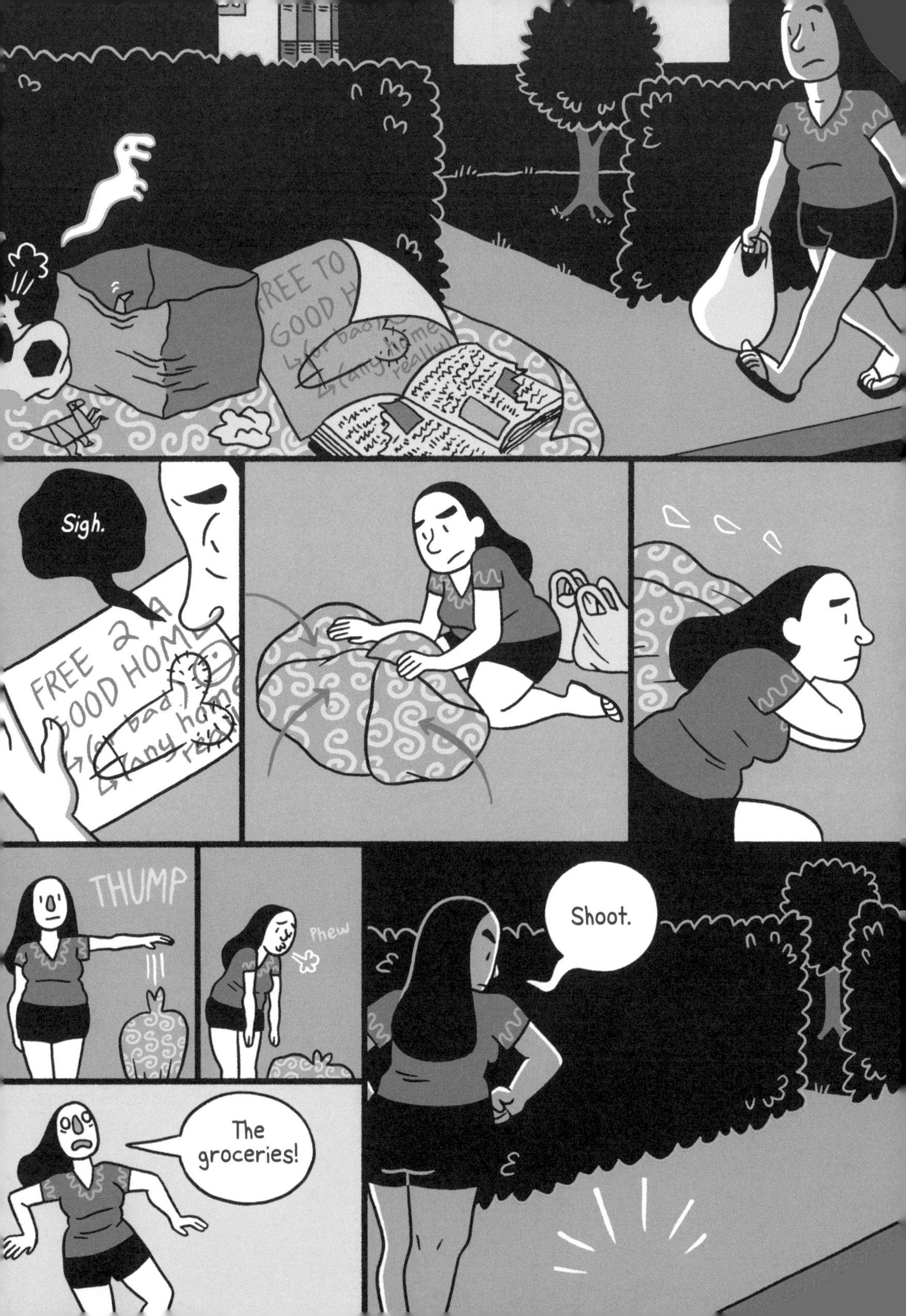

FREE TO
GOOD H
(or bad)
(any home
really)
Sigh.
FREE 2 A
GOOD HOME
THUMP
Phew
The groceries!
Shoot.

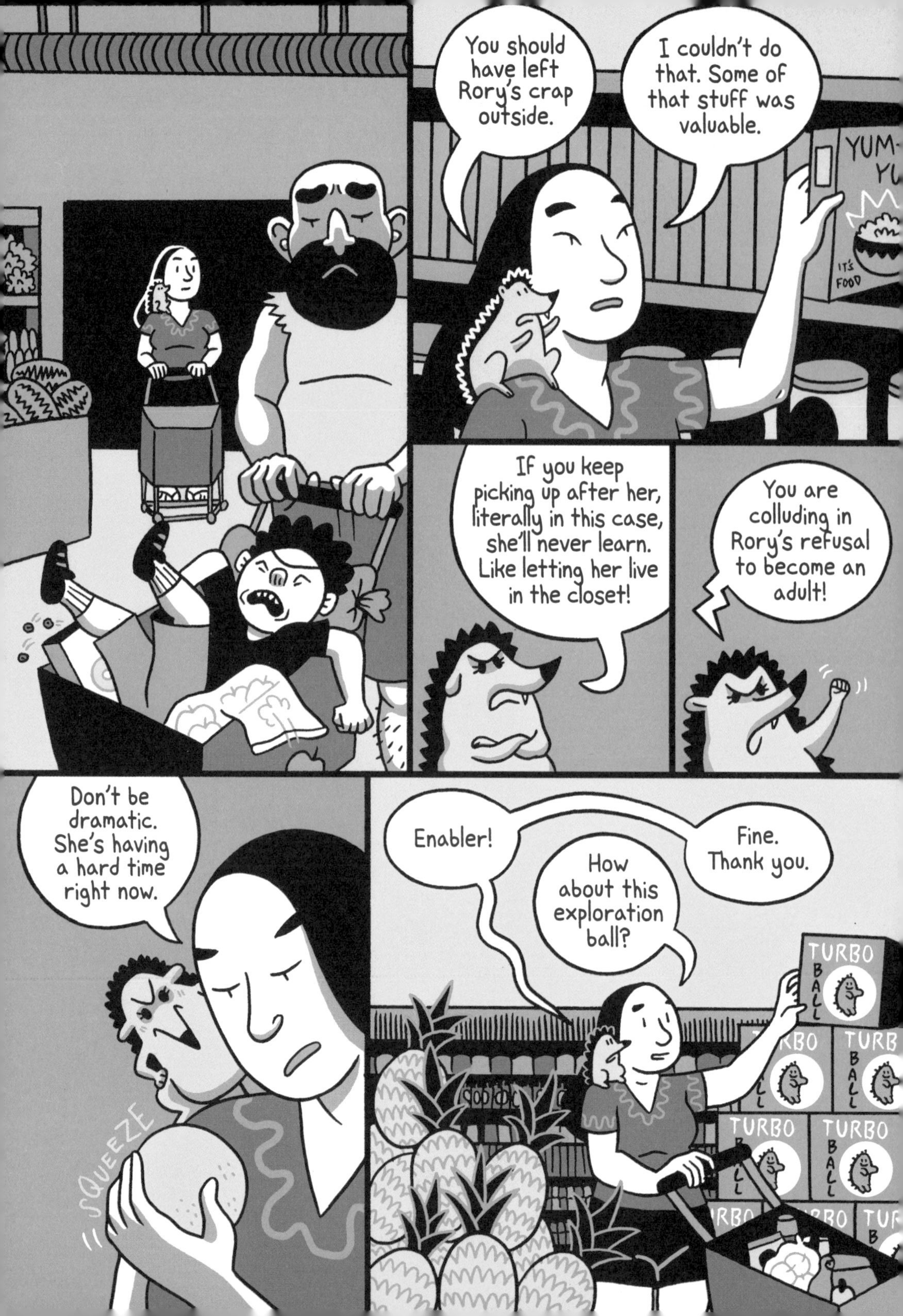
You should have left Rory's crap outside.
I couldn't do that. Some of that stuff was valuable.
YUM-YU
IT'S FOOD
If you keep picking up after her, literally in this case, she'll never learn. Like letting her live in the closet!
You are colluding in Rory's refusal to become an adult!
Don't be dramatic. She's having a hard time right now.
SQUEEZE
Enabler!
Fine. Thank you.
How about this exploration ball?
TURBO BALL

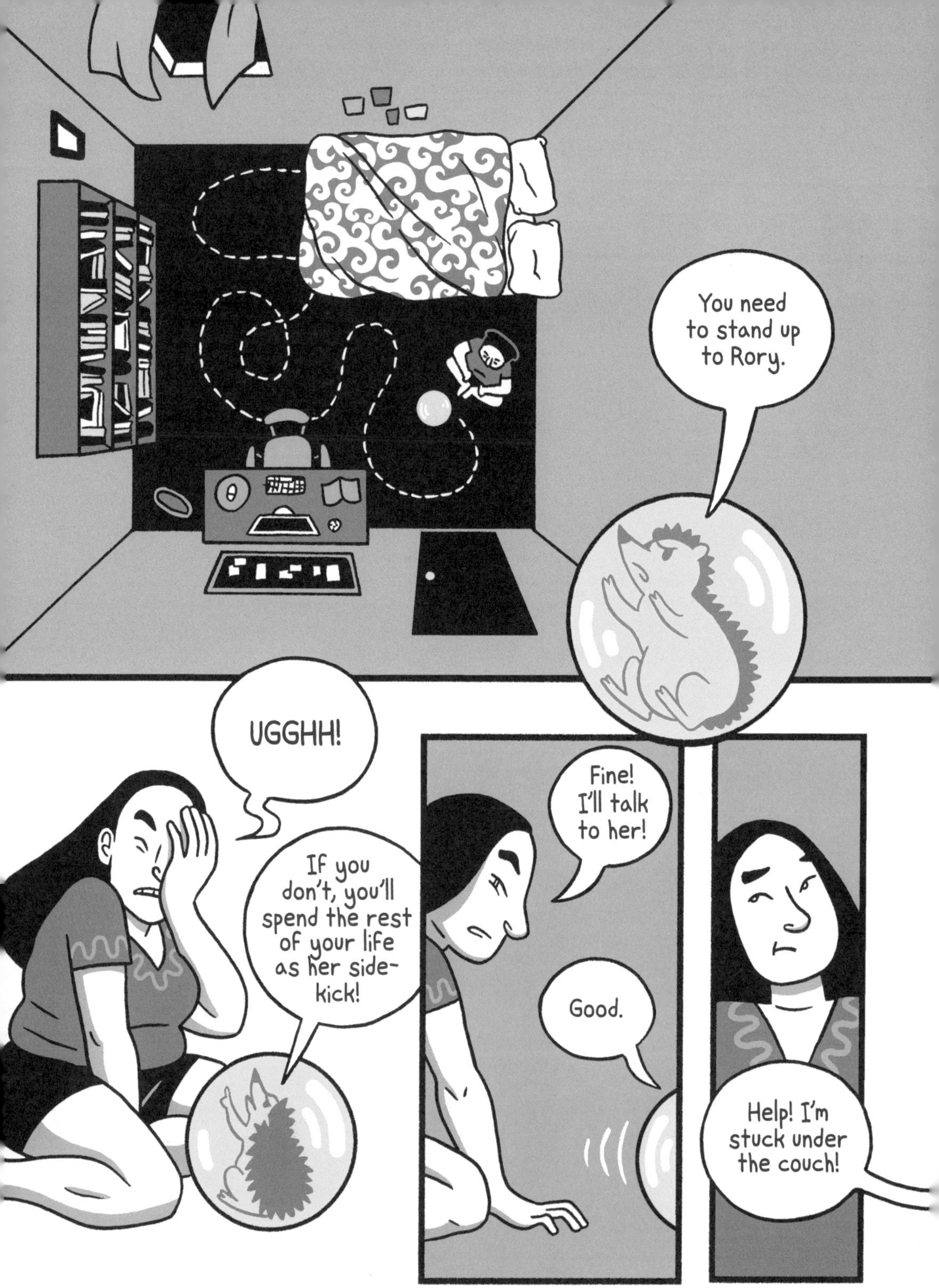
You need to stand up to Rory.
UGGHH!
If you don't, you'll spend the rest of your life as her side-kick!
Fine! I'll talk to her!
Good.
Help! I'm stuck under the couch!

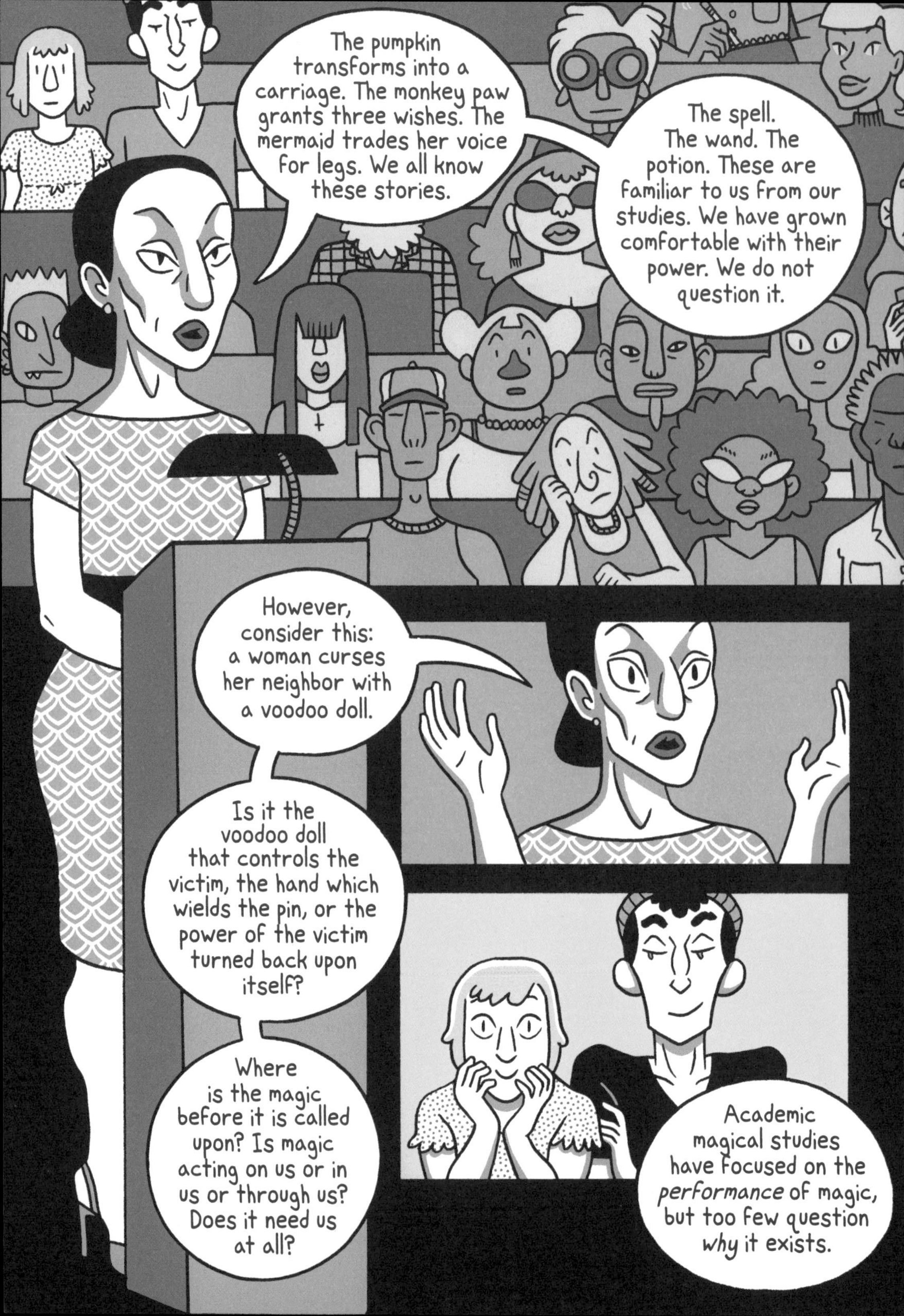

The pumpkin transforms into a carriage. The monkey paw grants three wishes. The mermaid trades her voice for legs. We all know these stories.
The spell. The wand. The potion. These are familiar to us from our studies. We have grown comfortable with their power. We do not question it.
However, consider this: a woman curses her neighbor with a voodoo doll.
Is it the voodoo doll that controls the victim, the hand which wields the pin, or the power of the victim turned back upon itself?
Where is the magic before it is called upon? Is magic acting on us or in us or through us? Does it need us at all?
Academic magical studies have focused on the *performance* of magic, but too few question *why* it exists.

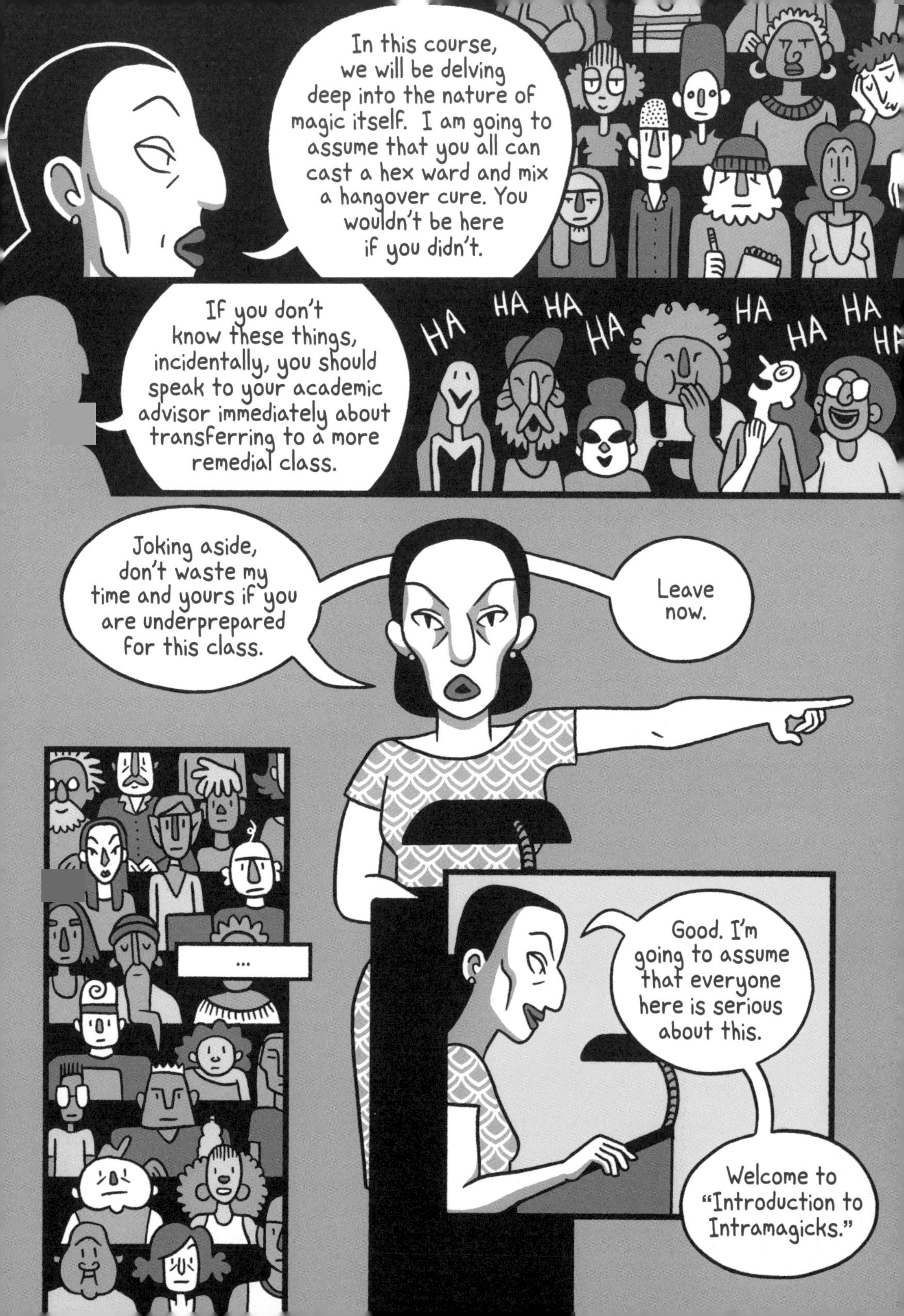

In this course, we will be delving deep into the nature of magic itself. I am going to assume that you all can cast a hex ward and mix a hangover cure. You wouldn't be here if you didn't.
If you don't know these things, incidentally, you should speak to your academic advisor immediately about transferring to a more remedial class.
HA HA HA HA HA HA HA HA
Joking aside, don't waste my time and yours if you are underprepared for this class.
Leave now.
...
Good. I'm going to assume that everyone here is serious about this.
Welcome to "Introduction to Intramagicks."

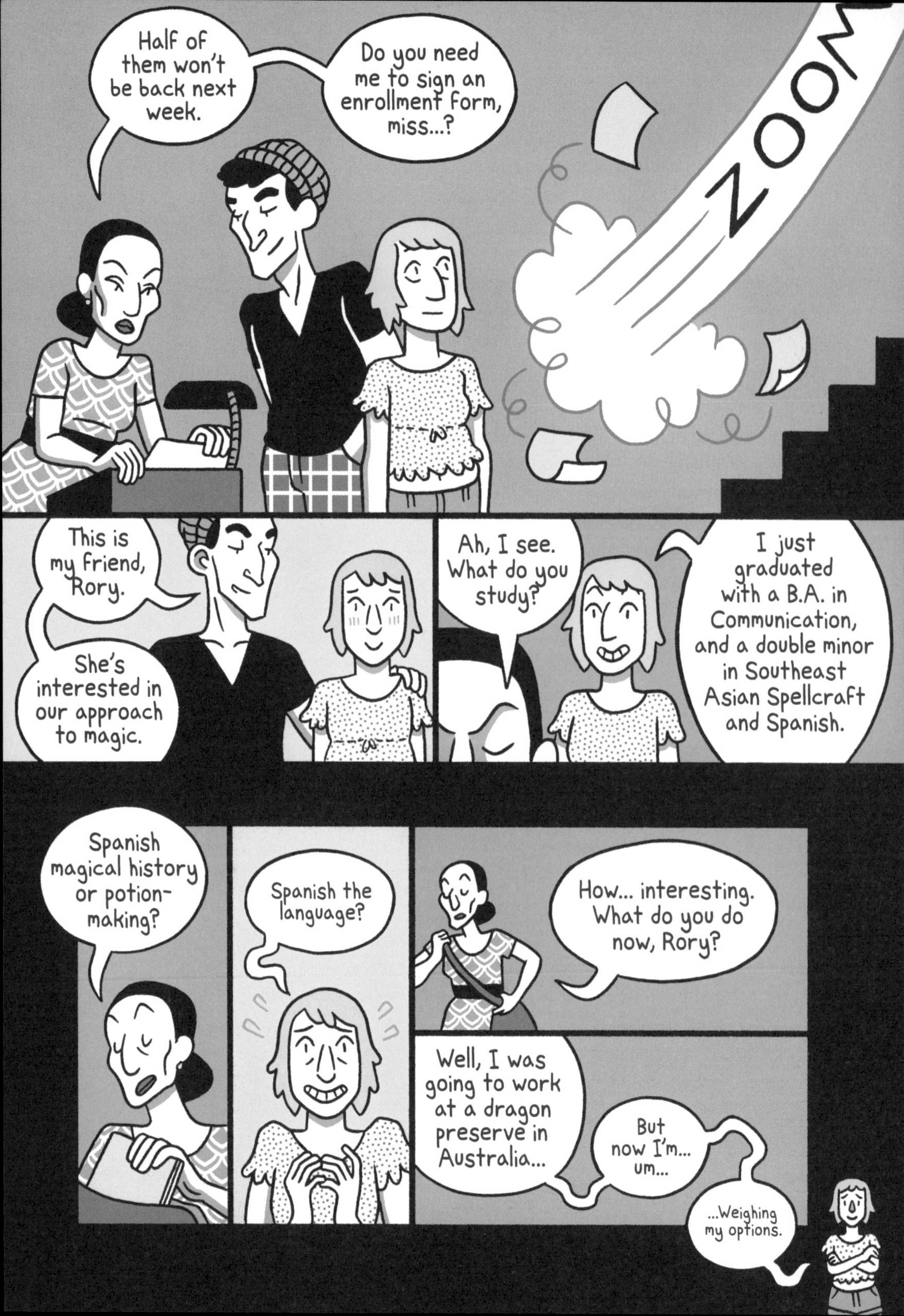
Half of them won't be back next week.
Do you need me to sign an enrollment form, miss...?
ZOOM
This is my friend, Rory.
She's interested in our approach to magic.
Ah, I see. What do you study?
I just graduated with a B.A. in Communication, and a double minor in Southeast Asian Spellcraft and Spanish.
Spanish magical history or potion-making?
Spanish the language?
How... interesting. What do you do now, Rory?
Well, I was going to work at a dragon preserve in Australia...
But now I'm... um...
...Weighing my options.

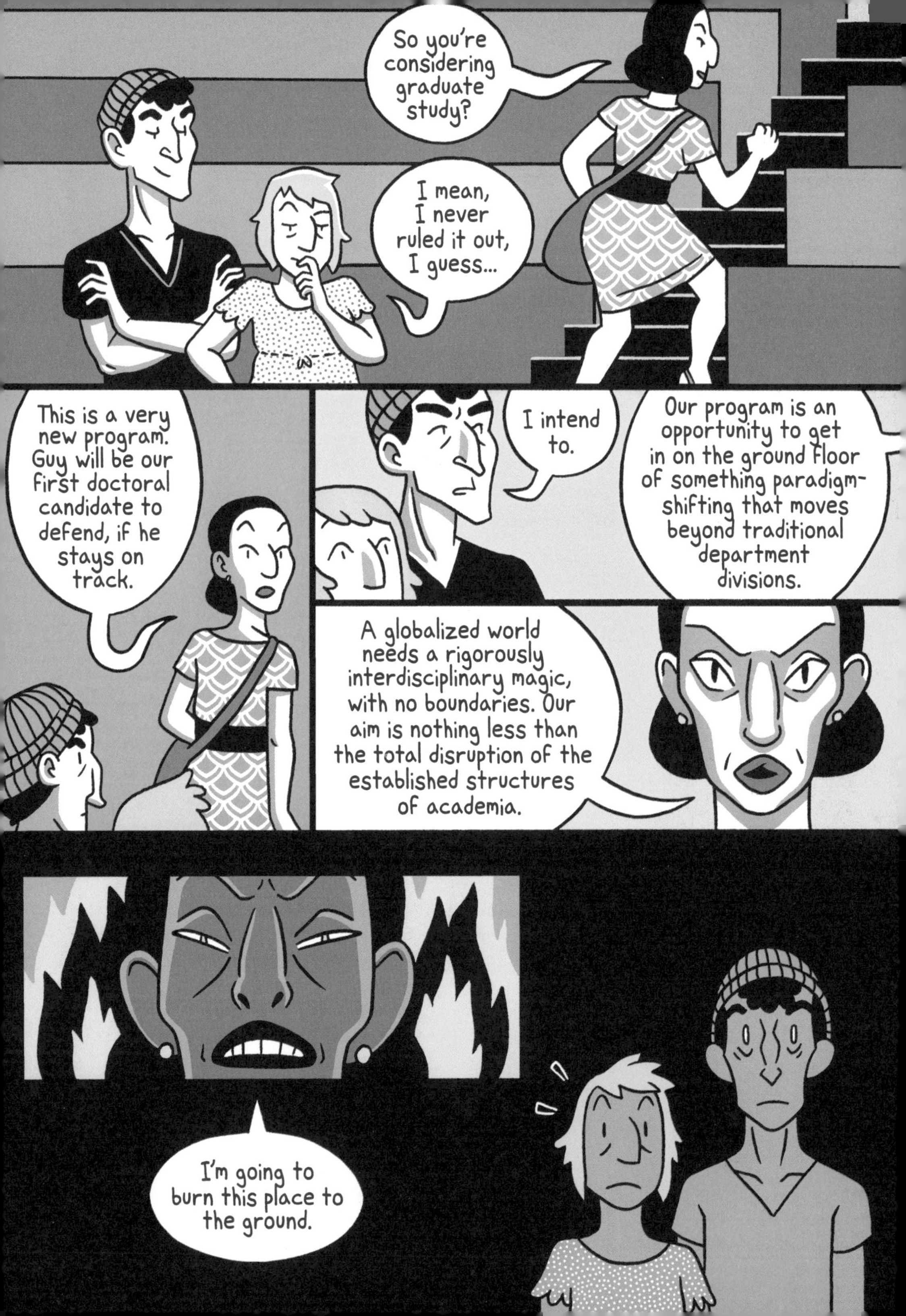
So you're considering graduate study?
I mean, I never ruled it out, I guess...
This is a very new program. Guy will be our first doctoral candidate to defend, if he stays on track.
I intend to.
Our program is an opportunity to get in on the ground floor of something paradigm-shifting that moves beyond traditional department divisions.
A globalized world needs a rigorously interdisciplinary magic, with no boundaries. Our aim is nothing less than the total disruption of the established structures of academia.
I'm going to burn this place to the ground.

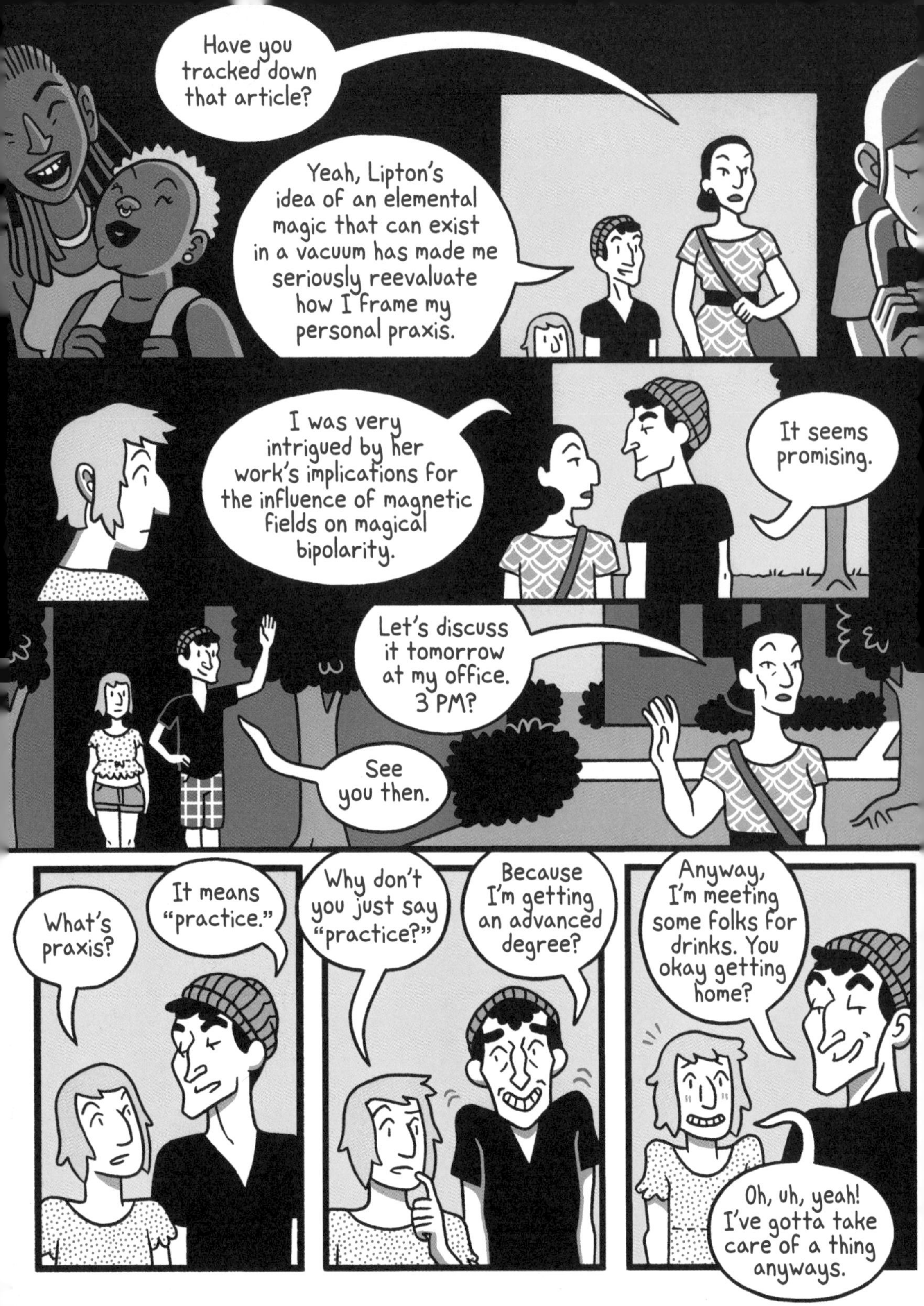
Have you tracked down that article?
Yeah, Lipton's idea of an elemental magic that can exist in a vacuum has made me seriously reevaluate how I frame my personal praxis.
I was very intrigued by her work's implications for the influence of magnetic fields on magical bipolarity.
It seems promising.
Let's discuss it tomorrow at my office. 3 PM?
See you then.
What's praxis?
It means "practice."
Why don't you just say "practice?"
Because I'm getting an advanced degree?
Anyway, I'm meeting some folks for drinks. You okay getting home?
Oh, uh, yeah! I've gotta take care of a thing anyways.

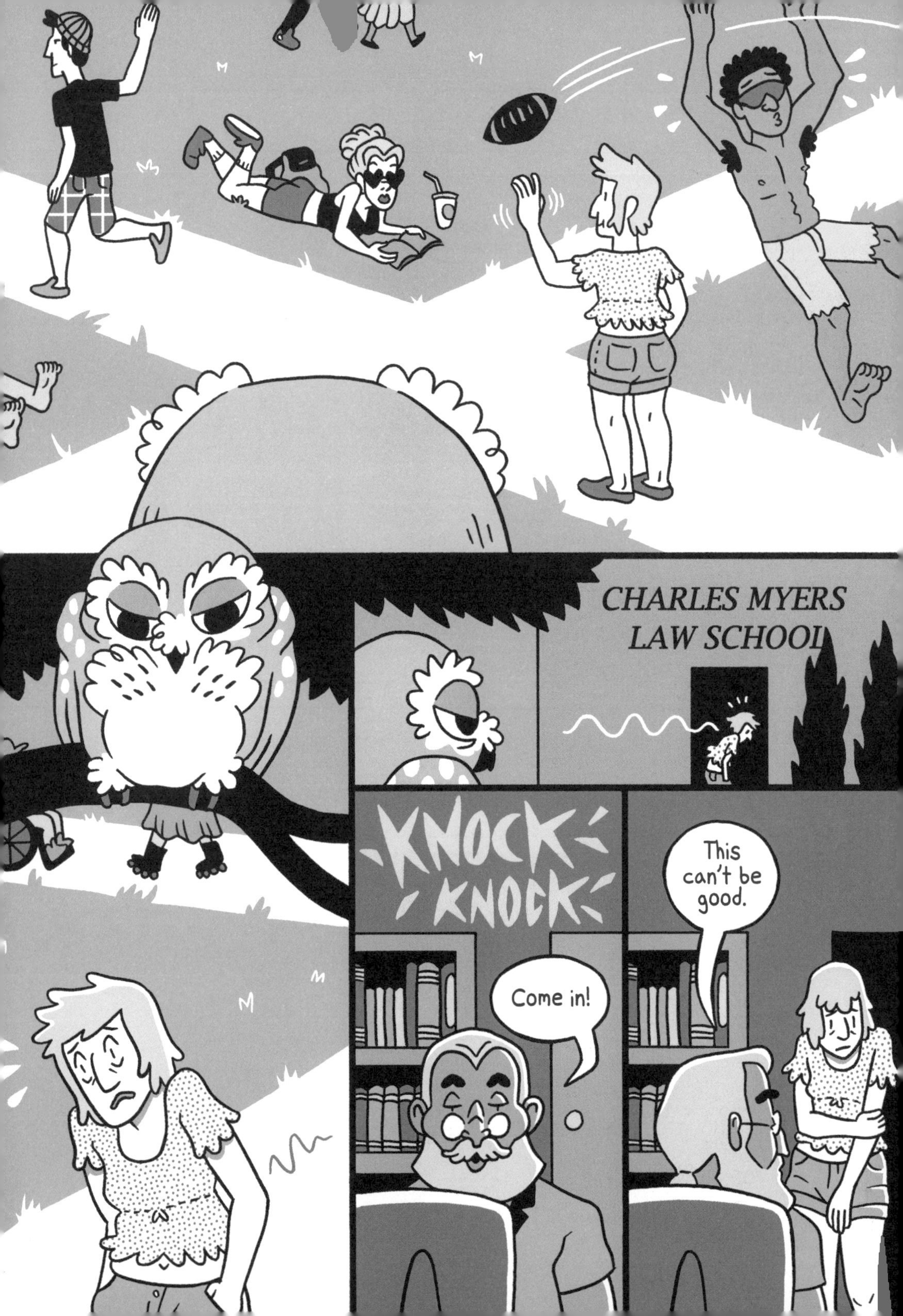
CHARLES MYERS
LAW SCHOOL
KNOCK
KNOCK
Come in!
This can't be good.

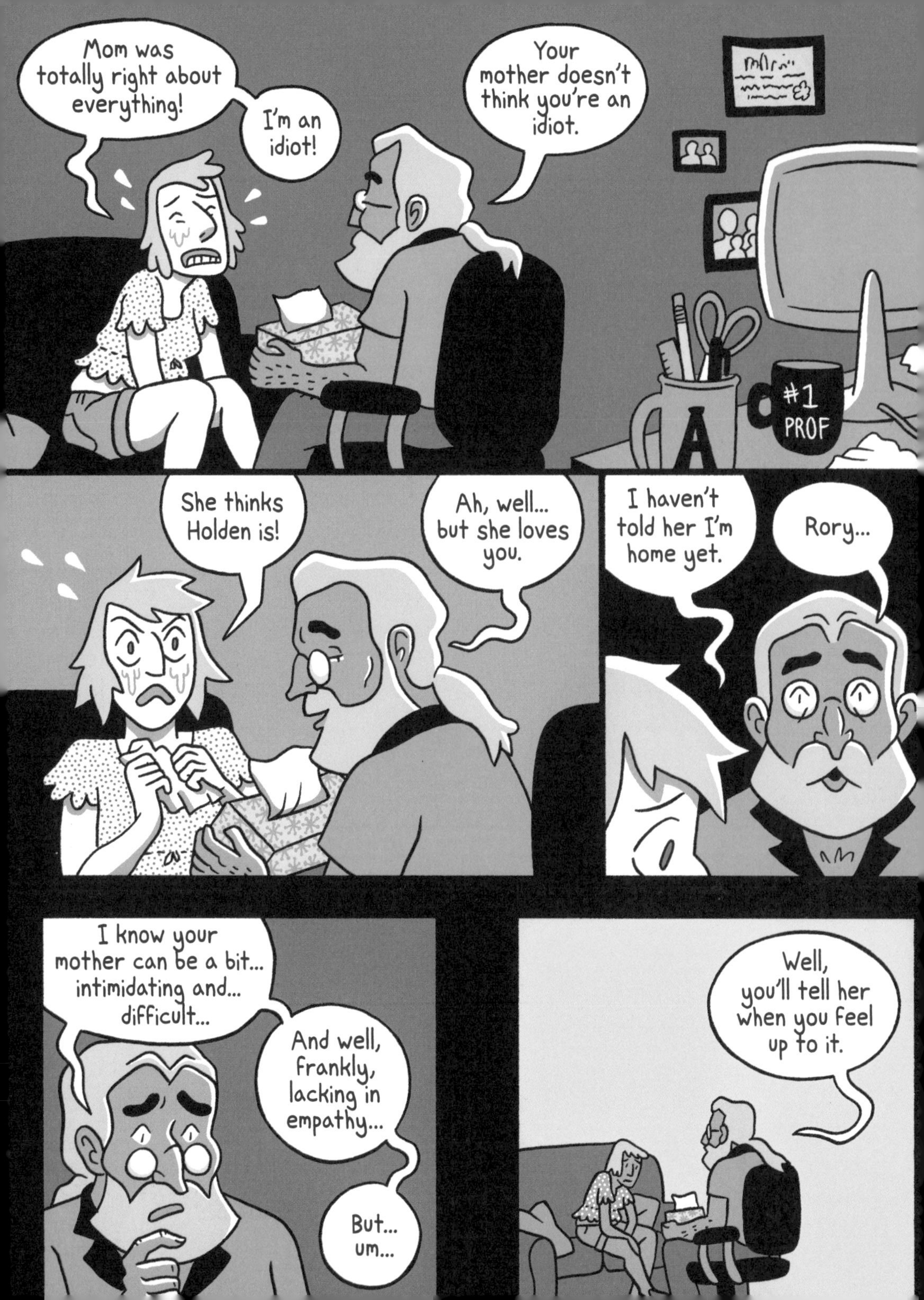
Mom was totally right about everything!
I'm an idiot!
Your mother doesn't think you're an idiot.
#1 PROF
She thinks Holden is!
Ah, well... but she loves you.
I haven't told her I'm home yet.
Rory...
I know your mother can be a bit... intimidating and... difficult...
And well, frankly, lacking in empathy...
But... um...
Well, you'll tell her when you feel up to it.

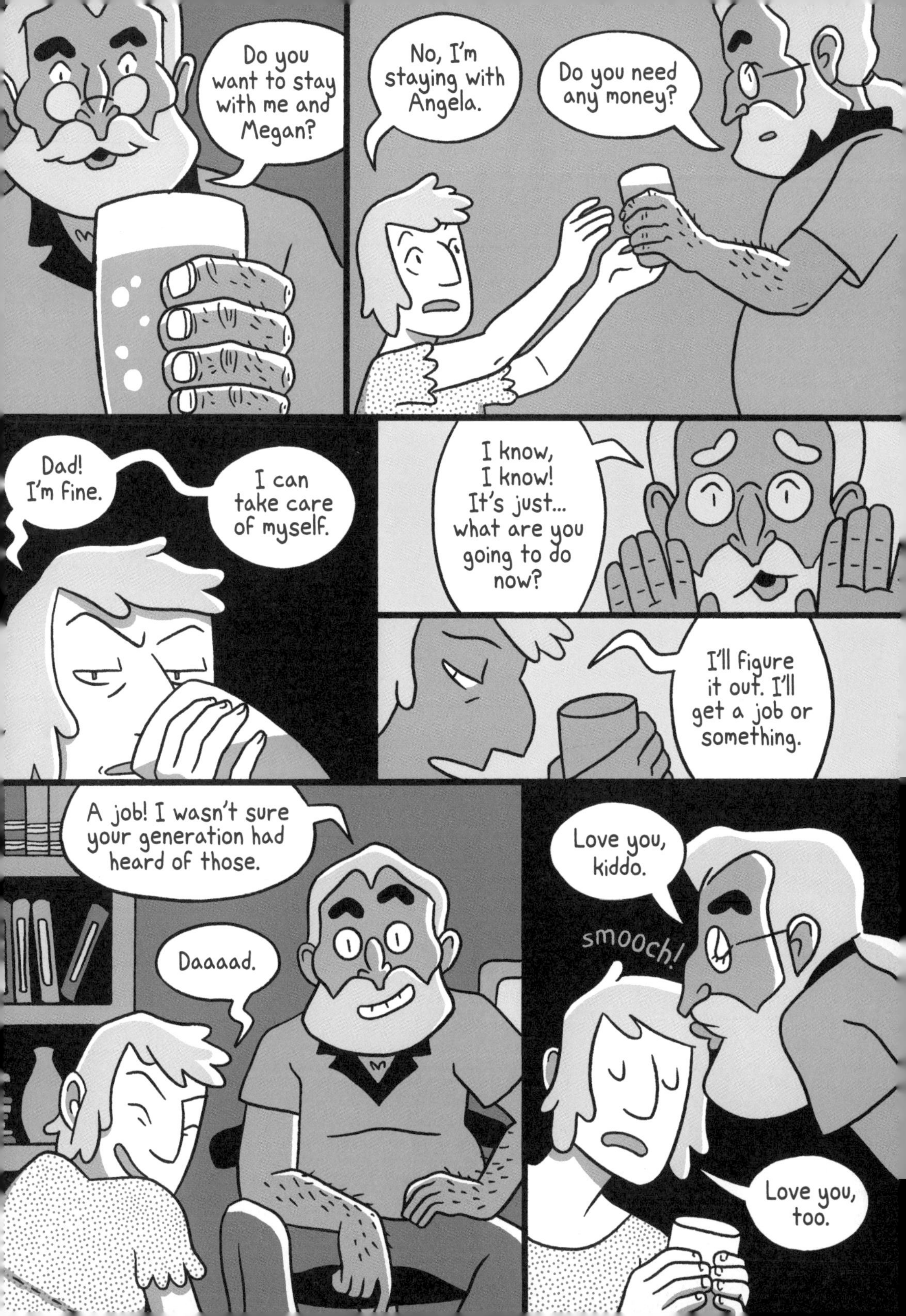
Do you want to stay with me and Megan?
No, I'm staying with Angela.
Do you need any money?
Dad! I'm fine.
I can take care of myself.
I know, I know! It's just... what are you going to do now?
I'll figure it out. I'll get a job or something.
A job! I wasn't sure your generation had heard of those.
Daaaad.
Love you, kiddo.
smooch!
Love you, too.

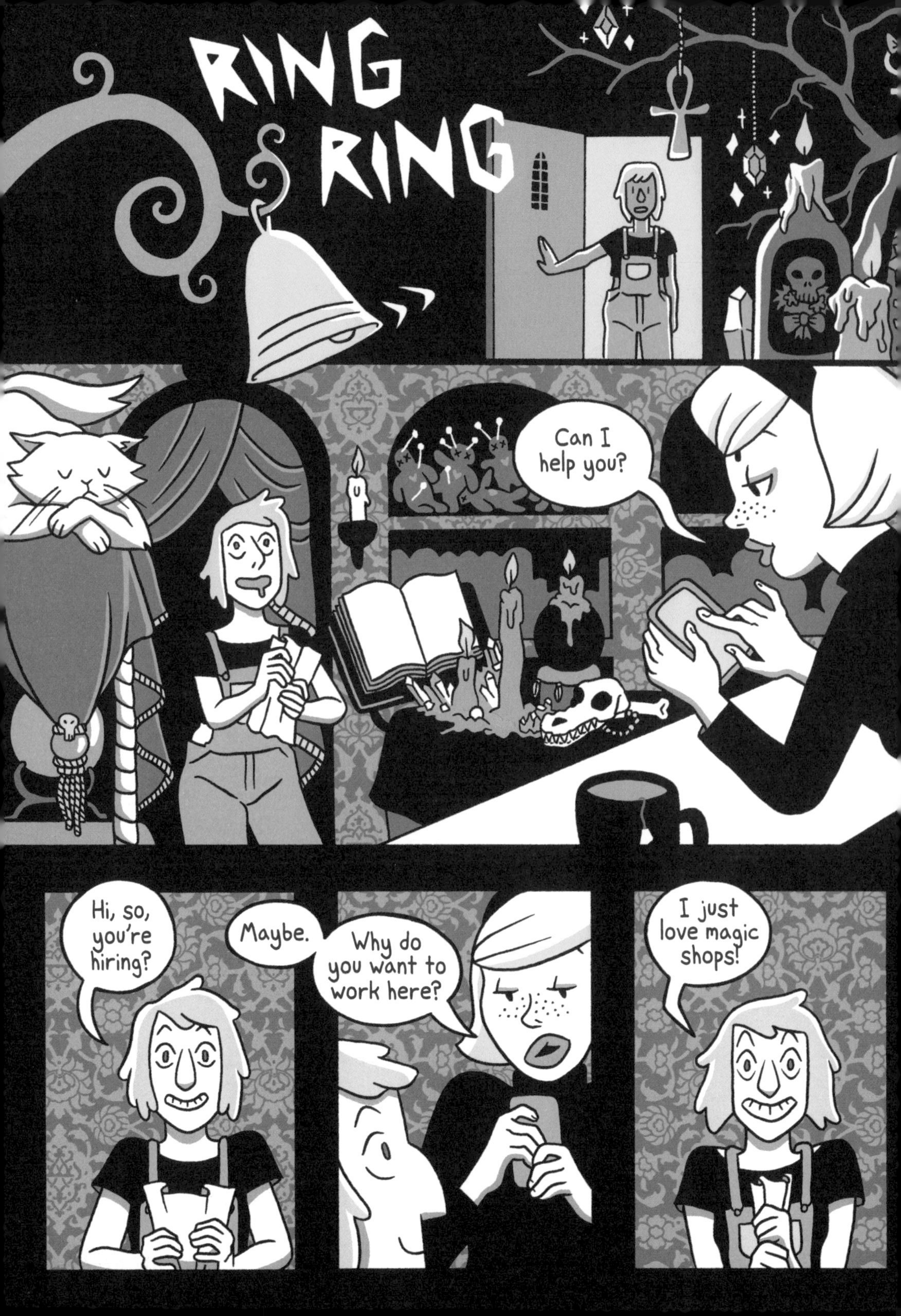

RING RING
Can I help you?
Hi, so, you're hiring?
Maybe.
Why do you want to work here?
I just love magic shops!

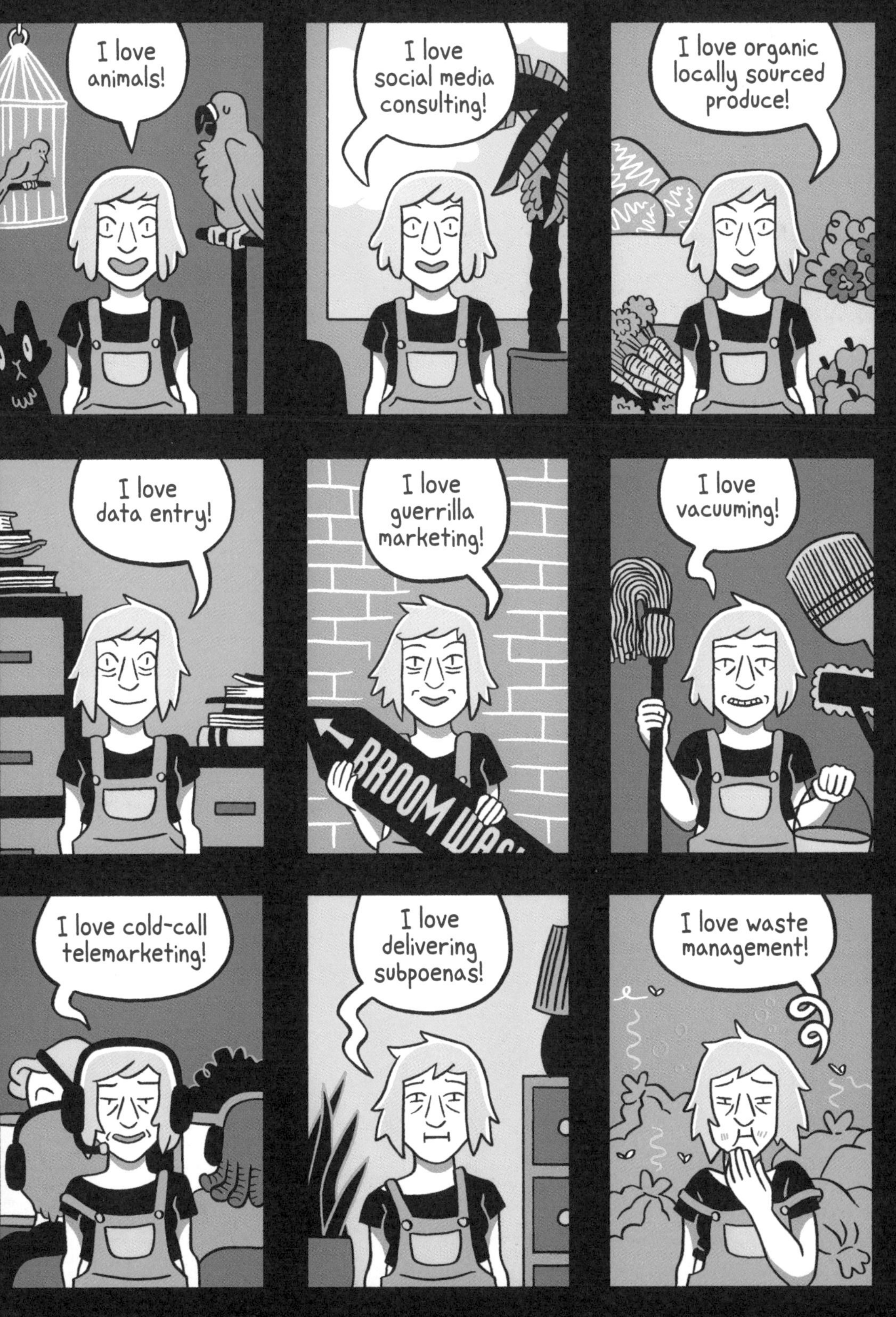
I love animals!
I love social media consulting!
I love organic locally sourced produce!
I love data entry!
I love guerrilla marketing!
BROOM WAS
I love vacuuming!
I love cold-call telemarketing!
I love delivering subpoenas!
I love waste management!

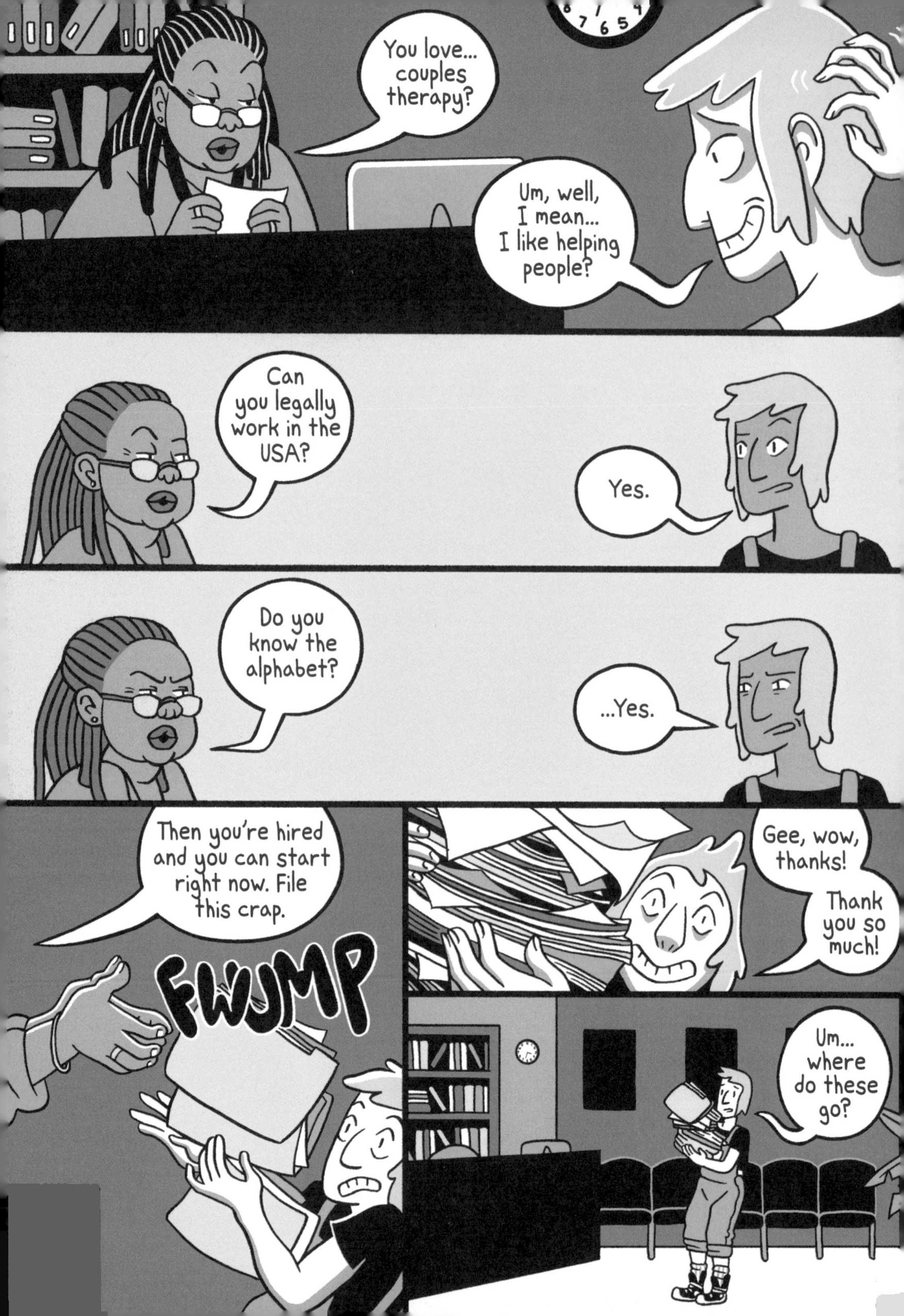
You love... couples therapy?
Um, well, I mean... I like helping people?
Can you legally work in the USA?
Yes.
Do you know the alphabet?
...Yes.
Then you're hired and you can start right now. File this crap.
FWUMP
Gee, wow, thanks!
Thank you so much!
Um... where do these go?

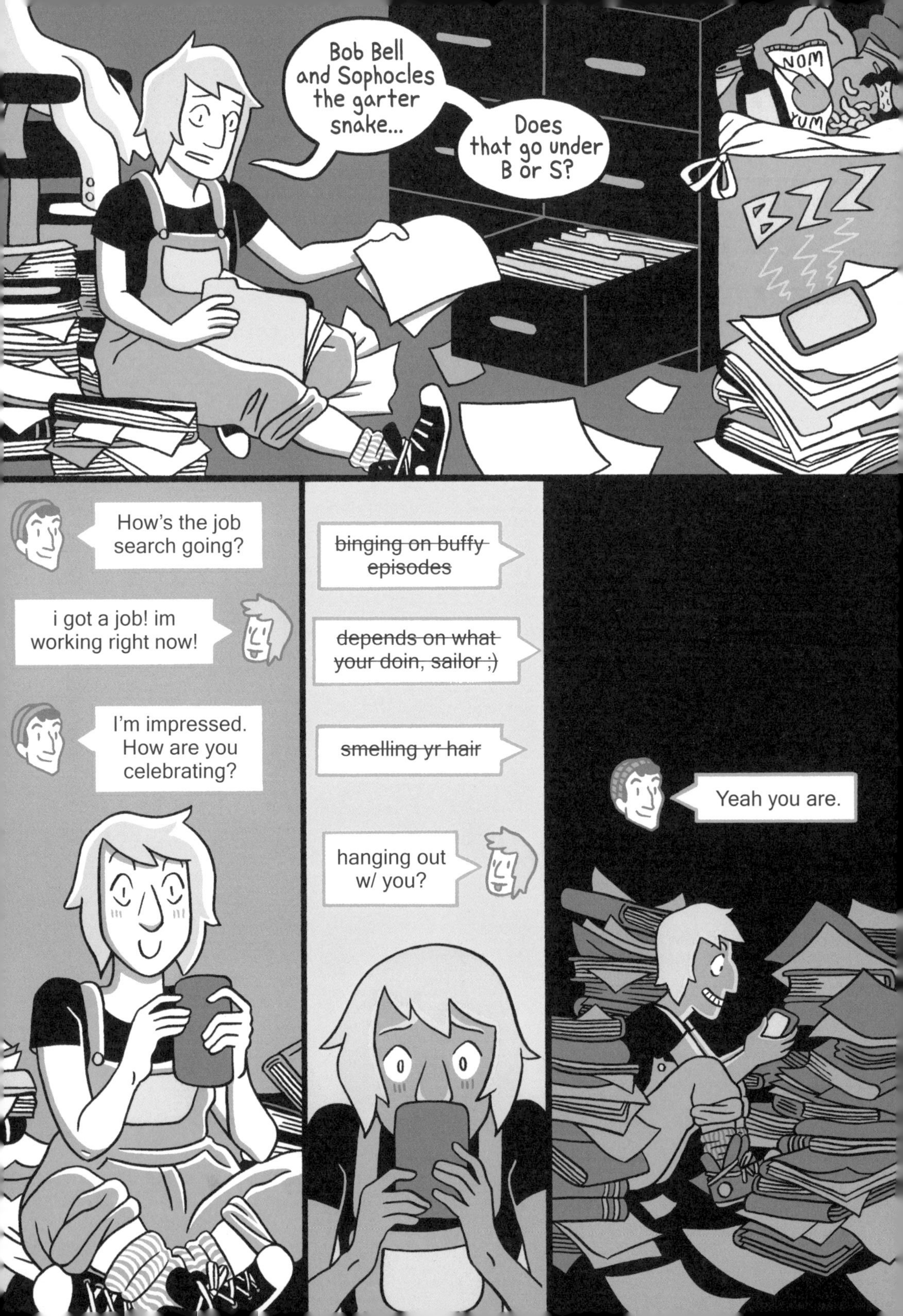

Bob Bell and Sophocles the garter snake...
Does that go under B or S?
NOM
YUM
BZZ
How's the job search going?
i got a job! im working right now!
I'm impressed. How are you celebrating?
binging on buffy episodes
depends on what your doin, sailor ;)
smelling yr hair
hanging out w/ you?
Yeah you are.

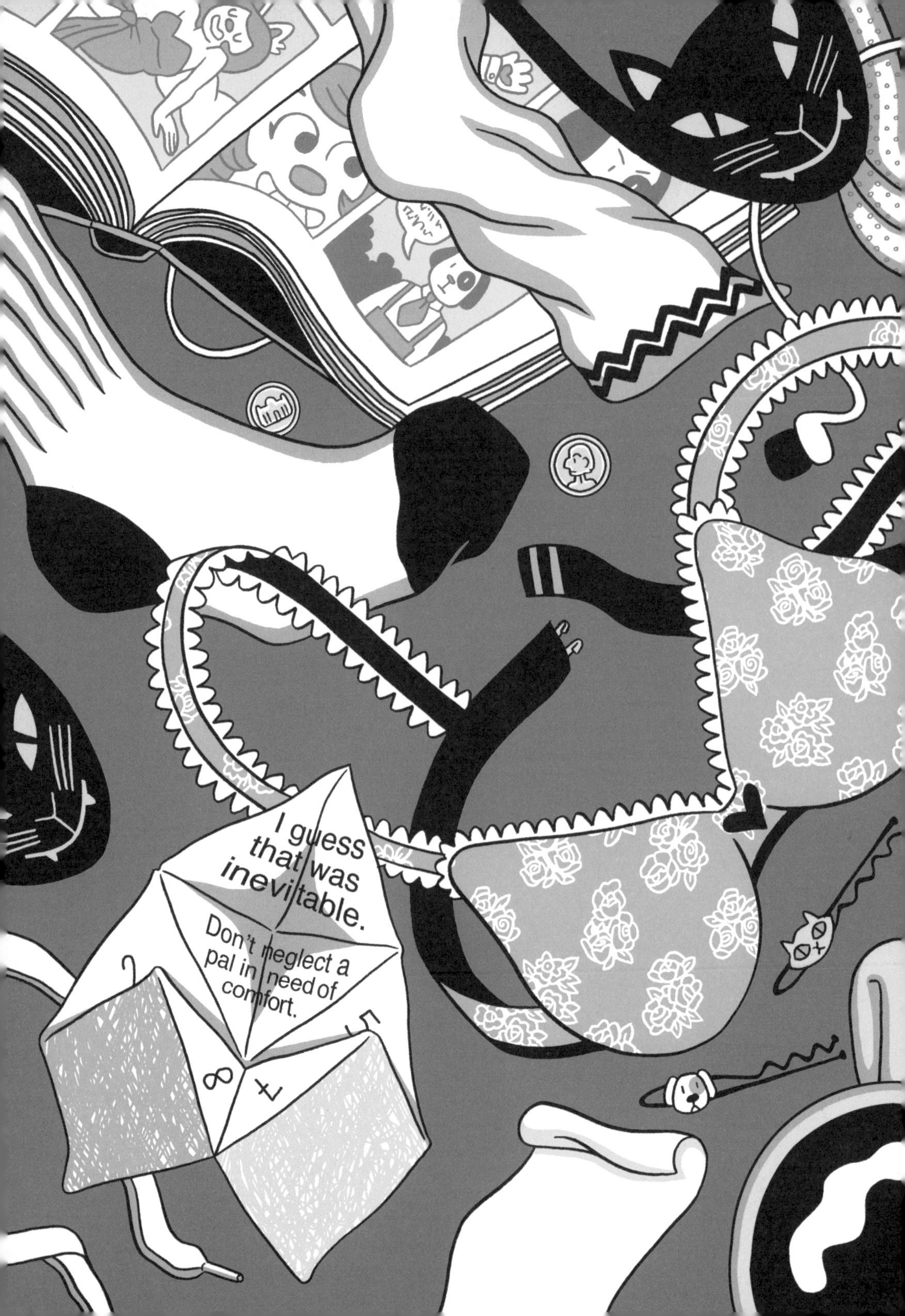

I guess that was inevitable.
Don't neglect a pal in need of comfort.

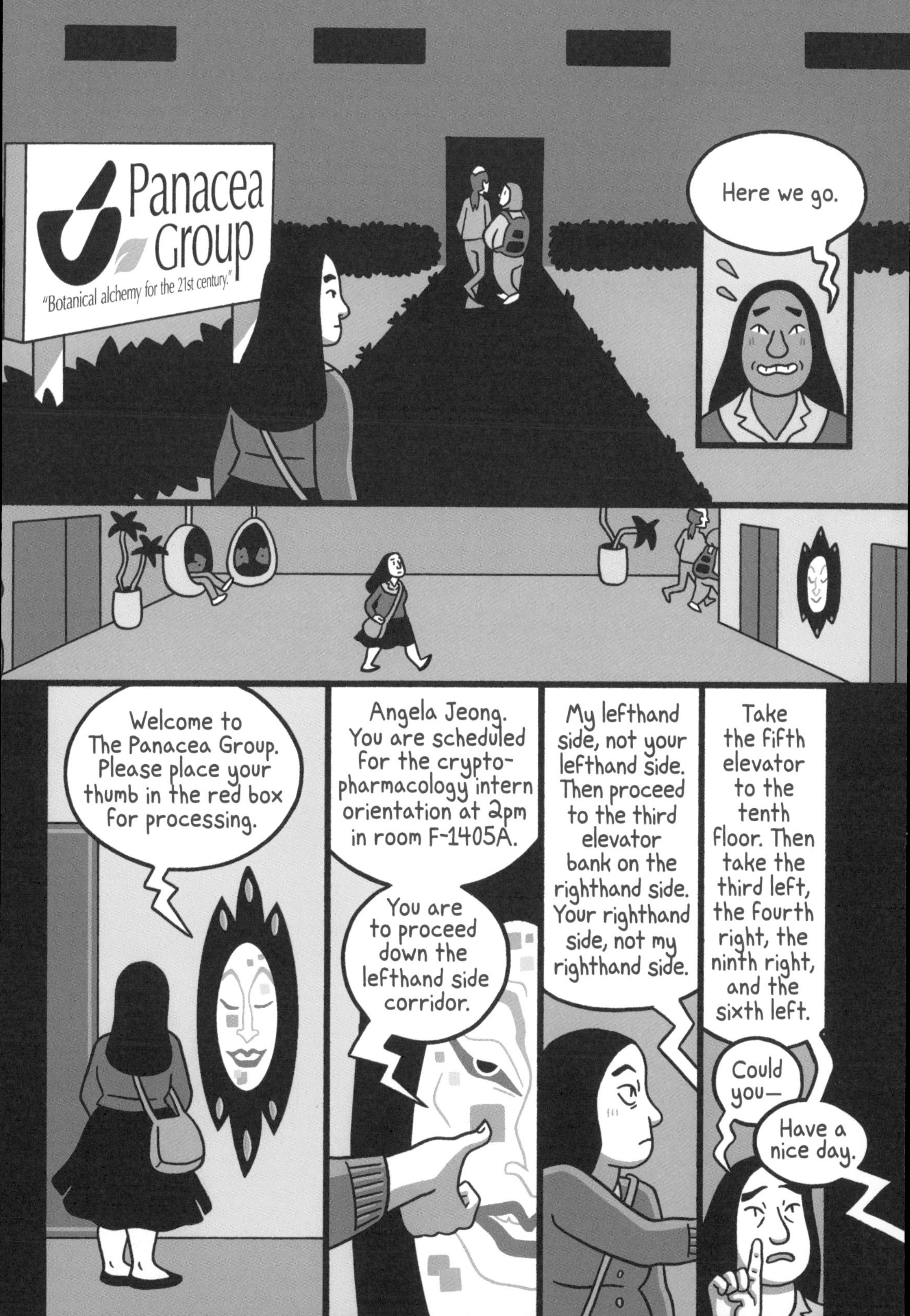
Panacea Group
"Botanical alchemy for the 21st century."
Here we go.
Welcome to The Panacea Group. Please place your thumb in the red box for processing.
Angela Jeong. You are scheduled for the crypto-pharmacology intern orientation at 2pm in room F-1405A.
You are to proceed down the lefthand side corridor.
My lefthand side, not your lefthand side. Then proceed to the third elevator bank on the righthand side. Your righthand side, not my righthand side.
Take the fifth elevator to the tenth floor. Then take the third left, the fourth right, the ninth right, and the sixth left.
Could you—
Have a nice day.

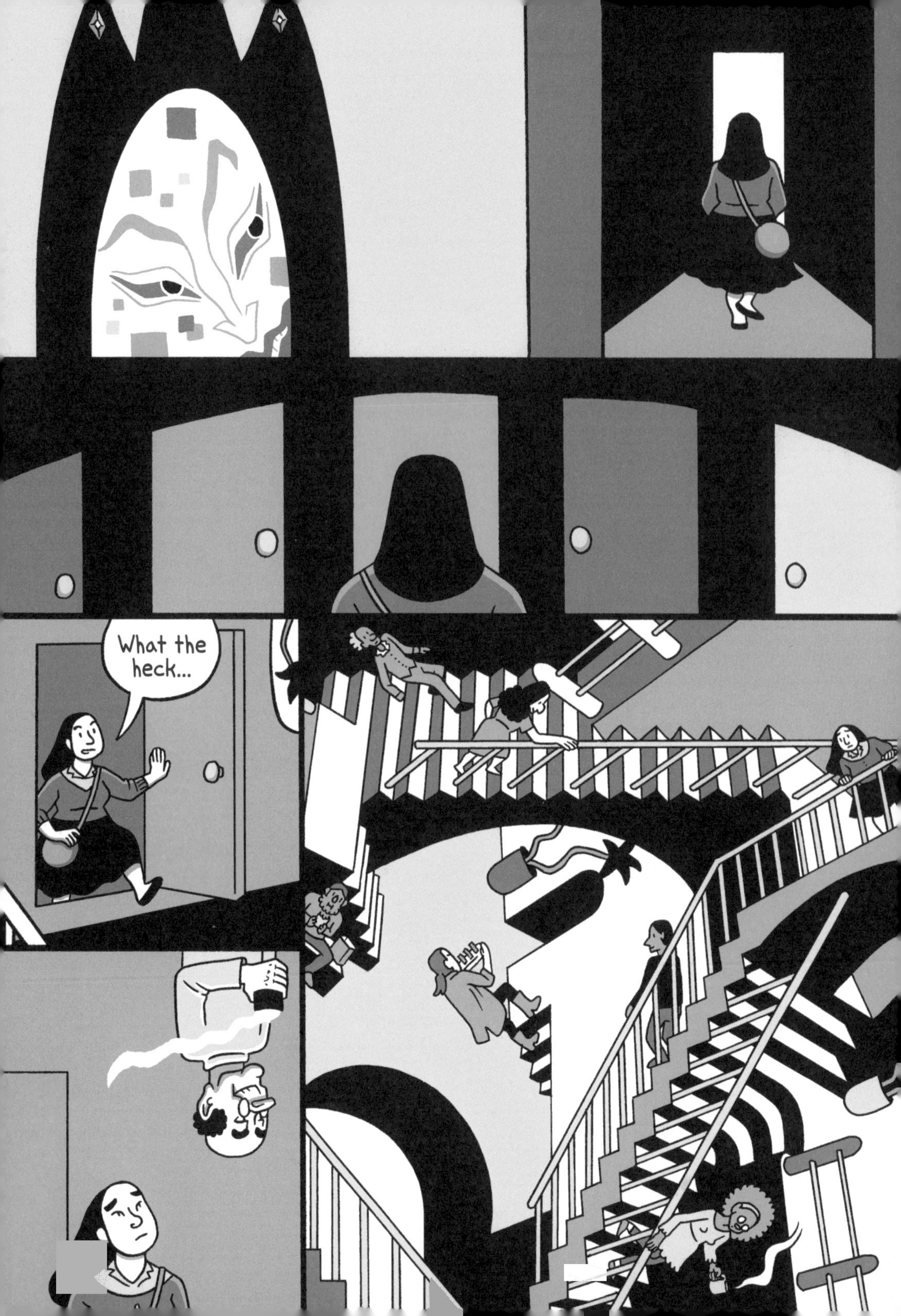
What the heck...

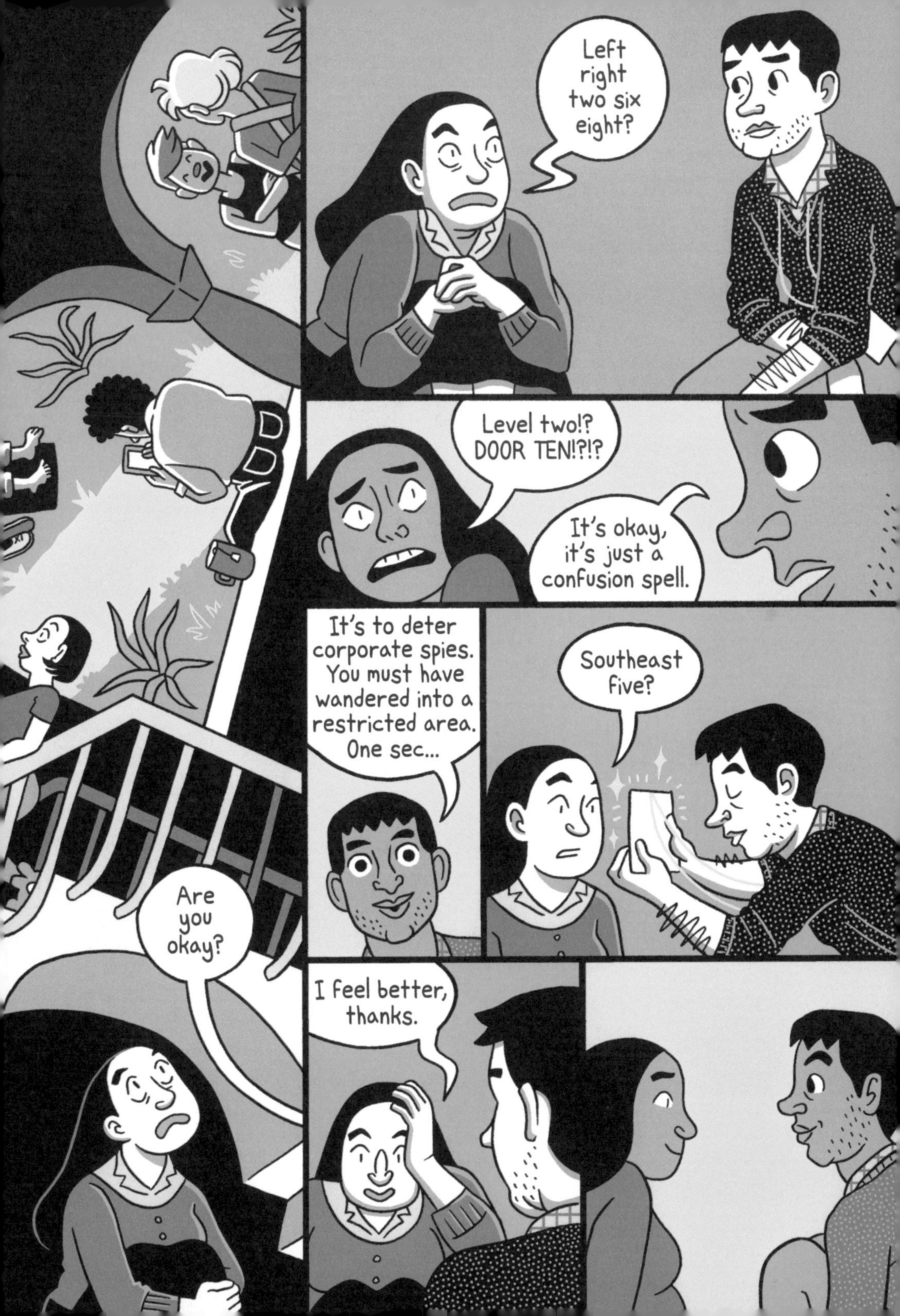
Left right two six eight?
Level two!? DOOR TEN!?!?
It's okay, it's just a confusion spell.
It's to deter corporate spies. You must have wandered into a restricted area. One sec...
Southeast five?
Are you okay?
I feel better, thanks.

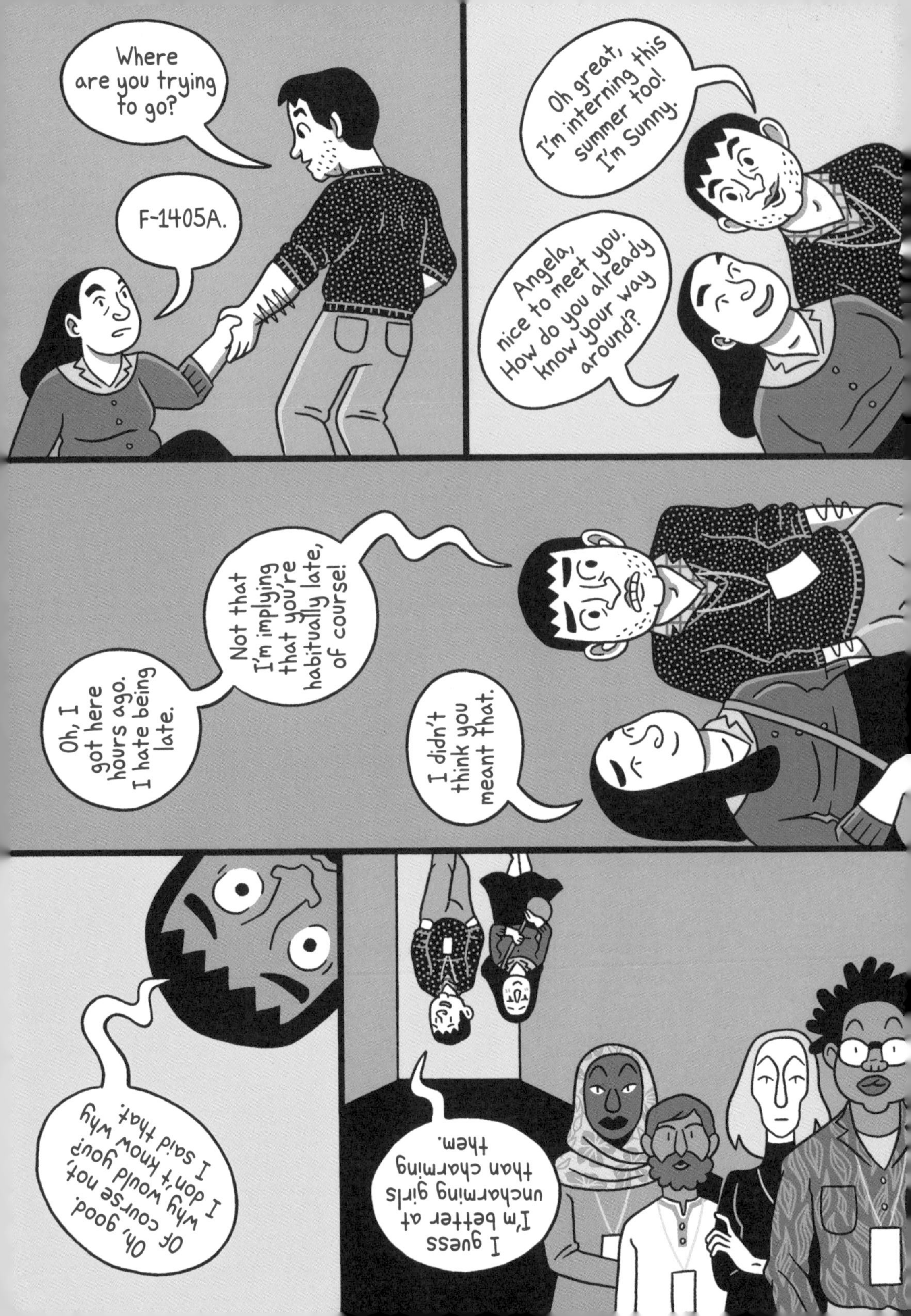

Where are you trying to go?
F-1405A.
Oh great, I'm interning this summer too! I'm Sunny.
Angela, nice to meet you. How do you already know your way around?
Oh, I got here hours ago. I hate being late.
Not that I'm implying that you're habitually late, of course!
I didn't think you meant that.
Oh, good. Of course not, why would you? I don't know why I said that.
I guess I'm better at uncharming girls than charming them.

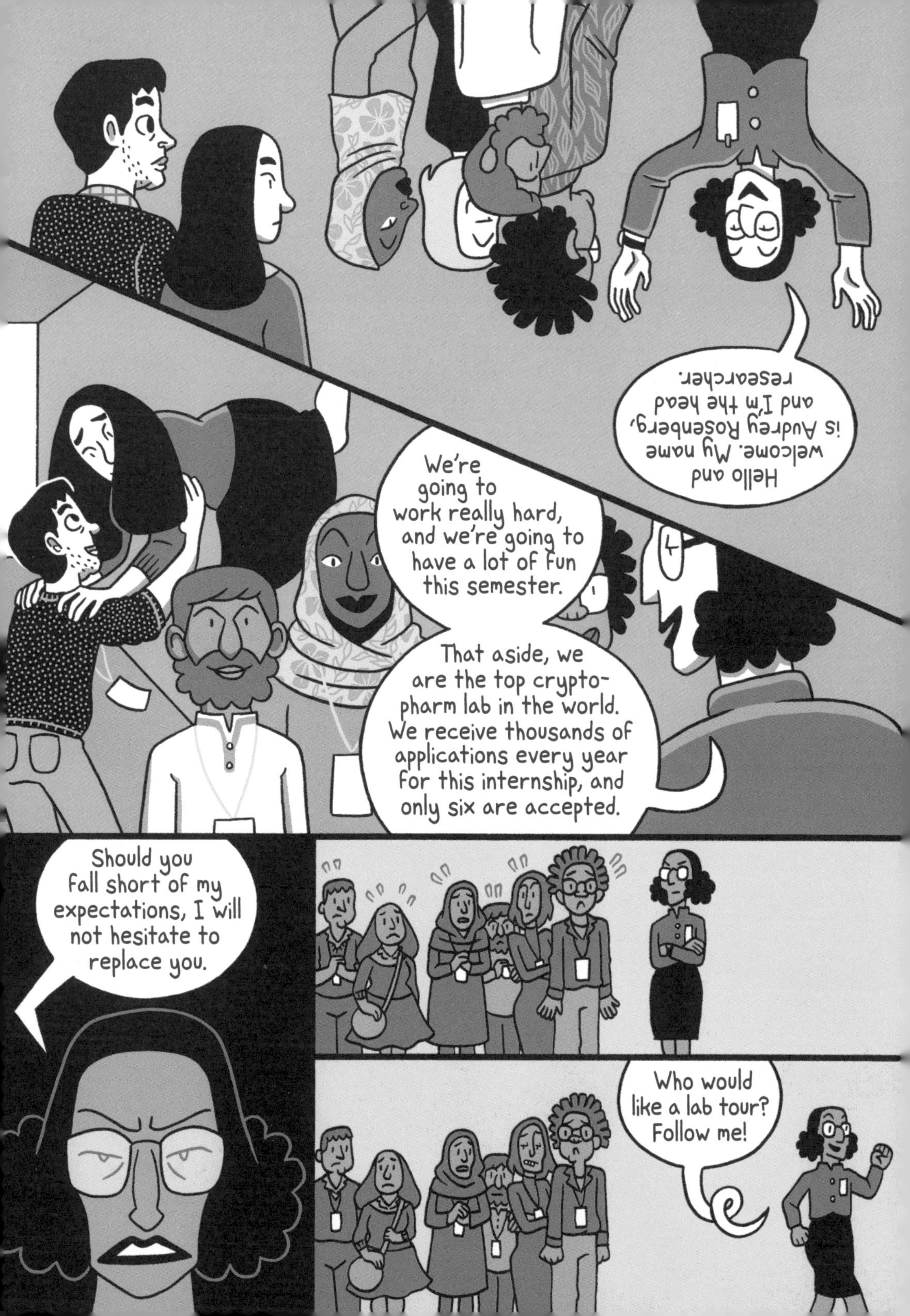
Hello and welcome. My name is Audrey Rosenberg, and I'm the head researcher.
We're going to work really hard, and we're going to have a lot of fun this semester.
That aside, we are the top crypto-pharm lab in the world. We receive thousands of applications every year for this internship, and only six are accepted.
Should you fall short of my expectations, I will not hesitate to replace you.
Who would like a lab tour? Follow me!

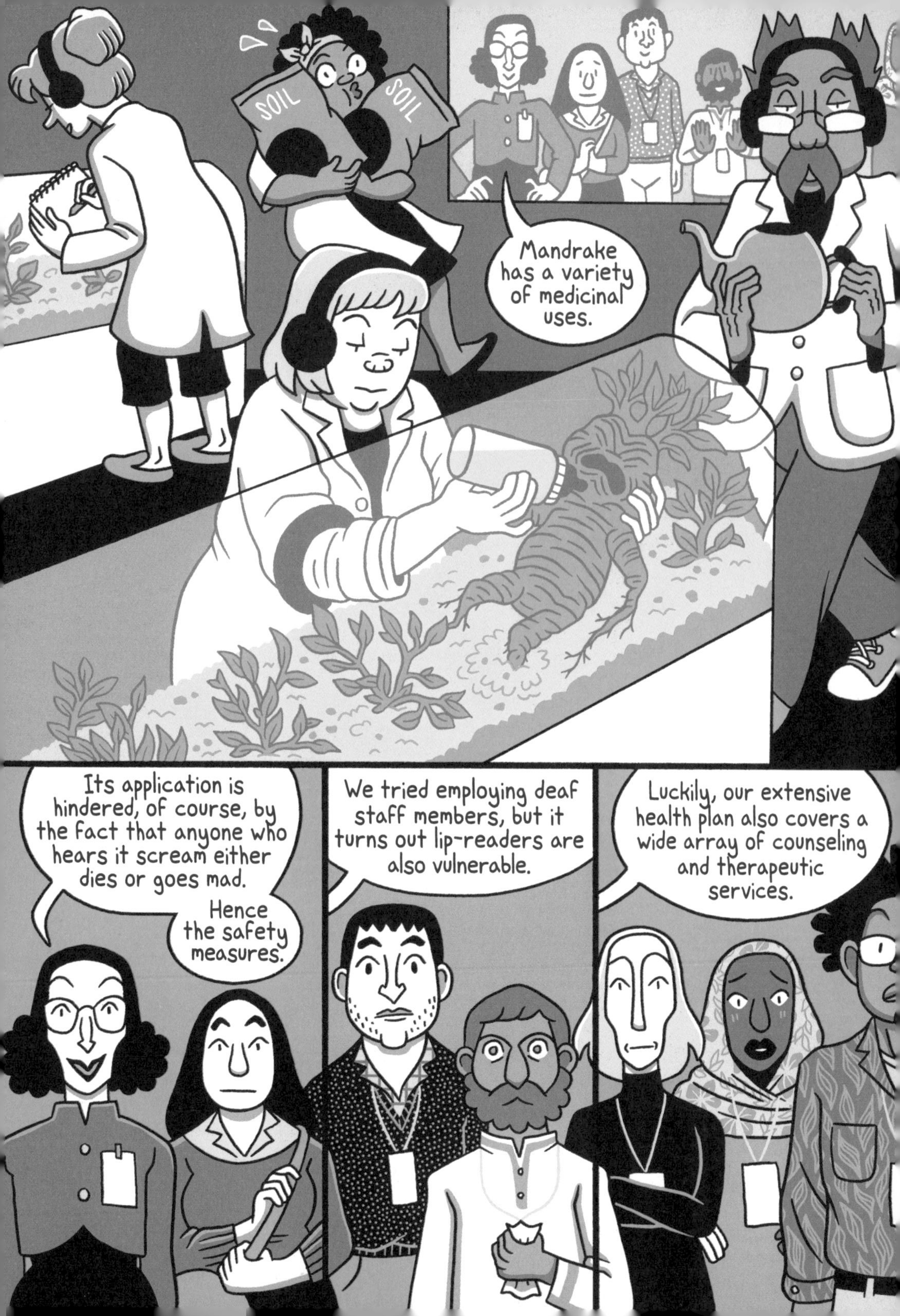
SOIL
SOIL
Mandrake has a variety of medicinal uses.
Its application is hindered, of course, by the fact that anyone who hears it scream either dies or goes mad.
Hence the safety measures.
We tried employing deaf staff members, but it turns out lip-readers are also vulnerable.
Luckily, our extensive health plan also covers a wide array of counseling and therapeutic services.

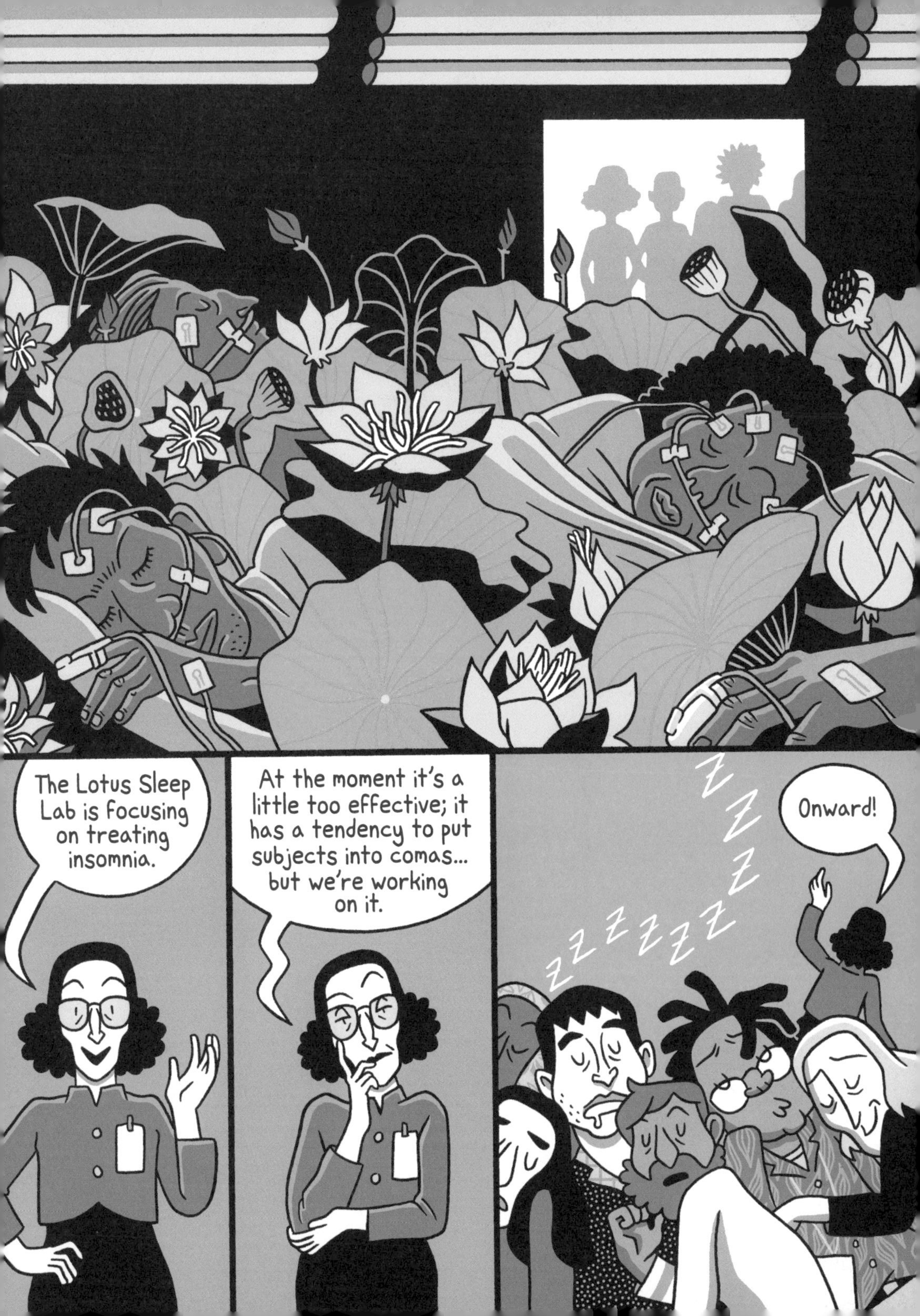
The Lotus Sleep Lab is focusing on treating insomnia.
At the moment it's a little too effective; it has a tendency to put subjects into comas... but we're working on it.
Z Z Z Z Z Z Z Z Z Z Z
Onward!

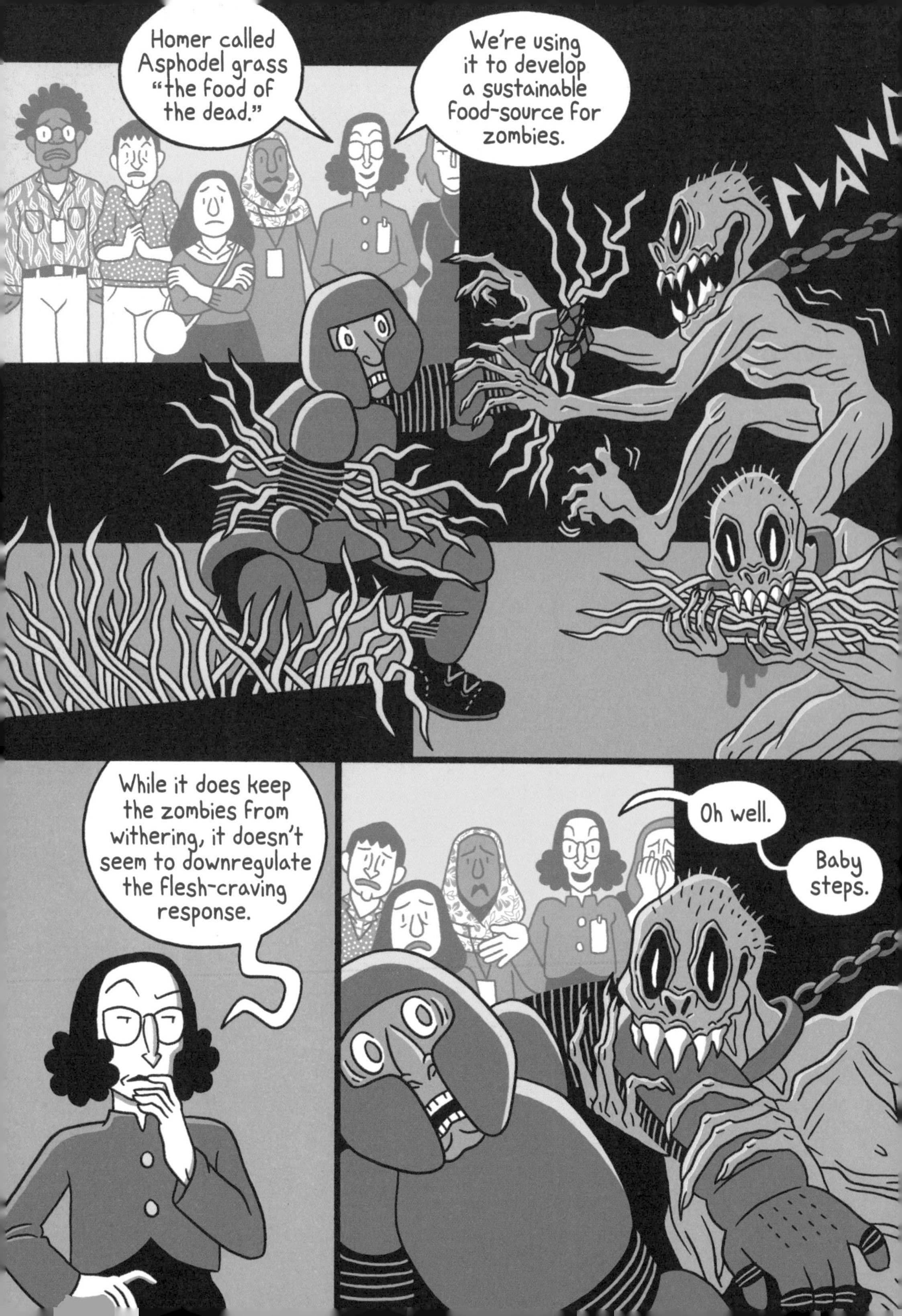
Homer called Asphodel grass "the food of the dead."
We're using it to develop a sustainable food-source for zombies.
CLANG
While it does keep the zombies from withering, it doesn't seem to downregulate the flesh-craving response.
Oh well.
Baby steps.

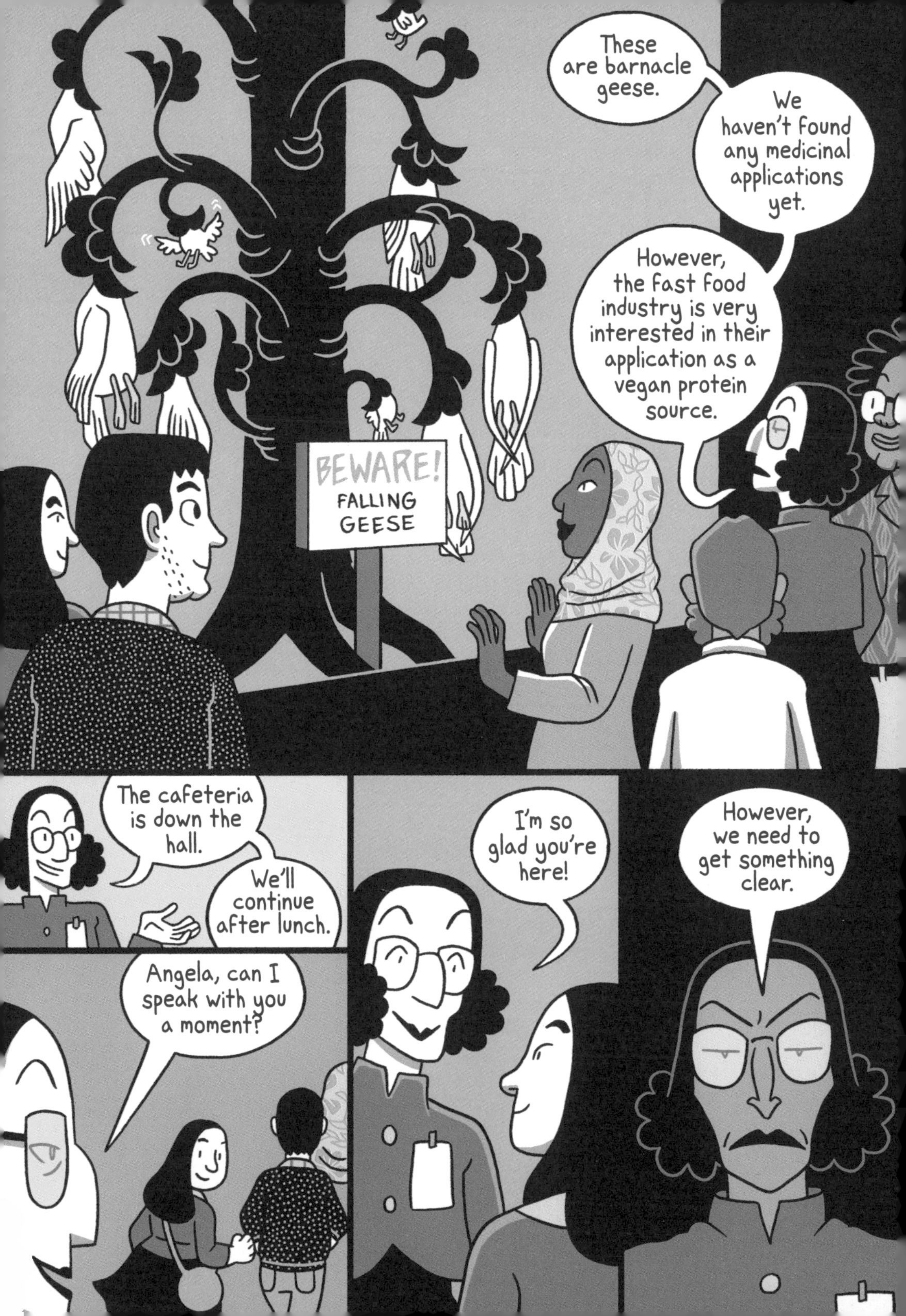
These are barnacle geese.
We haven't found any medicinal applications yet.
However, the fast food industry is very interested in their application as a vegan protein source.
BEWARE! FALLING GEESE
The cafeteria is down the hall.
We'll continue after lunch.
Angela, can I speak with you a moment?
I'm so glad you're here!
However, we need to get something clear.

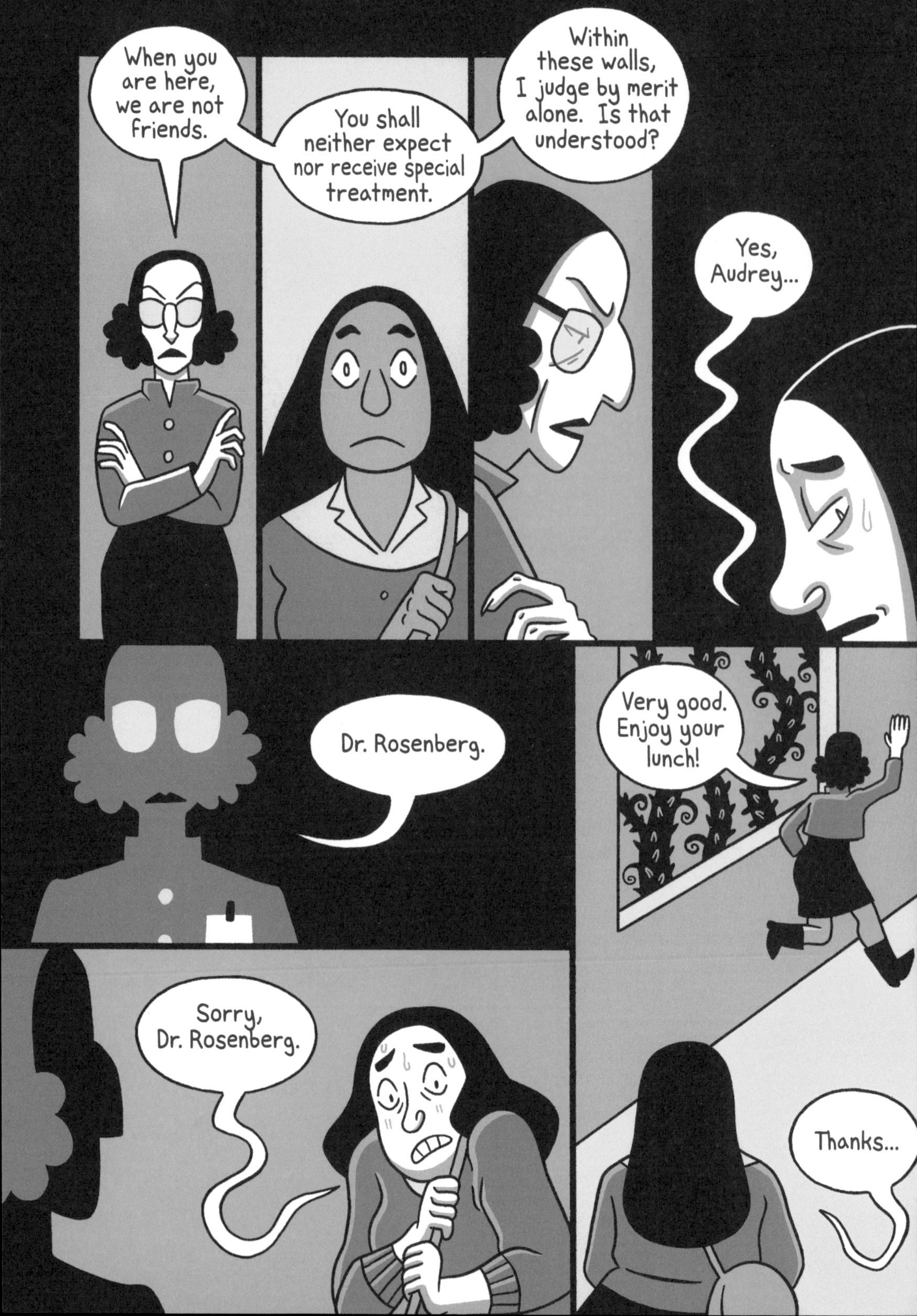
When you are here, we are not friends.
You shall neither expect nor receive special treatment.
Within these walls, I judge by merit alone. Is that understood?
Yes, Audrey...
Dr. Rosenberg.
Very good. Enjoy your lunch!
Sorry, Dr. Rosenberg.
Thanks...

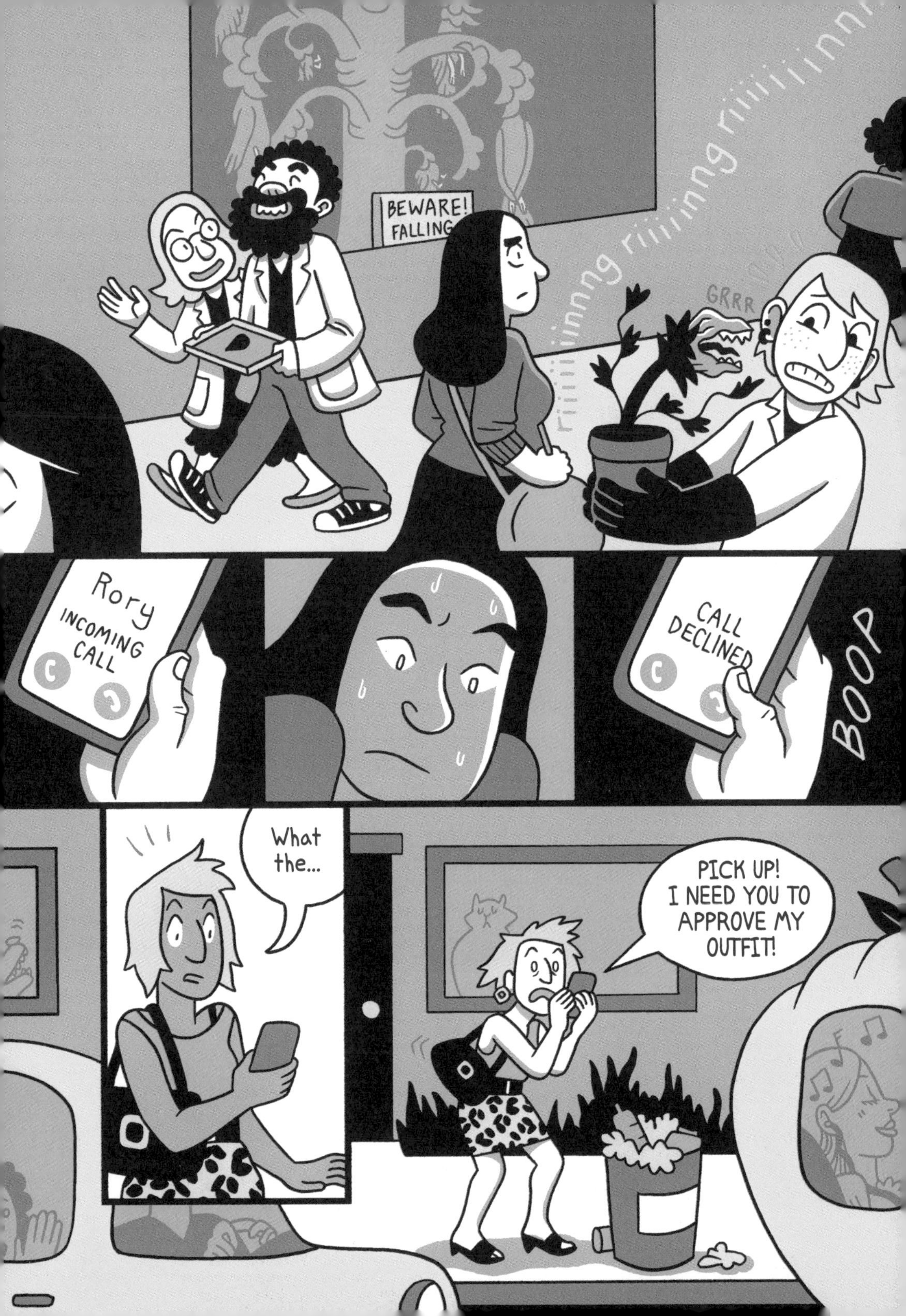
BEWARE! FALLING
riiiiinng riiiiinng riiiiiinnn
GRRR
Rory
INCOMING CALL
CALL DECLINED
BOOP
What the...
PICK UP! I NEED YOU TO APPROVE MY OUTFIT!

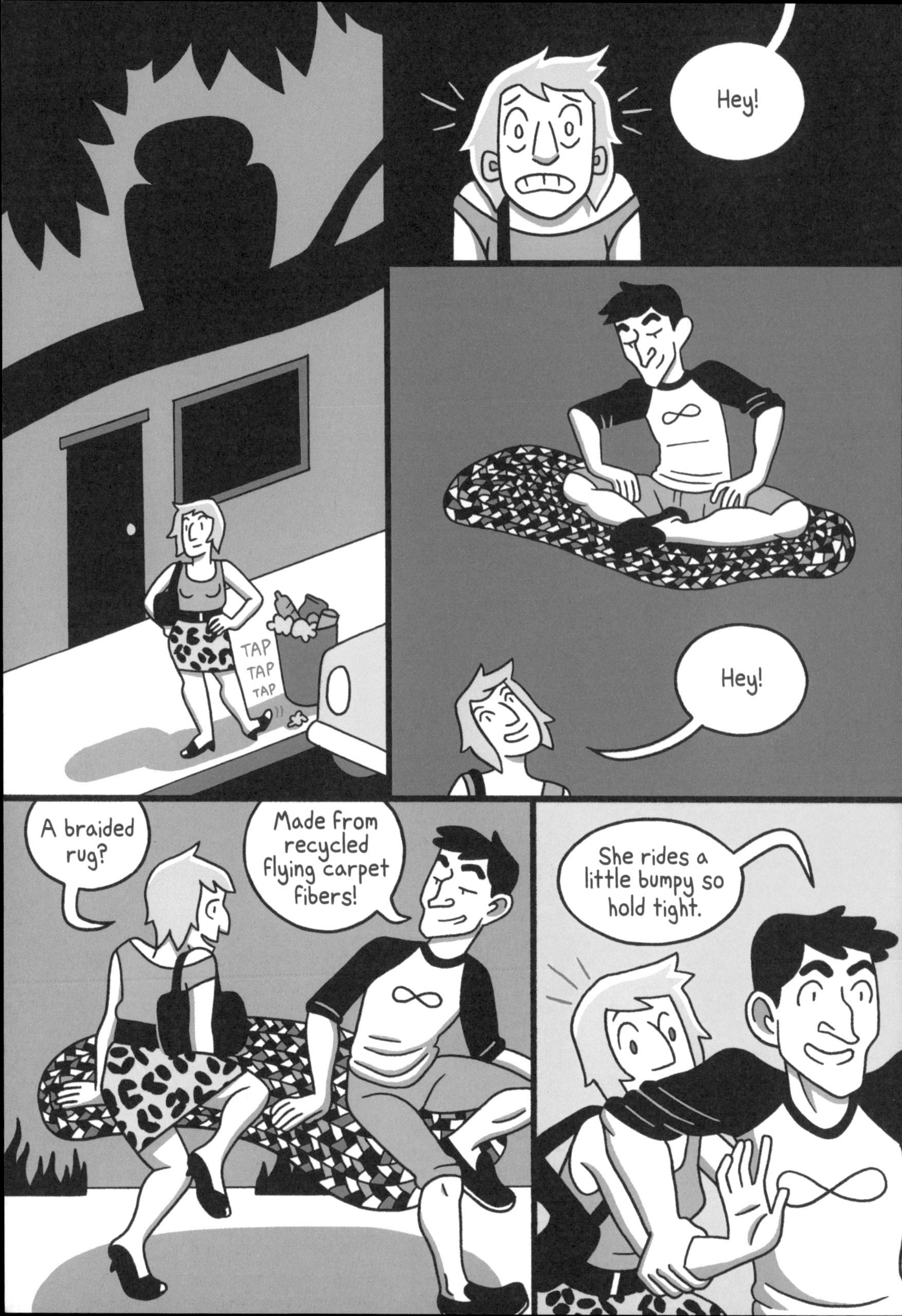
Hey!
TAP
TAP
TAP
Hey!
A braided rug?
Made from recycled flying carpet fibers!
She rides a little bumpy so hold tight.

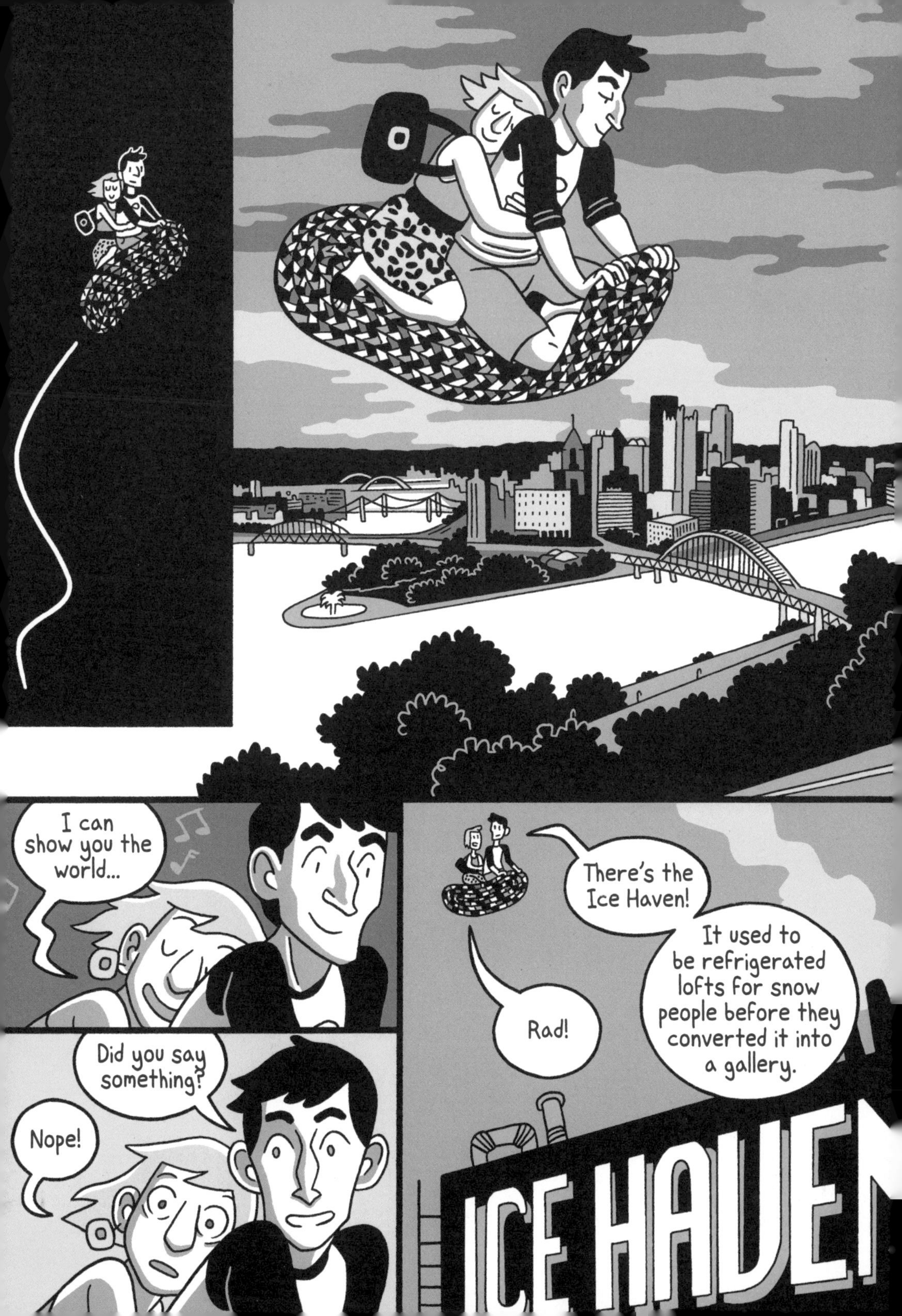

I can show you the world...
Did you say something?
Nope!
There's the Ice Haven!
It used to be refrigerated lofts for snow people before they converted it into a gallery.
Rad!
ICE HAVEN

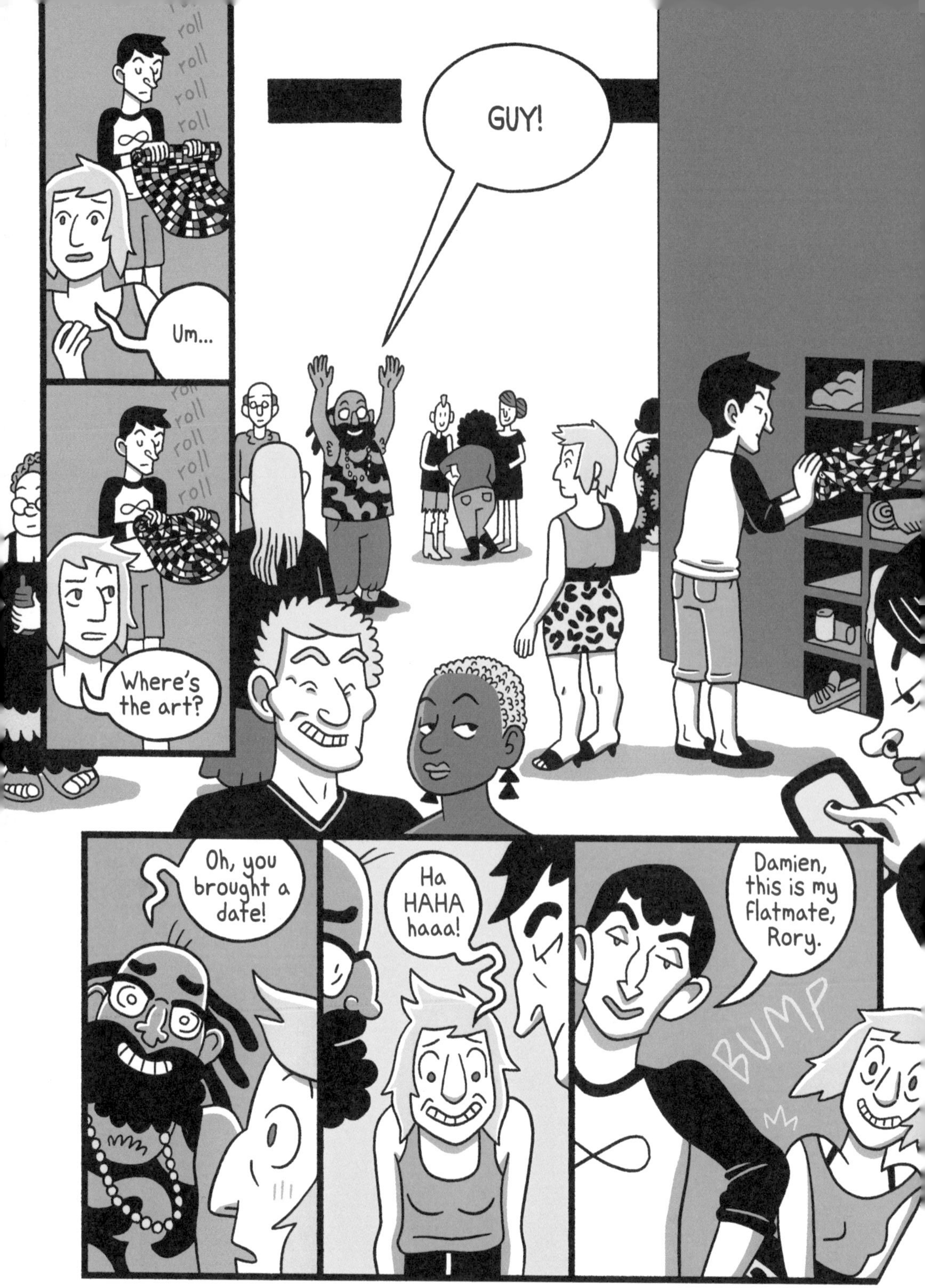

roll roll roll roll
Um...
roll roll roll roll roll
Where's the art?
GUY!
Oh, you brought a date!
Ha HAHA haaa!
Damien, this is my Flatmate, Rory.
BUMP

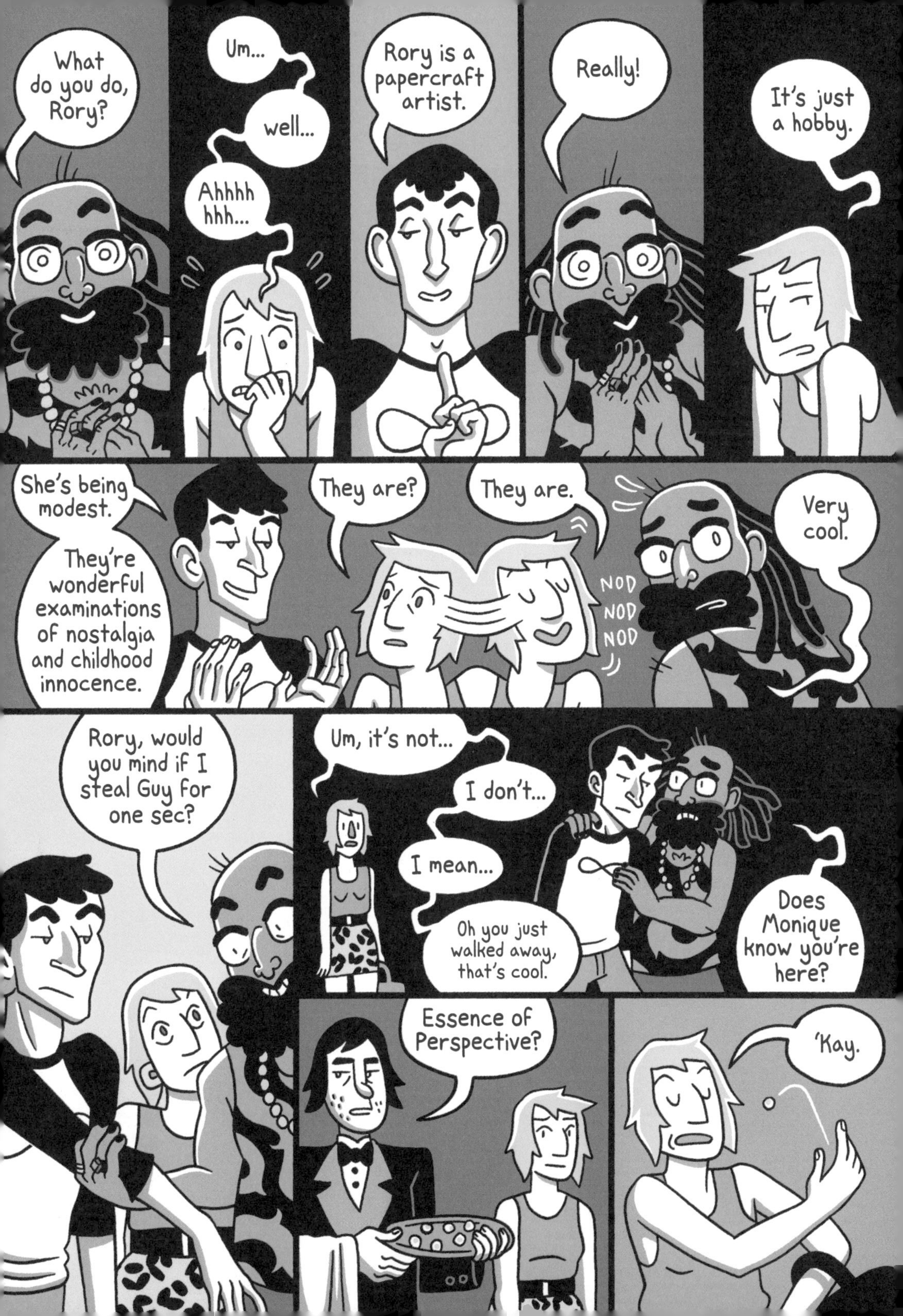

What do you do, Rory?
Um...
well...
Ahhhh hhh...
Rory is a papercraft artist.
Really!
It's just a hobby.
She's being modest.
They're wonderful examinations of nostalgia and childhood innocence.
They are?
They are.
NOD NOD NOD
Very cool.
Rory, would you mind if I steal Guy for one sec?
Um, it's not...
I don't...
I mean...
Oh you just walked away, that's cool.
Does Monique know you're here?
Essence of Perspective?
'Kay.

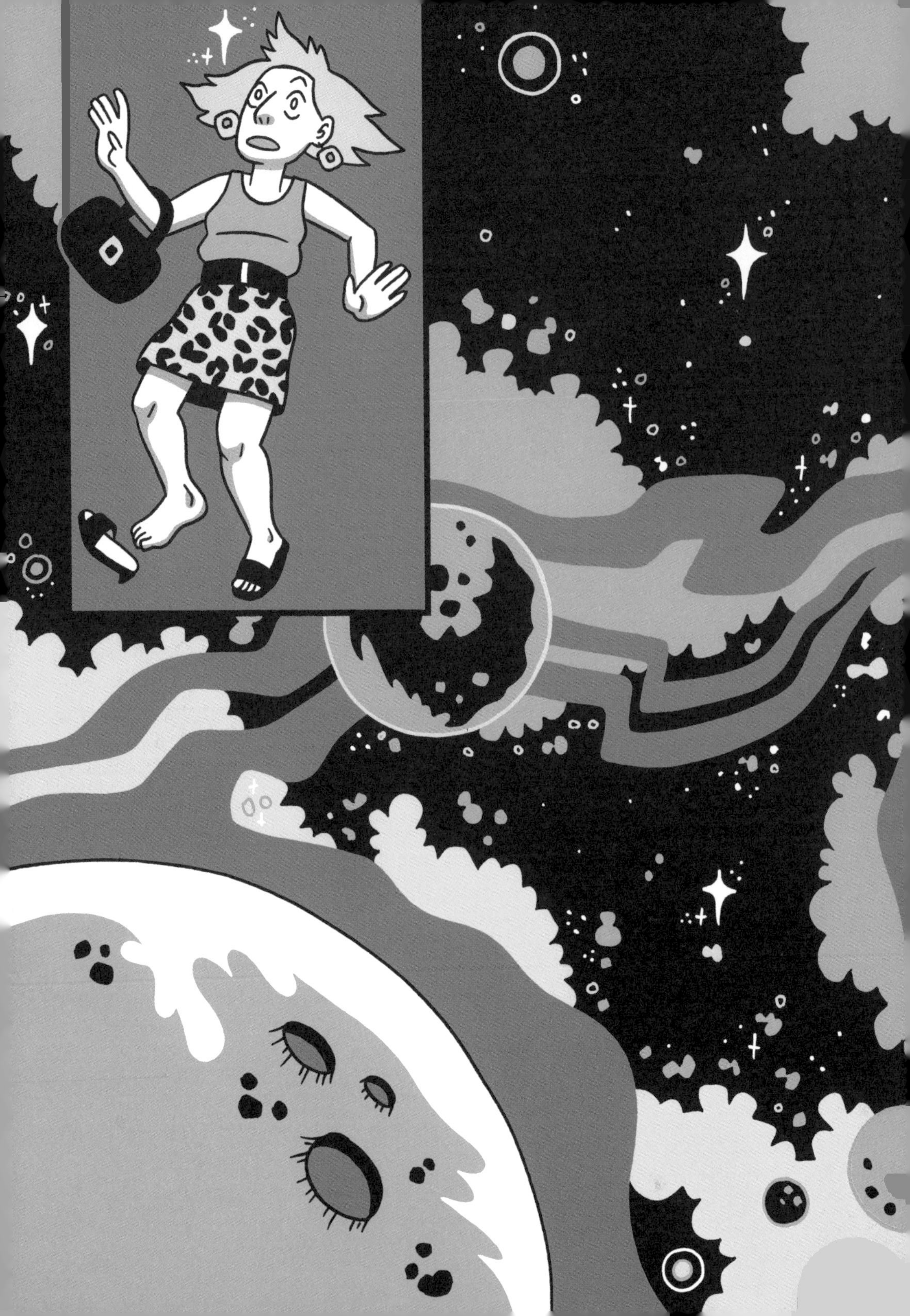

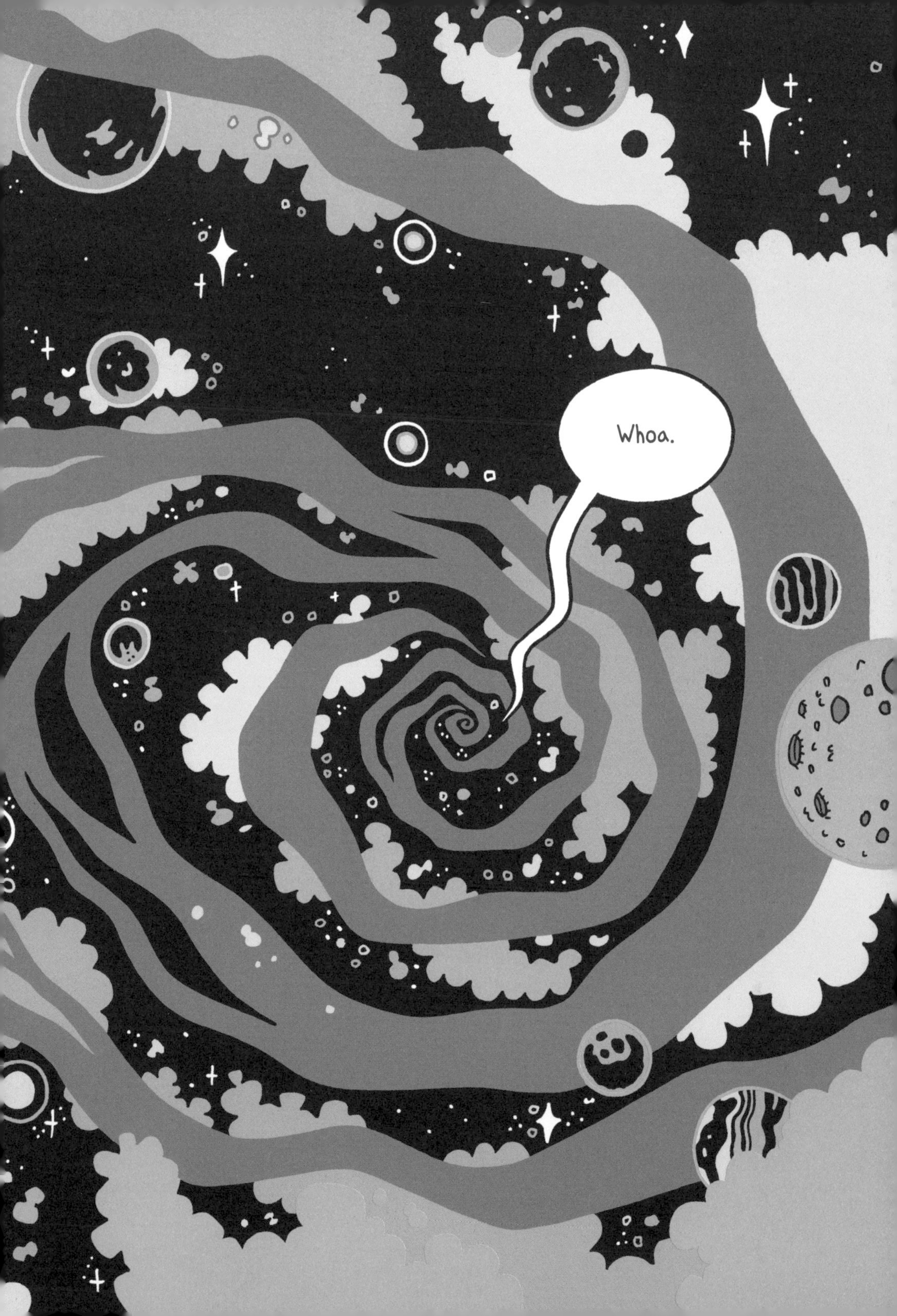
Whoa.

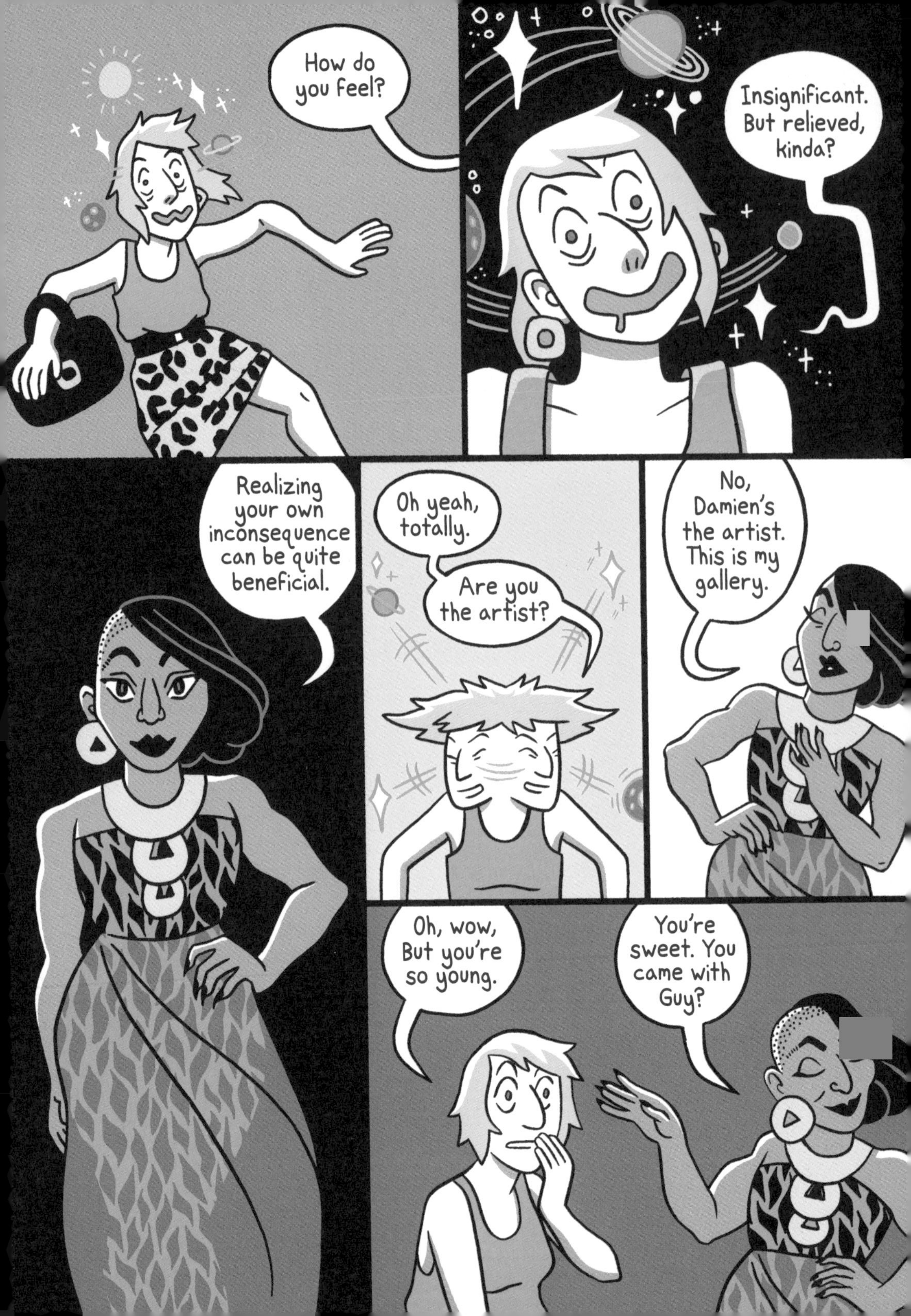
How do you feel?
Insignificant. But relieved, kinda?
Realizing your own inconsequence can be quite beneficial.
Oh yeah, totally.
Are you the artist?
No, Damien's the artist. This is my gallery.
Oh, wow, But you're so young.
You're sweet. You came with Guy?

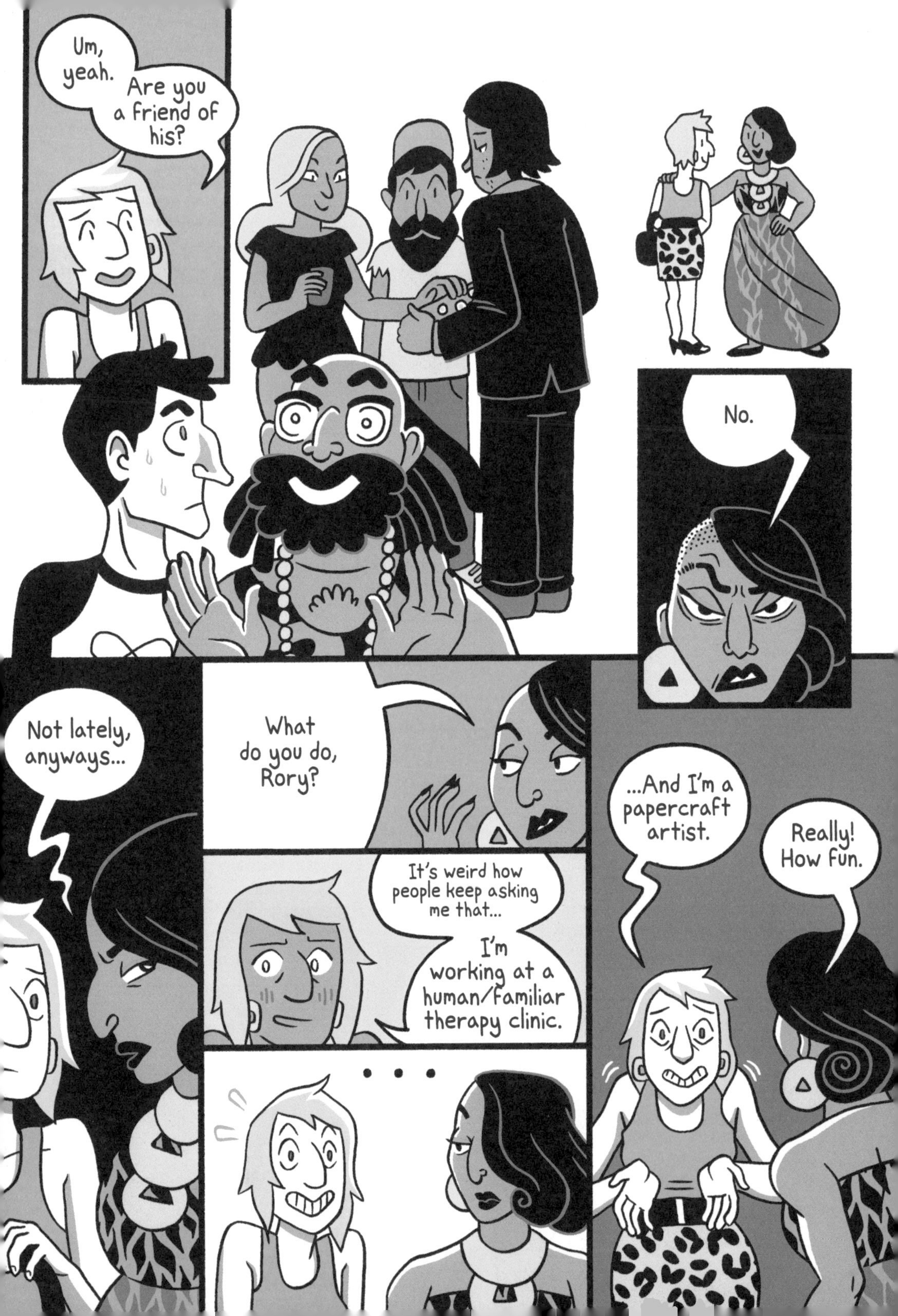

Um, yeah.
Are you a friend of his?
No.
Not lately, anyways...
What do you do, Rory?
It's weird how people keep asking me that...
I'm working at a human/familiar therapy clinic.
...
...And I'm a papercraft artist.
Really! How fun.

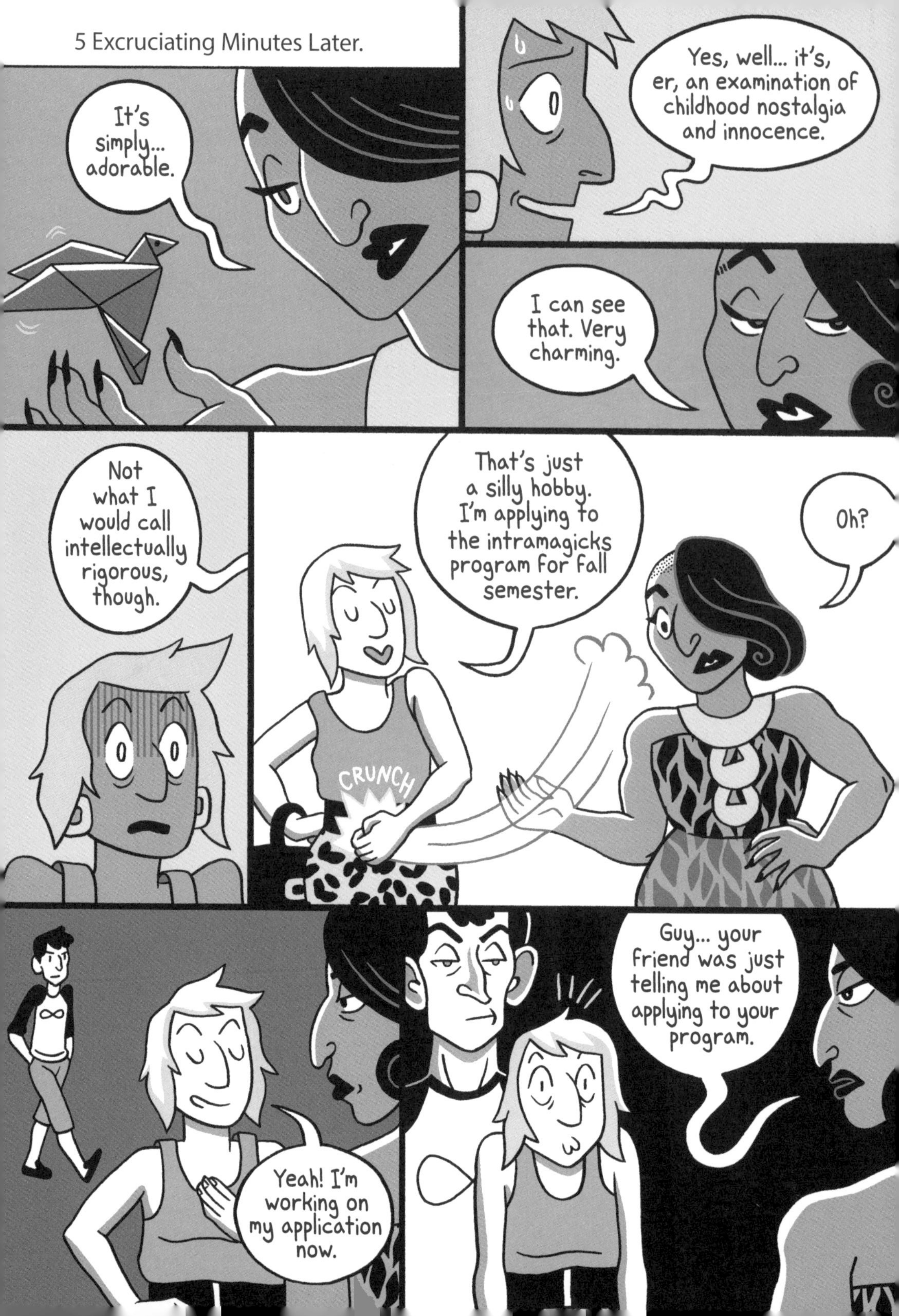
5 Excruciating Minutes Later.
It's simply... adorable.
Yes, well... it's, er, an examination of childhood nostalgia and innocence.
I can see that. Very charming.
Not what I would call intellectually rigorous, though.
That's just a silly hobby. I'm applying to the intramagicks program for fall semester.
Oh?
CRUNCH
Yeah! I'm working on my application now.
Guy... your friend was just telling me about applying to your program.

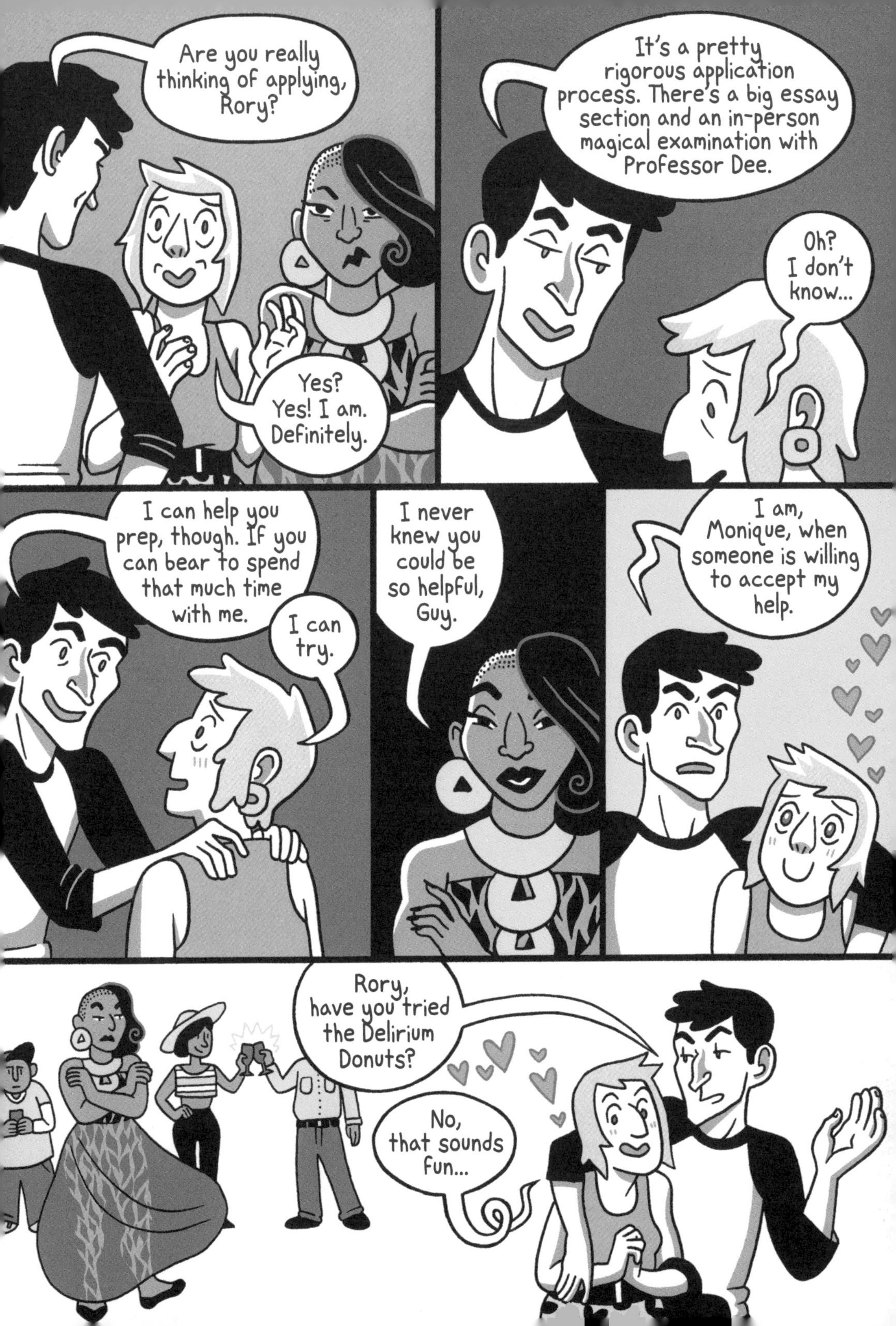

Are you really thinking of applying, Rory?
Yes? Yes! I am. Definitely.
It's a pretty rigorous application process. There's a big essay section and an in-person magical examination with Professor Dee.
Oh? I don't know...
I can help you prep, though. If you can bear to spend that much time with me.
I can try.
I never knew you could be so helpful, Guy.
I am, Monique, when someone is willing to accept my help.
Rory, have you tried the Delirium Donuts?
No, that sounds fun...

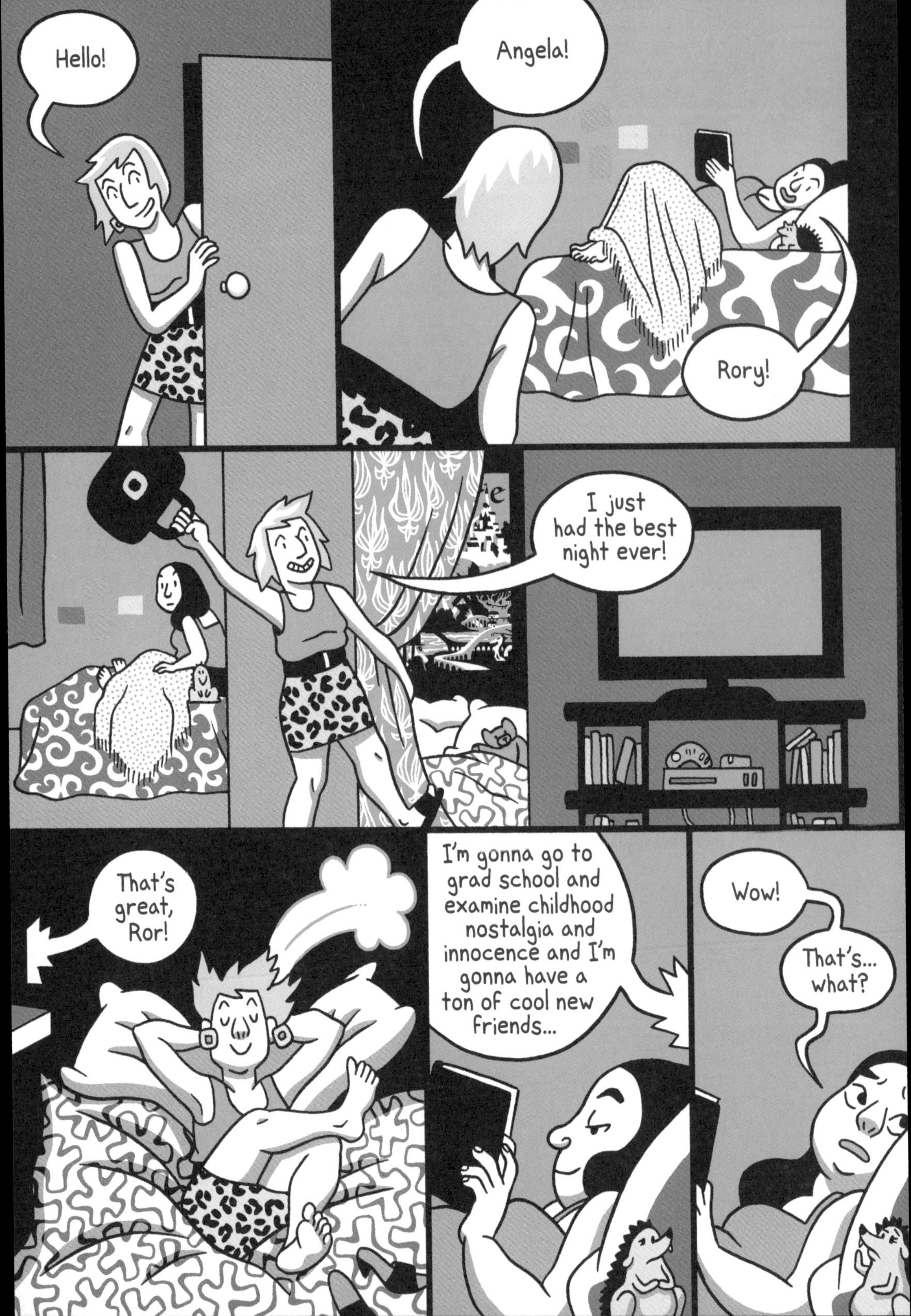
Hello!
Angela!
Rory!
I just had the best night ever!
That's great, Ror!
I'm gonna go to grad school and examine childhood nostalgia and innocence and I'm gonna have a ton of cool new friends...
Wow!
That's... what?

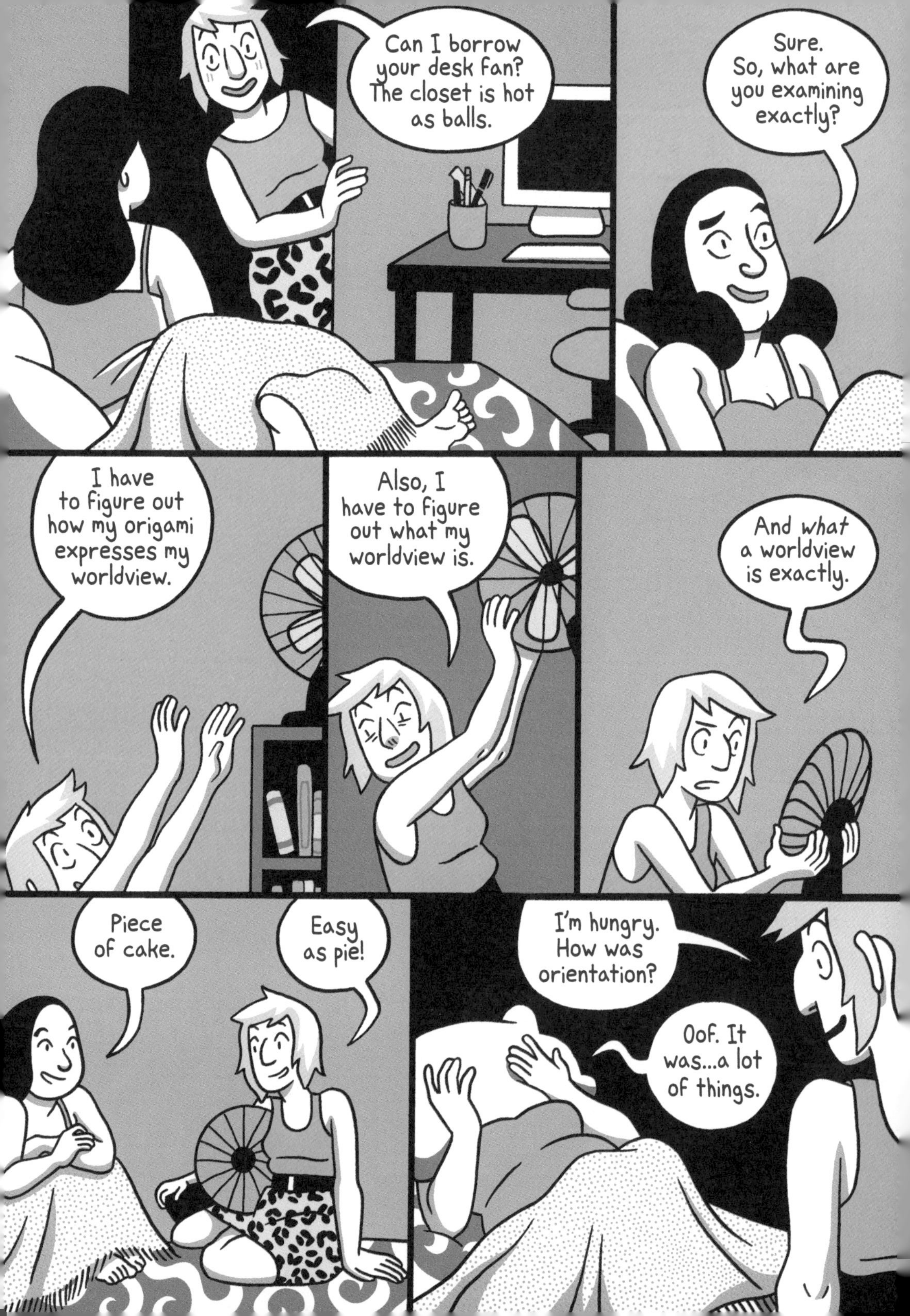
Can I borrow your desk fan? The closet is hot as balls.
Sure. So, what are you examining exactly?
I have to figure out how my origami expresses my worldview.
Also, I have to figure out what my worldview is.
And what a worldview is exactly.
Piece of cake.
Easy as pie!
I'm hungry. How was orientation?
Oof. It was...a lot of things.

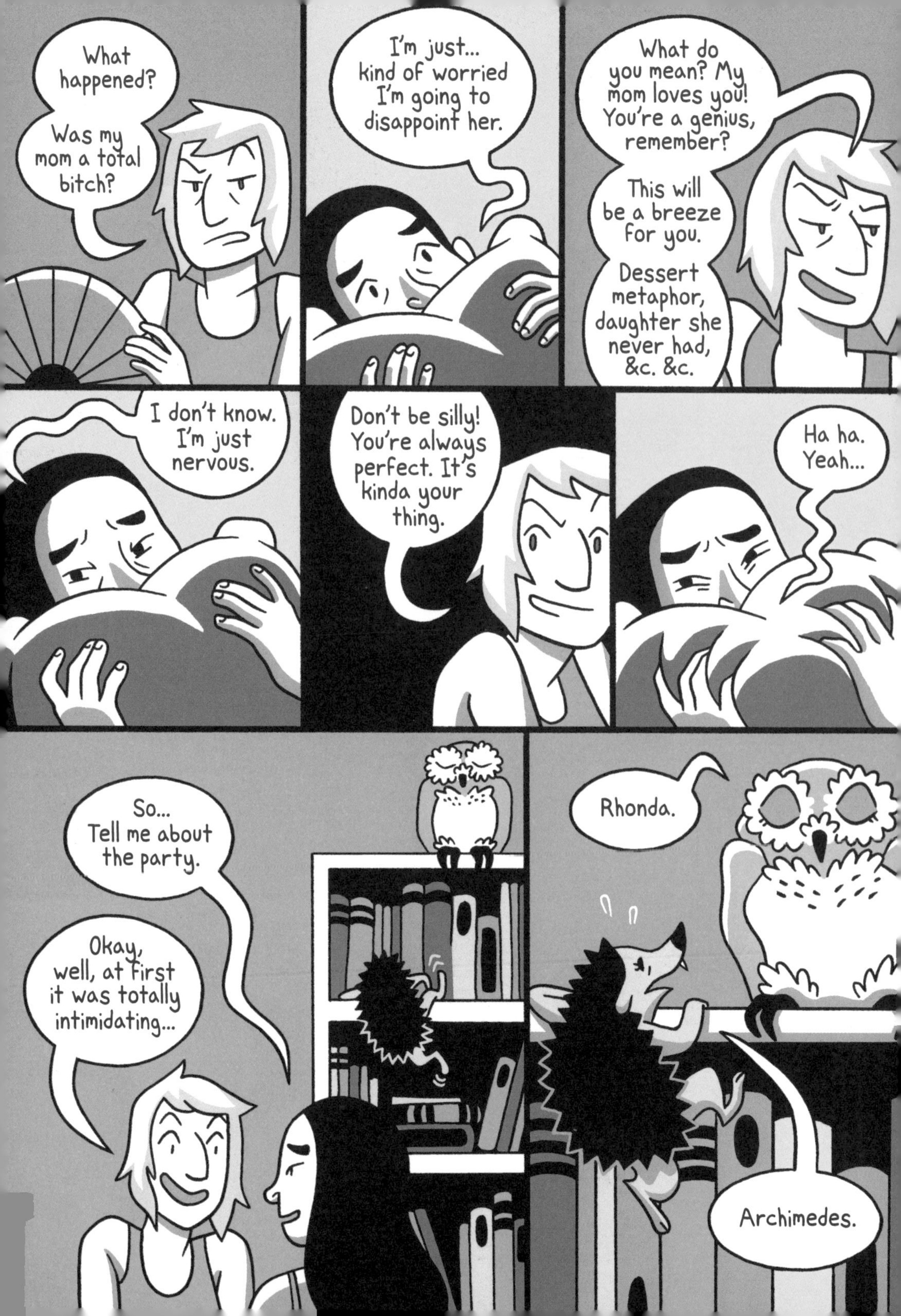
What happened?
Was my mom a total bitch?
I'm just... kind of worried I'm going to disappoint her.
What do you mean? My mom loves you! You're a genius, remember?
This will be a breeze for you.
Dessert metaphor, daughter she never had, &c. &c.
I don't know. I'm just nervous.
Don't be silly! You're always perfect. It's kinda your thing.
Ha ha. Yeah...
So... Tell me about the party.
Okay, well, at first it was totally intimidating...
Rhonda.
Archimedes.

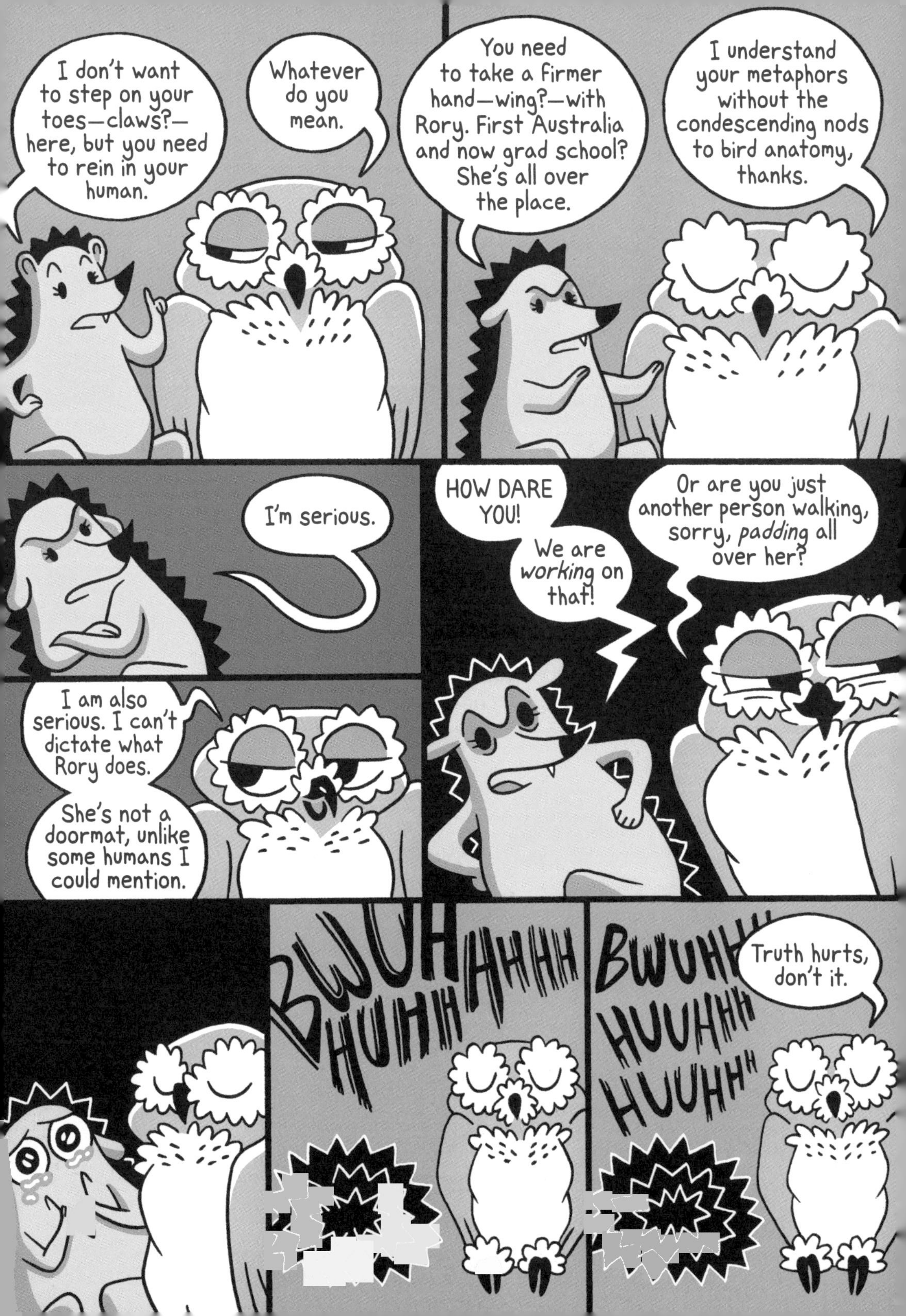
I don't want to step on your toes—claws?—here, but you need to rein in your human.
Whatever do you mean.
You need to take a firmer hand—wing?—with Rory. First Australia and now grad school? She's all over the place.
I understand your metaphors without the condescending nods to bird anatomy, thanks.
I'm serious.
I am also serious. I can't dictate what Rory does.
She's not a doormat, unlike some humans I could mention.
HOW DARE YOU!
We are *working* on that!
Or are you just another person walking, sorry, *padding* all over her?
BWUHHHHHH HUHHH
BWUHH HUUHHH HUUHHH
Truth hurts, don't it.

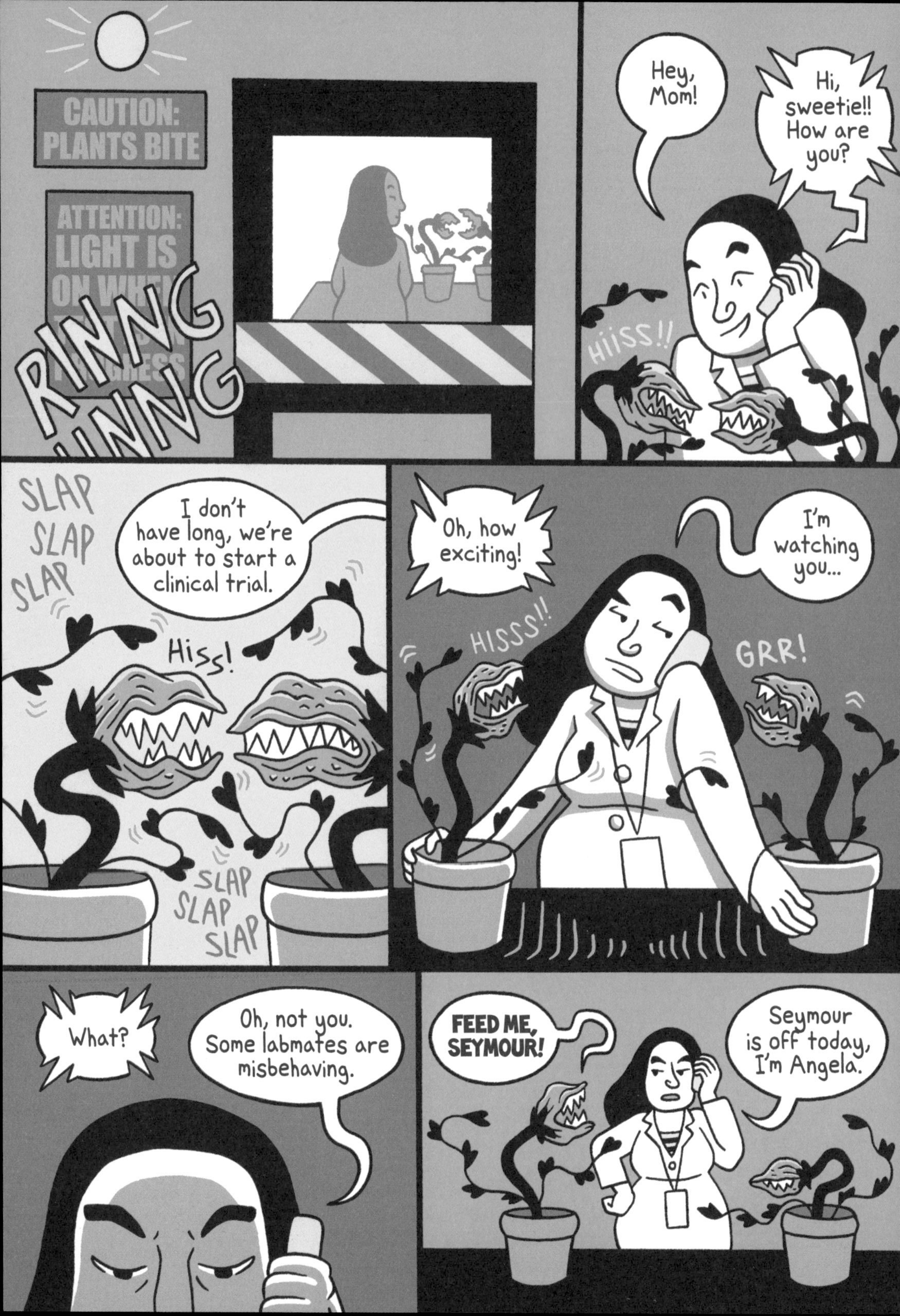
CAUTION: PLANTS BITE
ATTENTION: LIGHT IS
RINNG
Hey, Mom!
Hi, sweetie!! How are you?
HIISS!!
SLAP SLAP SLAP
I don't have long, we're about to start a clinical trial.
Hiss!
SLAP SLAP SLAP
Oh, how exciting!
I'm watching you...
HISSS!!
GRR!
What?
Oh, not you. Some labmates are misbehaving.
FEED ME, SEYMOUR!
Seymour is off today, I'm Angela.

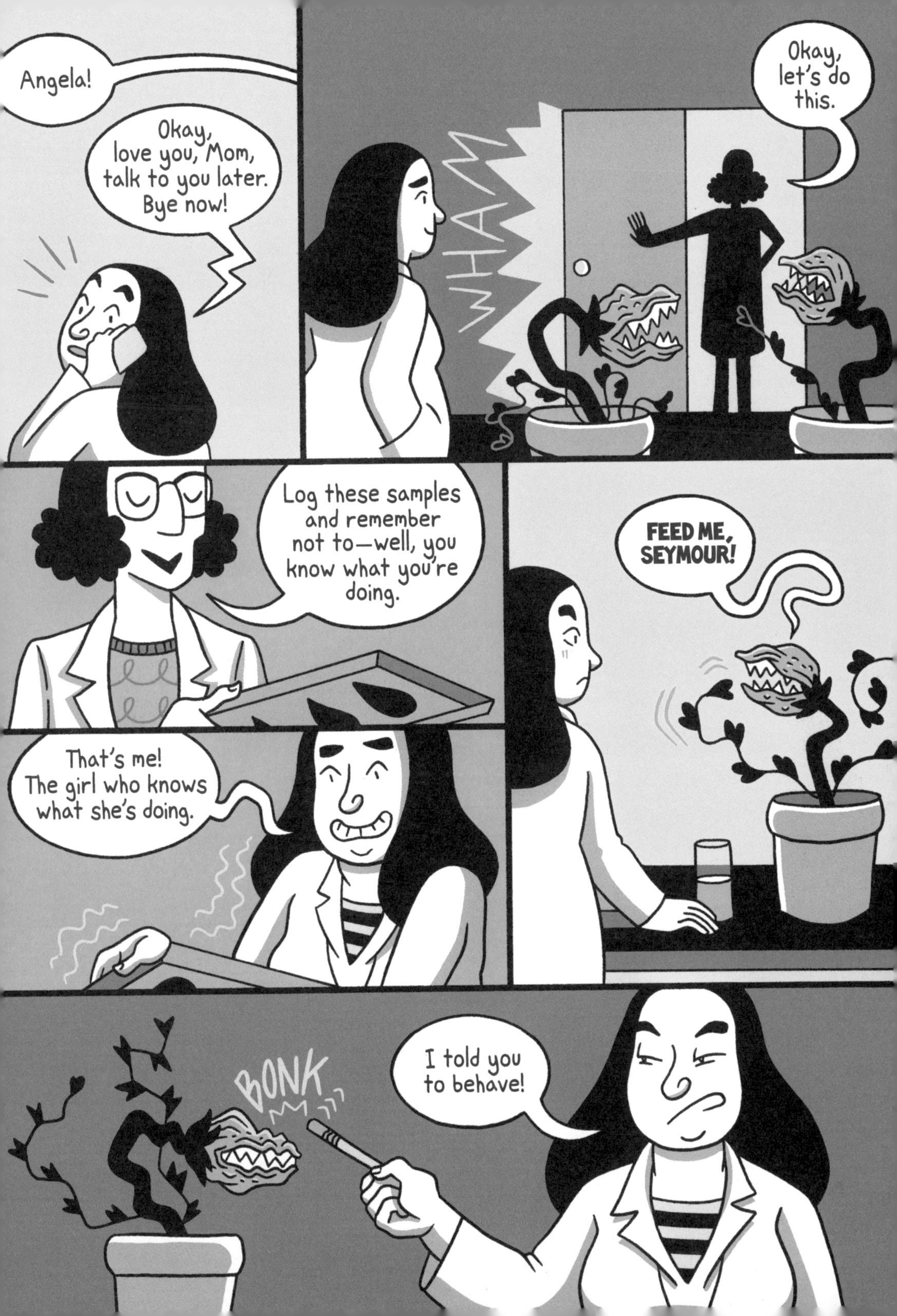
Angela!
Okay, love you, Mom, talk to you later. Bye now!
WHAM
Okay, let's do this.
Log these samples and remember not to—well, you know what you're doing.
That's me! The girl who knows what she's doing.
FEED ME, SEYMOUR!
BONK
I told you to behave!

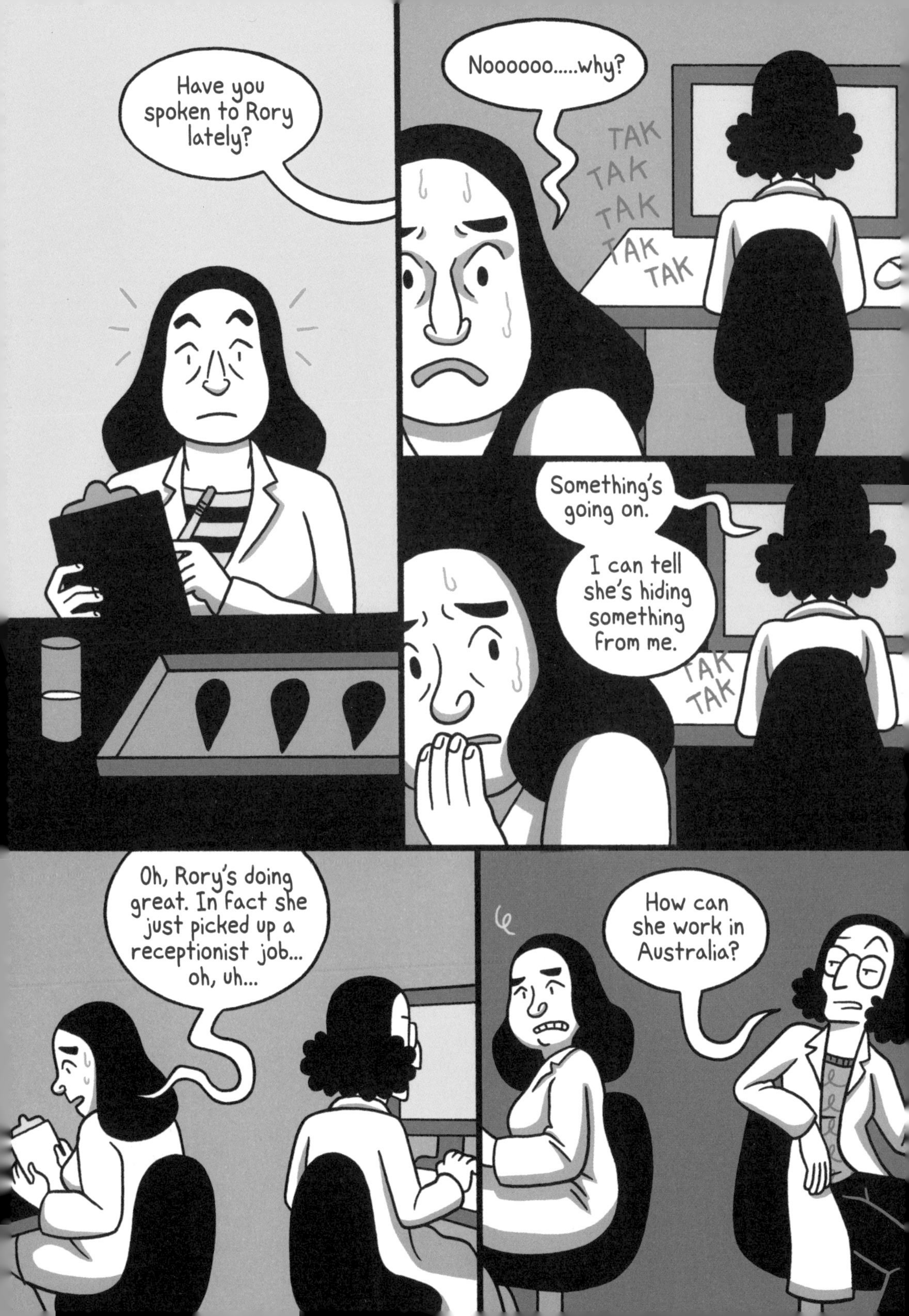
Have you spoken to Rory lately?
Noooooo.....why?
TAK TAK TAK TAK TAK
Something's going on.
I can tell she's hiding something from me.
TAK TAK
Oh, Rory's doing great. In fact she just picked up a receptionist job... oh, uh...
How can she work in Australia?

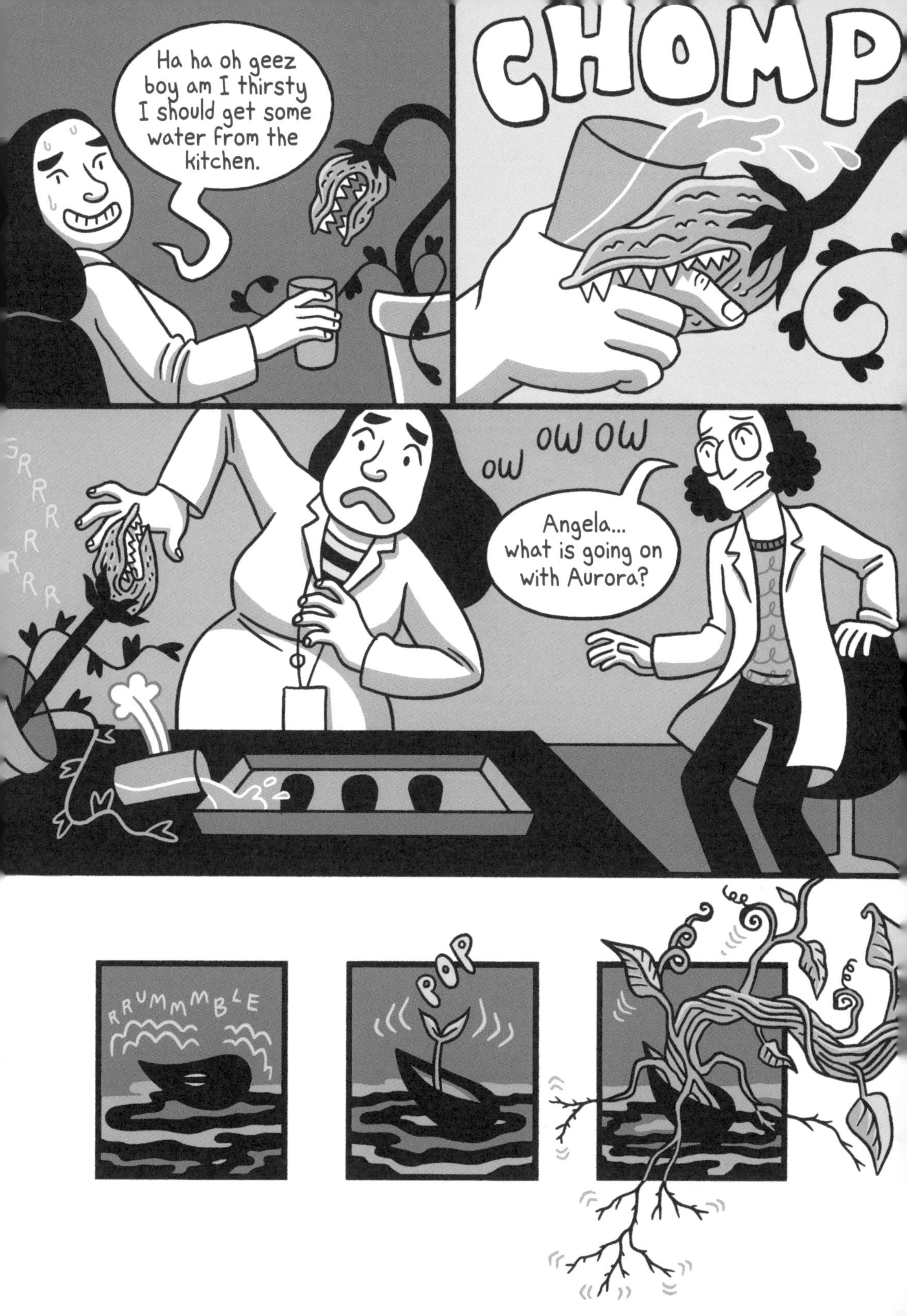
Ha ha oh geez boy am I thirsty I should get some water from the kitchen.
CHOMP
SRRRRRRRR
OW OW OW
Angela... what is going on with Aurora?
RRUMMMBLE
POP

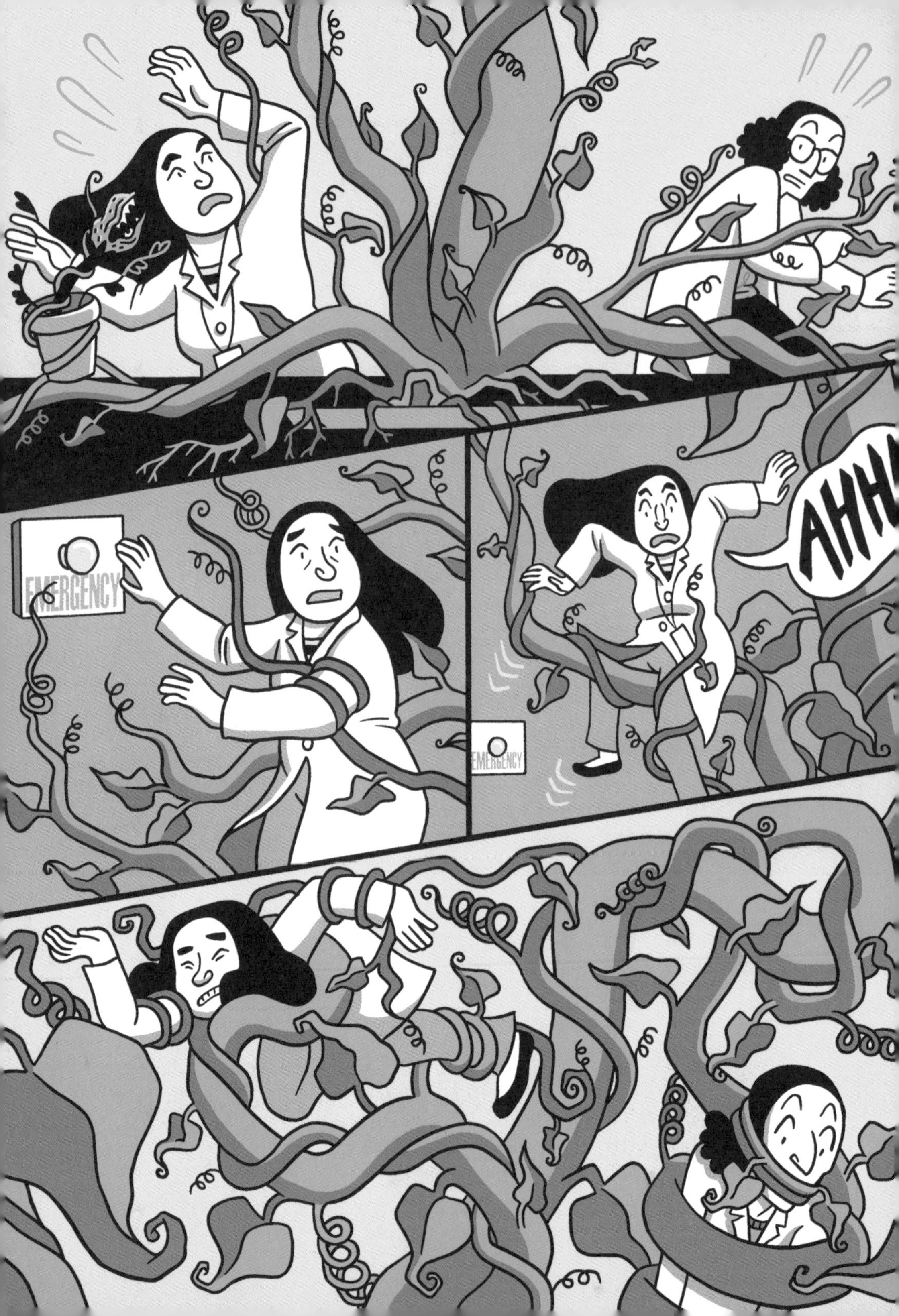
EMERGENCY
EMERGENCY
AHH

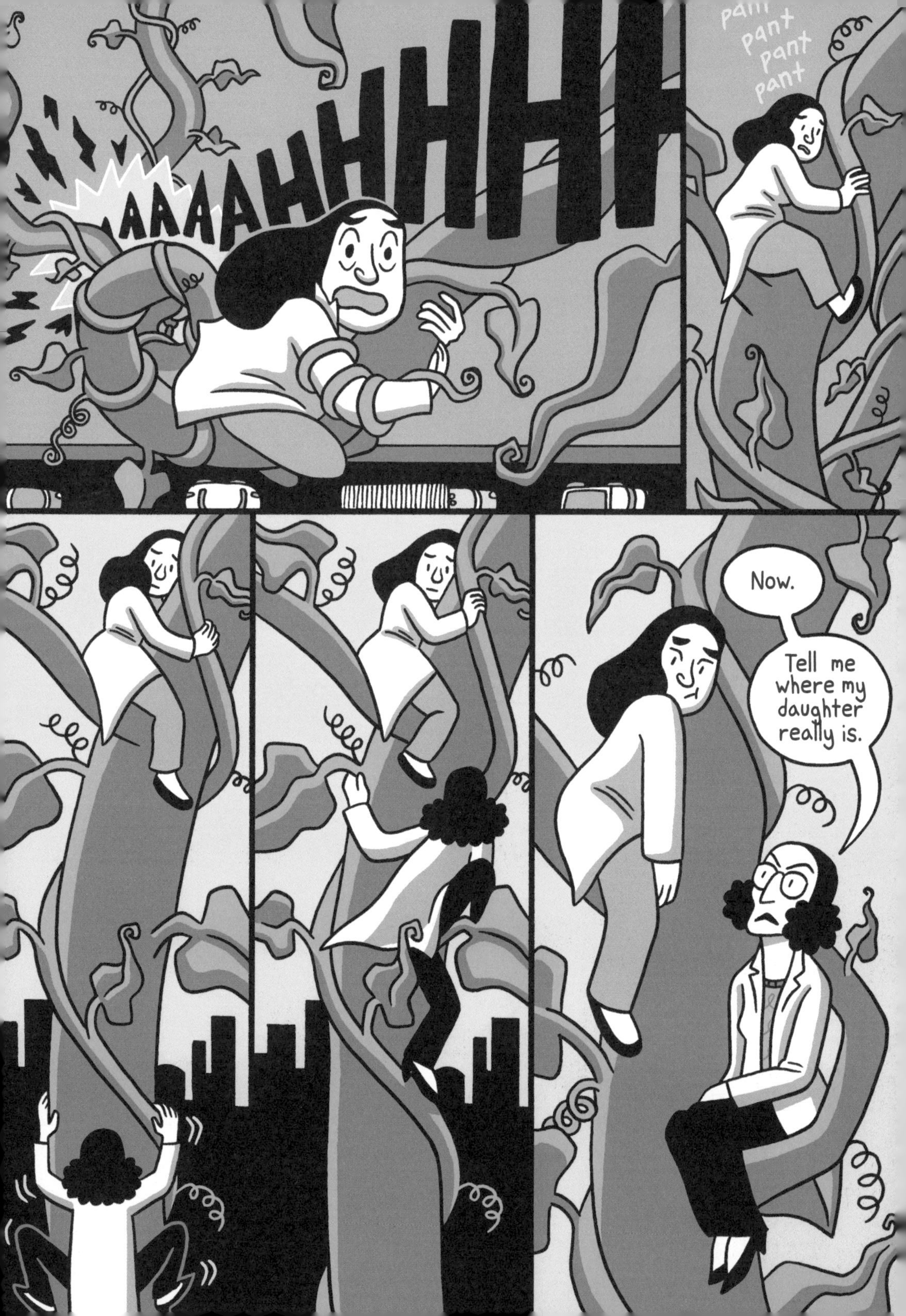
AAAAAHHHHHHH
pant
pant
pant
pant
Now.
Tell me where my daughter really is.

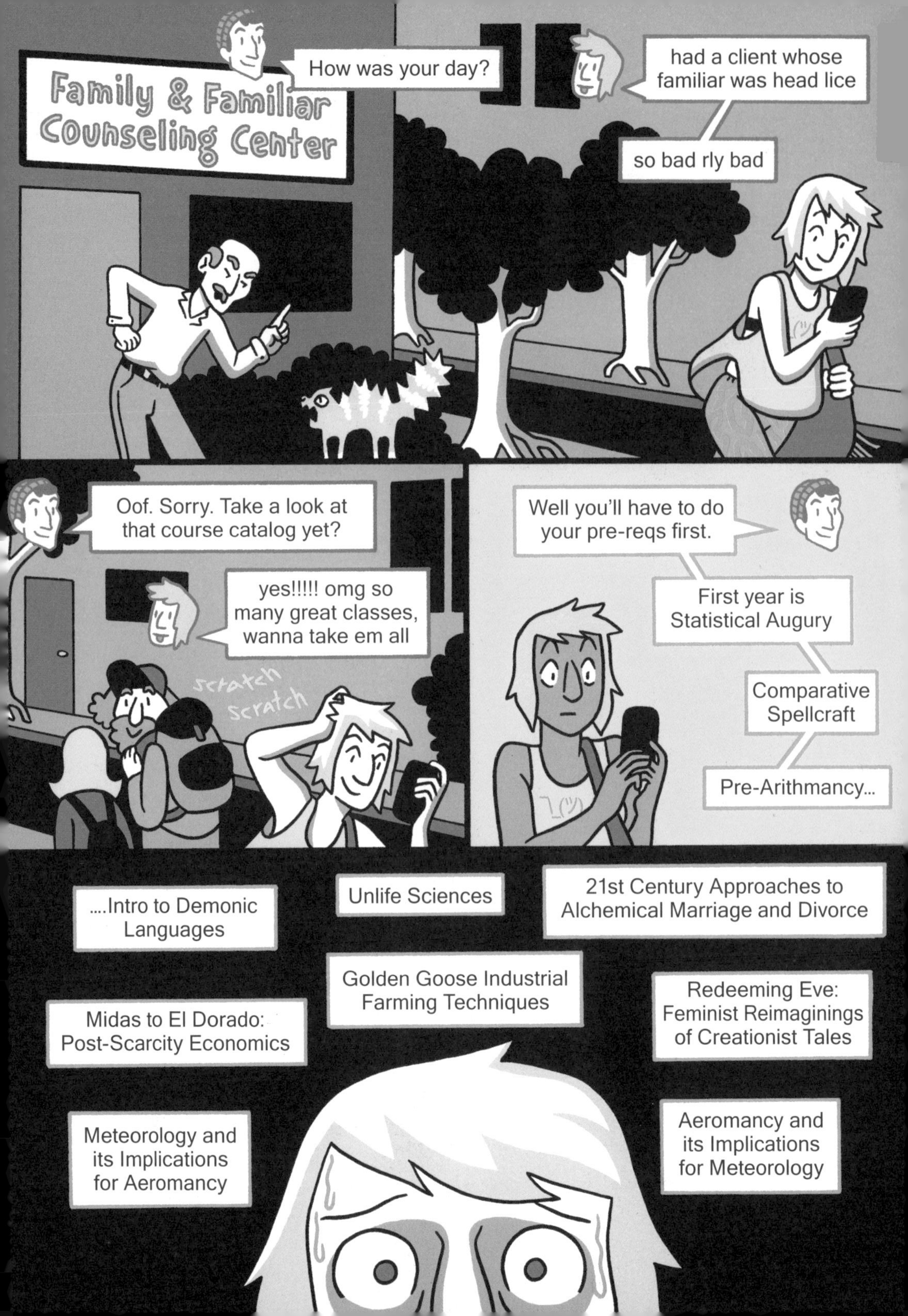
Family & Familiar Counseling Center
How was your day?
had a client whose familiar was head lice
so bad rly bad
Oof. Sorry. Take a look at that course catalog yet?
yes!!!!! omg so many great classes, wanna take em all
scratch scratch
Well you'll have to do your pre-reqs first.
First year is Statistical Augury
Comparative Spellcraft
Pre-Arithmancy...
....Intro to Demonic Languages
Unlife Sciences
21st Century Approaches to Alchemical Marriage and Divorce
Golden Goose Industrial Farming Techniques
Midas to El Dorado: Post-Scarcity Economics
Redeeming Eve: Feminist Reimaginings of Creationist Tales
Meteorology and its Implications for Aeromancy
Aeromancy and its Implications for Meteorology

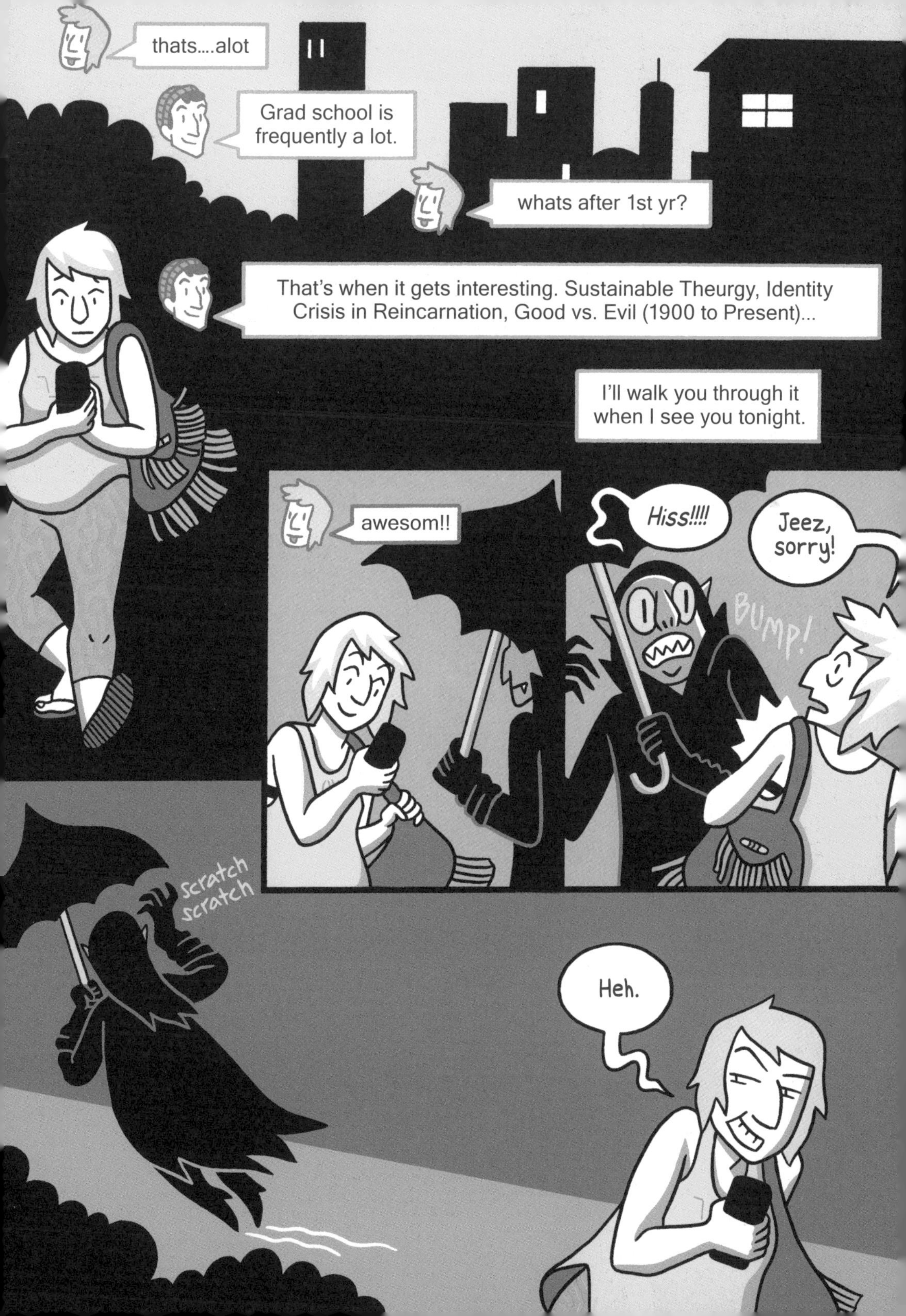
thats....alot
Grad school is frequently a lot.
whats after 1st yr?
That's when it gets interesting. Sustainable Theurgy, Identity Crisis in Reincarnation, Good vs. Evil (1900 to Present)...
I'll walk you through it when I see you tonight.
awesom!!
Hiss!!!!
Jeez, sorry!
BUMP!
scratch scratch
Heh.

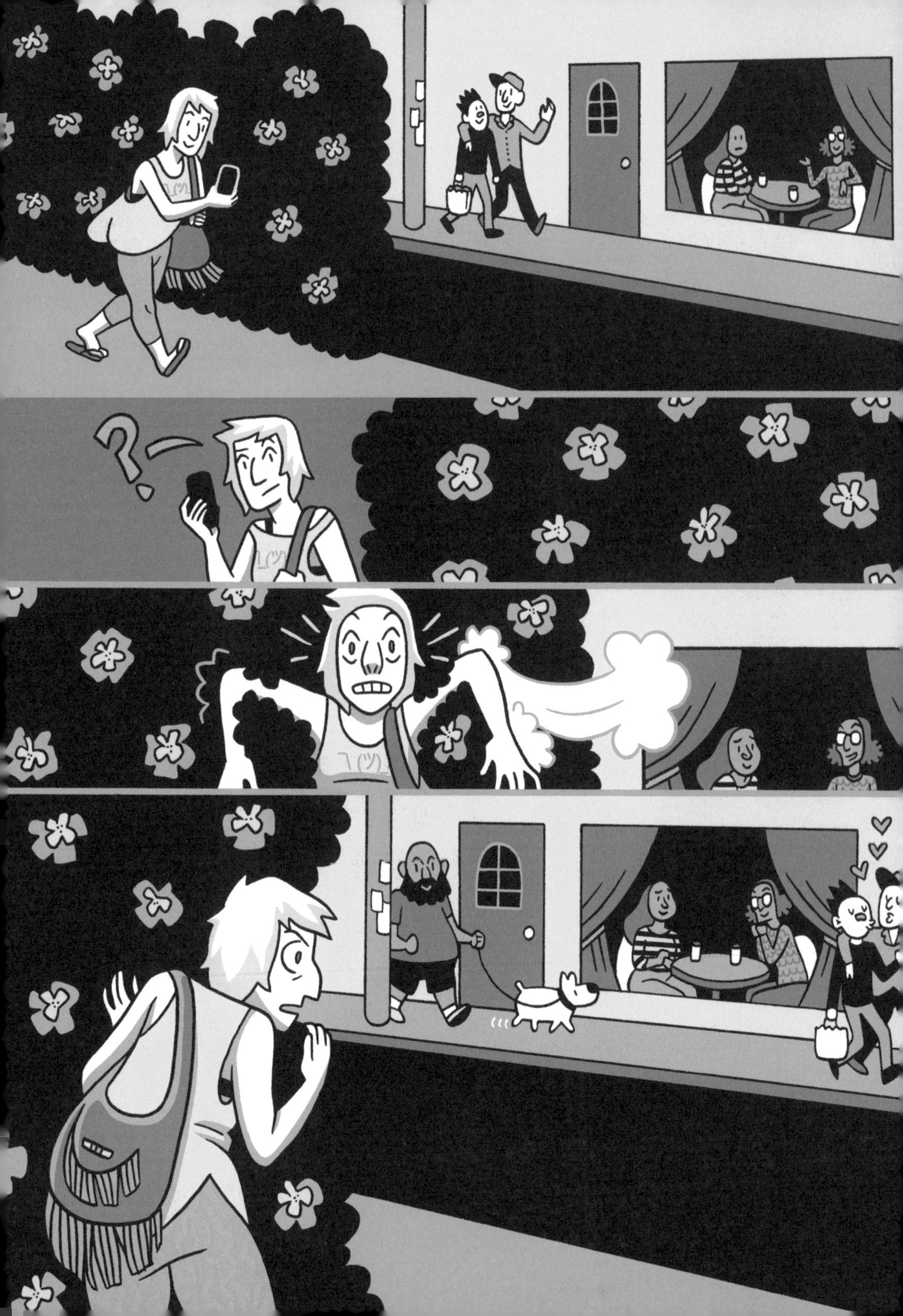

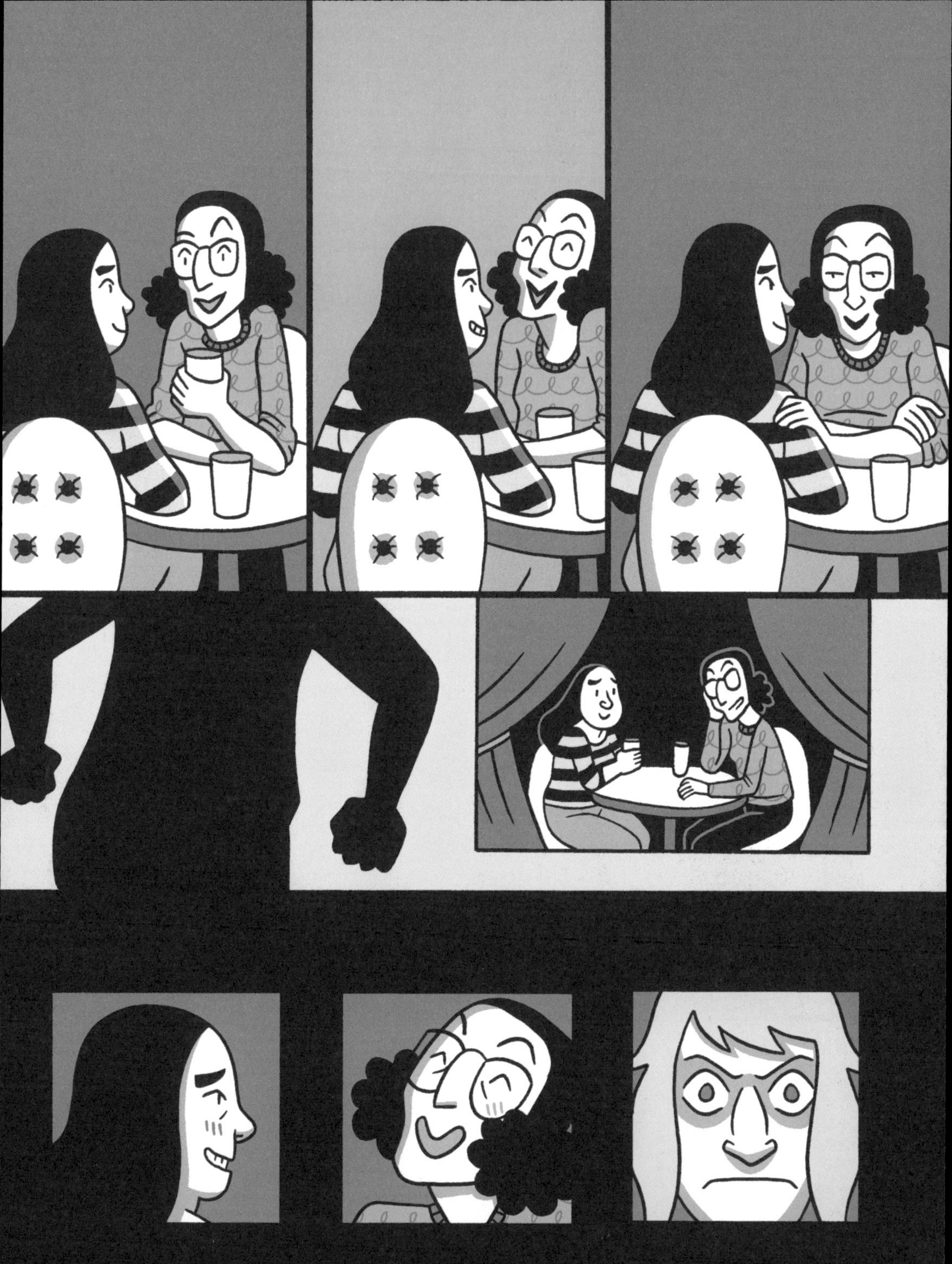

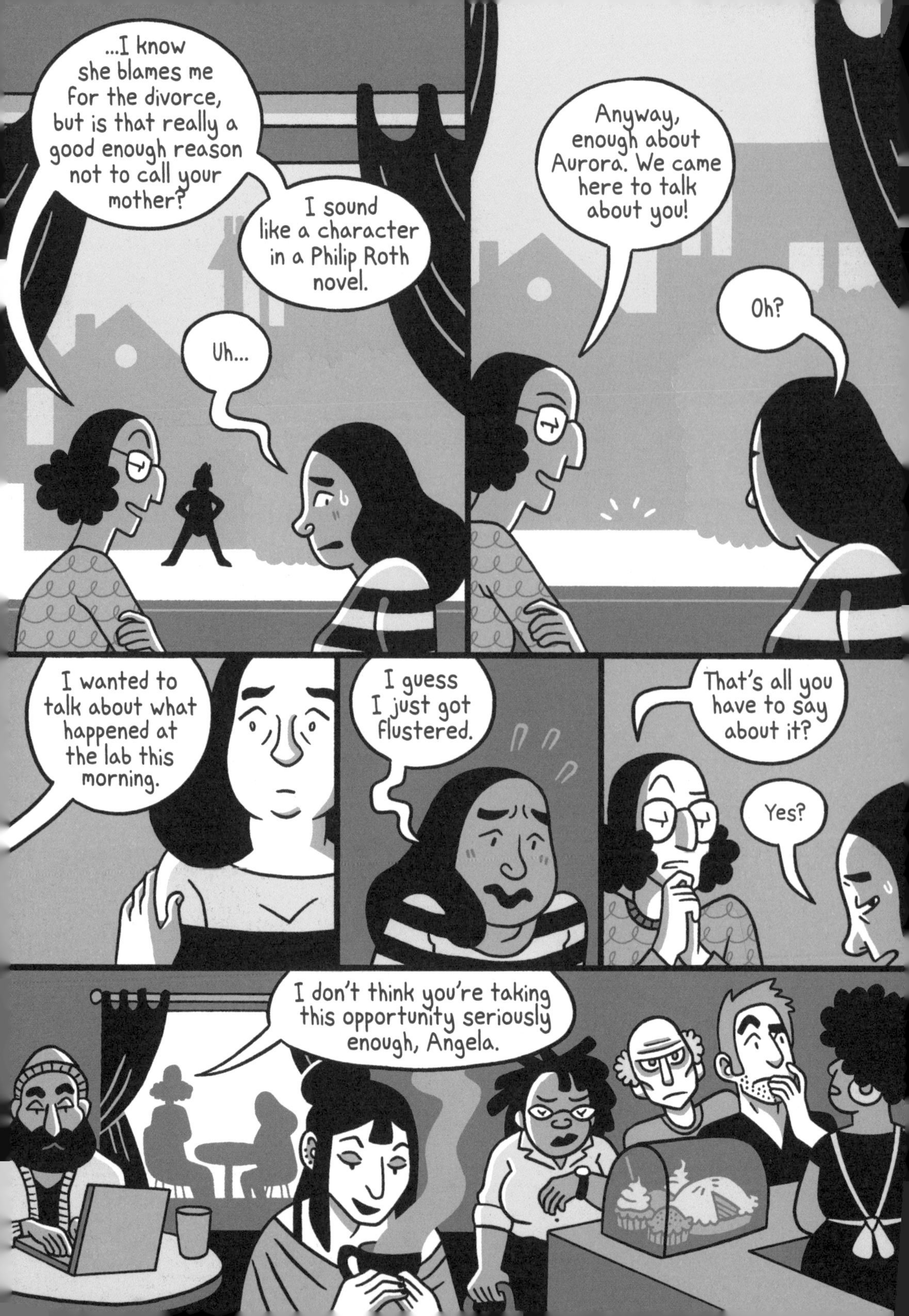
...I know she blames me for the divorce, but is that really a good enough reason not to call your mother?
I sound like a character in a Philip Roth novel.
Uh...
Anyway, enough about Aurora. We came here to talk about you!
Oh?
I wanted to talk about what happened at the lab this morning.
I guess I just got flustered.
That's all you have to say about it?
Yes?
I don't think you're taking this opportunity seriously enough, Angela.

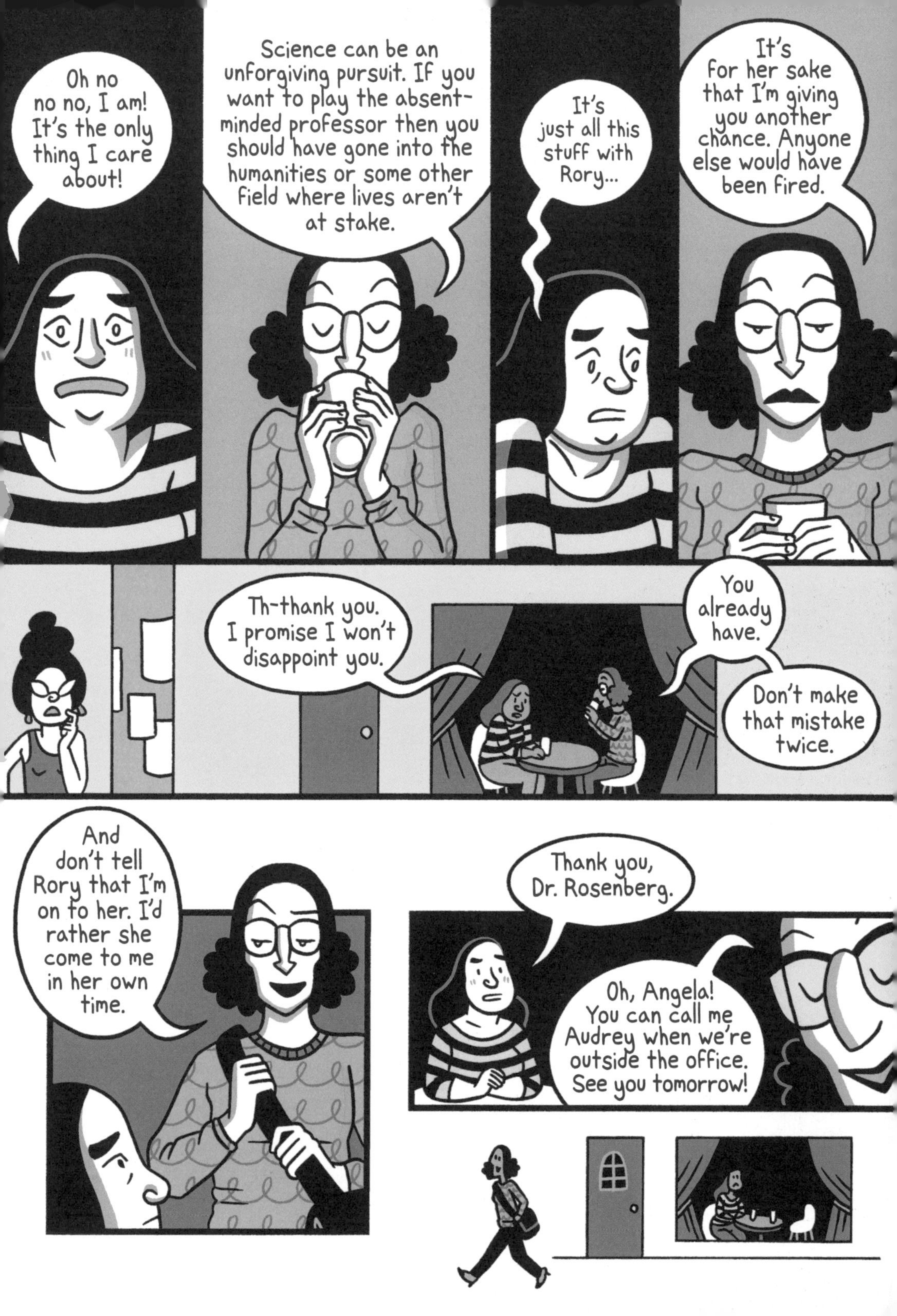
Oh no no no, I am! It's the only thing I care about!
Science can be an unforgiving pursuit. If you want to play the absent-minded professor then you should have gone into the humanities or some other field where lives aren't at stake.
It's just all this stuff with Rory...
It's for her sake that I'm giving you another chance. Anyone else would have been fired.
Th-thank you. I promise I won't disappoint you.
You already have.
Don't make that mistake twice.
And don't tell Rory that I'm on to her. I'd rather she come to me in her own time.
Thank you, Dr. Rosenberg.
Oh, Angela! You can call me Audrey when we're outside the office. See you tomorrow!

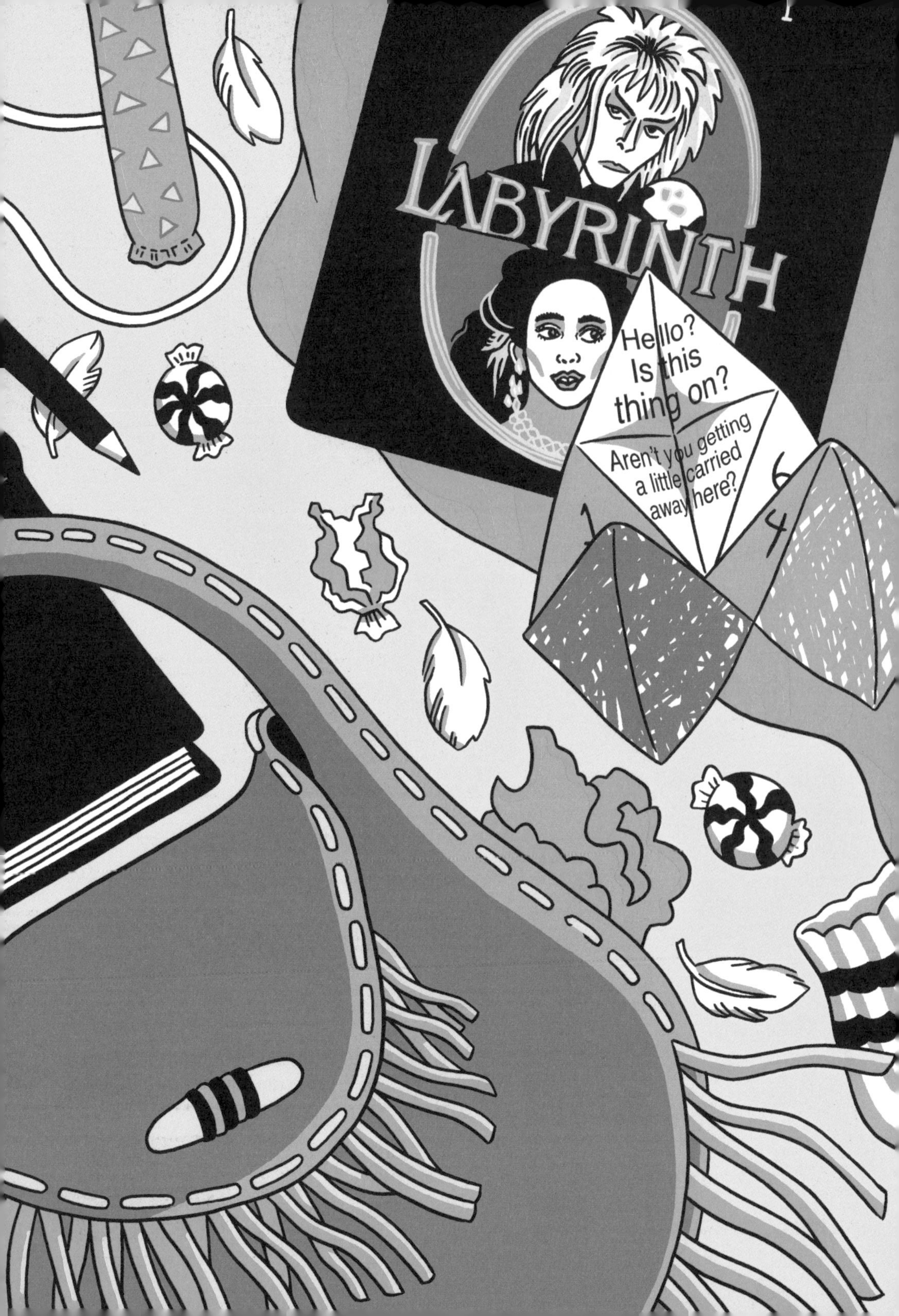
LABYRINTH
Hello? Is this thing on?
Aren't you getting a little carried away here?
6
1
4

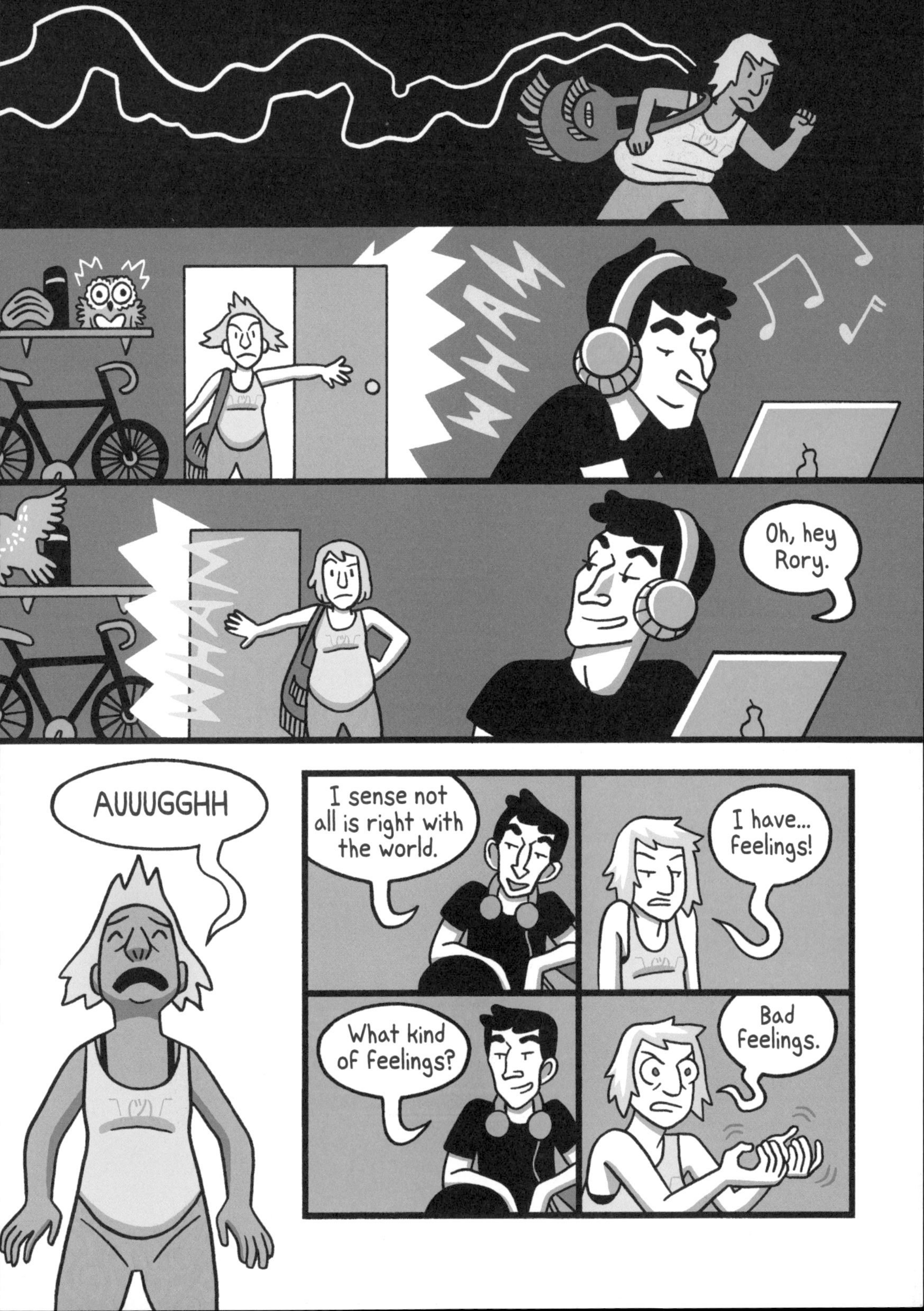
WHAM
WHAM
Oh, hey Rory.
AUUUGGHH
I sense not all is right with the world.
I have... feelings!
What kind of feelings?
Bad feelings.

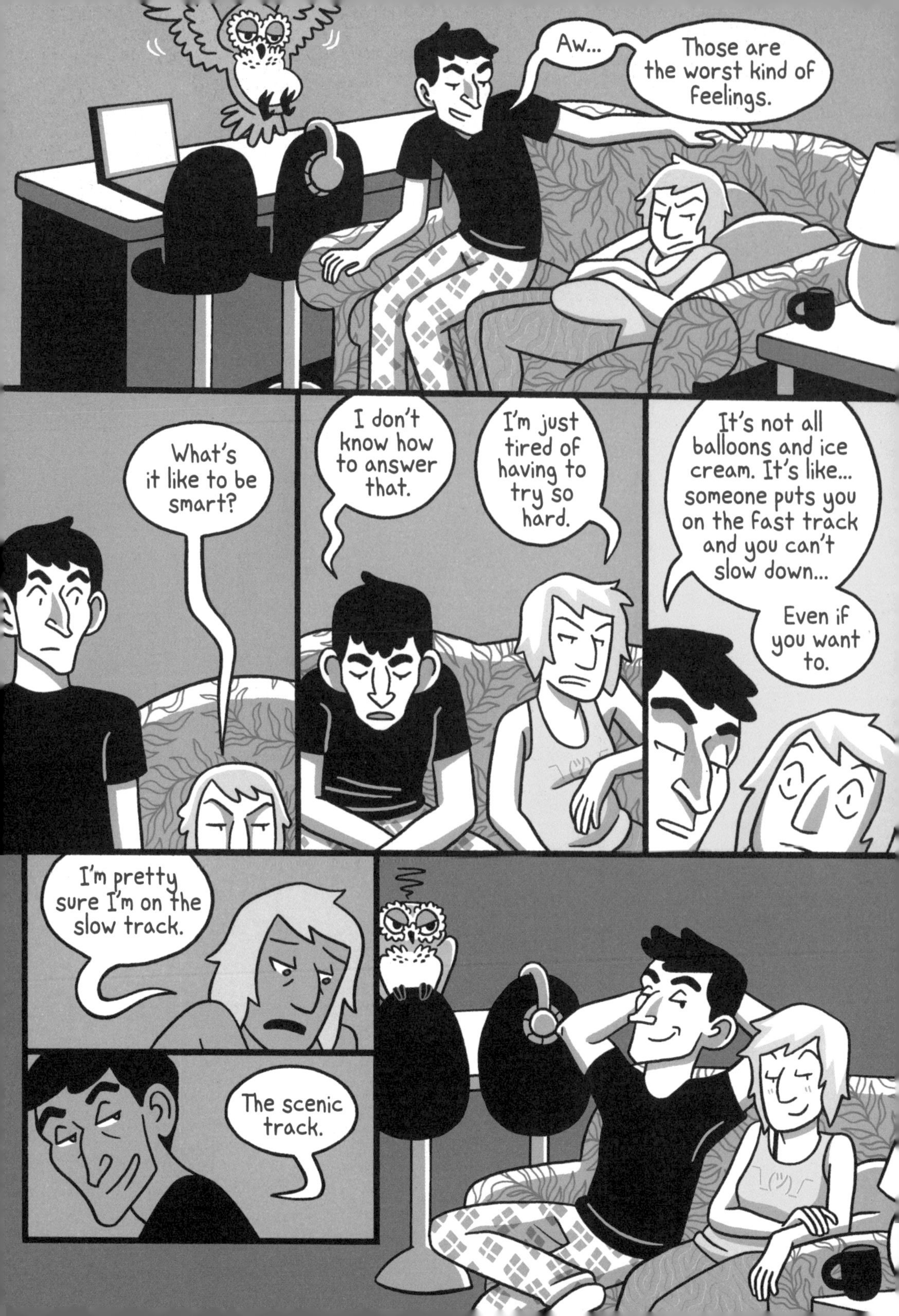
Aw...
Those are the worst kind of feelings.
What's it like to be smart?
I don't know how to answer that.
I'm just tired of having to try so hard.
It's not all balloons and ice cream. It's like... someone puts you on the fast track and you can't slow down...
Even if you want to.
I'm pretty sure I'm on the slow track.
The scenic track.

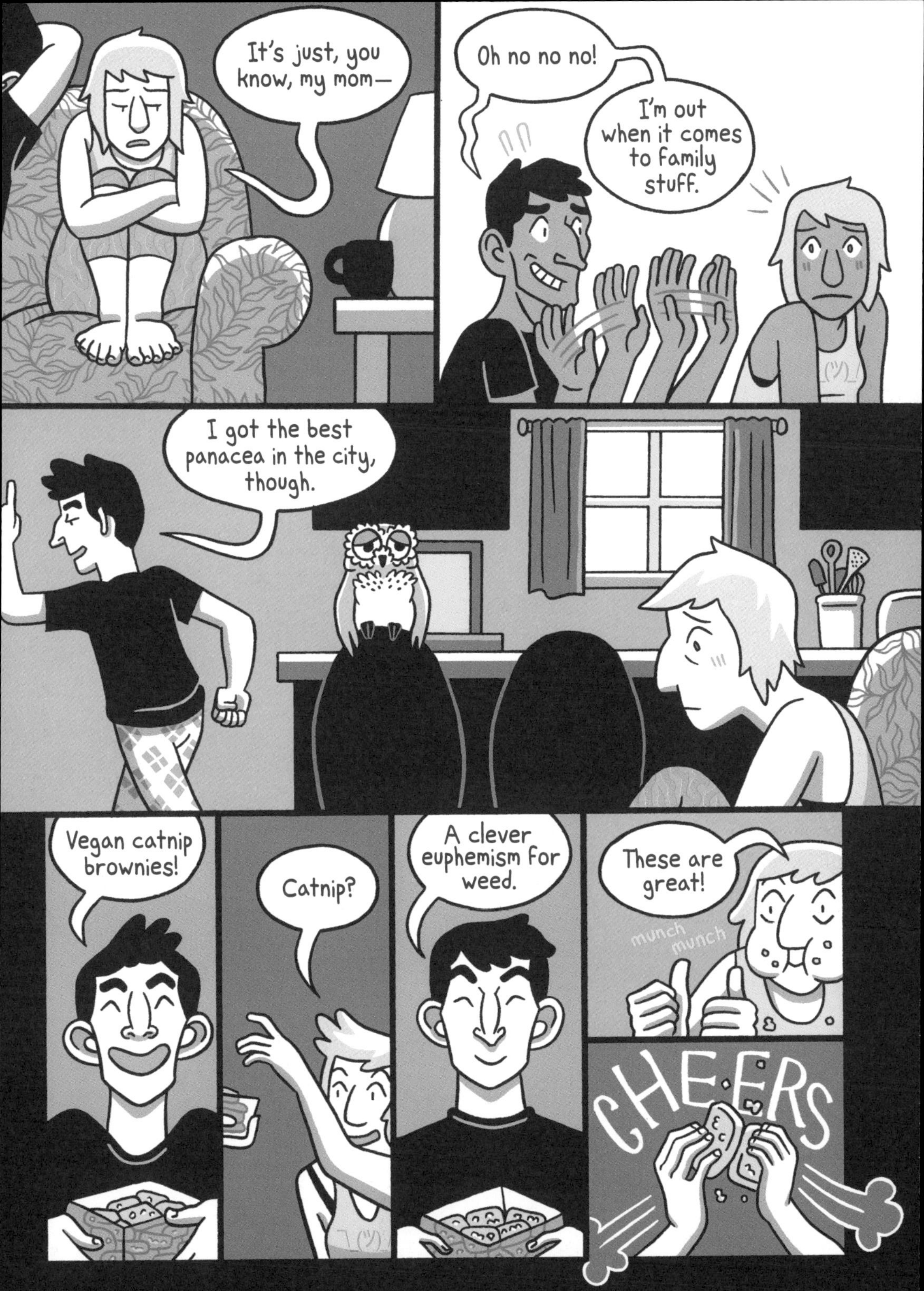
It's just, you know, my mom—
Oh no no no!
I'm out when it comes to family stuff.
I got the best panacea in the city, though.
Vegan catnip brownies!
Catnip?
A clever euphemism for weed.
These are great!
munch munch
CHEERS

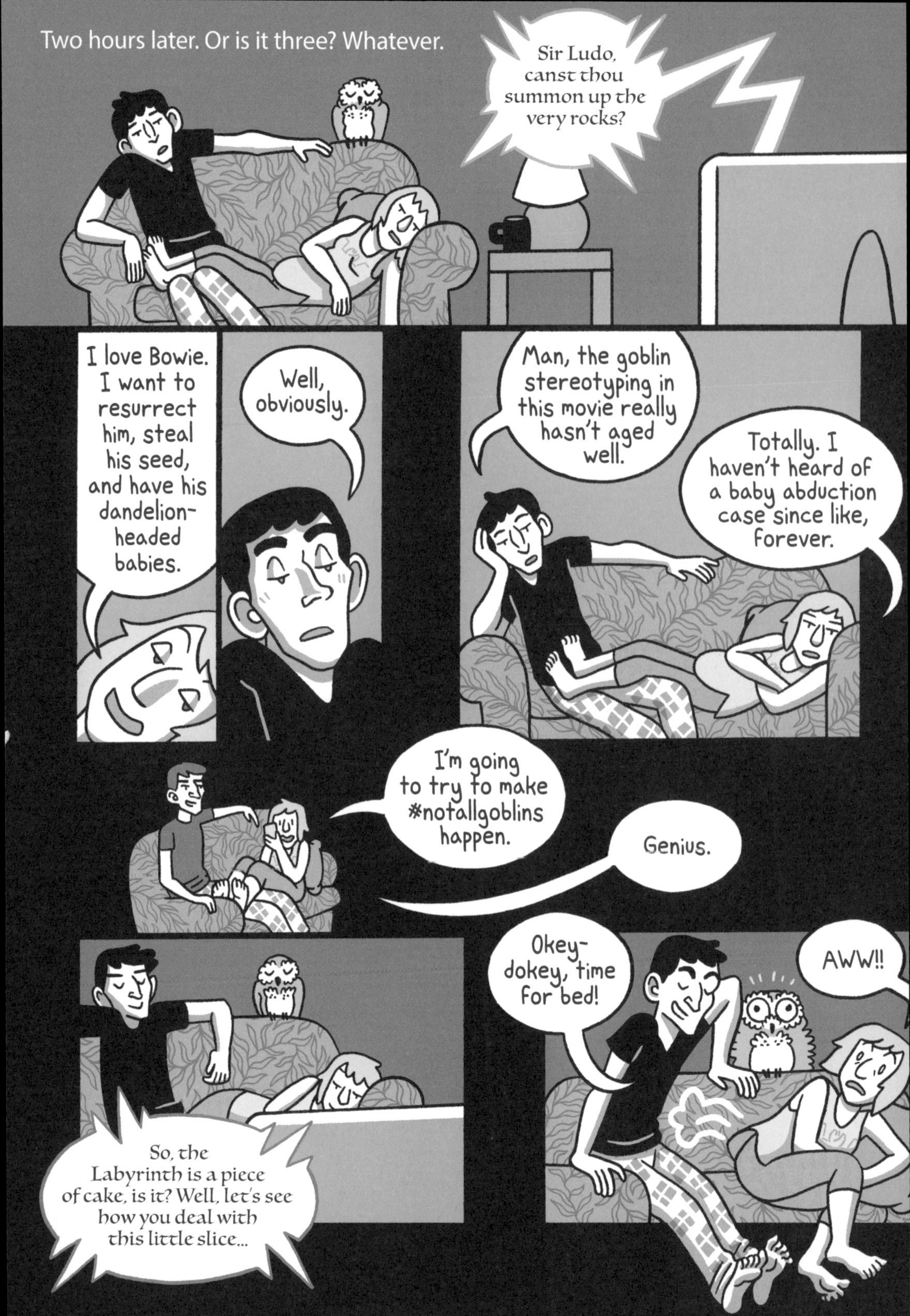
Two hours later. Or is it three? Whatever.
Sir Ludo, canst thou summon up the very rocks?
I love Bowie. I want to resurrect him, steal his seed, and have his dandelion-headed babies.
Well, obviously.
Man, the goblin stereotyping in this movie really hasn't aged well.
Totally. I haven't heard of a baby abduction case since like, forever.
I'm going to try to make #notallgoblins happen.
Genius.
So, the Labyrinth is a piece of cake, is it? Well, let's see how you deal with this little slice...
Okey-dokey, time for bed!
AWW!!

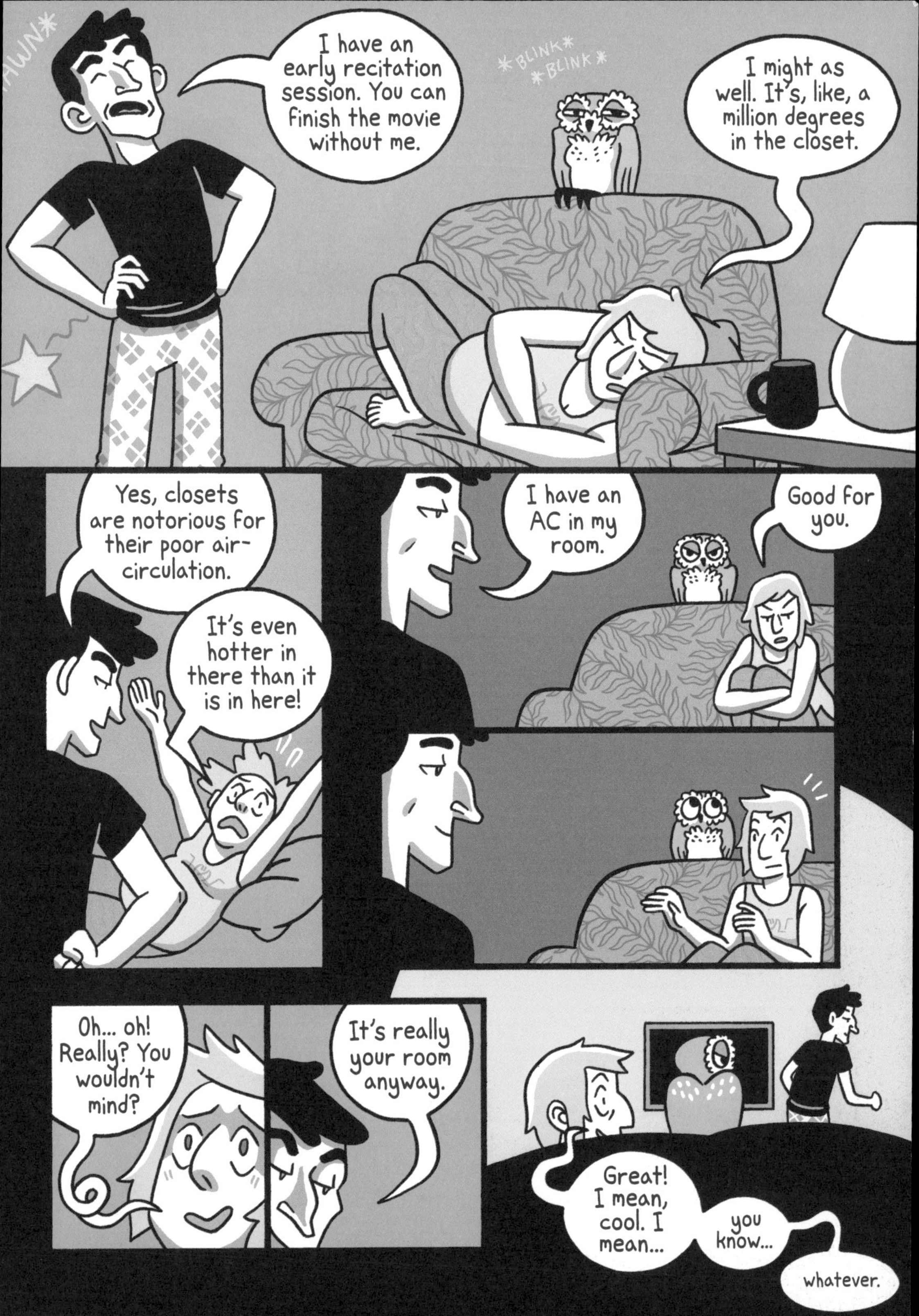
YAWN
I have an early recitation session. You can finish the movie without me.
BLINK *BLINK*
I might as well. It's, like, a million degrees in the closet.
Yes, closets are notorious for their poor air-circulation.
It's even hotter in there than it is in here!
I have an AC in my room.
Good for you.
Oh... oh! Really? You wouldn't mind?
It's really your room anyway.
Great! I mean, cool. I mean...
you know...
whatever.

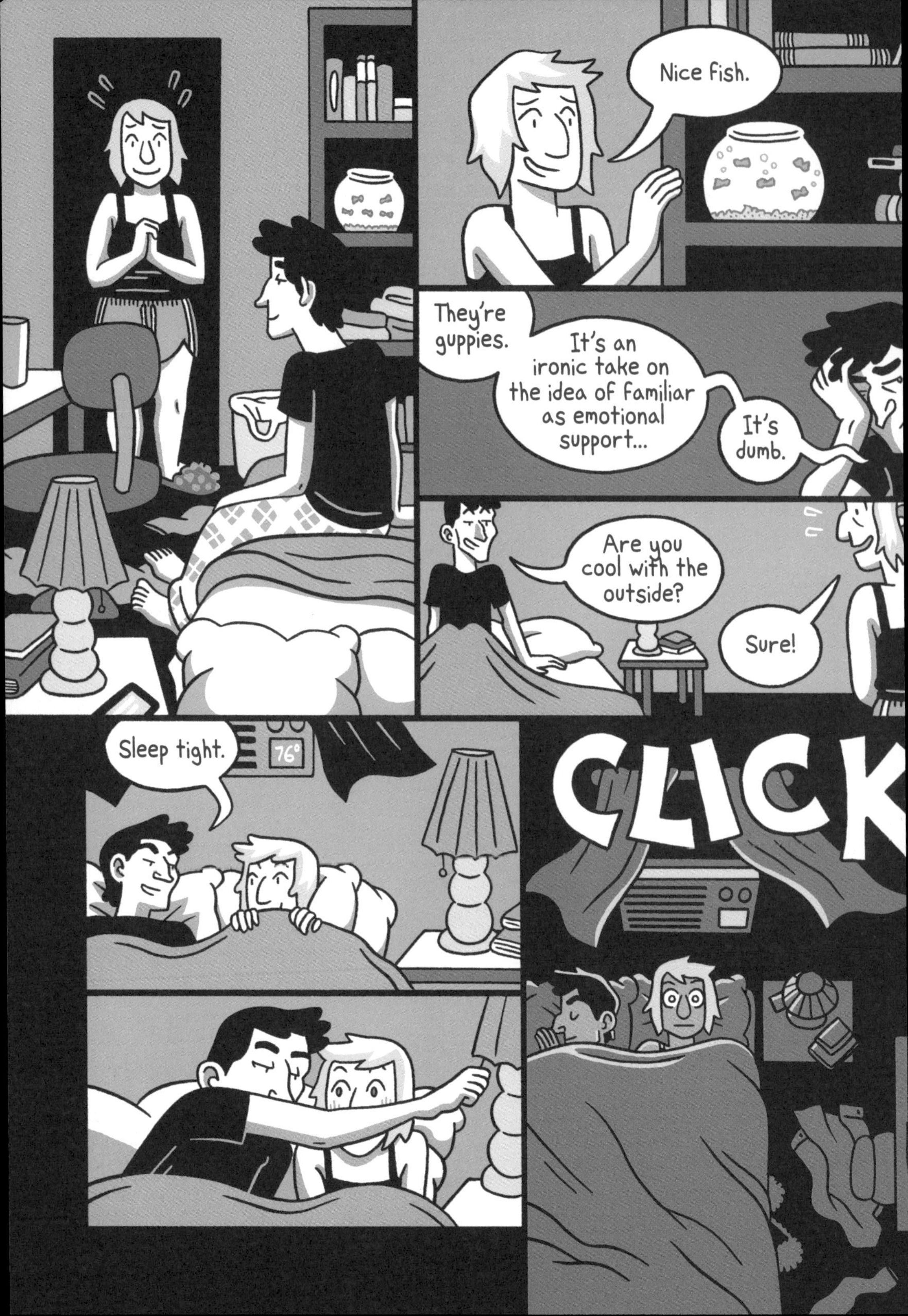
Nice fish.
They're guppies.
It's an ironic take on the idea of familiar as emotional support...
It's dumb.
Are you cool with the outside?
Sure!
Sleep tight.
76°
CLICK

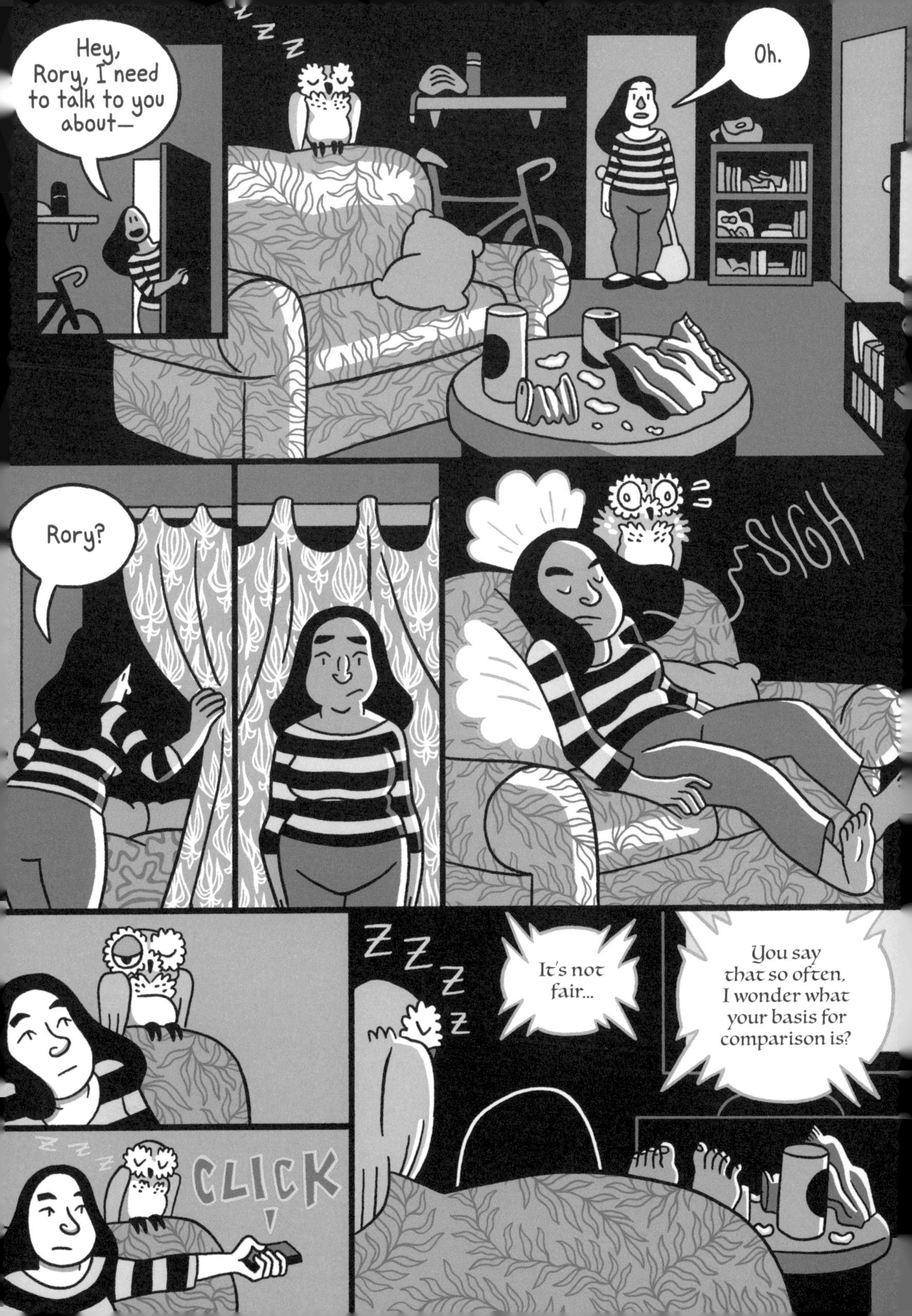
Hey, Rory, I need to talk to you about—
Z Z Z
Oh.
Rory?
SIGH
It's not fair...
You say that so often, I wonder what your basis for comparison is?
CLICK

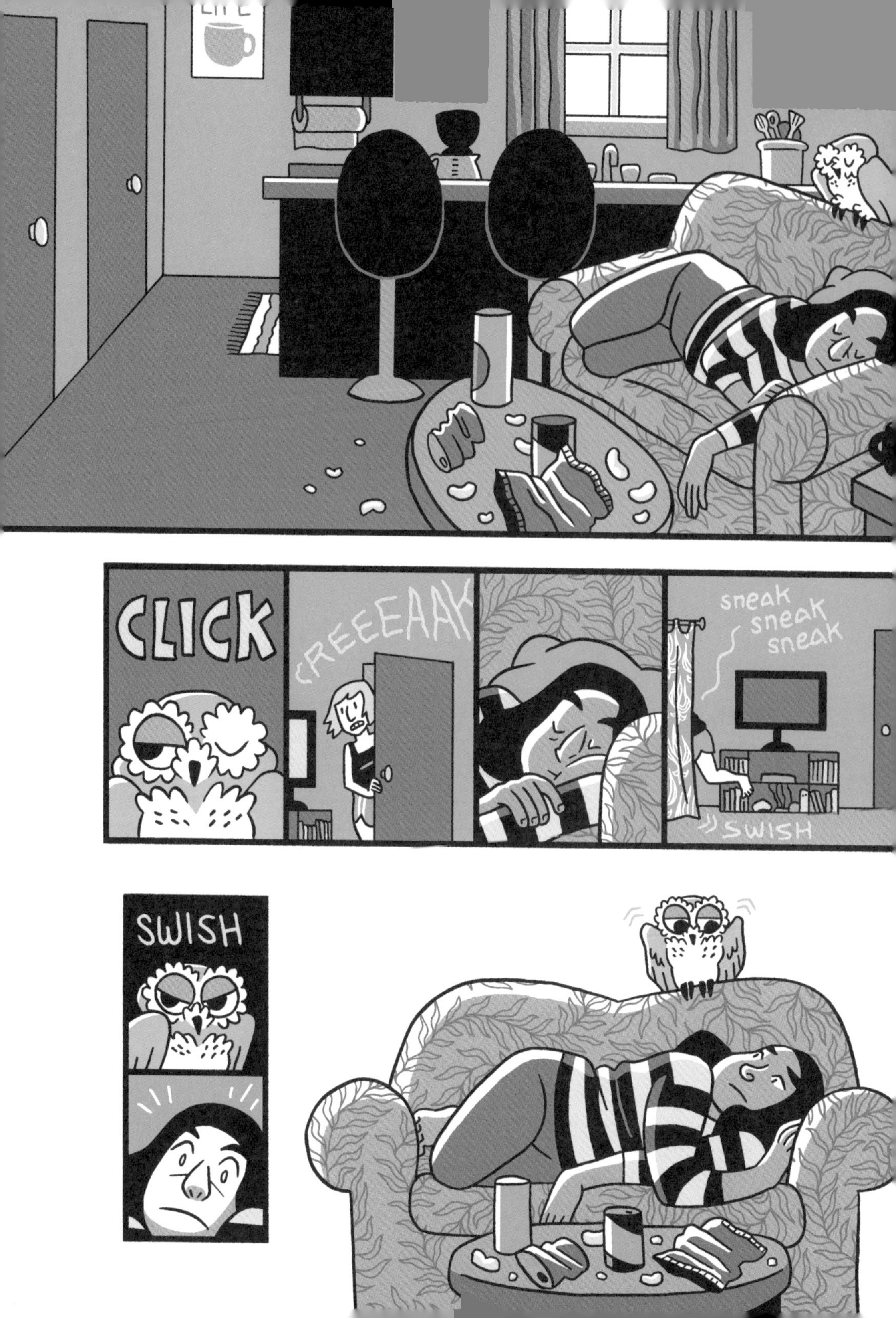
CLICK
CREEEAAK
sneak
sneak
sneak
SWISH
SWISH

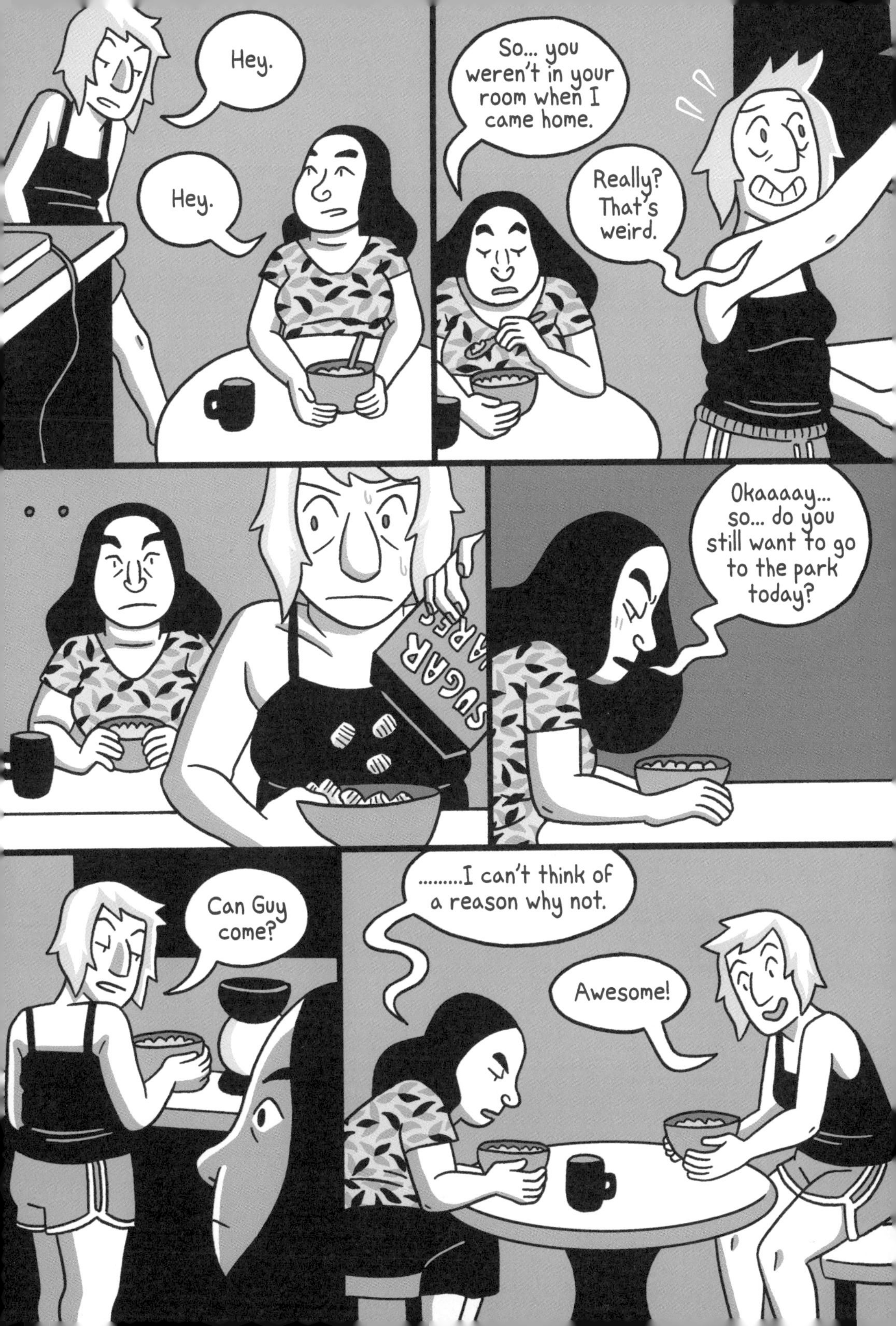
Hey.
Hey.
So... you weren't in your room when I came home.
Really? That's weird.
SUGAR FLAKES
Okaaaay... so... do you still want to go to the park today?
Can Guy come?
.........I can't think of a reason why not.
Awesome!

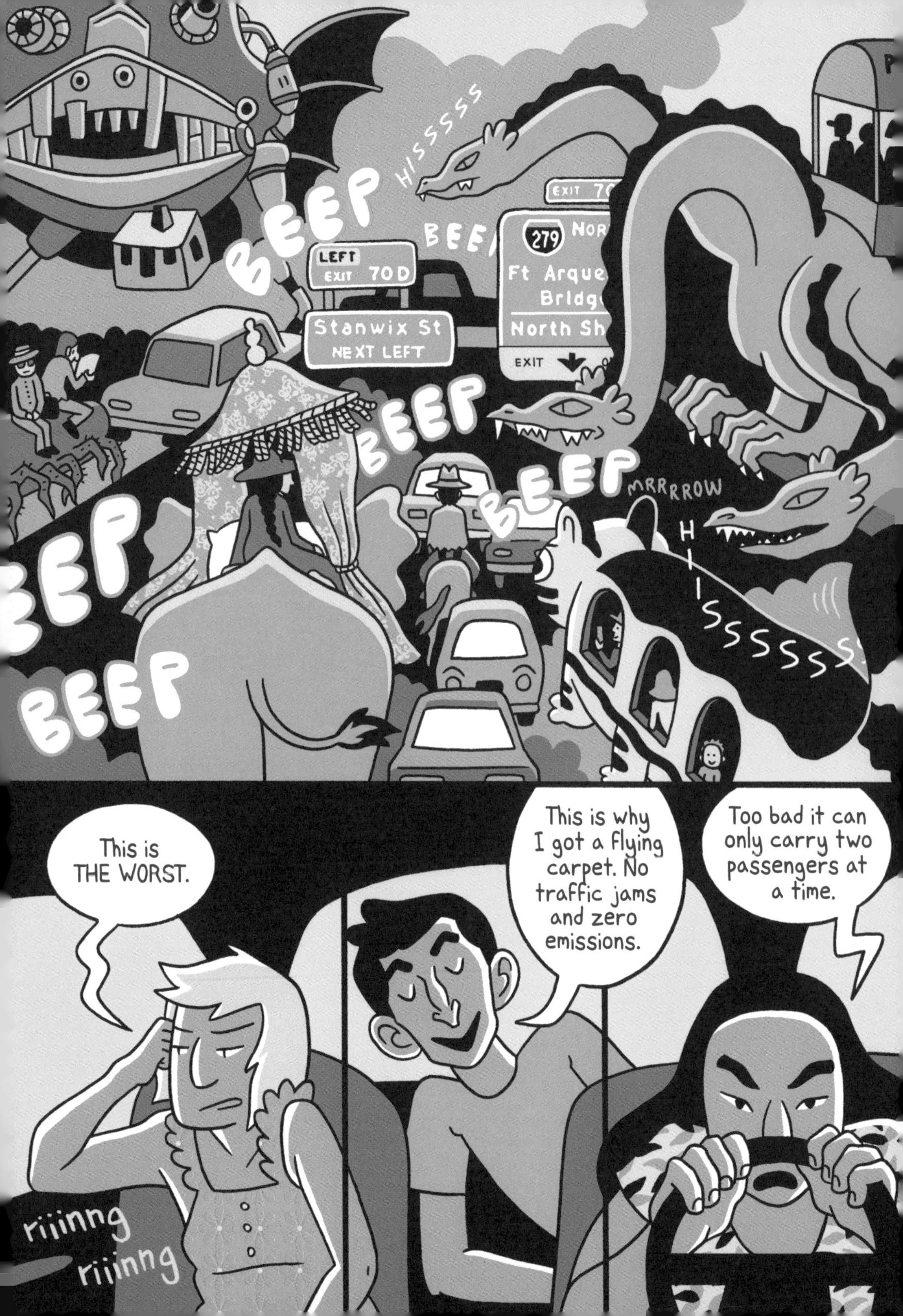
HISSSSS
BEEP
BEE
EXIT 70
279 NOR
Ft Arque
Bridg
North Sh
EXIT
LEFT EXIT 70D
Stanwix St NEXT LEFT
BEEP
BEEP
MRRRROW
HISSSSSSS
EEP
BEEP
This is THE WORST.
This is why I got a flying carpet. No traffic jams and zero emissions.
Too bad it can only carry two passengers at a time.
riiinng riiinng

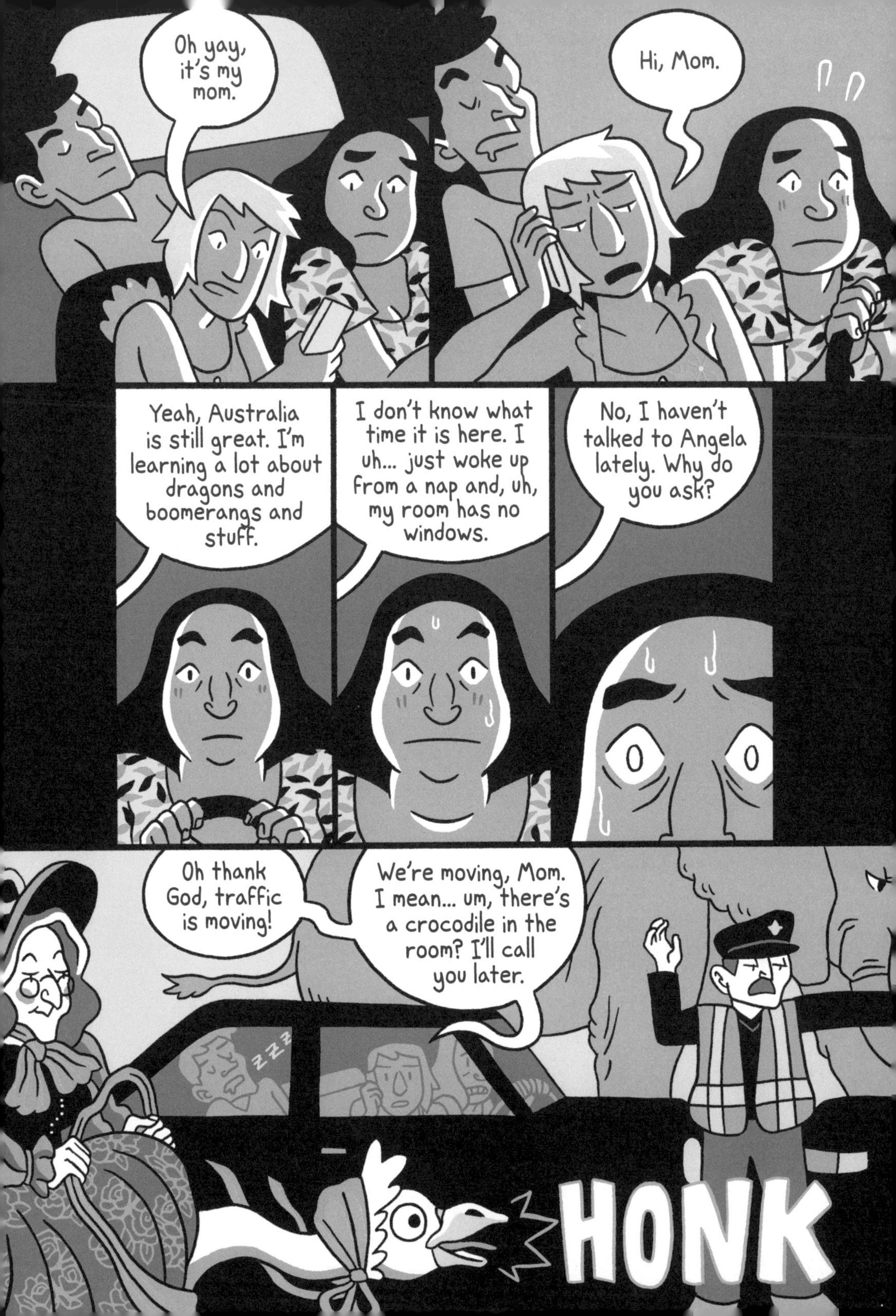
Oh yay, it's my mom.
Hi, Mom.
Yeah, Australia is still great. I'm learning a lot about dragons and boomerangs and stuff.
I don't know what time it is here. I uh... just woke up from a nap and, uh, my room has no windows.
No, I haven't talked to Angela lately. Why do you ask?
Oh thank God, traffic is moving!
We're moving, Mom. I mean... um, there's a crocodile in the room? I'll call you later.
ZZZ
HONK

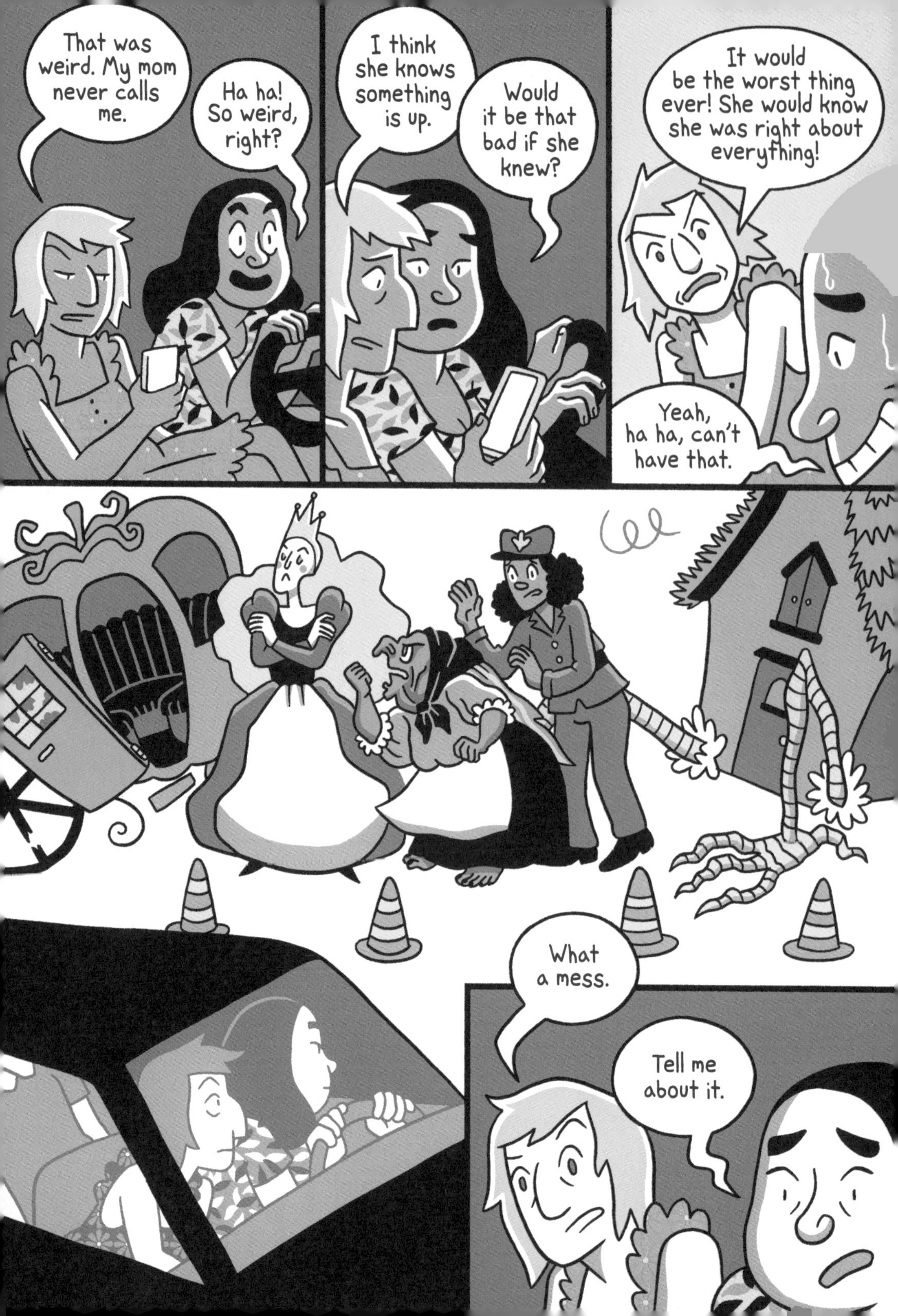
That was weird. My mom never calls me.
Ha ha! So weird, right?
I think she knows something is up.
Would it be that bad if she knew?
It would be the worst thing ever! She would know she was right about everything!
Yeah, ha ha, can't have that.
What a mess.
Tell me about it.

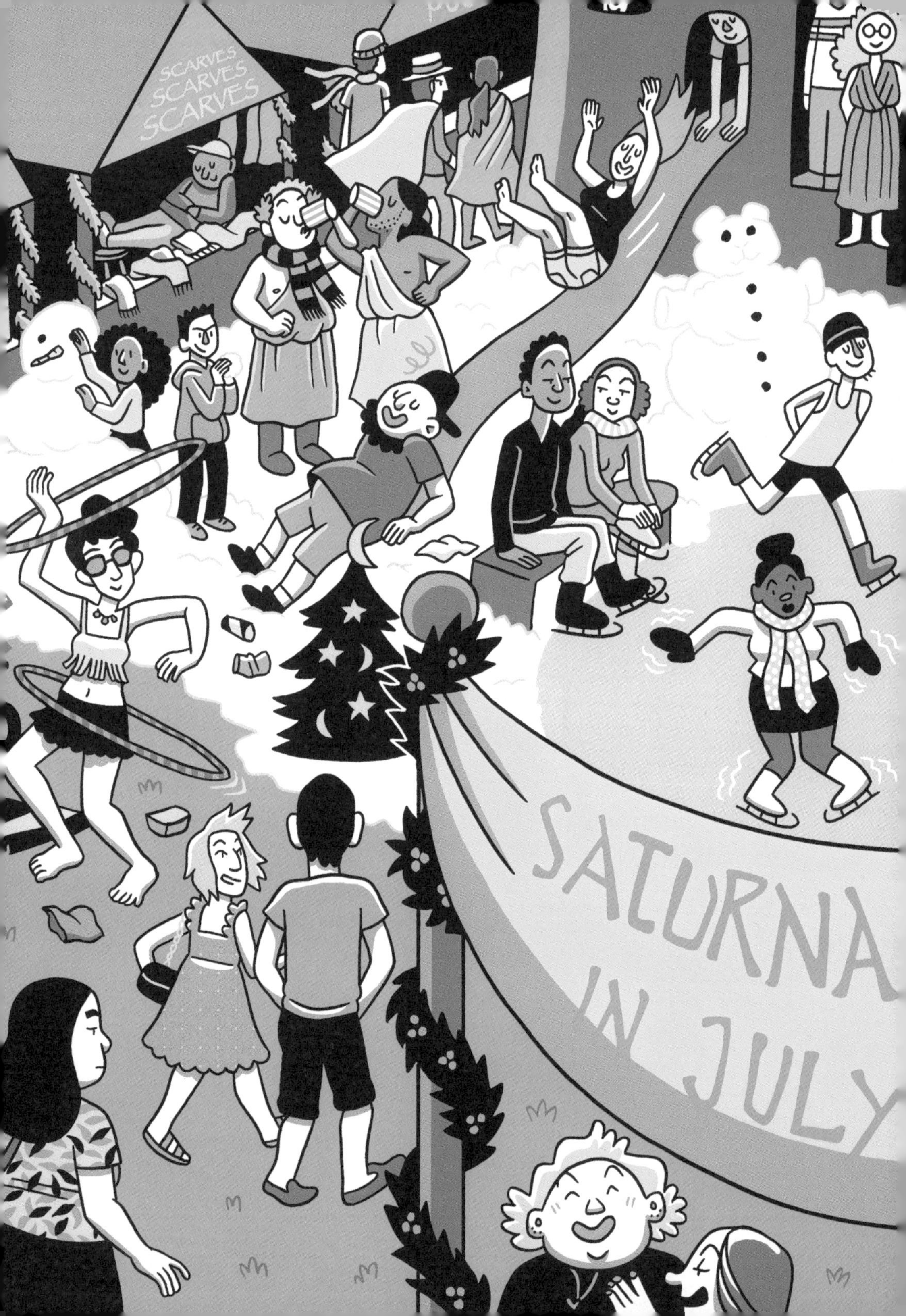
SCARVES
SCARVES
SCARVES
SATURNA
IN JULY

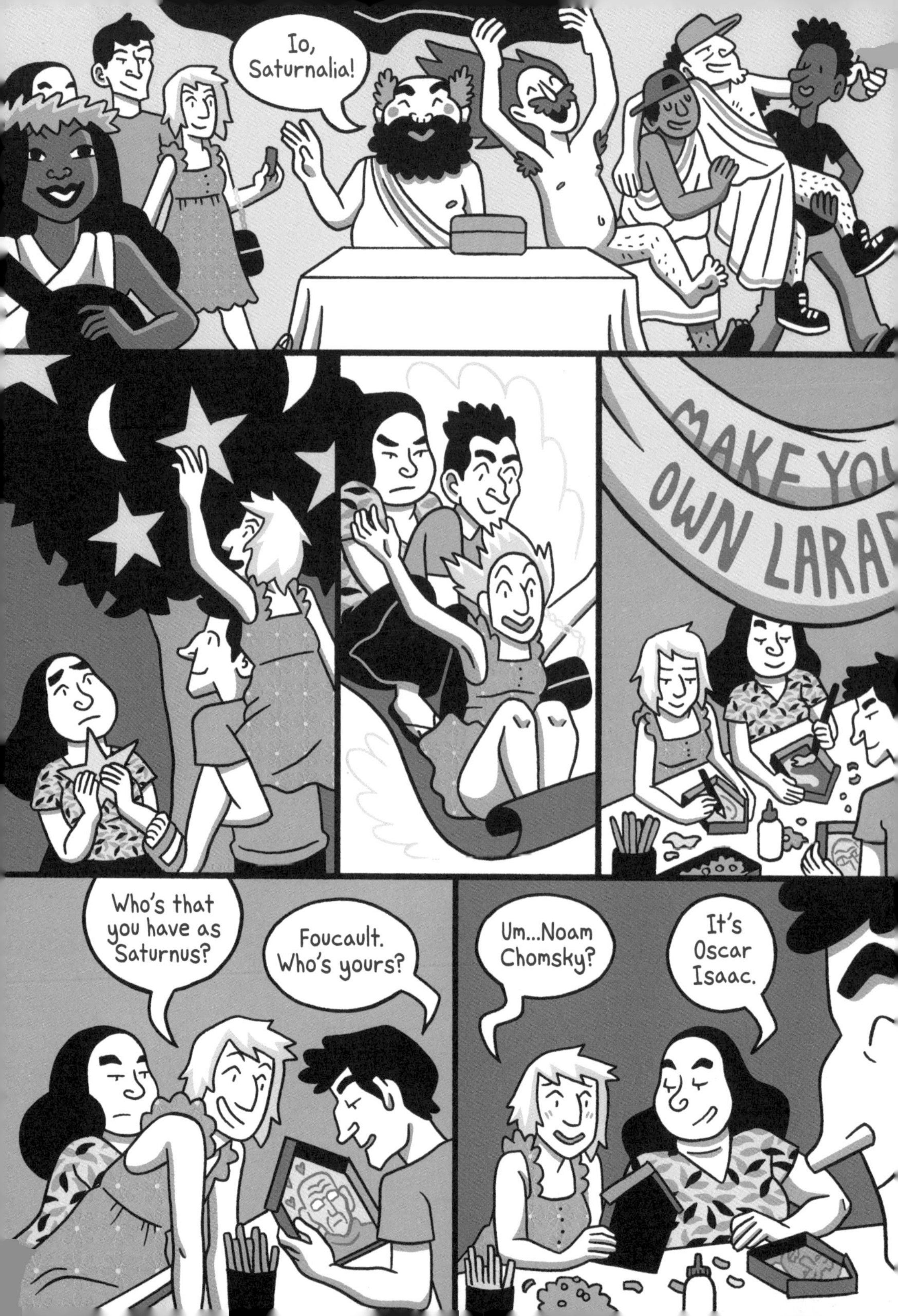
Io, Saturnalia!
MAKE YOU
OWN LARA
Who's that you have as Saturnus?
Foucault. Who's yours?
Um...Noam Chomsky?
It's Oscar Isaac.

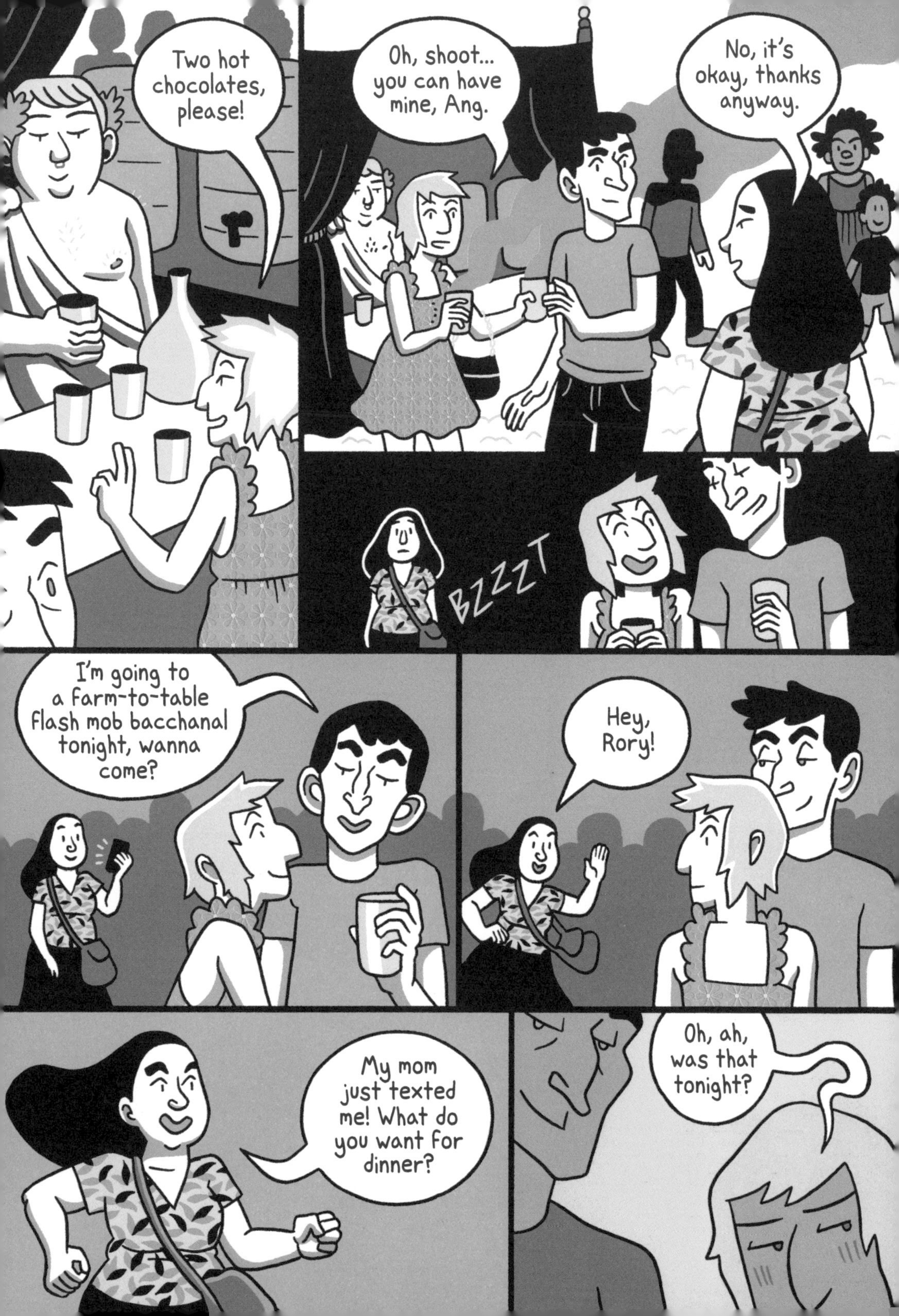
Two hot chocolates, please!
Oh, shoot... you can have mine, Ang.
No, it's okay, thanks anyway.
BZZZT
I'm going to a farm-to-table flash mob bacchanal tonight, wanna come?
Hey, Rory!
My mom just texted me! What do you want for dinner?
Oh, ah, was that tonight?

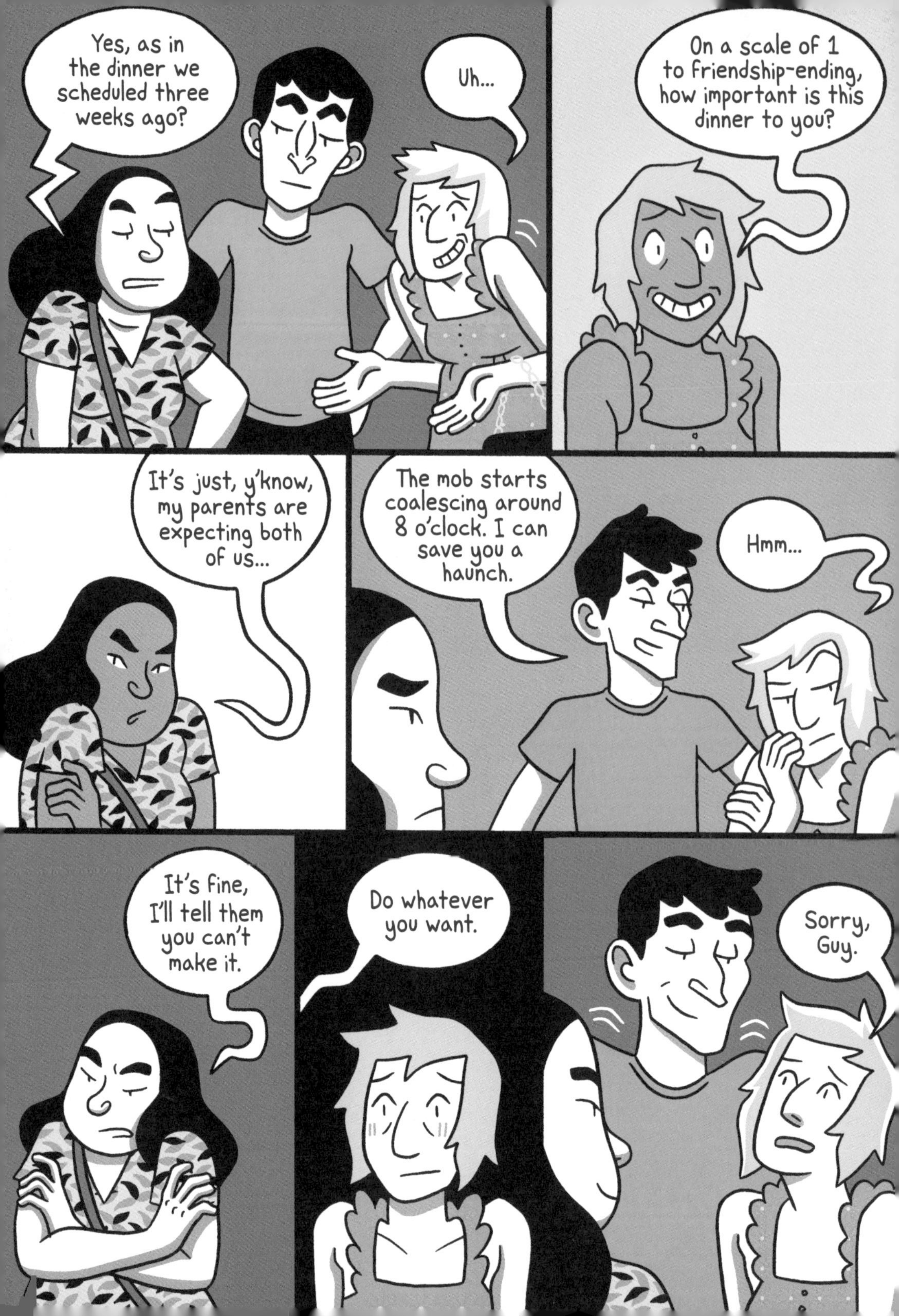
Yes, as in the dinner we scheduled three weeks ago?
Uh...
On a scale of 1 to friendship-ending, how important is this dinner to you?
It's just, y'know, my parents are expecting both of us...
The mob starts coalescing around 8 o'clock. I can save you a haunch.
Hmm...
It's fine, I'll tell them you can't make it.
Do whatever you want.
Sorry, Guy.

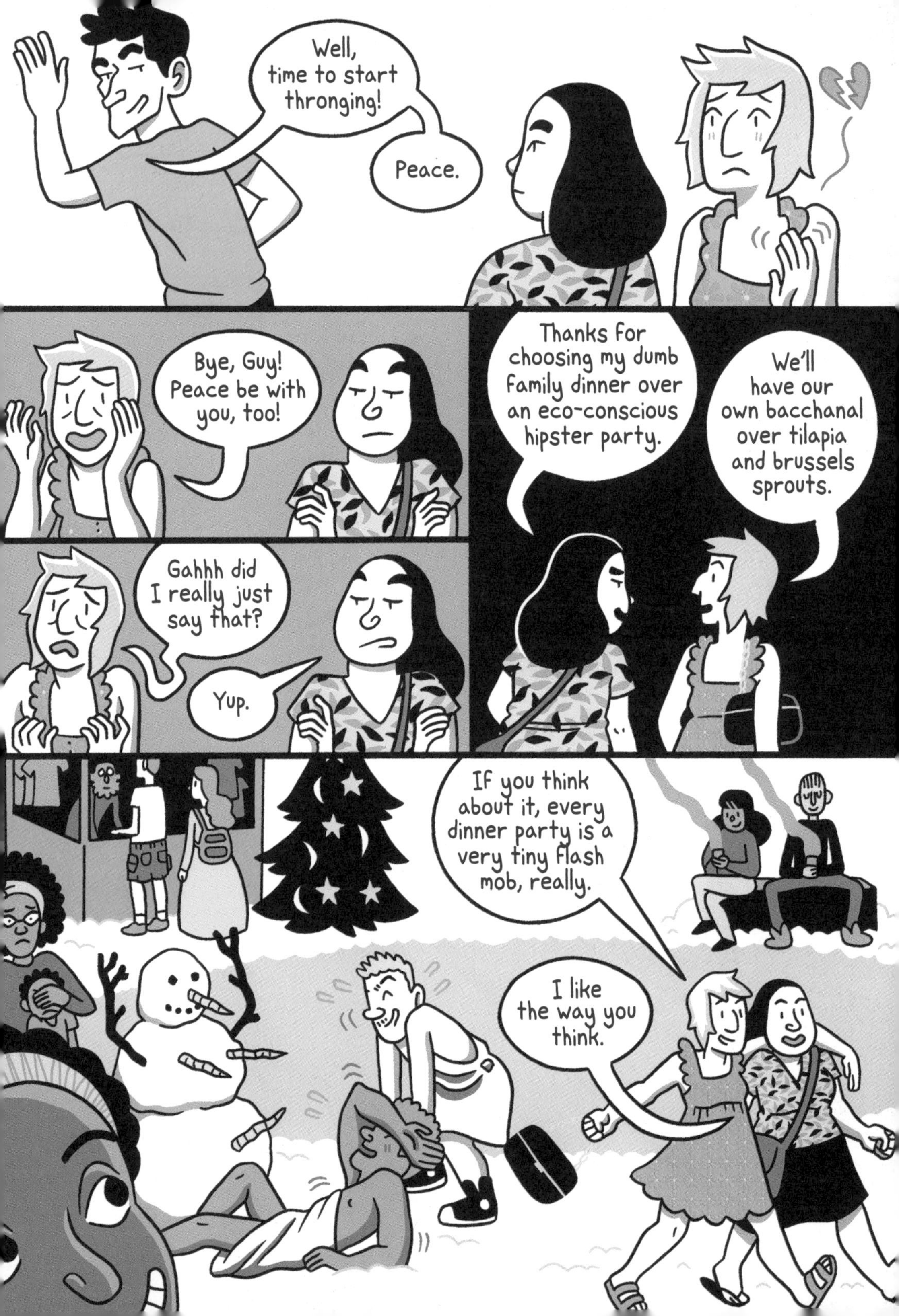
Well, time to start thronging!
Peace.
Bye, Guy! Peace be with you, too!
Gahhh did I really just say that?
Yup.
Thanks for choosing my dumb family dinner over an eco-conscious hipster party.
We'll have our own bacchanal over tilapia and brussels sprouts.
If you think about it, every dinner party is a very tiny flash mob, really.
I like the way you think.

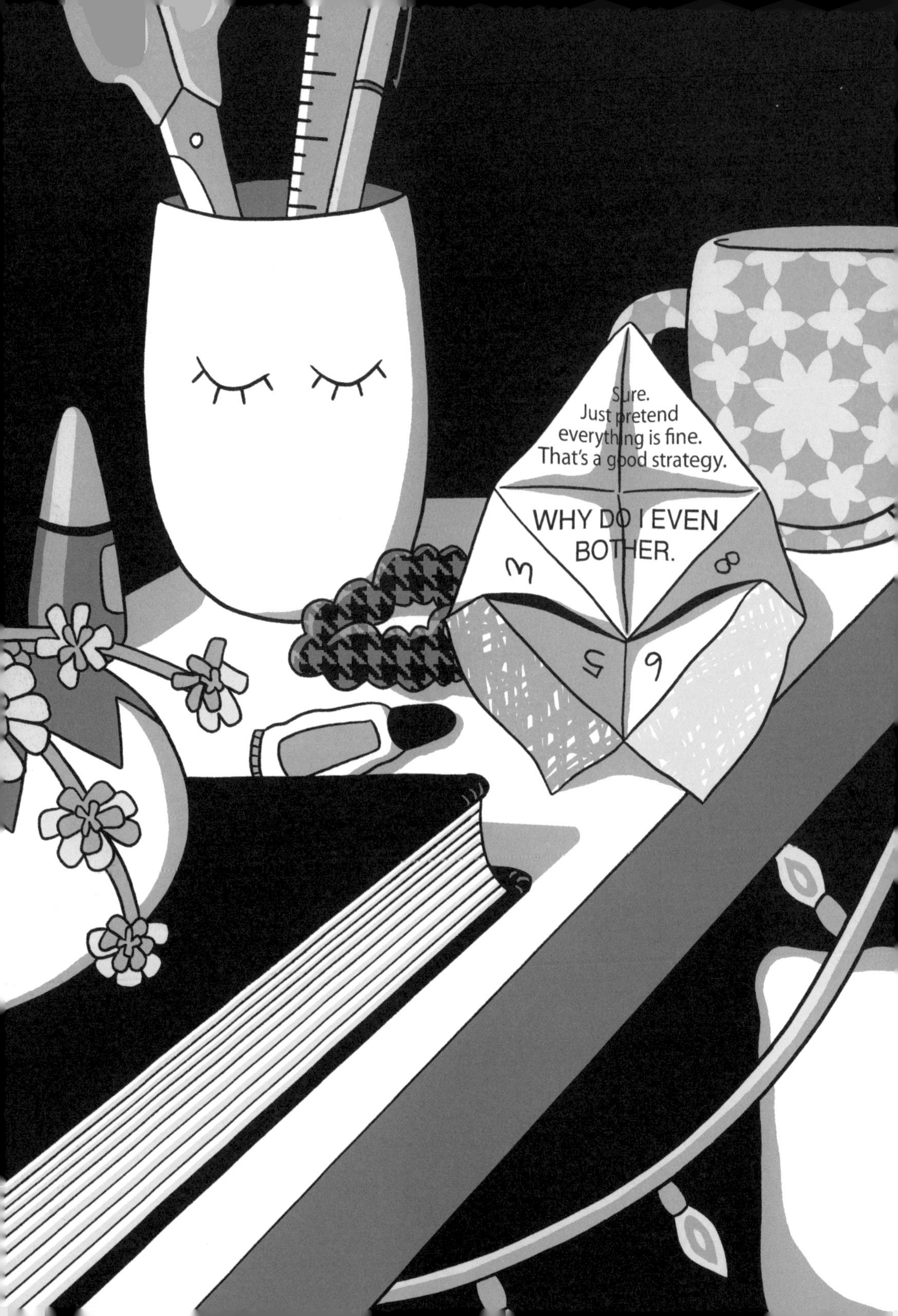
Sure.
Just pretend
everything is fine.
That's a good strategy.
WHY DO I EVEN
BOTHER.
3
8
5
6

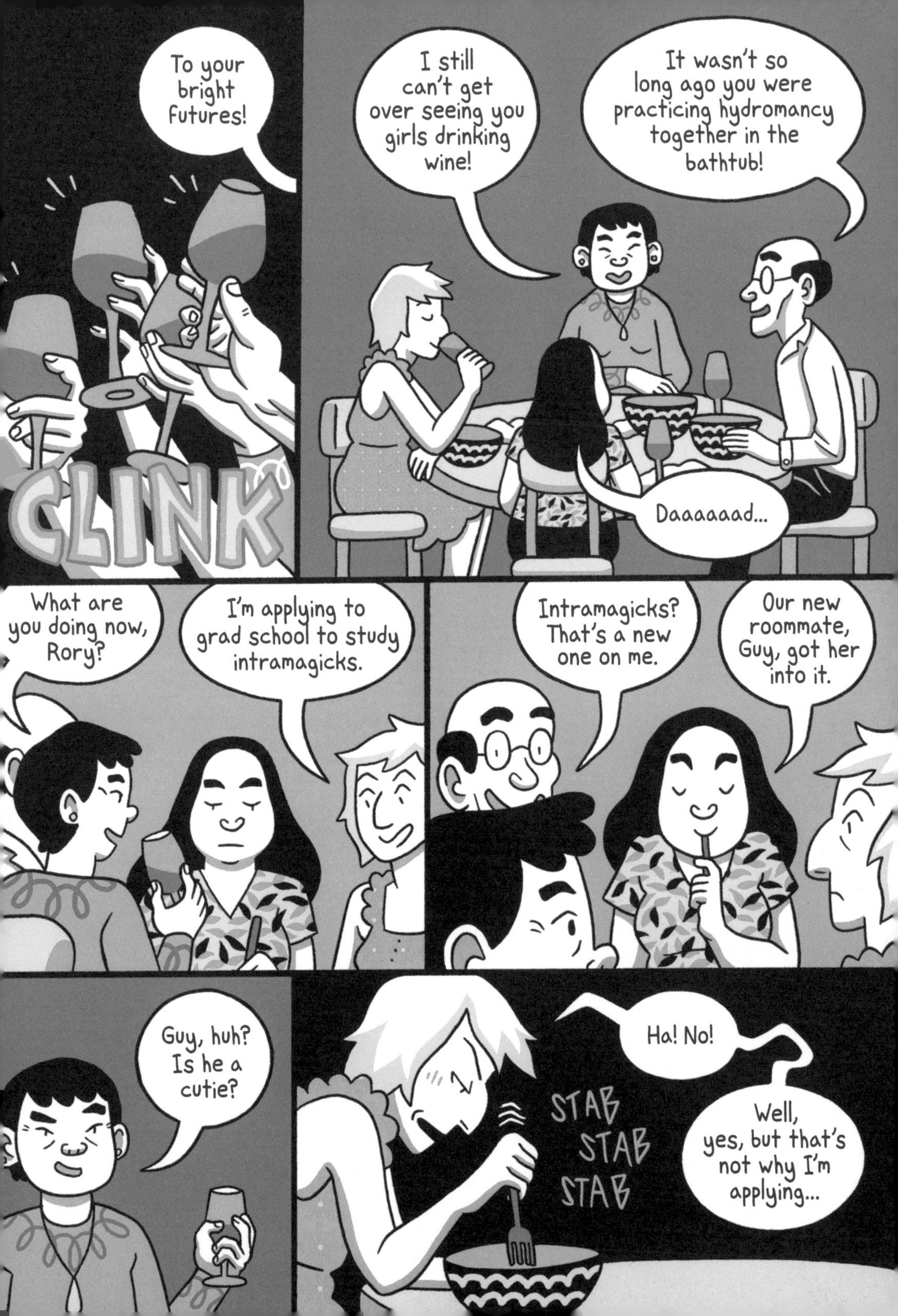

To your bright futures!
CLINK
I still can't get over seeing you girls drinking wine!
It wasn't so long ago you were practicing hydromancy together in the bathtub!
Daaaaaad...
What are you doing now, Rory?
I'm applying to grad school to study intramagicks.
Intramagicks? That's a new one on me.
Our new roommate, Guy, got her into it.
Guy, huh? Is he a cutie?
Ha! No!
Well, yes, but that's not why I'm applying...
STAB
STAB
STAB

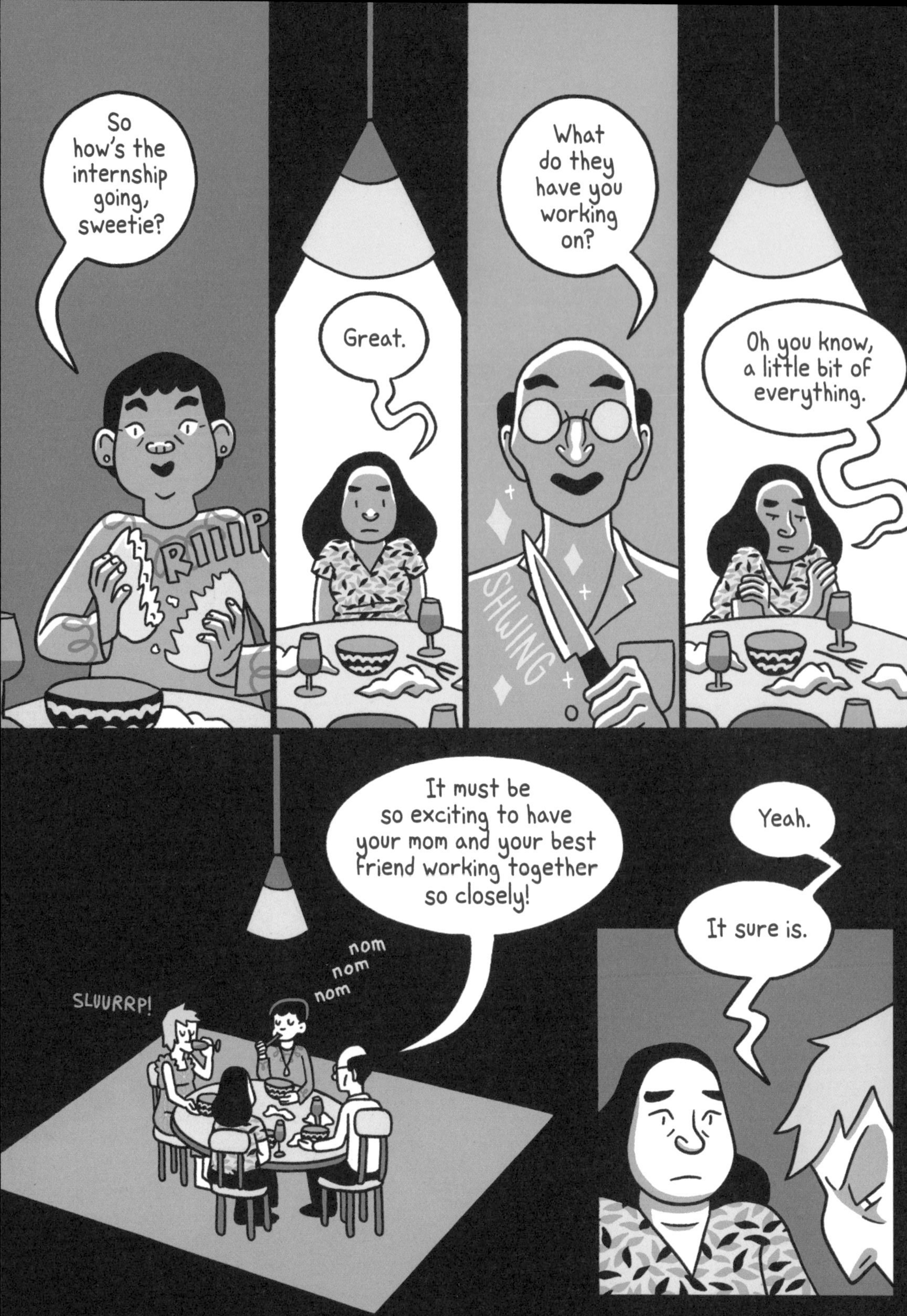
So how's the internship going, sweetie?
RIIIP
Great.
What do they have you working on?
SHWING
Oh you know, a little bit of everything.
SLUURRP!
nom nom nom
It must be so exciting to have your mom and your best friend working together so closely!
Yeah.
It sure is.

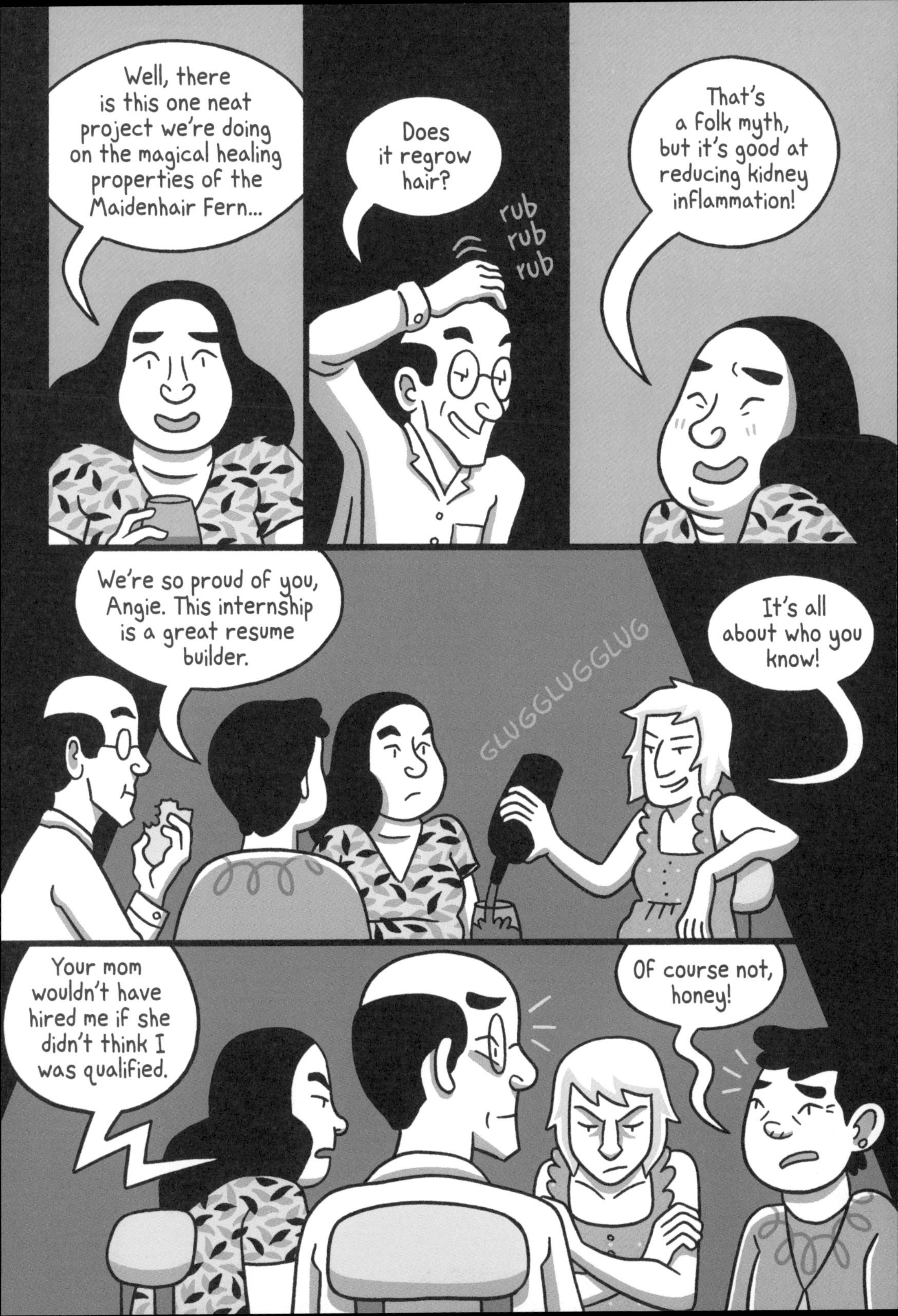
Well, there is this one neat project we're doing on the magical healing properties of the Maidenhair Fern...
Does it regrow hair?
rub rub rub
That's a folk myth, but it's good at reducing kidney inflammation!
We're so proud of you, Angie. This internship is a great resume builder.
GLUGGLUGGLUG
It's all about who you know!
Your mom wouldn't have hired me if she didn't think I was qualified.
Of course not, honey!

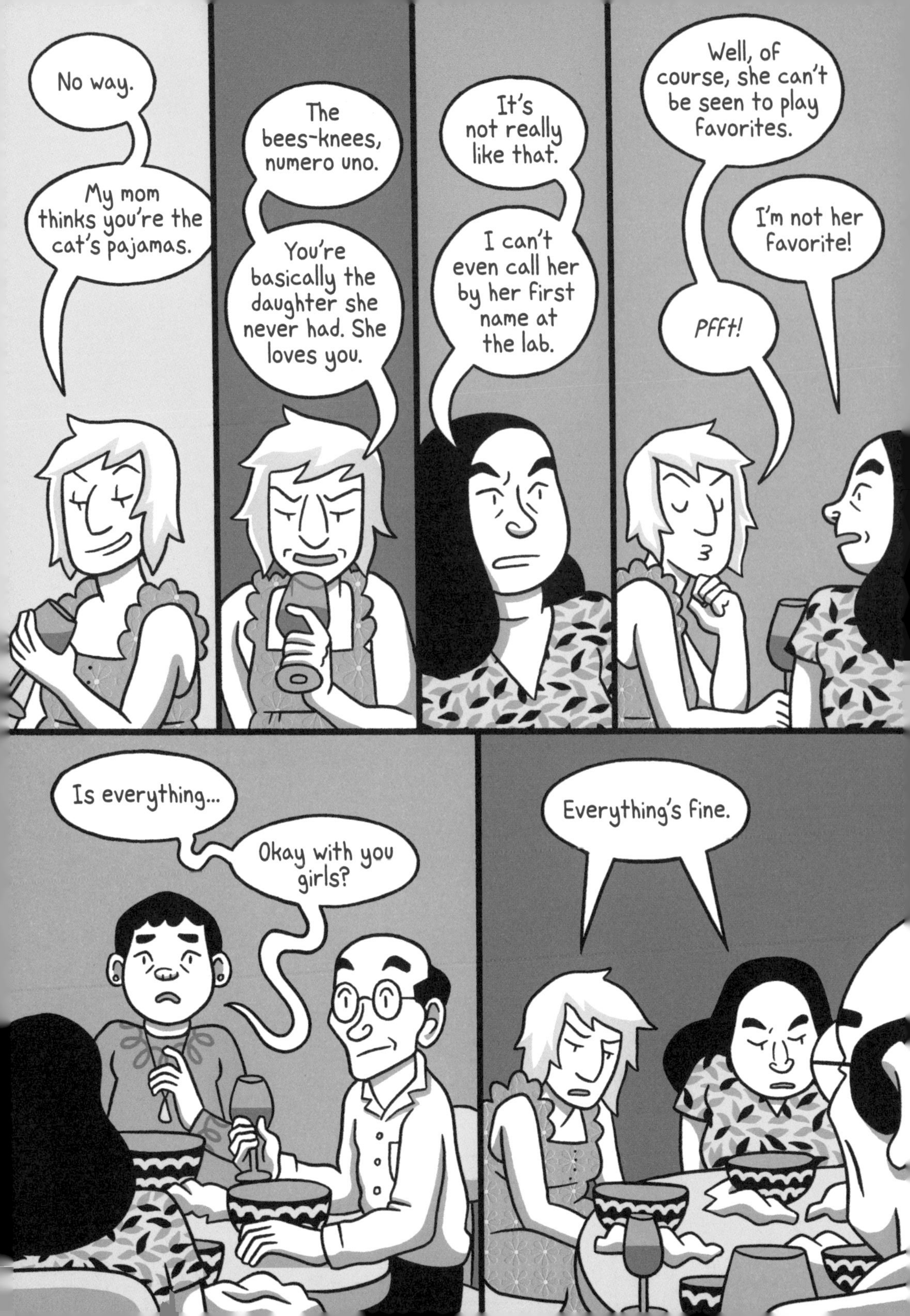
No way.
My mom thinks you're the cat's pajamas.
The bees-knees, numero uno.
You're basically the daughter she never had. She loves you.
It's not really like that.
I can't even call her by her first name at the lab.
Well, of course, she can't be seen to play favorites.
PFFT!
I'm not her favorite!
Is everything...
Okay with you girls?
Everything's fine.

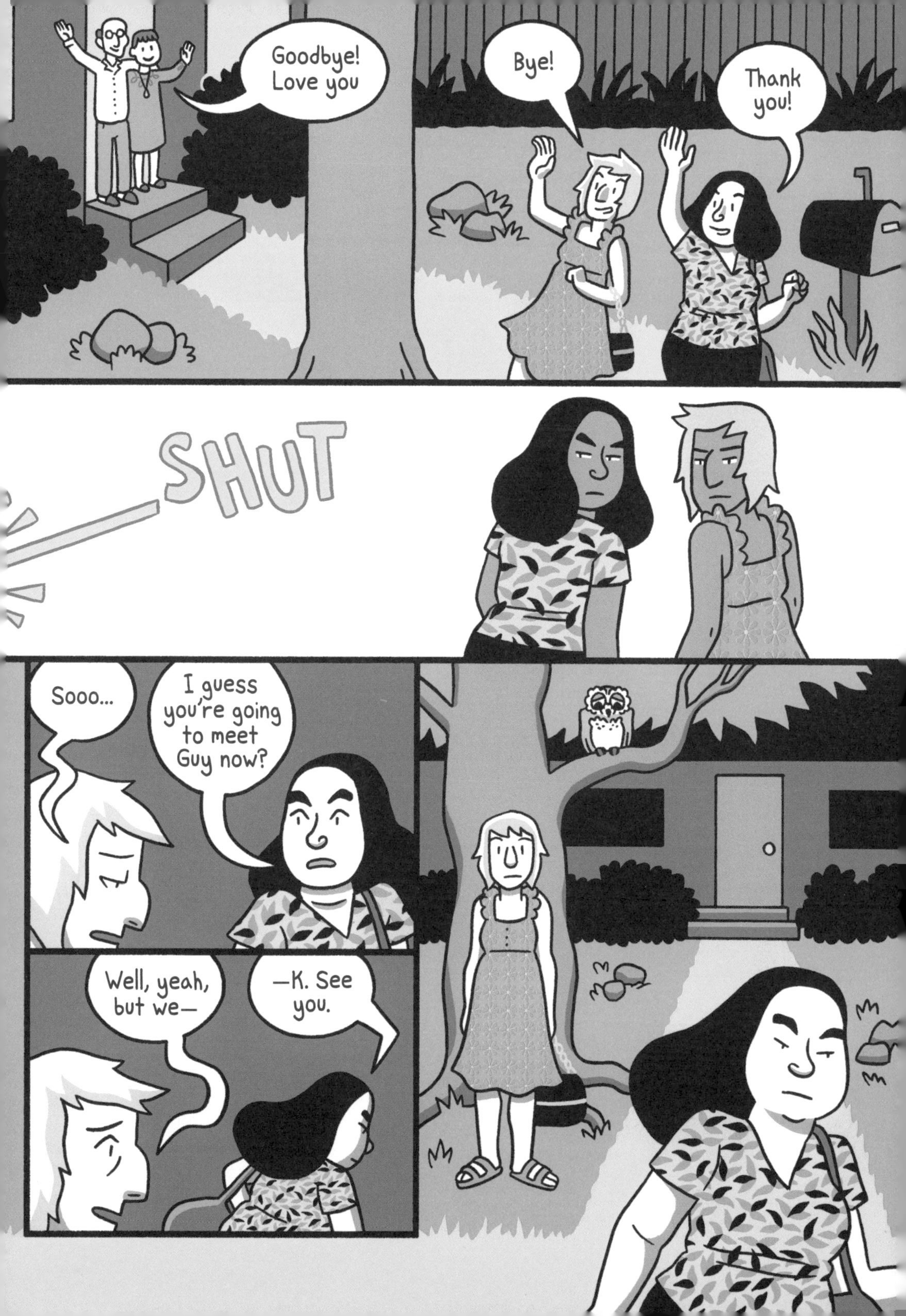

Goodbye! Love you
Bye!
Thank you!
SHUT
Sooo...
I guess you're going to meet Guy now?
Well, yeah, but we—
—K. See you.

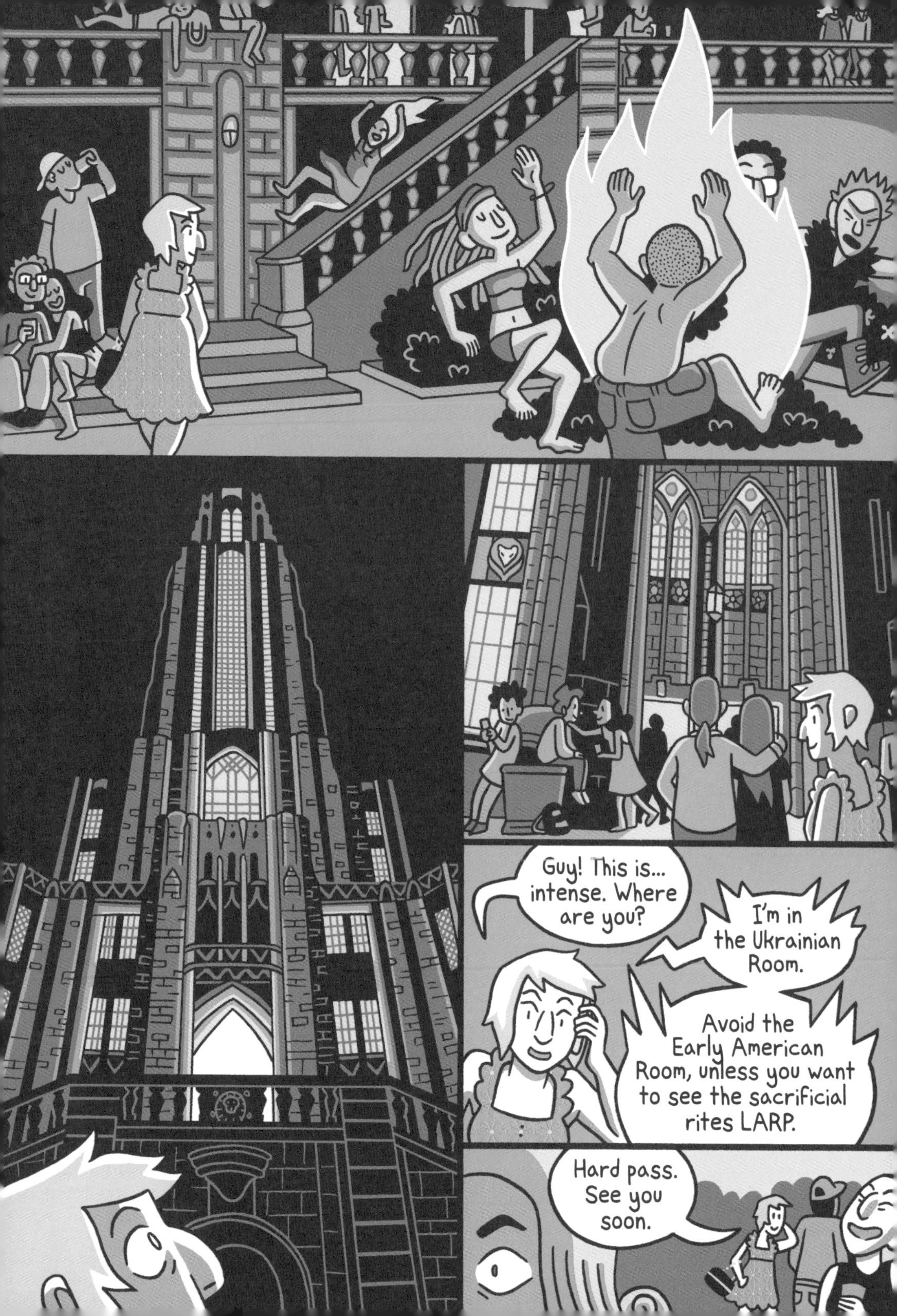
Guy! This is... intense. Where are you?
I'm in the Ukrainian Room.
Avoid the Early American Room, unless you want to see the sacrificial rites LARP.
Hard pass. See you soon.

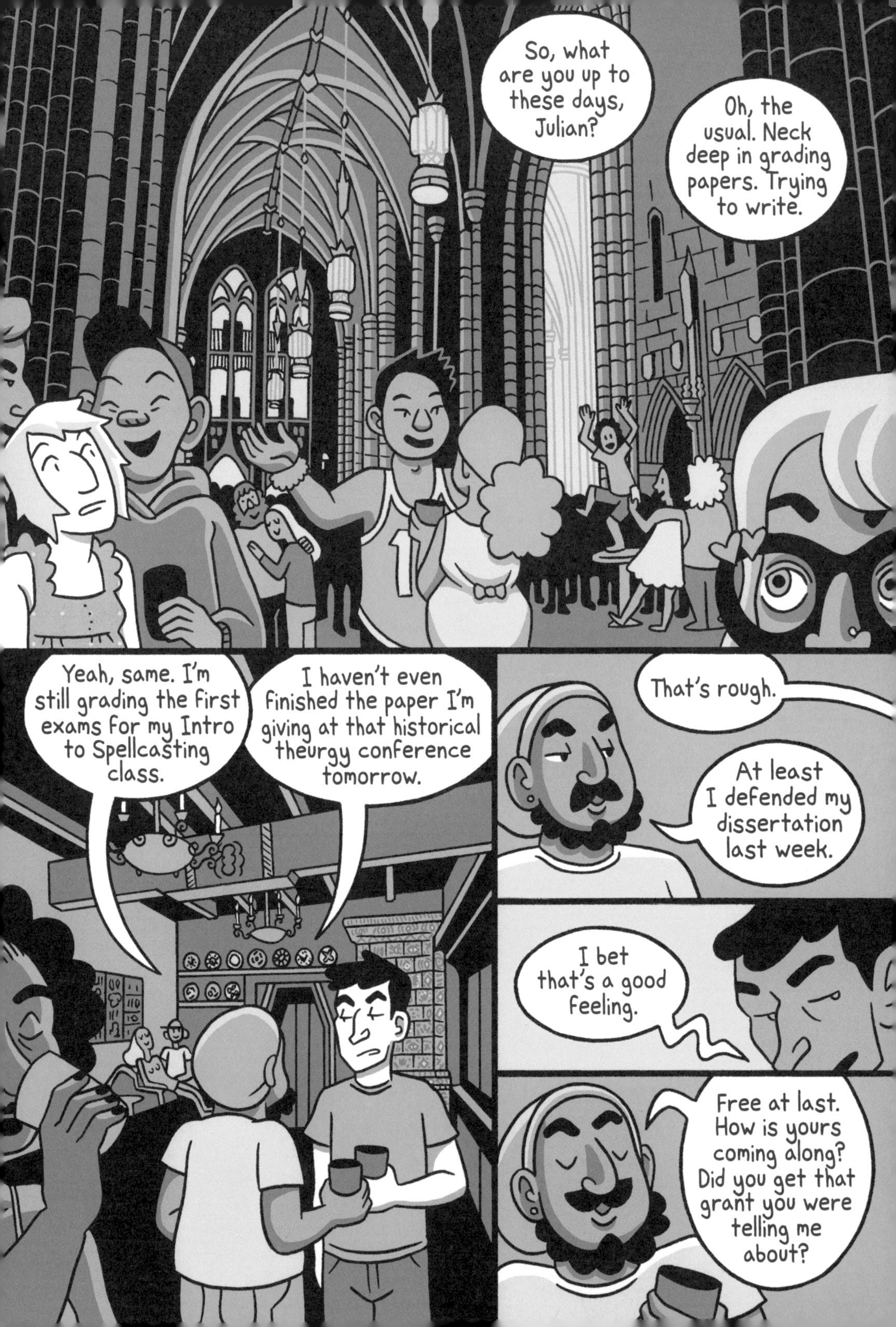

So, what are you up to these days, Julian?
Oh, the usual. Neck deep in grading papers. Trying to write.
Yeah, same. I'm still grading the first exams for my Intro to Spellcasting class.
I haven't even finished the paper I'm giving at that historical theurgy conference tomorrow.
That's rough.
At least I defended my dissertation last week.
I bet that's a good feeling.
Free at last. How is yours coming along? Did you get that grant you were telling me about?

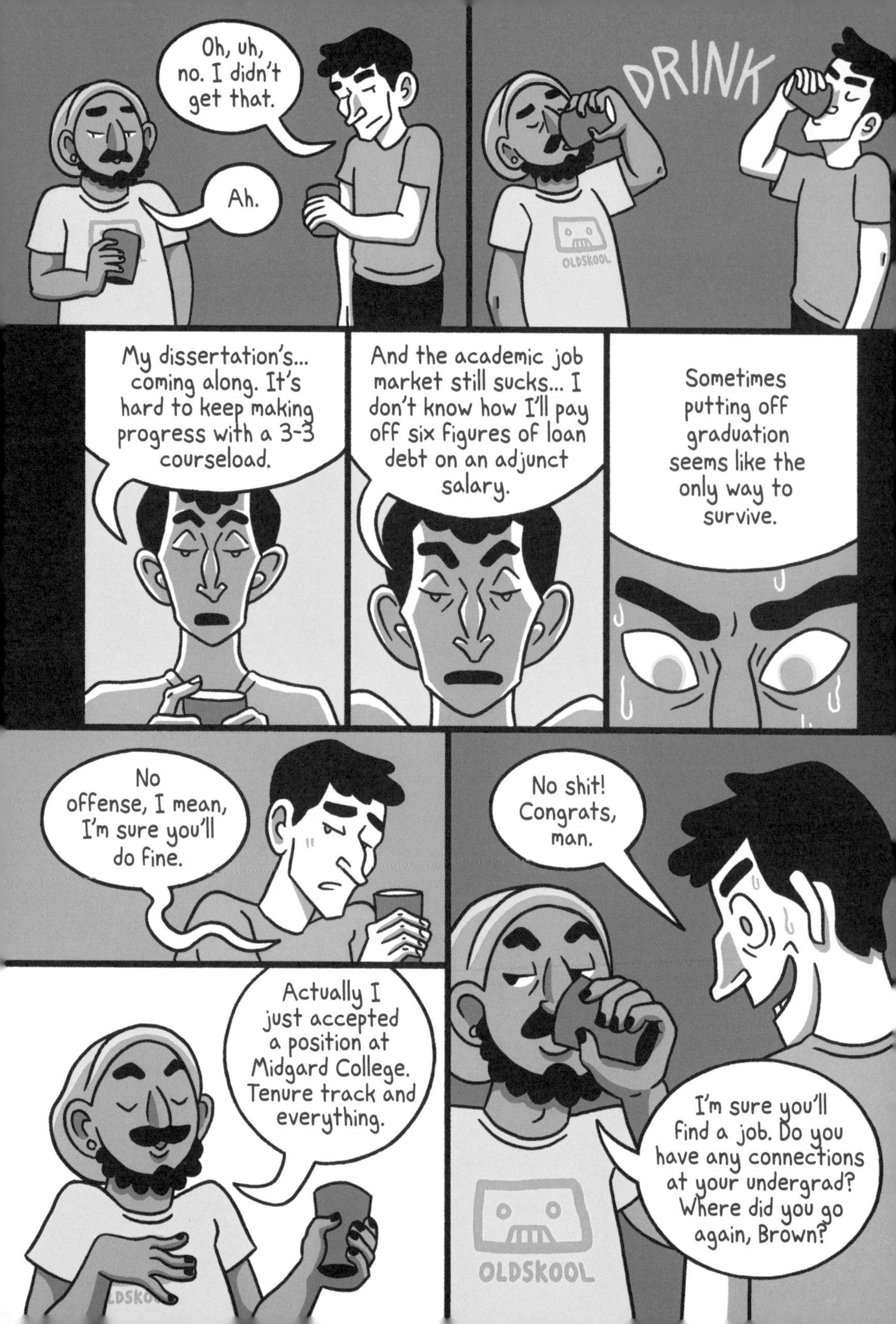
Oh, uh, no. I didn't get that.
Ah.
DRINK
OLDSKOOL
My dissertation's... coming along. It's hard to keep making progress with a 3-3 courseload.
And the academic job market still sucks... I don't know how I'll pay off six figures of loan debt on an adjunct salary.
Sometimes putting off graduation seems like the only way to survive.
No offense, I mean, I'm sure you'll do fine.
Actually I just accepted a position at Midgard College. Tenure track and everything.
No shit! Congrats, man.
I'm sure you'll find a job. Do you have any connections at your undergrad? Where did you go again, Brown?
OLDSKOOL

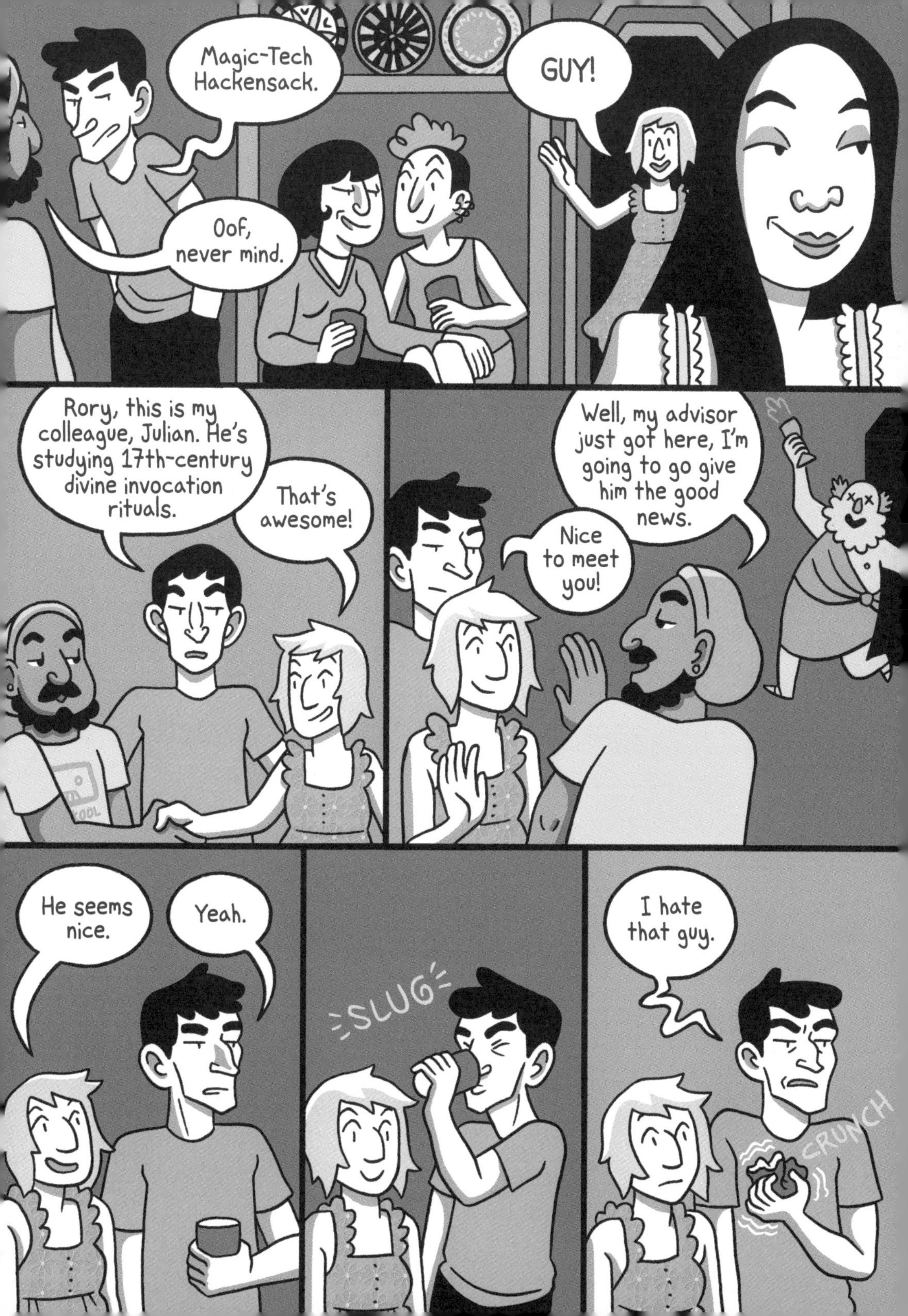
Magic-Tech Hackensack.
Oof, never mind.
GUY!
Rory, this is my colleague, Julian. He's studying 17th-century divine invocation rituals.
That's awesome!
Well, my advisor just got here, I'm going to go give him the good news.
Nice to meet you!
He seems nice.
Yeah.
SLUG
I hate that guy.
CRUNCH

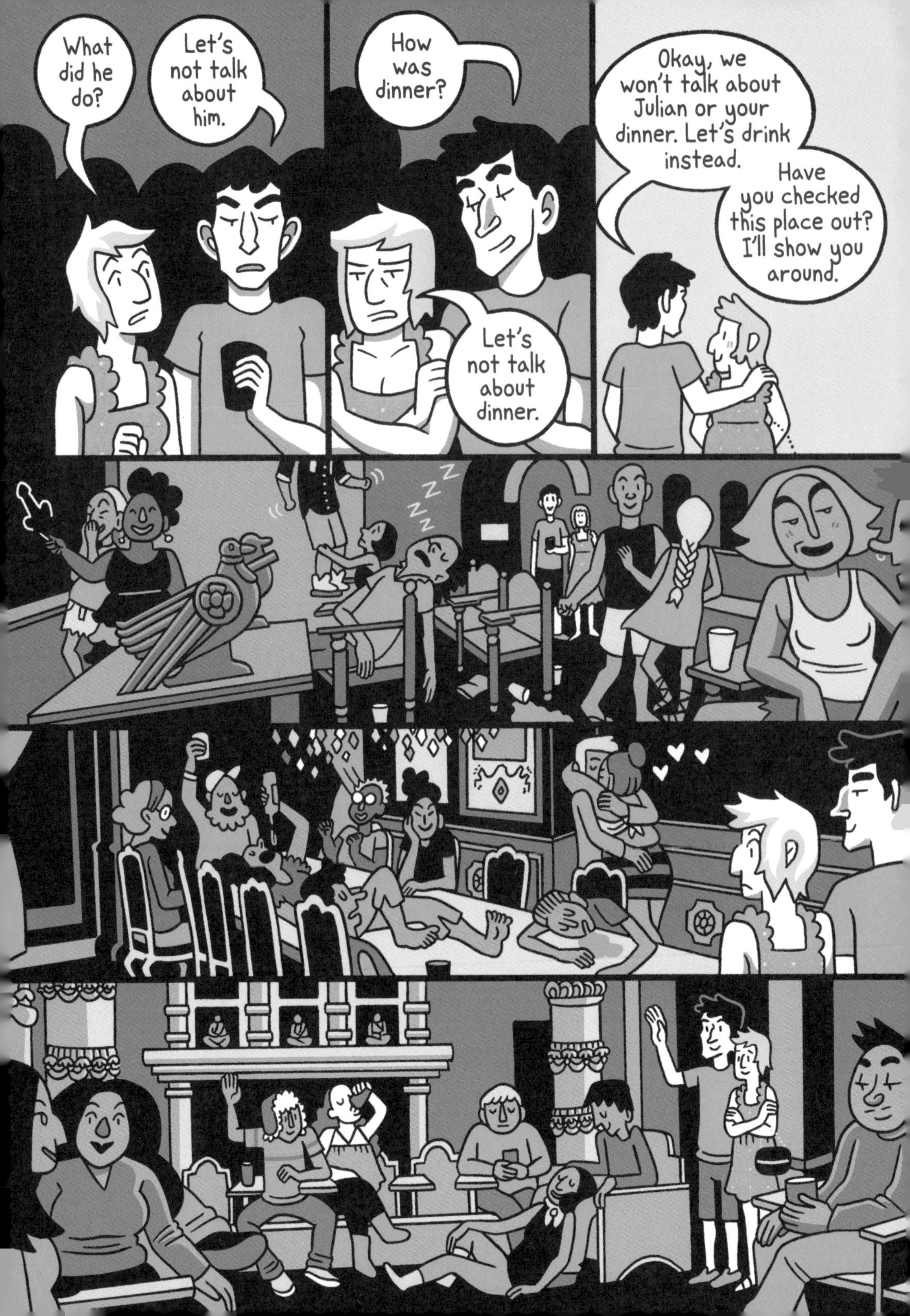
What did he do?
Let's not talk about him.
How was dinner?
Let's not talk about dinner.
Okay, we won't talk about Julian or your dinner. Let's drink instead.
Have you checked this place out? I'll show you around.

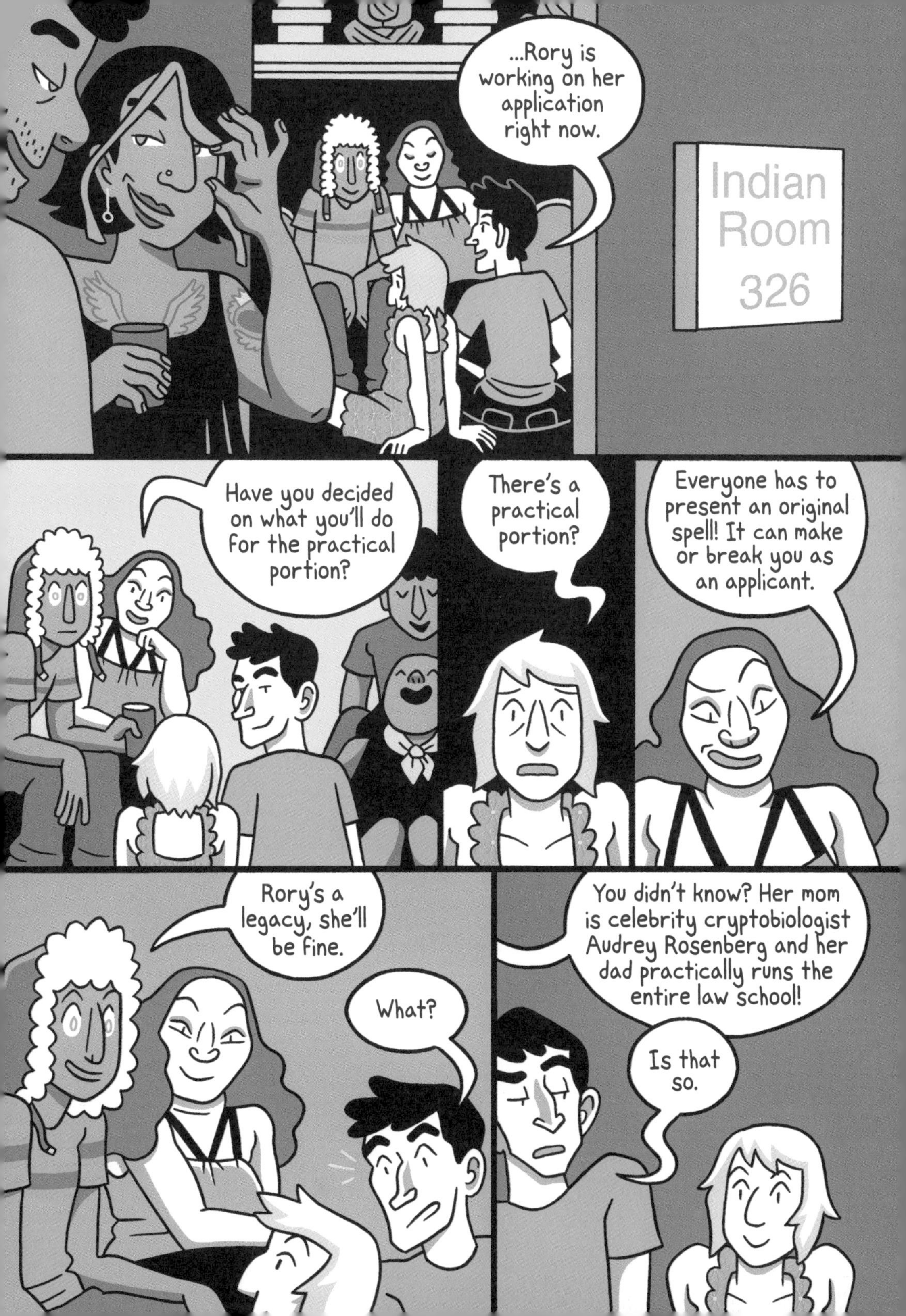
...Rory is working on her application right now.
Indian Room 326
Have you decided on what you'll do for the practical portion?
There's a practical portion?
Everyone has to present an original spell! It can make or break you as an applicant.
Rory's a legacy, she'll be fine.
What?
You didn't know? Her mom is celebrity cryptobiologist Audrey Rosenberg and her dad practically runs the entire law school!
Is that so.

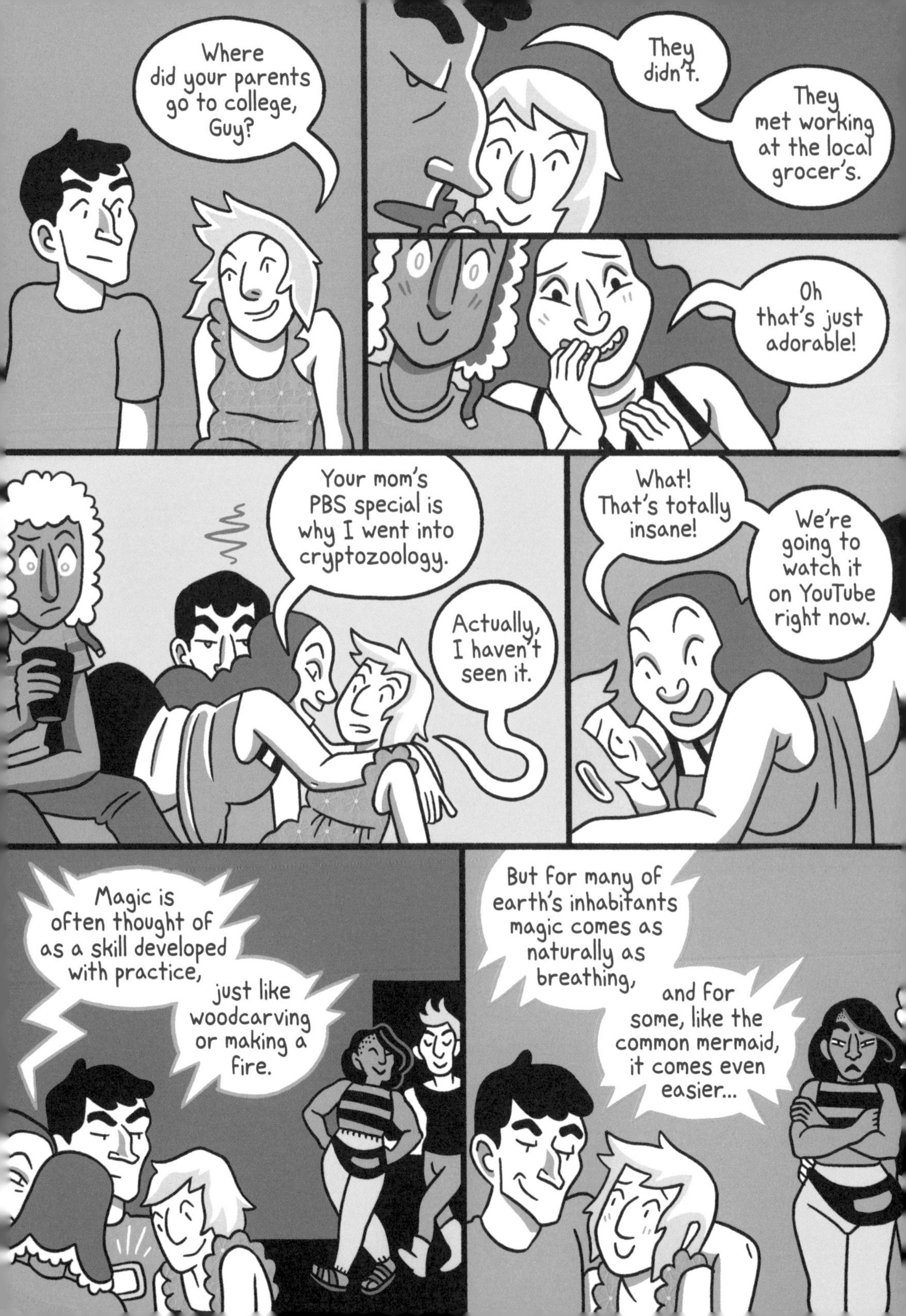
Where did your parents go to college, Guy?
They didn't.
They met working at the local grocer's.
Oh that's just adorable!
Your mom's PBS special is why I went into cryptozoology.
Actually, I haven't seen it.
What! That's totally insane!
We're going to watch it on YouTube right now.
Magic is often thought of as a skill developed with practice,
just like woodcarving or making a fire.
But for many of earth's inhabitants magic comes as naturally as breathing,
and for some, like the common mermaid, it comes even easier...

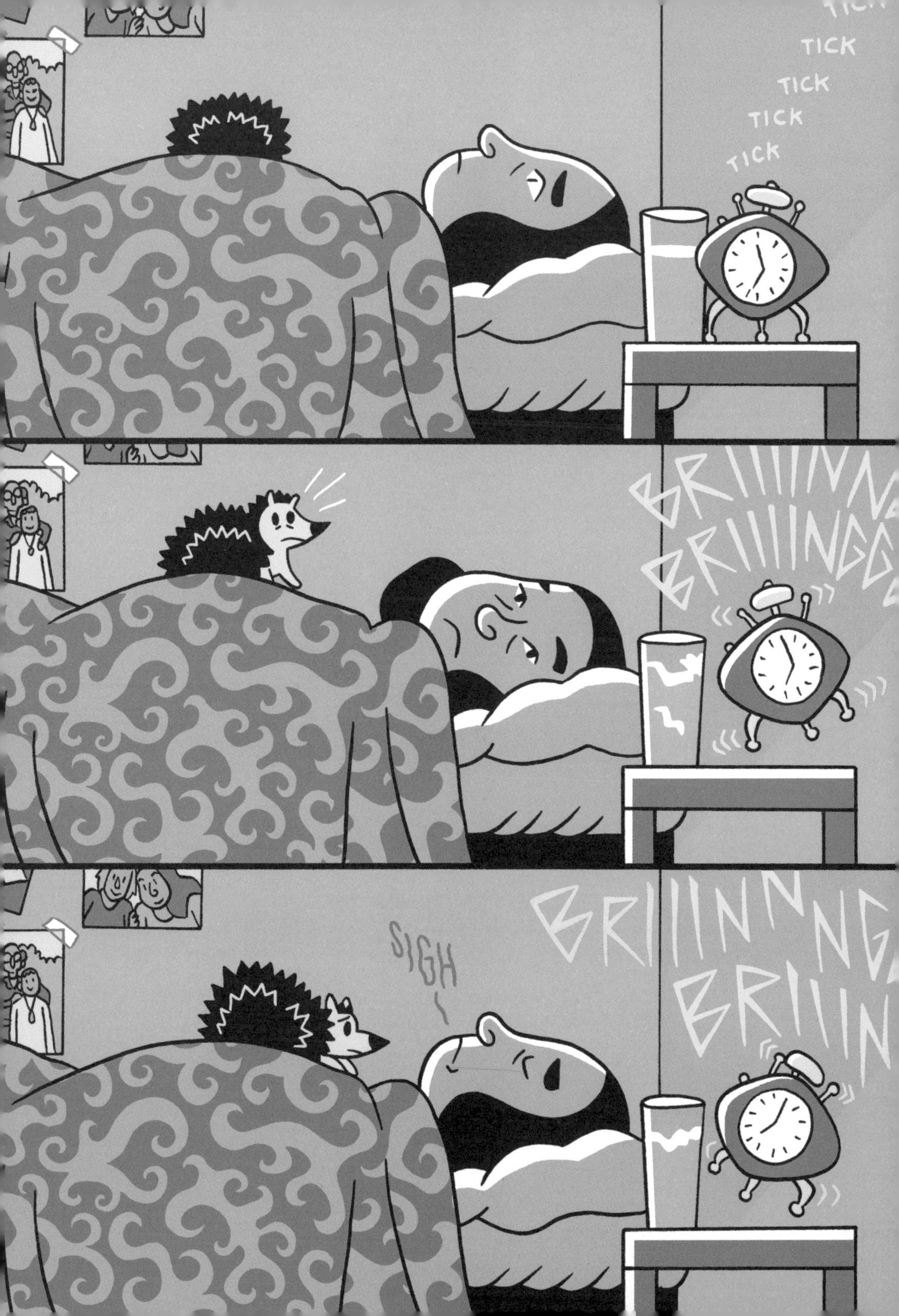
TICK
TICK
TICK
TICK
SIGH

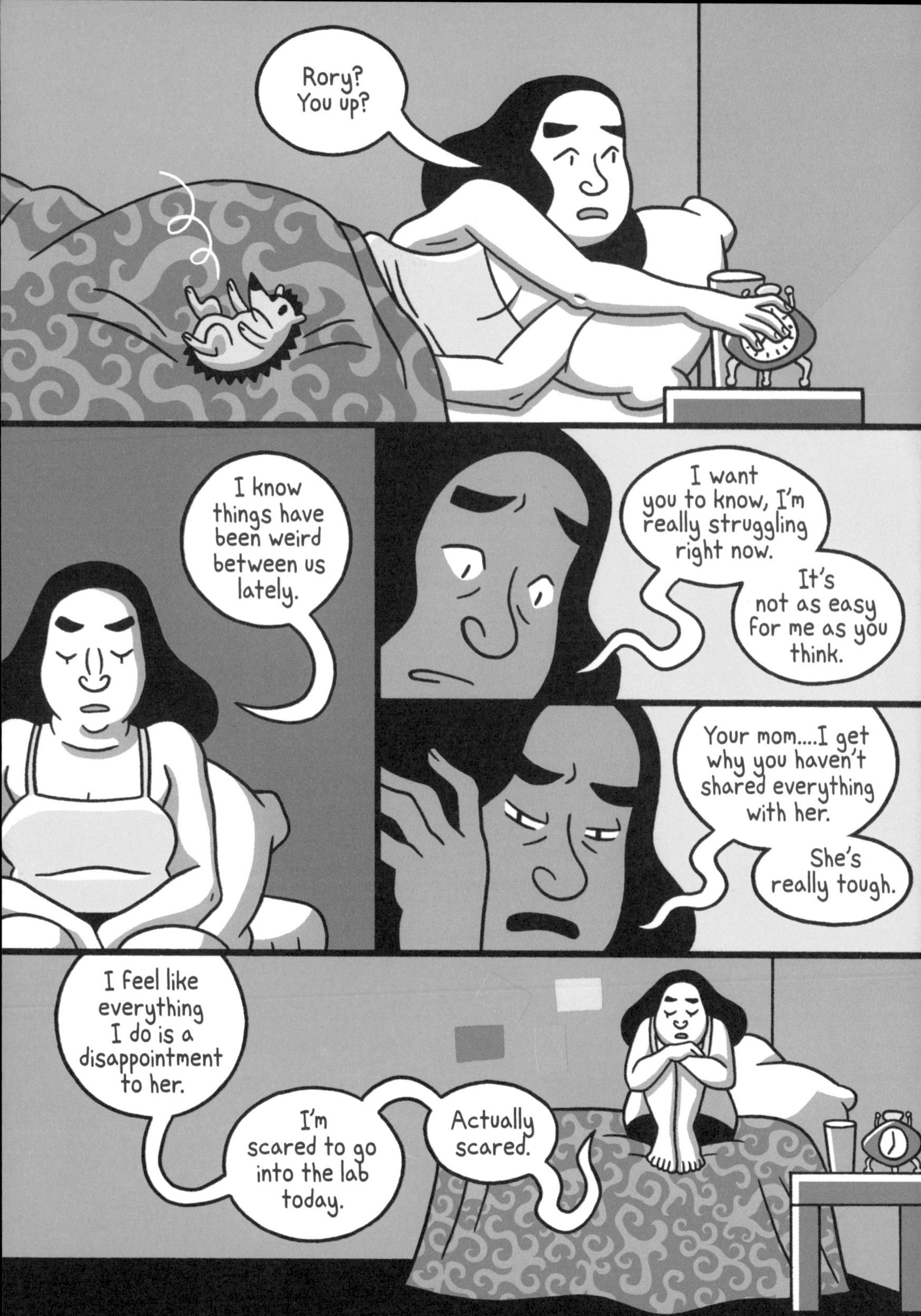
Rory? You up?
I know things have been weird between us lately.
I want you to know, I'm really struggling right now.
It's not as easy for me as you think.
Your mom....I get why you haven't shared everything with her.
She's really tough.
I feel like everything I do is a disappointment to her.
I'm scared to go into the lab today.
Actually scared.

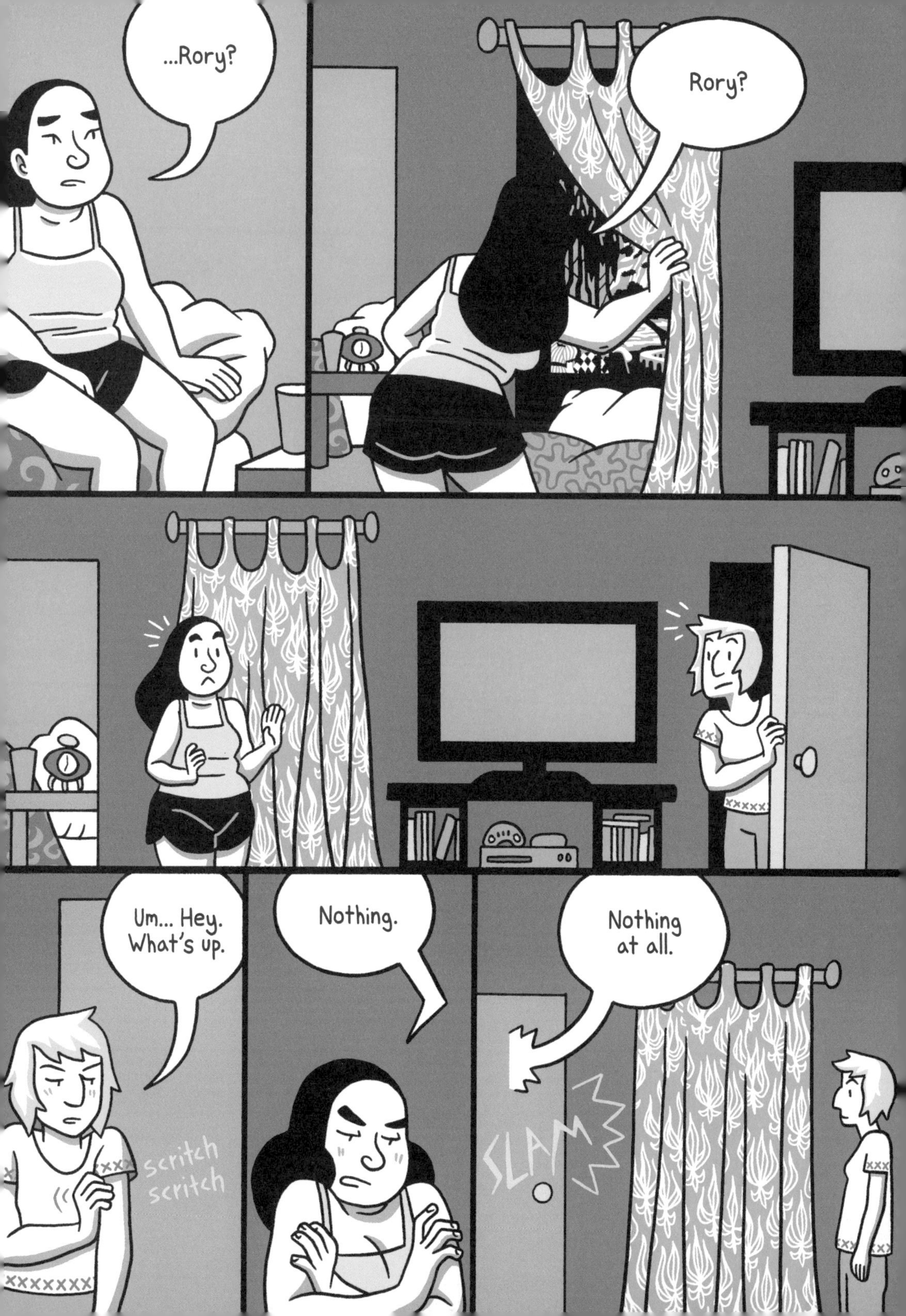
...Rory?
Rory?
Um... Hey. What's up.
scritch scritch
Nothing.
Nothing at all.
SLAM

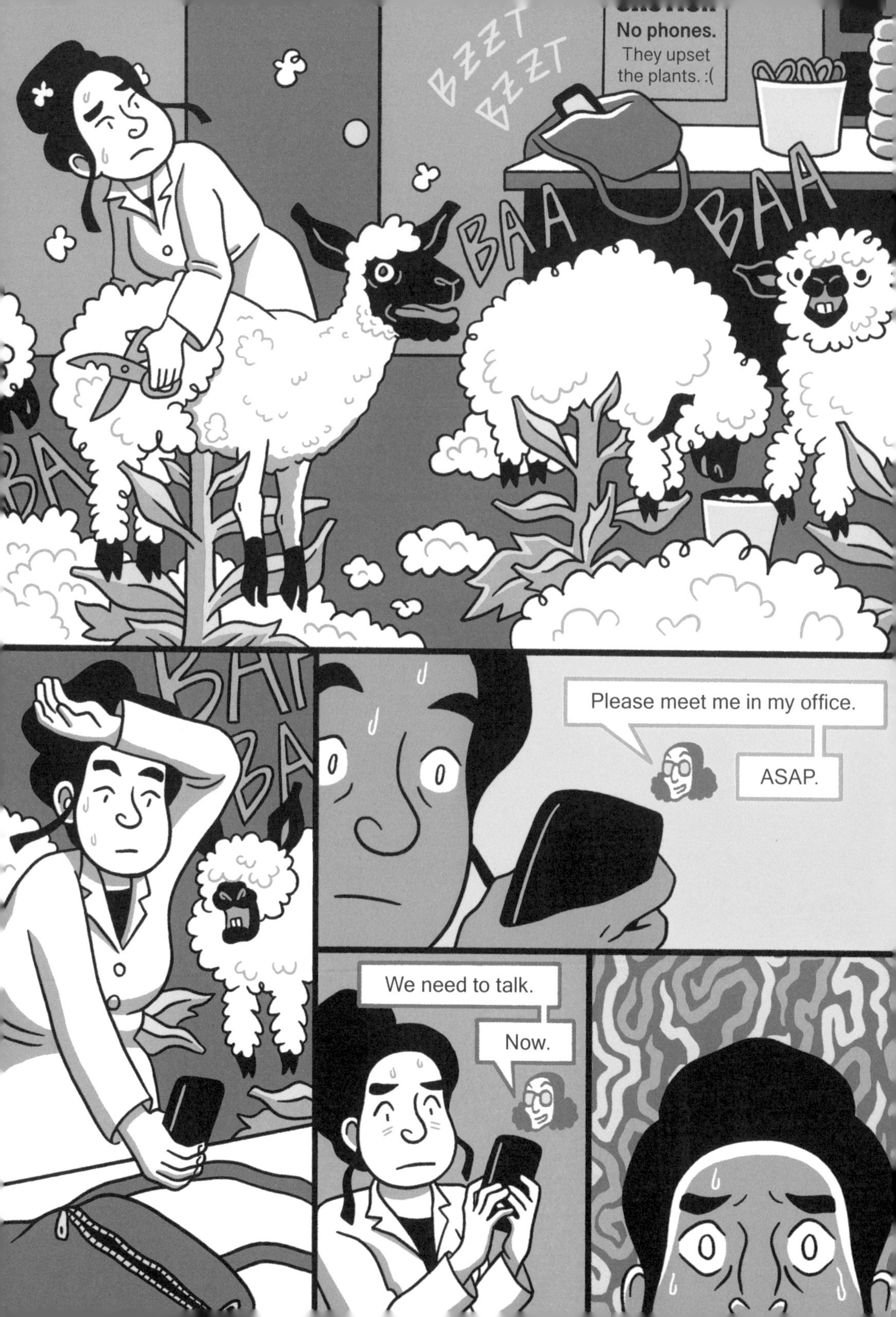
No phones.
They upset the plants. :(
BZZT BZZT
BAA
BAA
BA
BAA
BA
Please meet me in my office.
ASAP.
We need to talk.
Now.

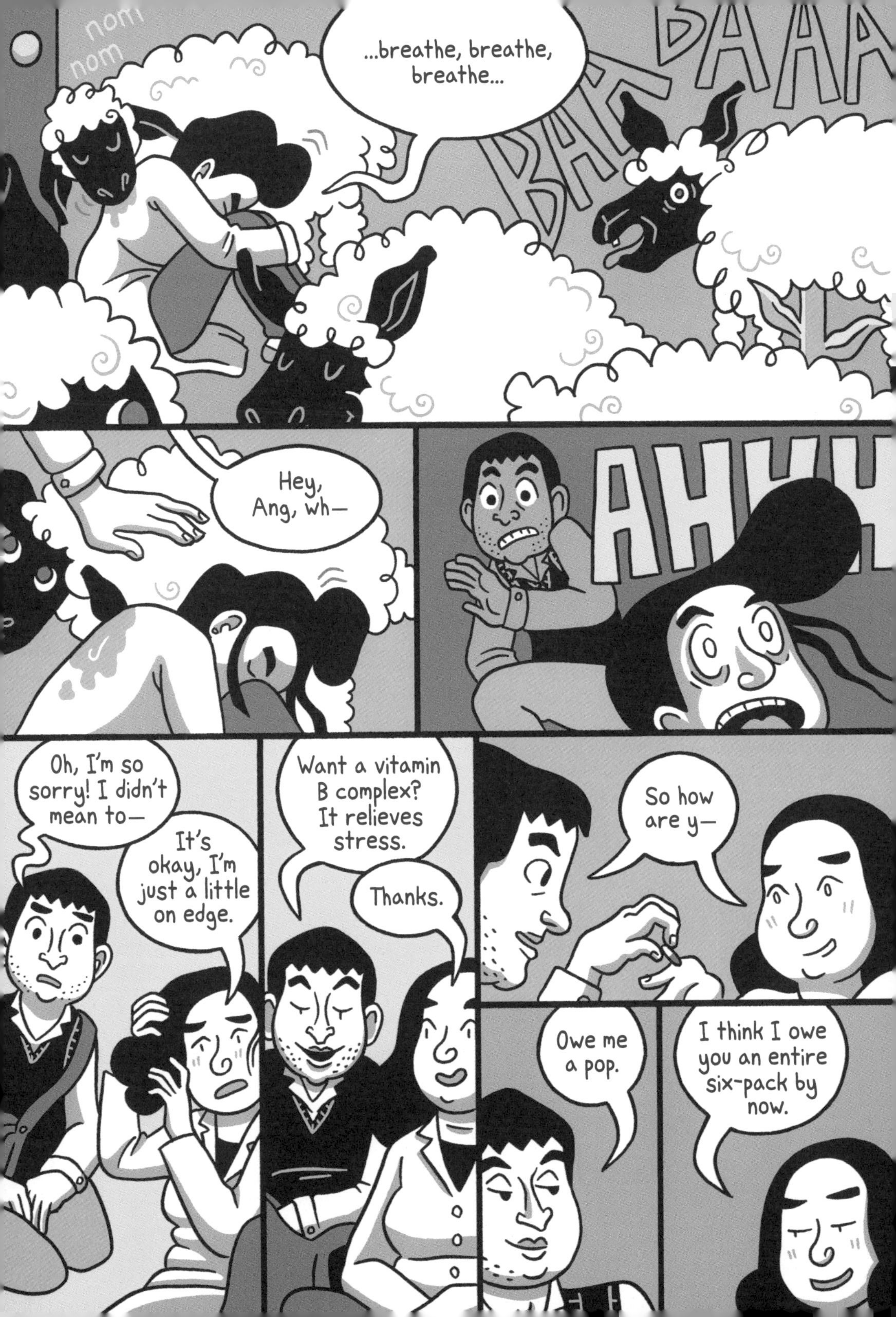
nom nom
...breathe, breathe, breathe...
BAA BAAA
Hey, Ang, wh—
AHHH
Oh, I'm so sorry! I didn't mean to—
It's okay, I'm just a little on edge.
Want a vitamin B complex? It relieves stress.
Thanks.
So how are y—
Owe me a pop.
I think I owe you an entire six-pack by now.

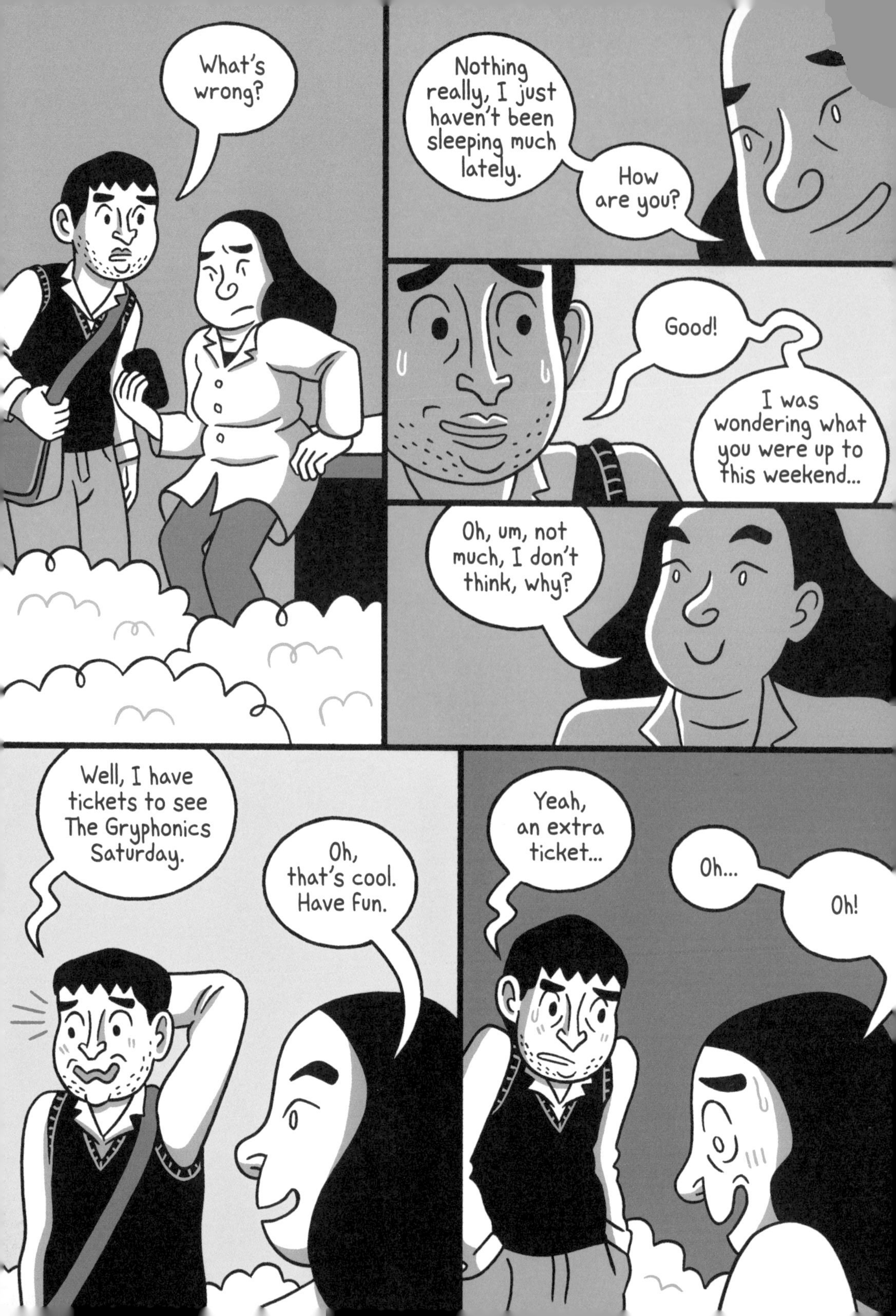
What's wrong?
Nothing really, I just haven't been sleeping much lately.
How are you?
Good!
I was wondering what you were up to this weekend...
Oh, um, not much, I don't think, why?
Well, I have tickets to see The Gryphonics Saturday.
Oh, that's cool. Have fun.
Yeah, an extra ticket...
Oh...
Oh!

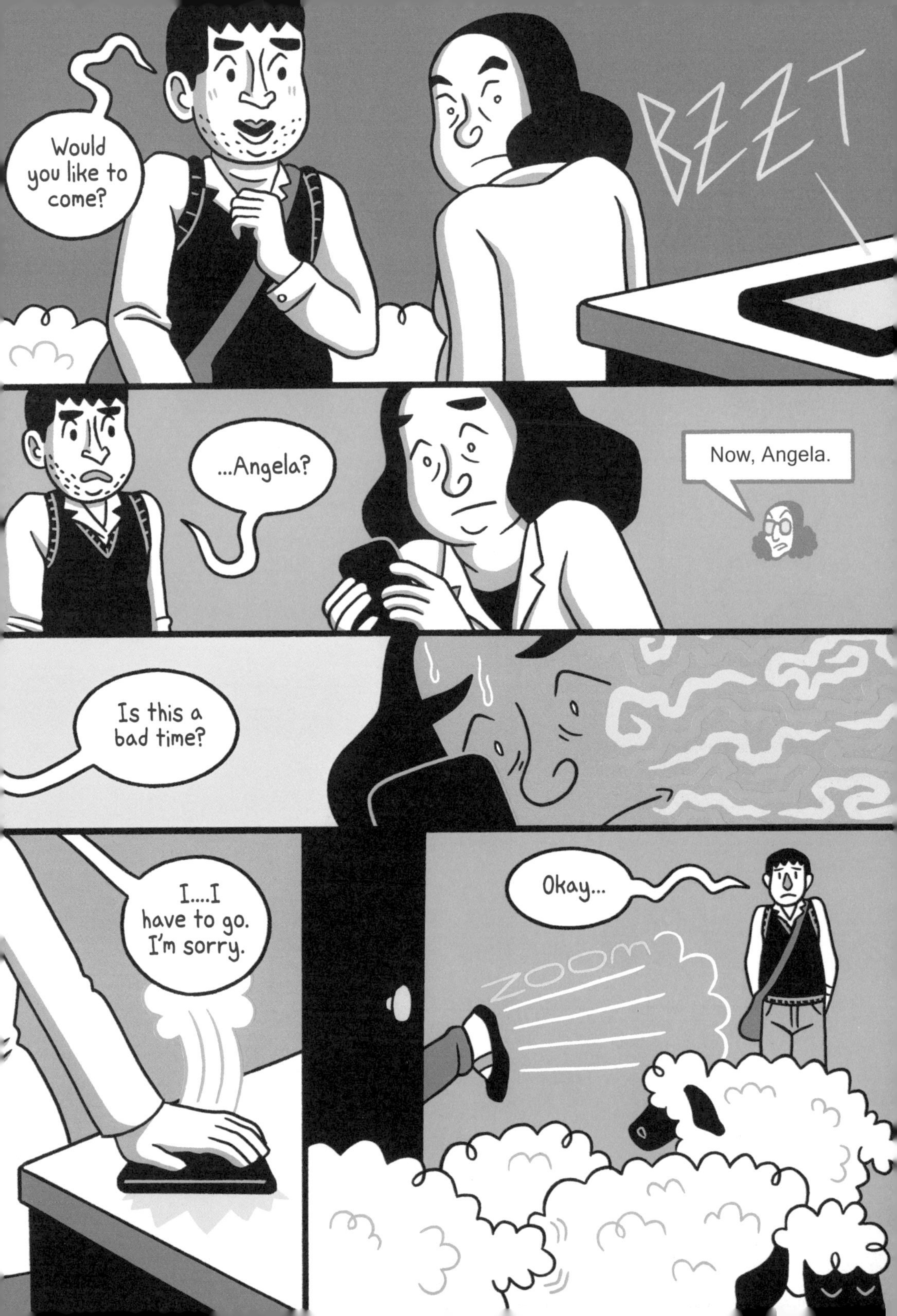
Would you like to come?
BZZT
...Angela?
Now, Angela.
Is this a bad time?
I....I have to go. I'm sorry.
Okay...
ZOOM

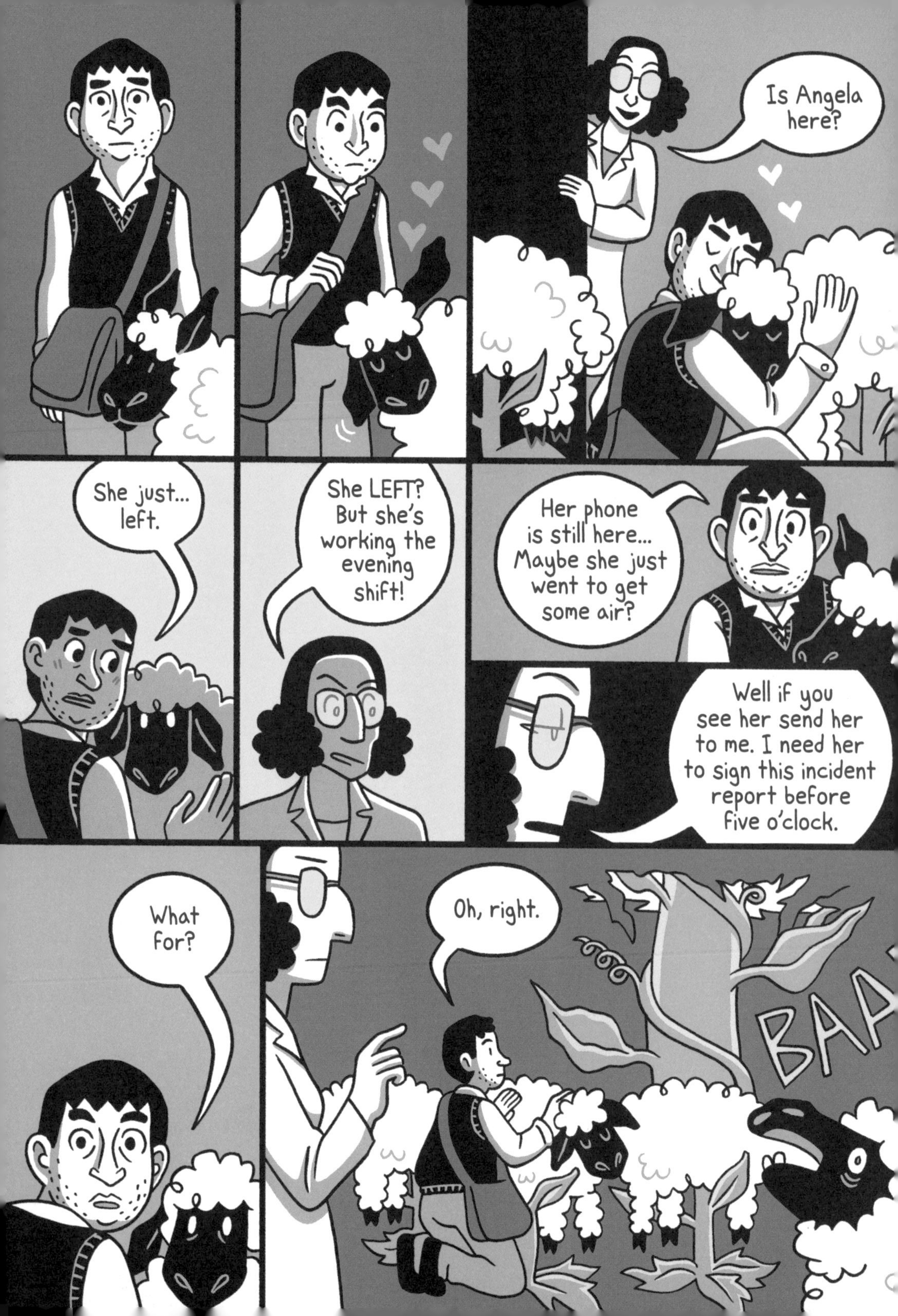
Is Angela here?
She just... left.
She LEFT? But she's working the evening shift!
Her phone is still here... Maybe she just went to get some air?
Well if you see her send her to me. I need her to sign this incident report before five o'clock.
What for?
Oh, right.
BAA

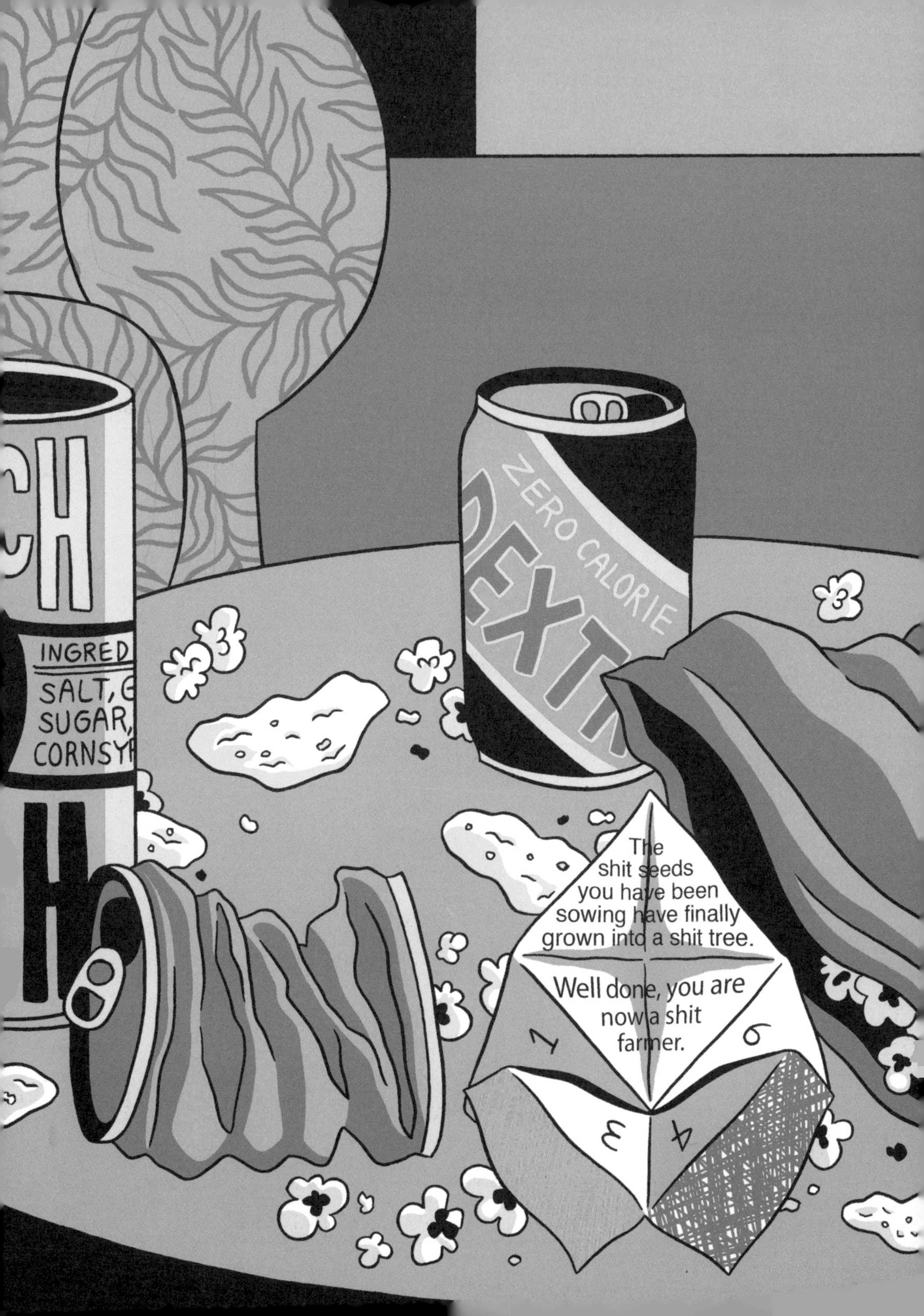
CH
INGRED
SALT, G
SUGAR,
CORNSYR
H
ZERO CALORIE
EXTR
The shit seeds you have been sowing have finally grown into a shit tree.
Well done, you are now a shit farmer.
1
6
3
4

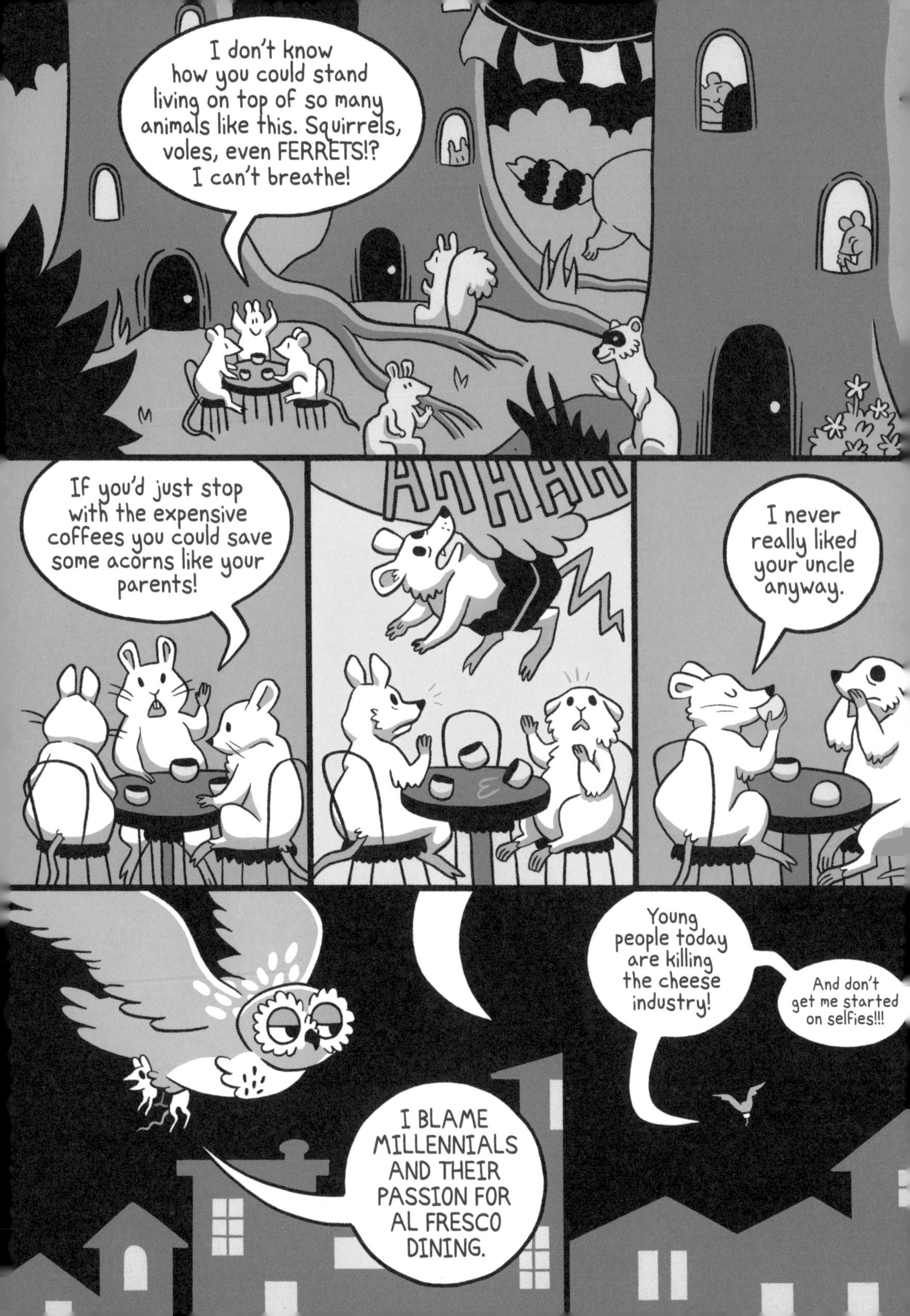

I don't know how you could stand living on top of so many animals like this. Squirrels, voles, even FERRETS!? I can't breathe!
If you'd just stop with the expensive coffees you could save some acorns like your parents!
AAHAAH
I never really liked your uncle anyway.
Young people today are killing the cheese industry!
And don't get me started on selfies!!!
I BLAME MILLENNIALS AND THEIR PASSION FOR AL FRESCO DINING.

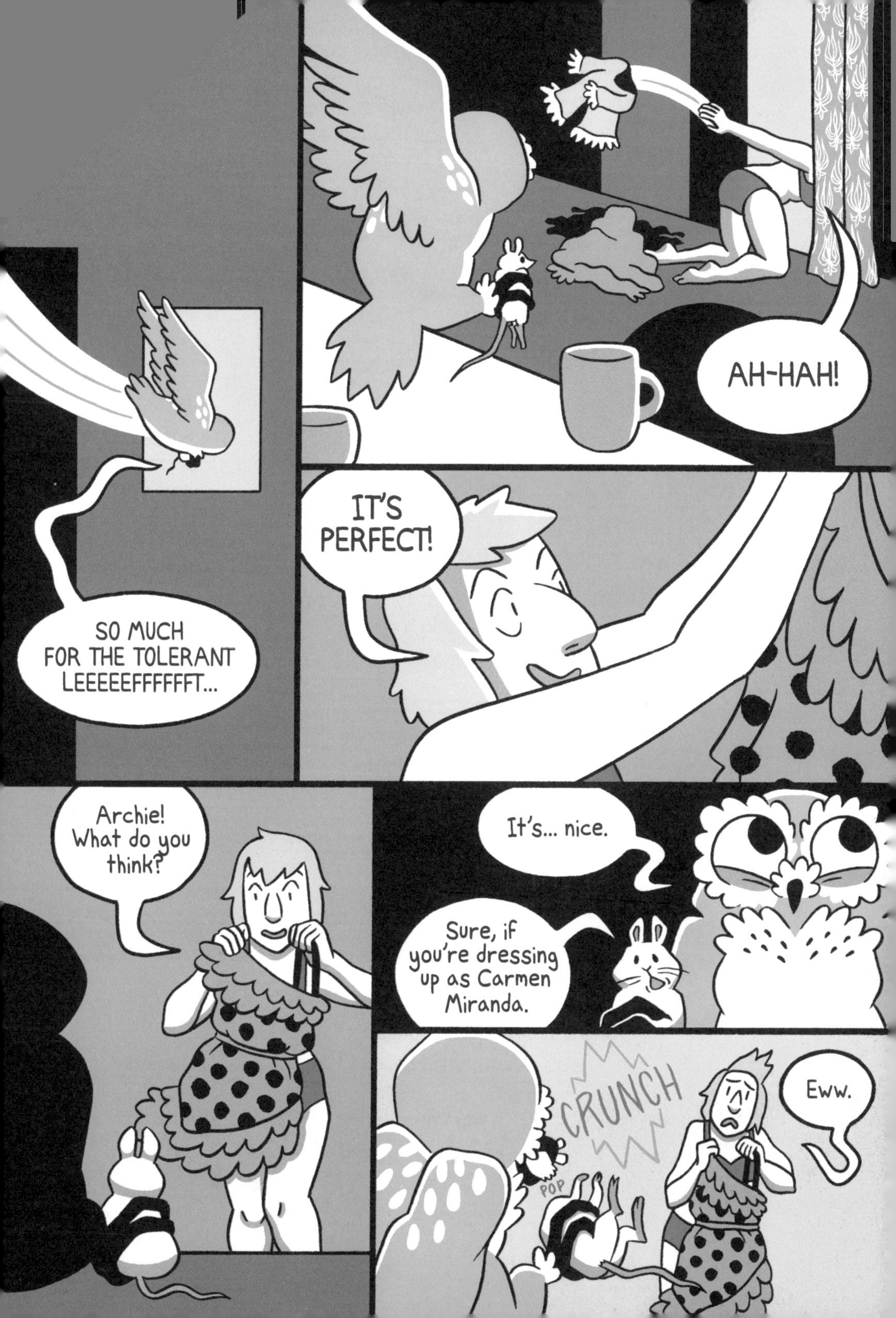
AH-HAH!
SO MUCH FOR THE TOLERANT LEEEEEFFFFFFT...
IT'S PERFECT!
Archie! What do you think?
It's... nice.
Sure, if you're dressing up as Carmen Miranda.
CRUNCH
POP
Eww.

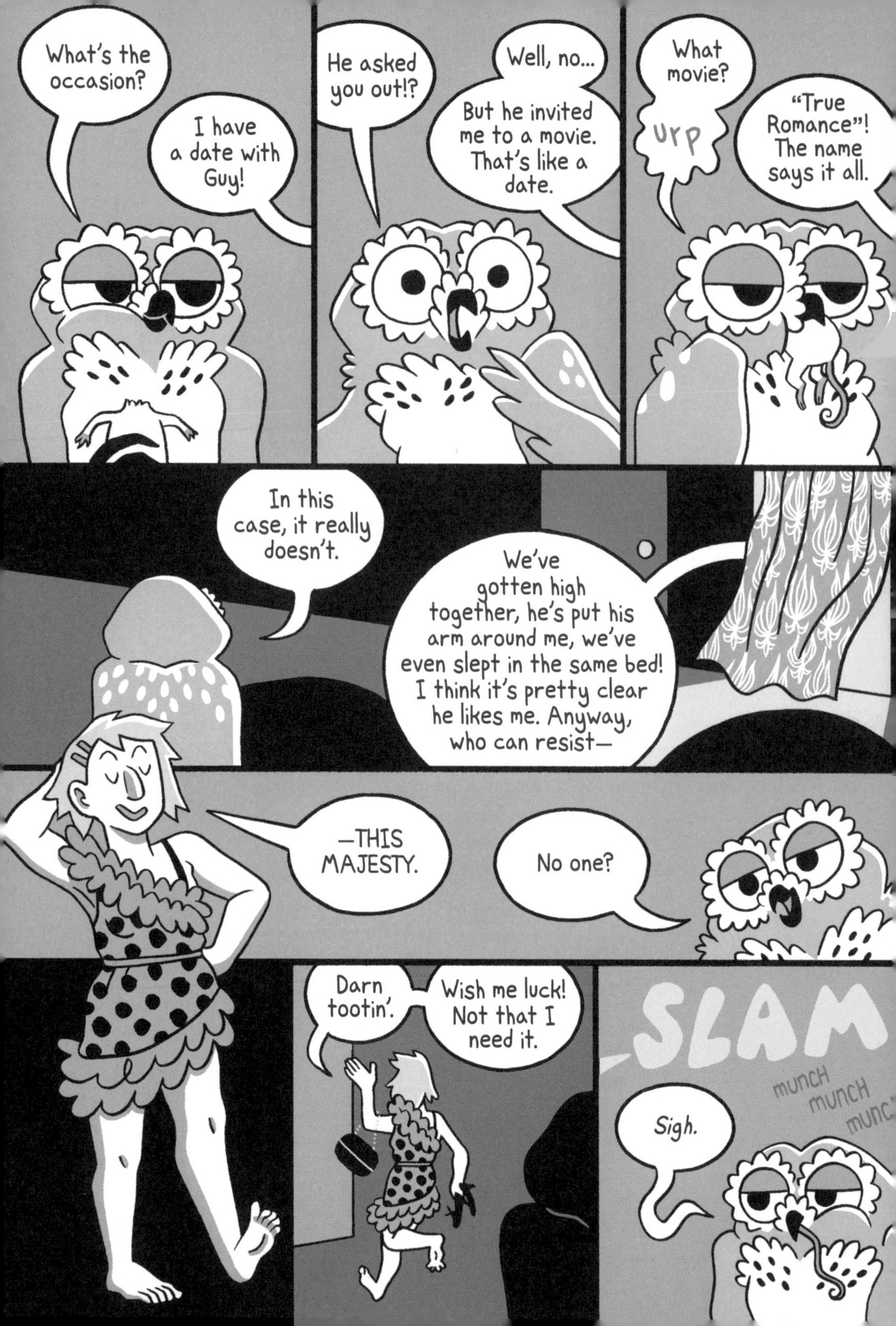
What's the occasion?
I have a date with Guy!
He asked you out!?
Well, no...
But he invited me to a movie. That's like a date.
What movie?
Urp
"True Romance"! The name says it all.
In this case, it really doesn't.
We've gotten high together, he's put his arm around me, we've even slept in the same bed! I think it's pretty clear he likes me. Anyway, who can resist—
—THIS MAJESTY.
No one?
Darn tootin'.
Wish me luck! Not that I need it.
SLAM
munch
munch
Sigh.

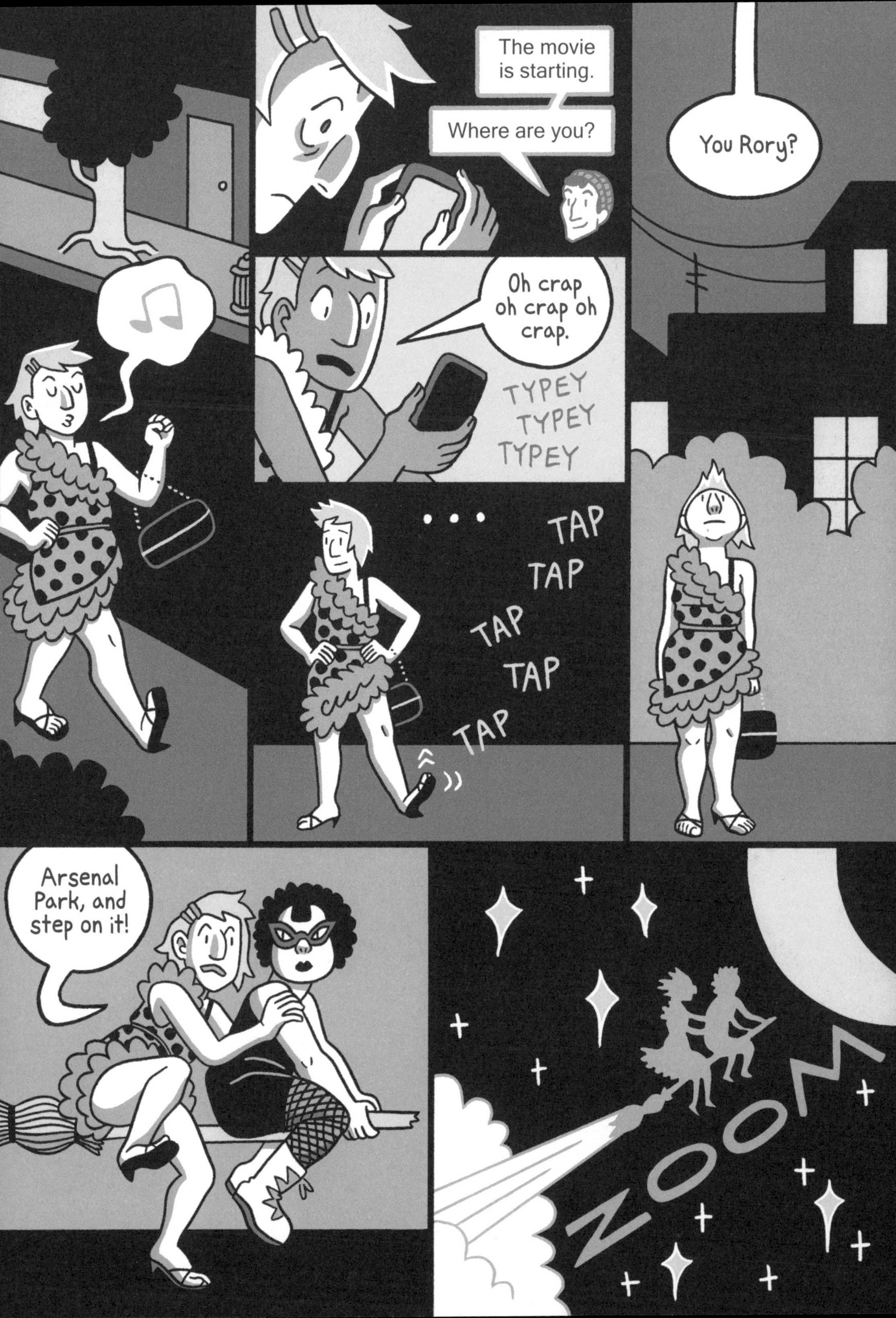
The movie is starting.
Where are you?
You Rory?
Oh crap oh crap oh crap.
TYPEY TYPEY TYPEY
. . .
TAP TAP TAP TAP TAP
Arsenal Park, and step on it!
ZOOM

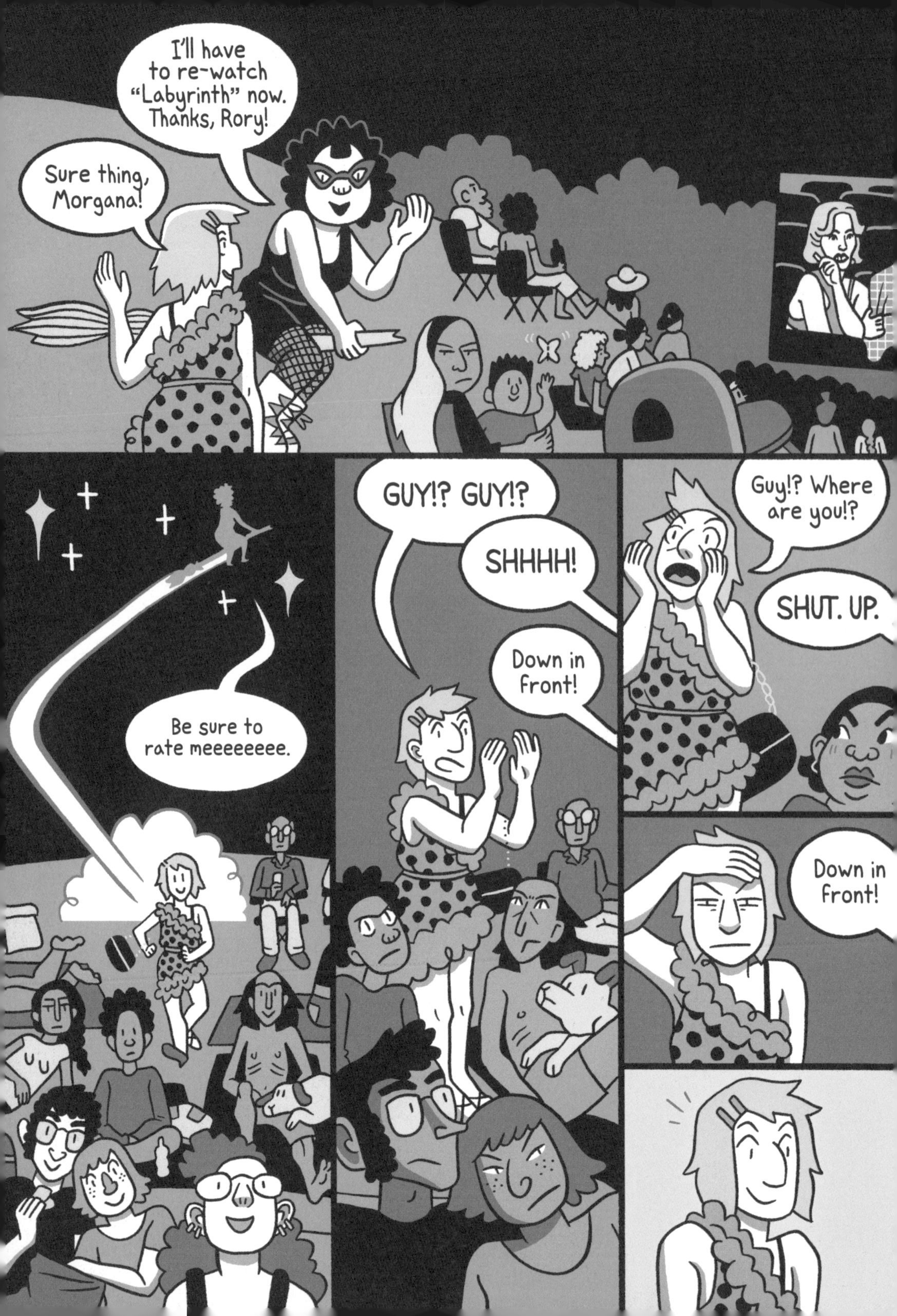
I'll have to re-watch "Labyrinth" now. Thanks, Rory!
Sure thing, Morgana!
Be sure to rate meeeeeeee.
GUY!? GUY!?
SHHHH!
Down in front!
Guy!? Where are you!?
SHUT. UP.
Down in front!

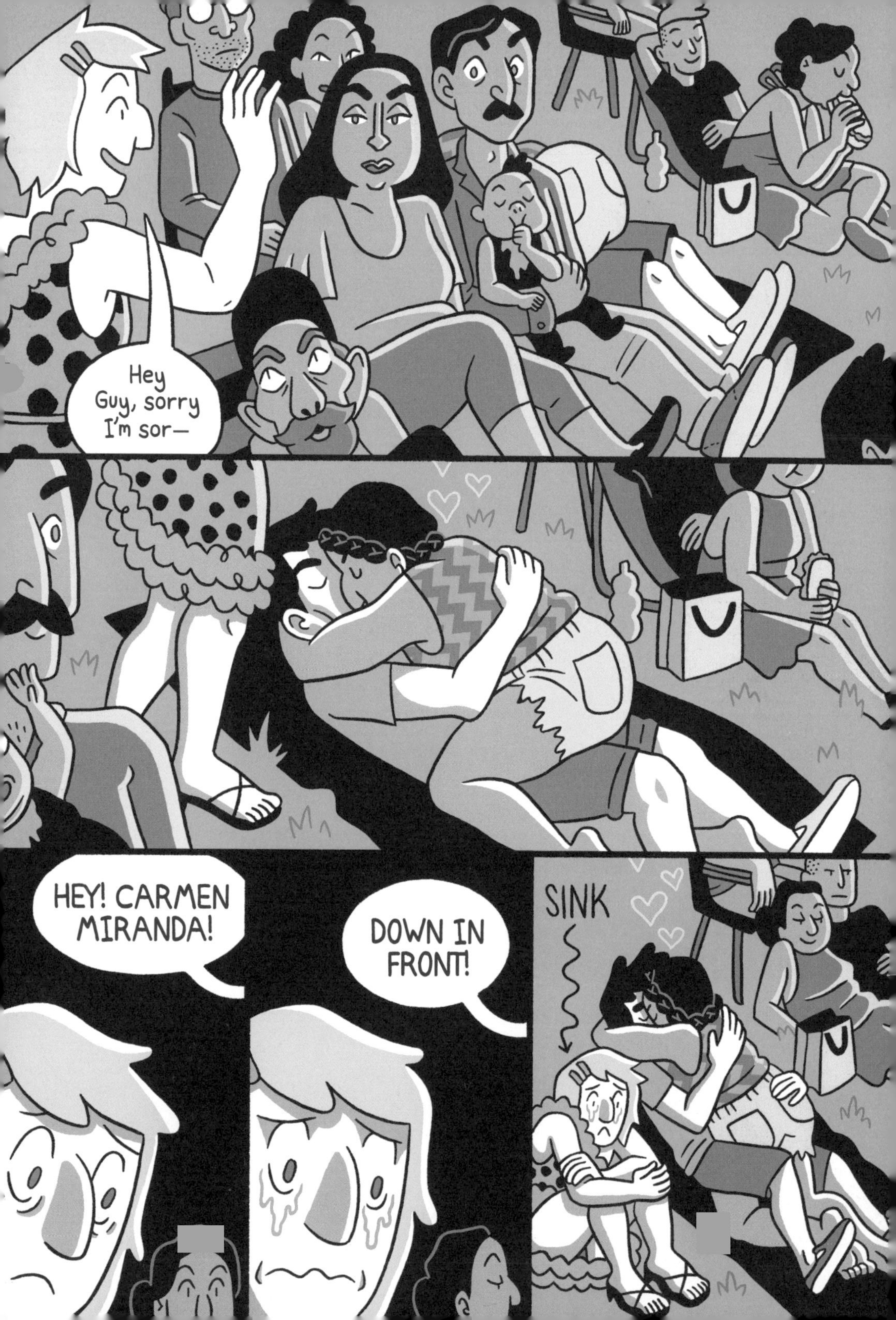
Hey Guy, sorry I'm sor—
HEY! CARMEN MIRANDA!
DOWN IN FRONT!
SINK

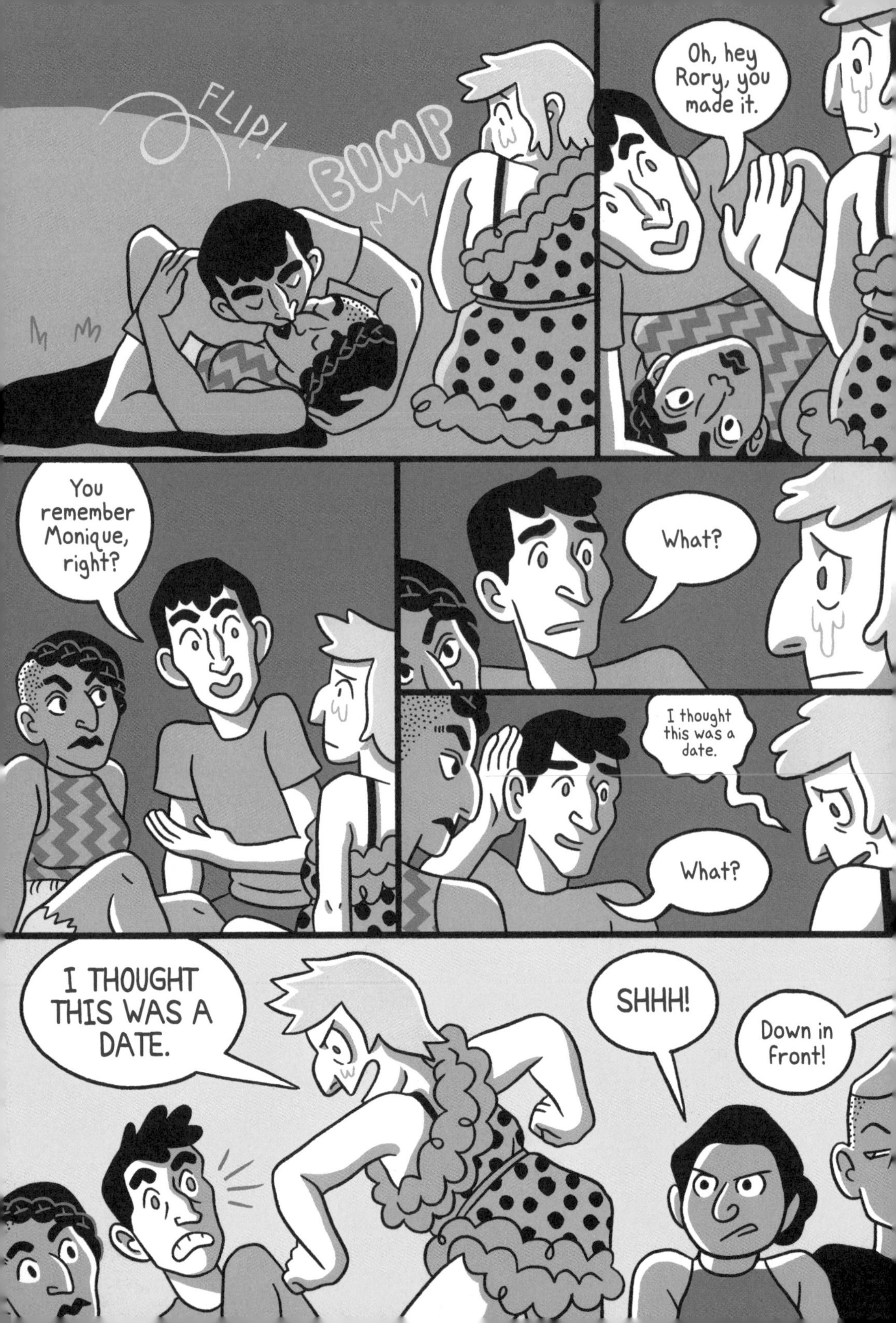
FLIP!
BUMP
Oh, hey Rory, you made it.
You remember Monique, right?
What?
I thought this was a date.
What?
I THOUGHT THIS WAS A DATE.
SHHH!
Down in front!

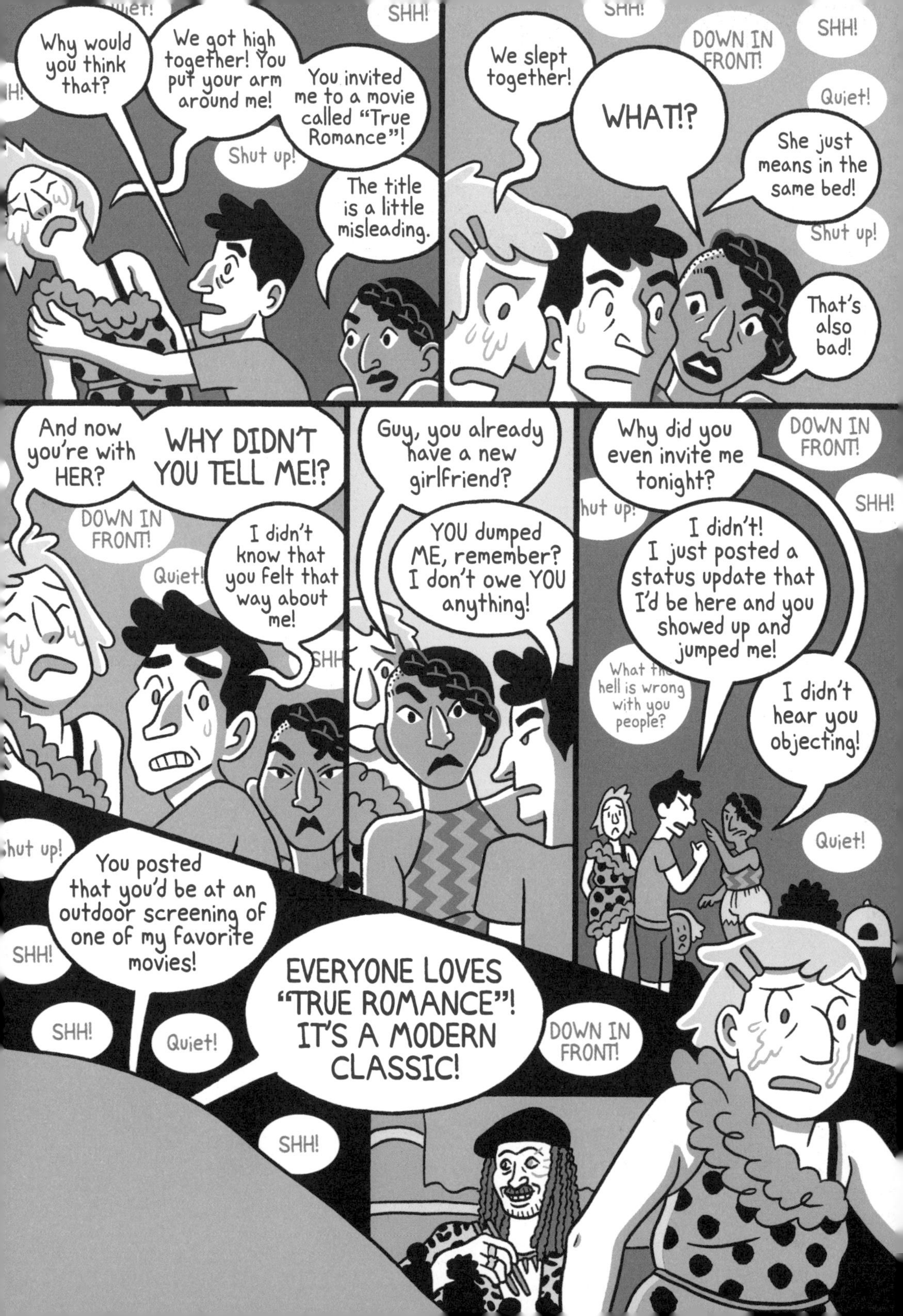
Quiet!
SHH!
Why would you think that?
We got high together! You put your arm around me!
You invited me to a movie called "True Romance"!
Shut up!
The title is a little misleading.
SHH!
DOWN IN FRONT!
SHH!
We slept together!
WHAT!?
Quiet!
She just means in the same bed!
Shut up!
That's also bad!
And now you're with HER?
WHY DIDN'T YOU TELL ME!?
DOWN IN FRONT!
Quiet!
I didn't know that you felt that way about me!
SHH
Guy, you already have a new girlfriend?
YOU dumped ME, remember? I don't owe YOU anything!
Why did you even invite me tonight?
DOWN IN FRONT!
SHH!
Shut up!
I didn't! I just posted a status update that I'd be here and you showed up and jumped me!
What the hell is wrong with you people?
I didn't hear you objecting!
Quiet!
Shut up!
You posted that you'd be at an outdoor screening of one of my favorite movies!
SHH!
EVERYONE LOVES "TRUE ROMANCE"! IT'S A MODERN CLASSIC!
SHH!
Quiet!
DOWN IN FRONT!
SHH!

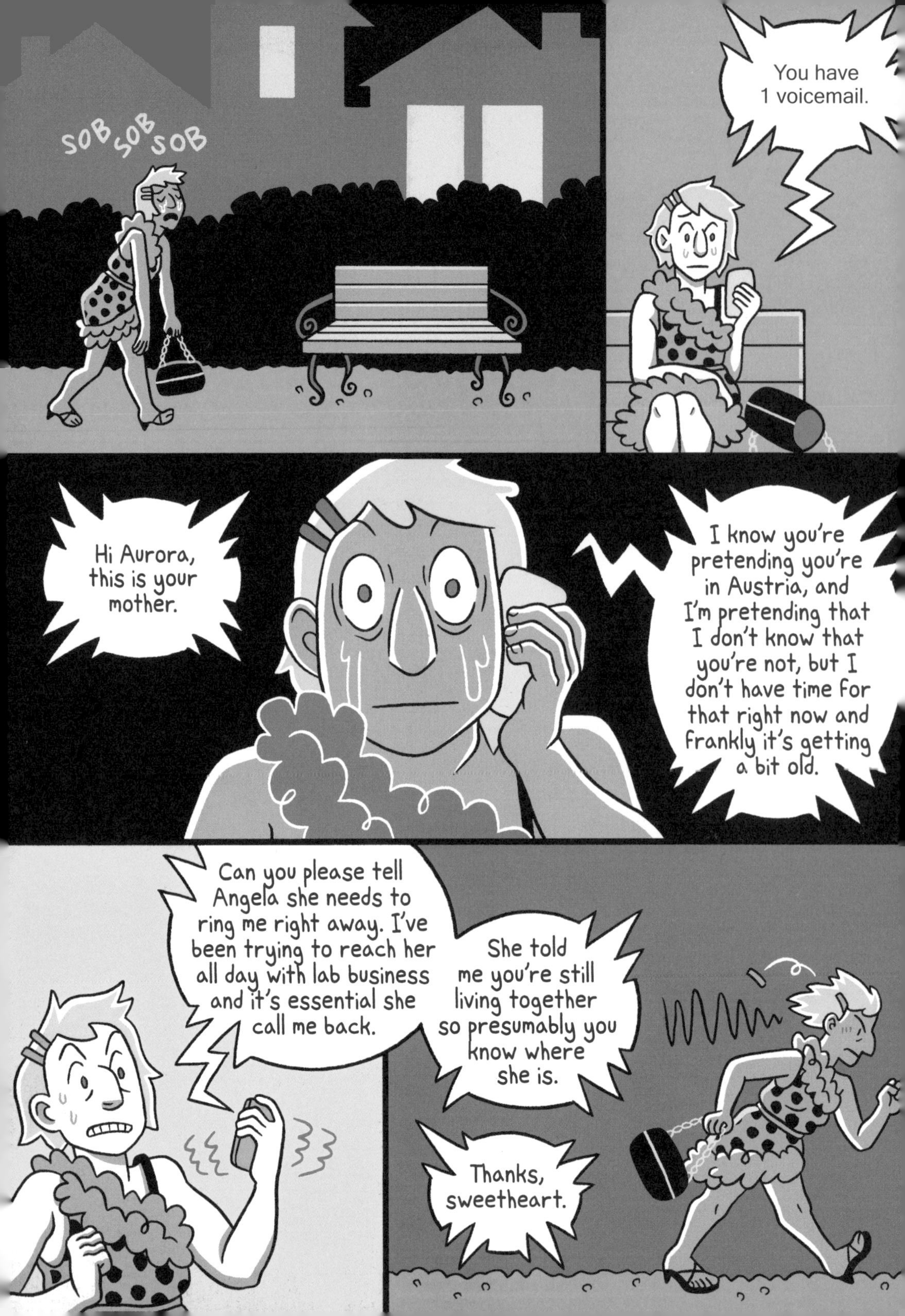
SOB SOB SOB
You have 1 voicemail.
Hi Aurora, this is your mother.
I know you're pretending you're in Austria, and I'm pretending that I don't know that you're not, but I don't have time for that right now and frankly it's getting a bit old.
Can you please tell Angela she needs to ring me right away. I've been trying to reach her all day with lab business and it's essential she call me back.
She told me you're still living together so presumably you know where she is.
Thanks, sweetheart.

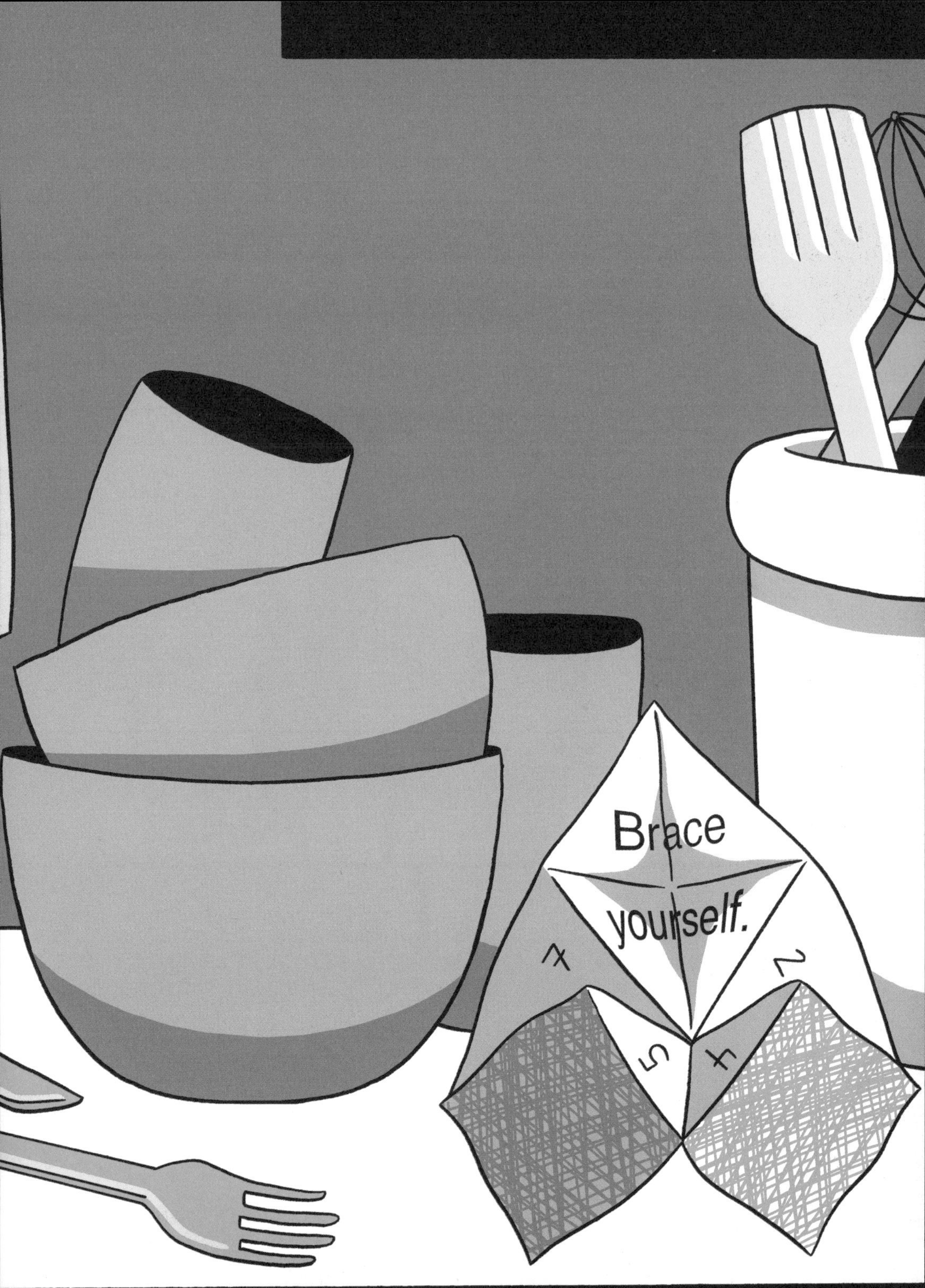
Brace
yourself.

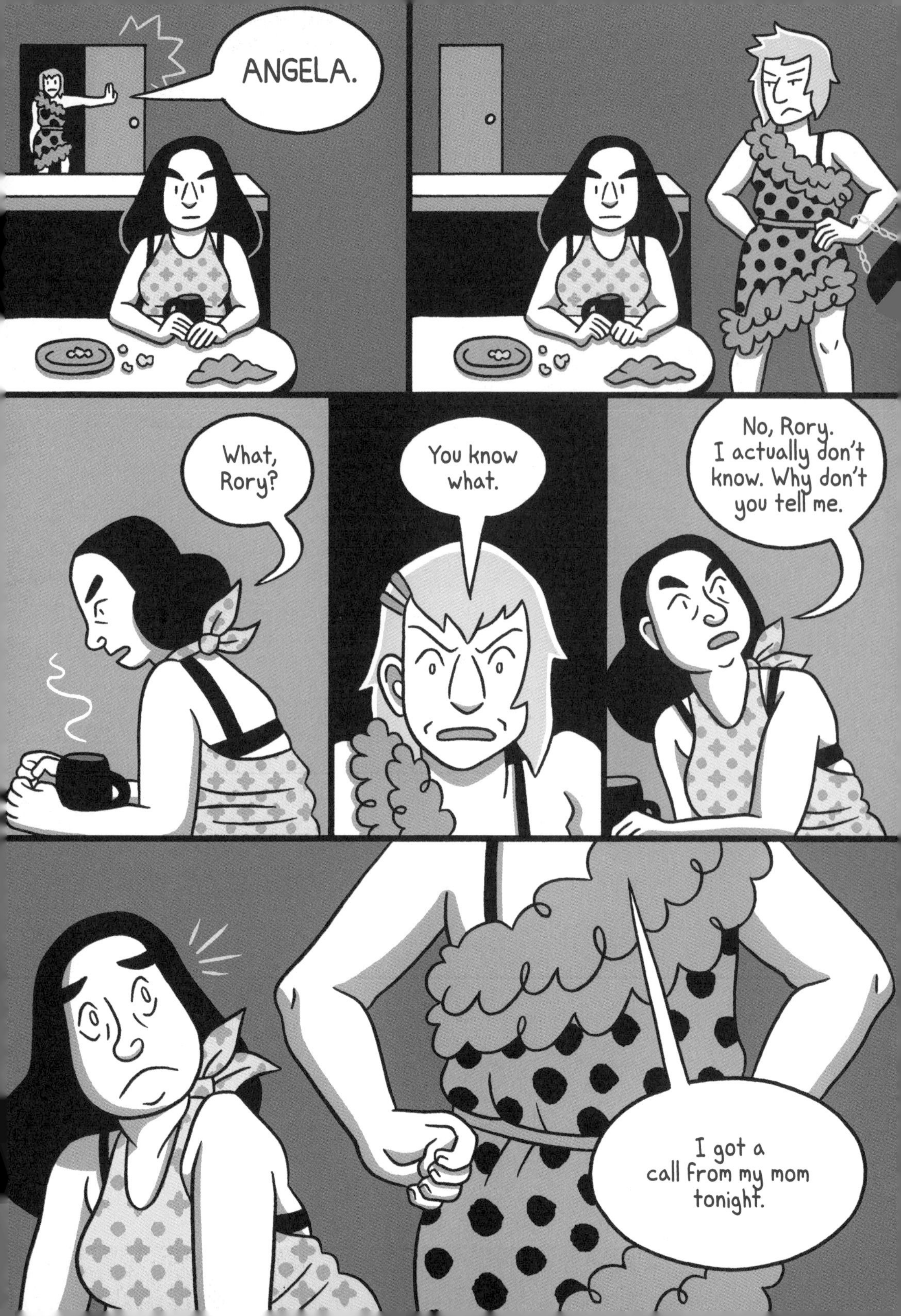
ANGELA.
What, Rory?
You know what.
No, Rory. I actually don't know. Why don't you tell me.
I got a call from my mom tonight.

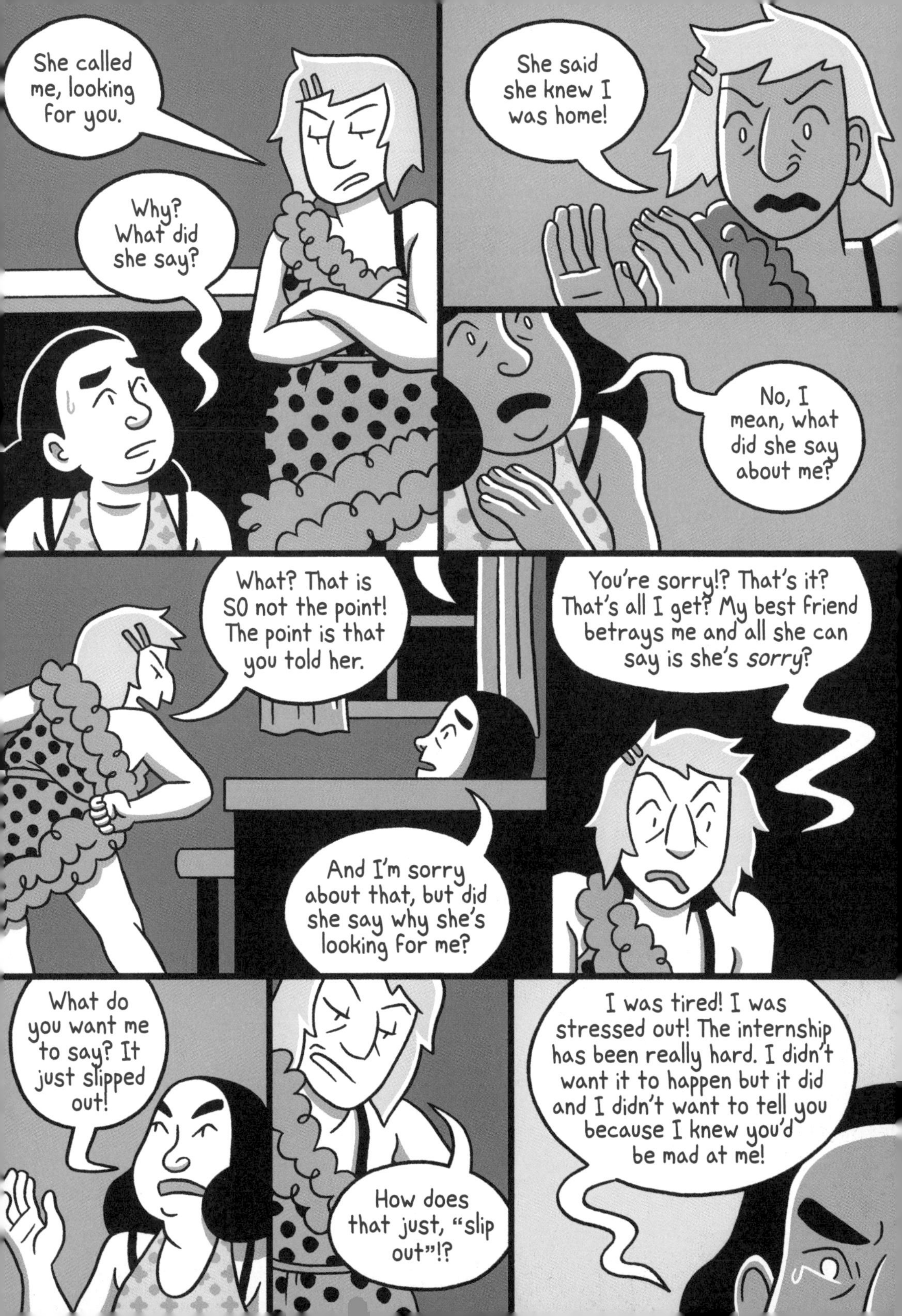
She called me, looking for you.
Why? What did she say?
She said she knew I was home!
No, I mean, what did she say about me?
What? That is SO not the point! The point is that you told her.
And I'm sorry about that, but did she say why she's looking for me?
You're sorry!? That's it? That's all I get? My best friend betrays me and all she can say is she's *sorry*?
What do you want me to say? It just slipped out!
How does that just, "slip out"!?
I was tired! I was stressed out! The internship has been really hard. I didn't want it to happen but it did and I didn't want to tell you because I knew you'd be mad at me!

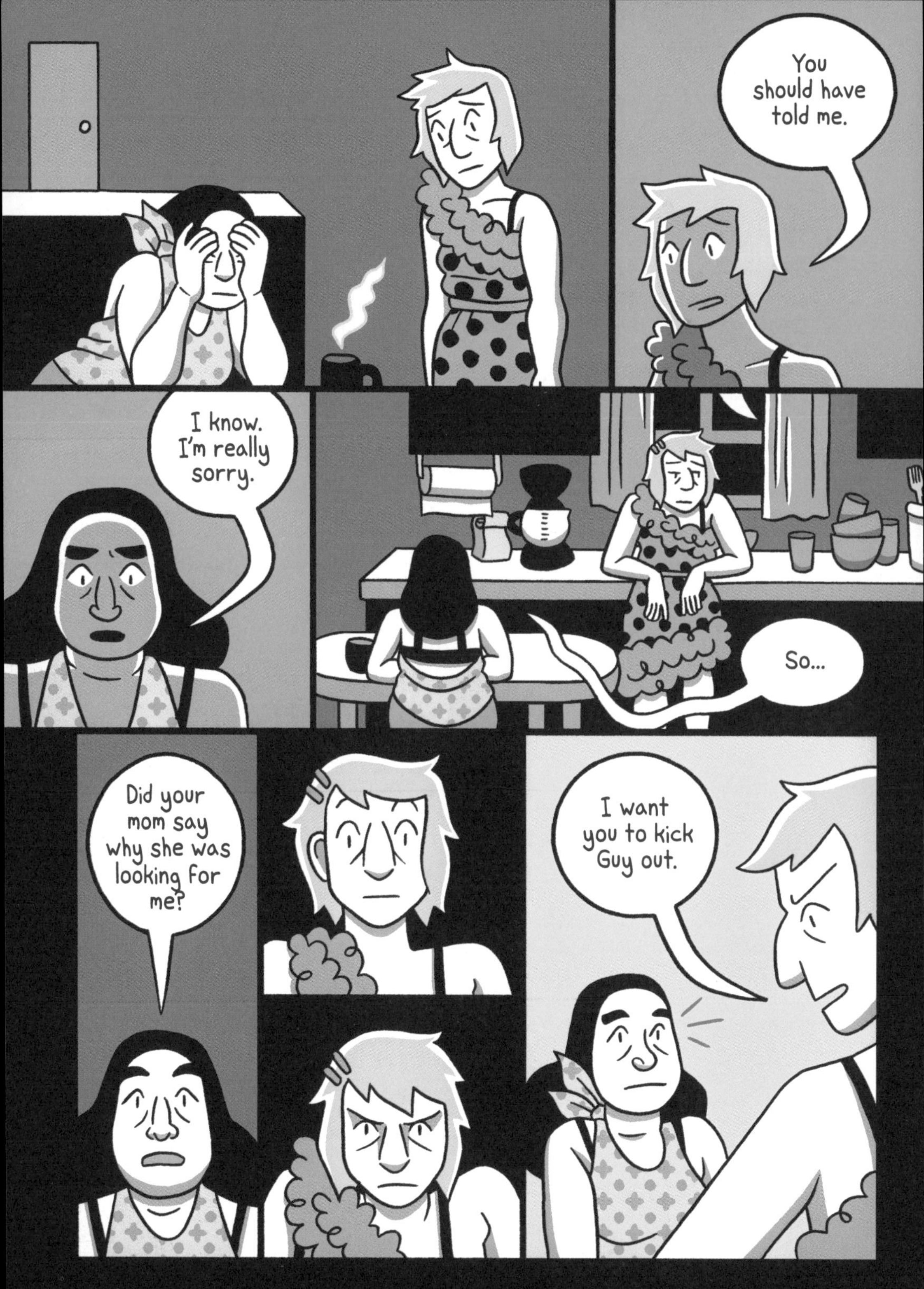
You should have told me.
I know. I'm really sorry.
So...
Did your mom say why she was looking for me?
I want you to kick Guy out.

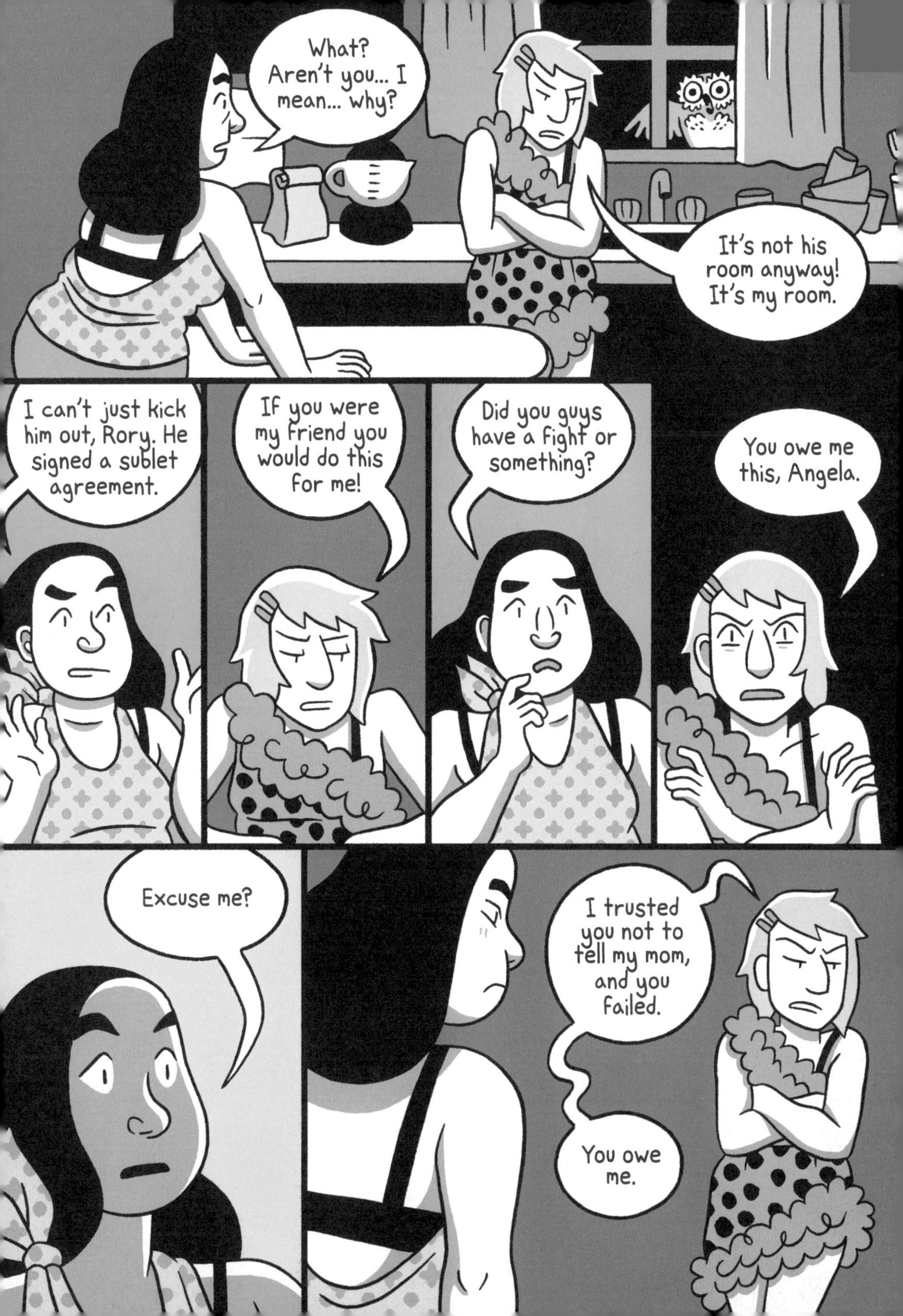

What? Aren't you... I mean... why?
It's not his room anyway! It's my room.
I can't just kick him out, Rory. He signed a sublet agreement.
If you were my friend you would do this for me!
Did you guys have a fight or something?
You owe me this, Angela.
Excuse me?
I trusted you not to tell my mom, and you failed.
You owe me.

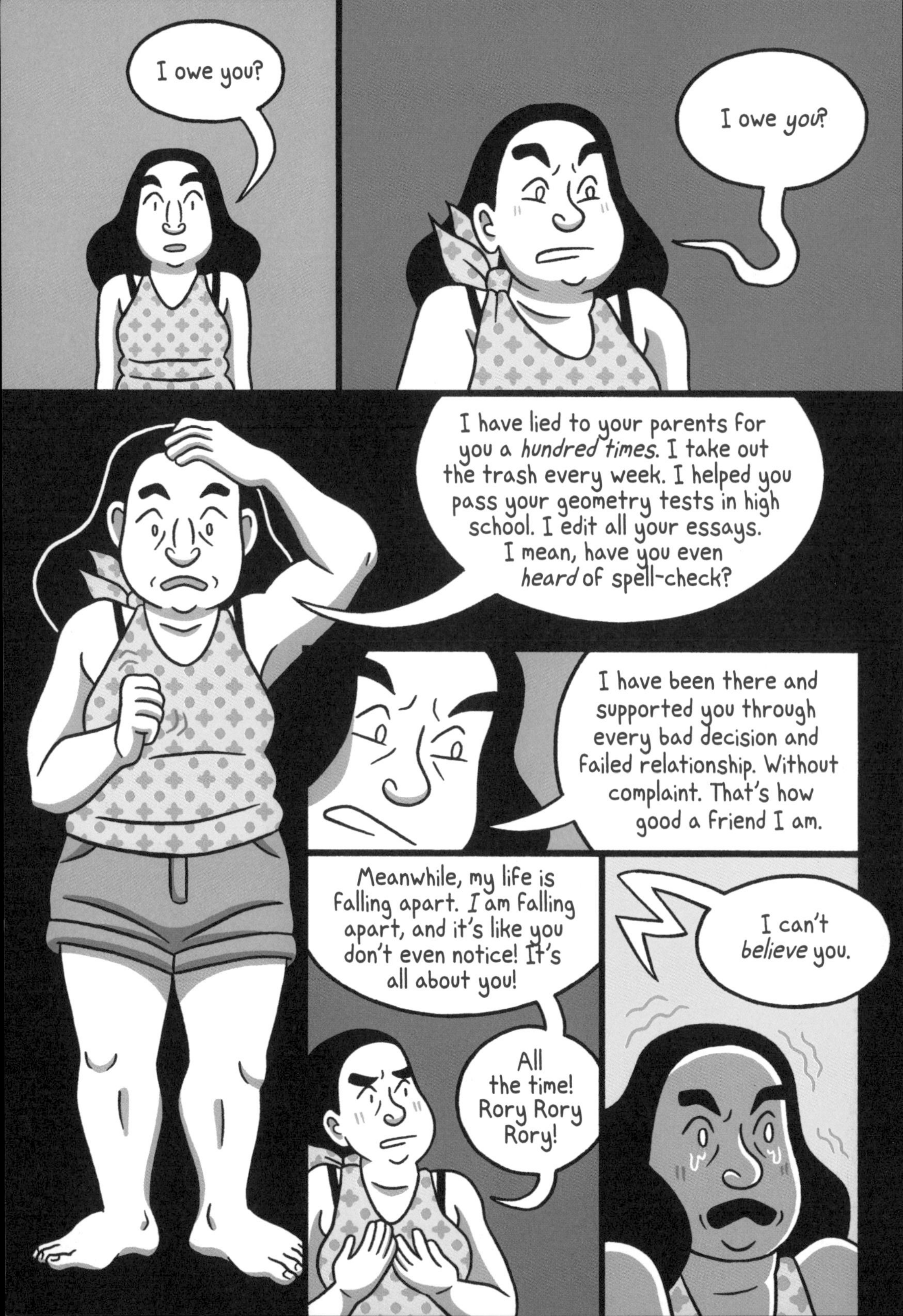
I owe you?
I owe *you*?
I have lied to your parents for you a *hundred times*. I take out the trash every week. I helped you pass your geometry tests in high school. I edit all your essays. I mean, have you even *heard* of spell-check?
I have been there and supported you through every bad decision and failed relationship. Without complaint. That's how good a friend I am.
Meanwhile, my life is falling apart. *I* am falling apart, and it's like you don't even notice! It's all about you!
All the time! Rory Rory Rory!
I can't *believe* you.

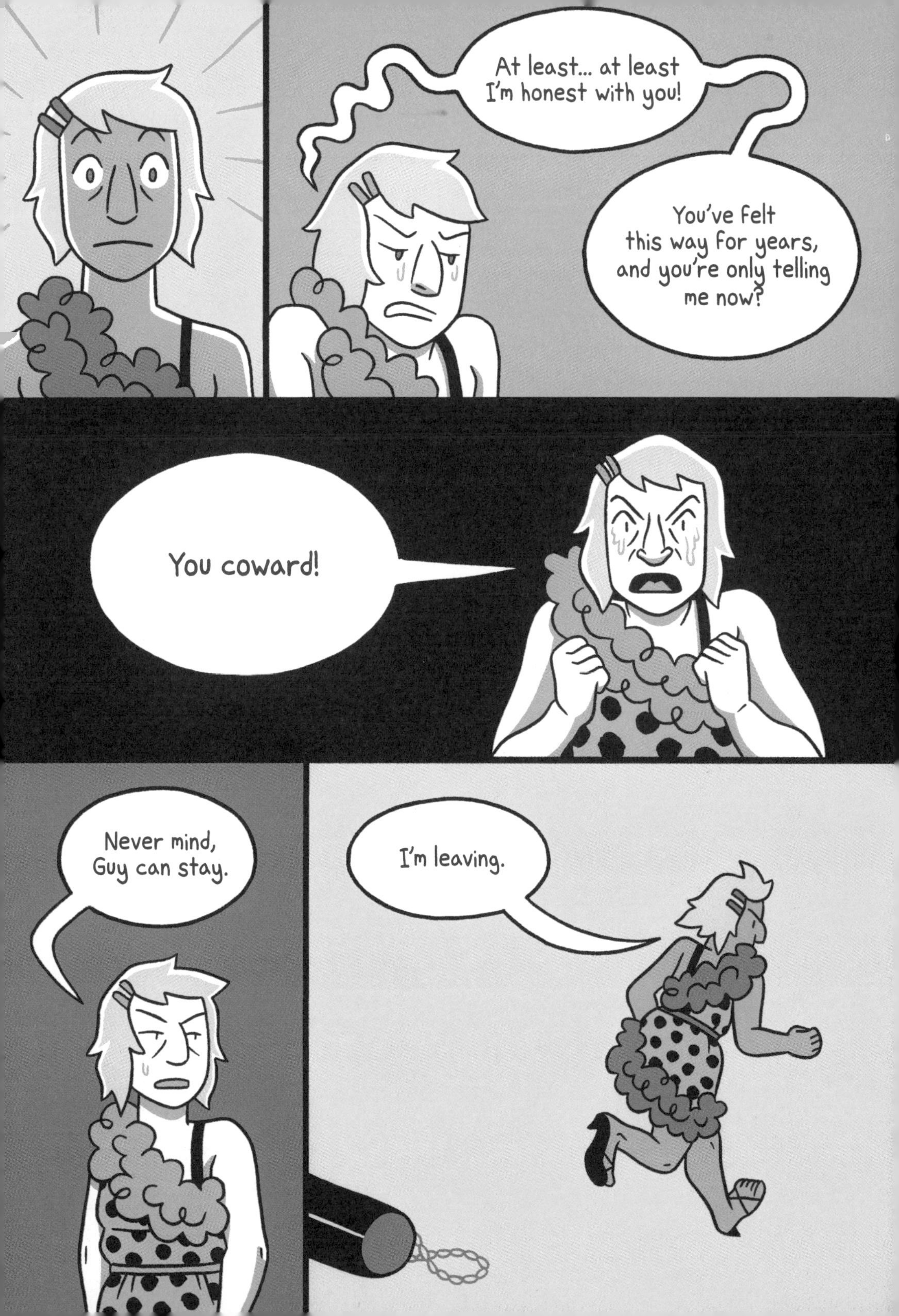

At least... at least I'm honest with you!
You've felt this way for years, and you're only telling me now?
You coward!
Never mind, Guy can stay.
I'm leaving.

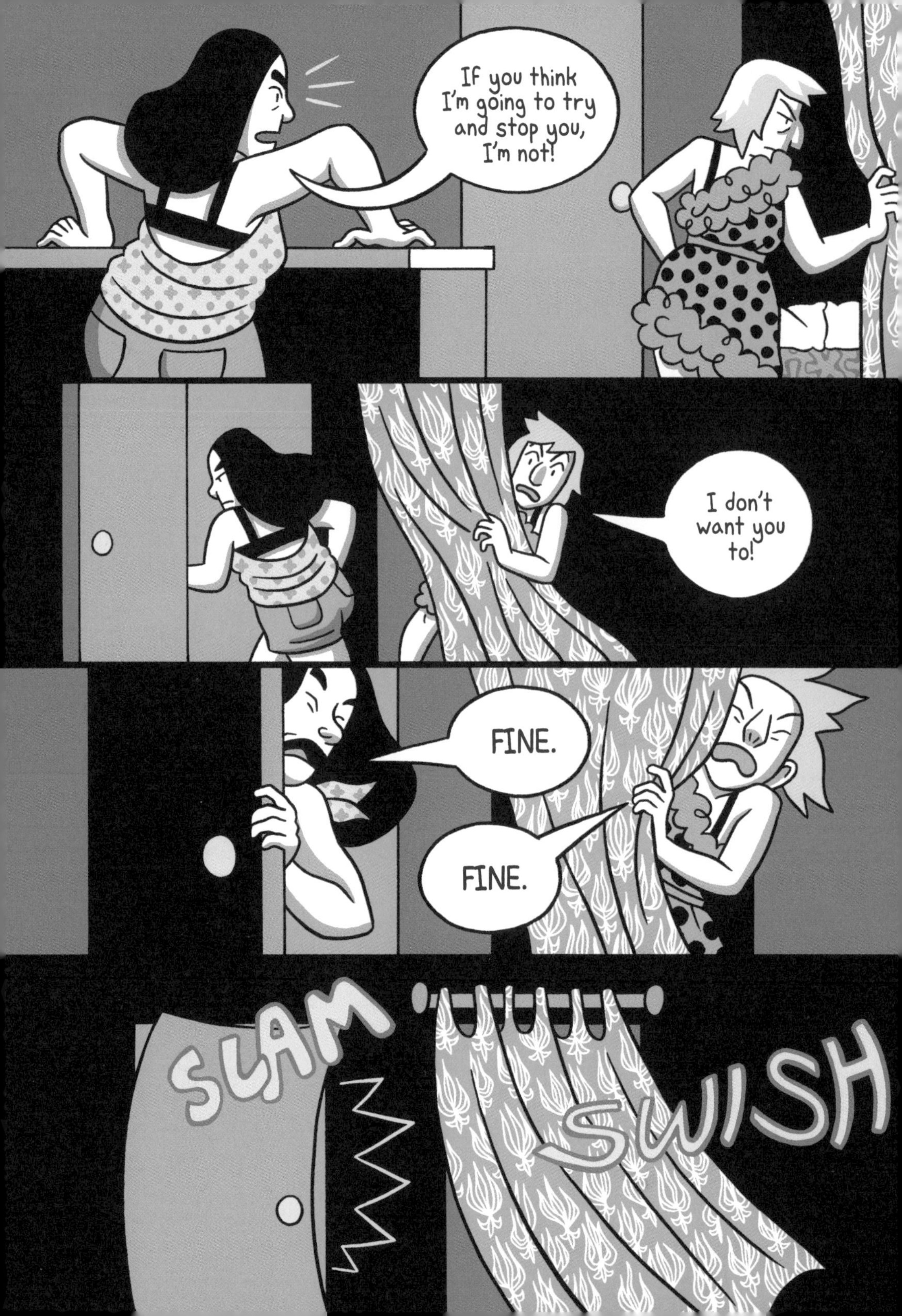
If you think I'm going to try and stop you, I'm not!
I don't want you to!
FINE.
FINE.
SLAM
SWISH

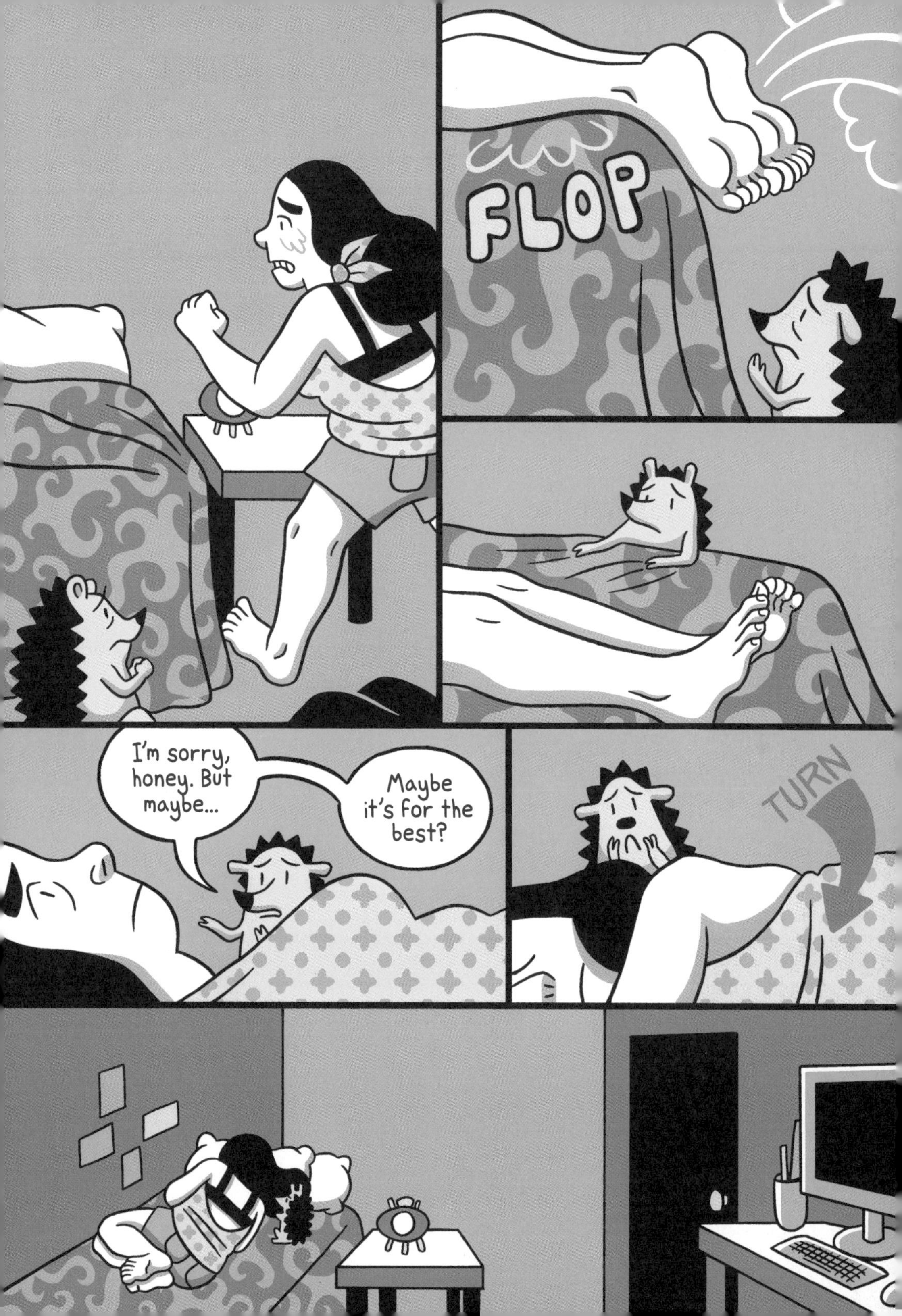
FLOP
I'm sorry, honey. But maybe...
Maybe it's for the best?
TURN

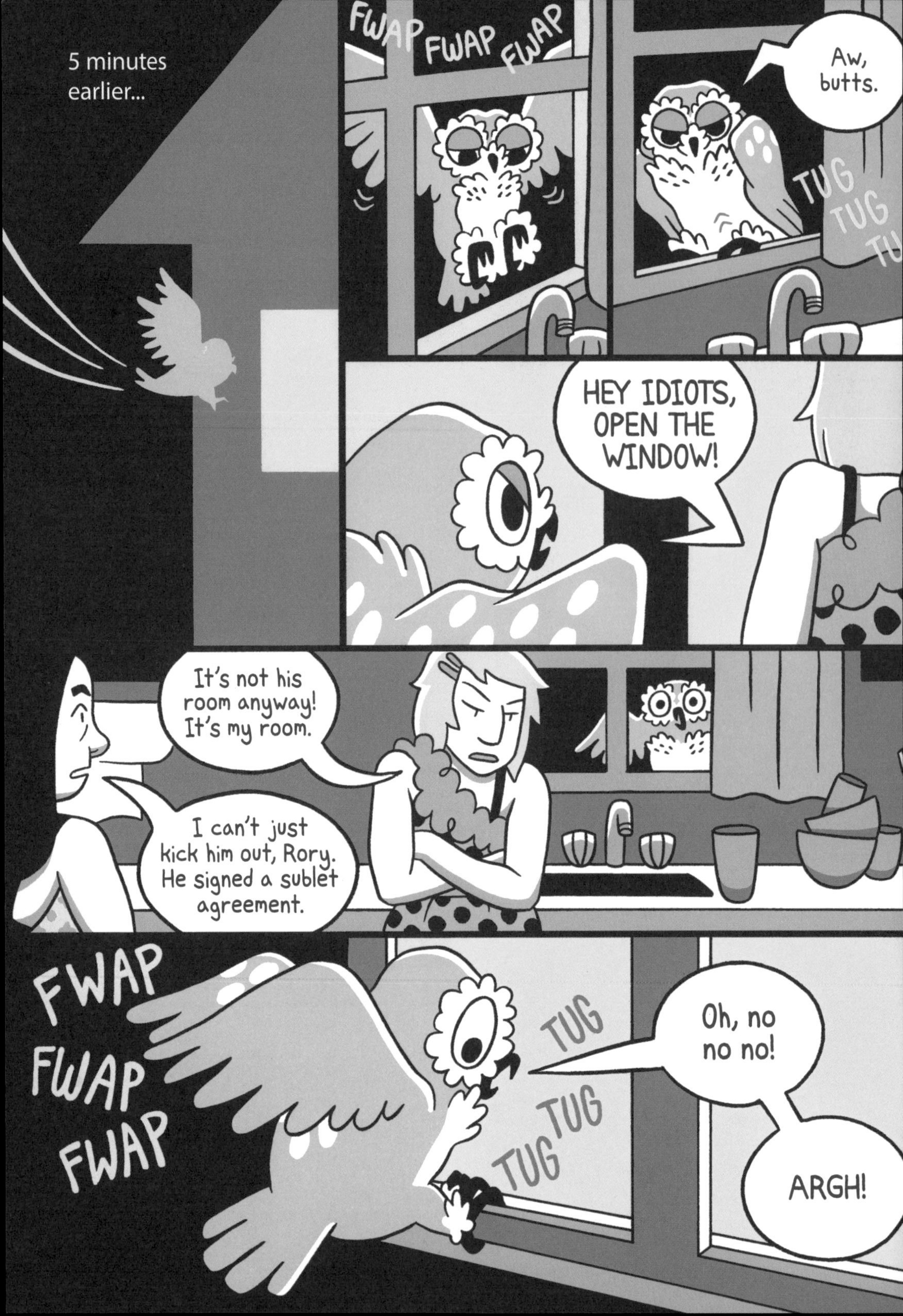
5 minutes earlier...
FWAP FWAP FWAP
Aw, butts.
TUG TUG TU
HEY IDIOTS, OPEN THE WINDOW!
It's not his room anyway! It's my room.
I can't just kick him out, Rory. He signed a sublet agreement.
FWAP FWAP FWAP
TUG
Oh, no no no!
TUG TUG
ARGH!

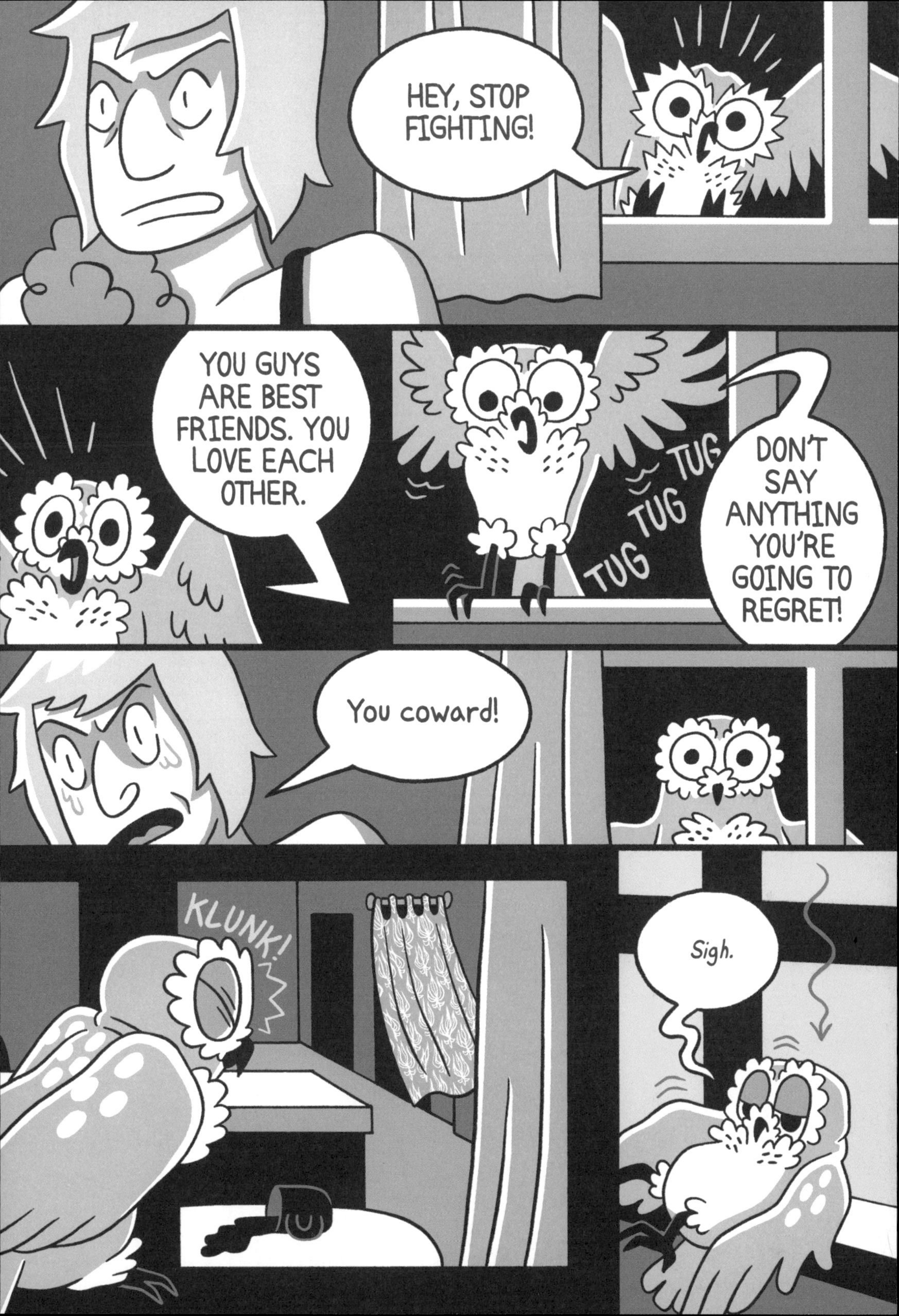
HEY, STOP FIGHTING!
YOU GUYS ARE BEST FRIENDS. YOU LOVE EACH OTHER.
TUG TUG TUG
DON'T SAY ANYTHING YOU'RE GOING TO REGRET!
You coward!
KLUNK!
Sigh.

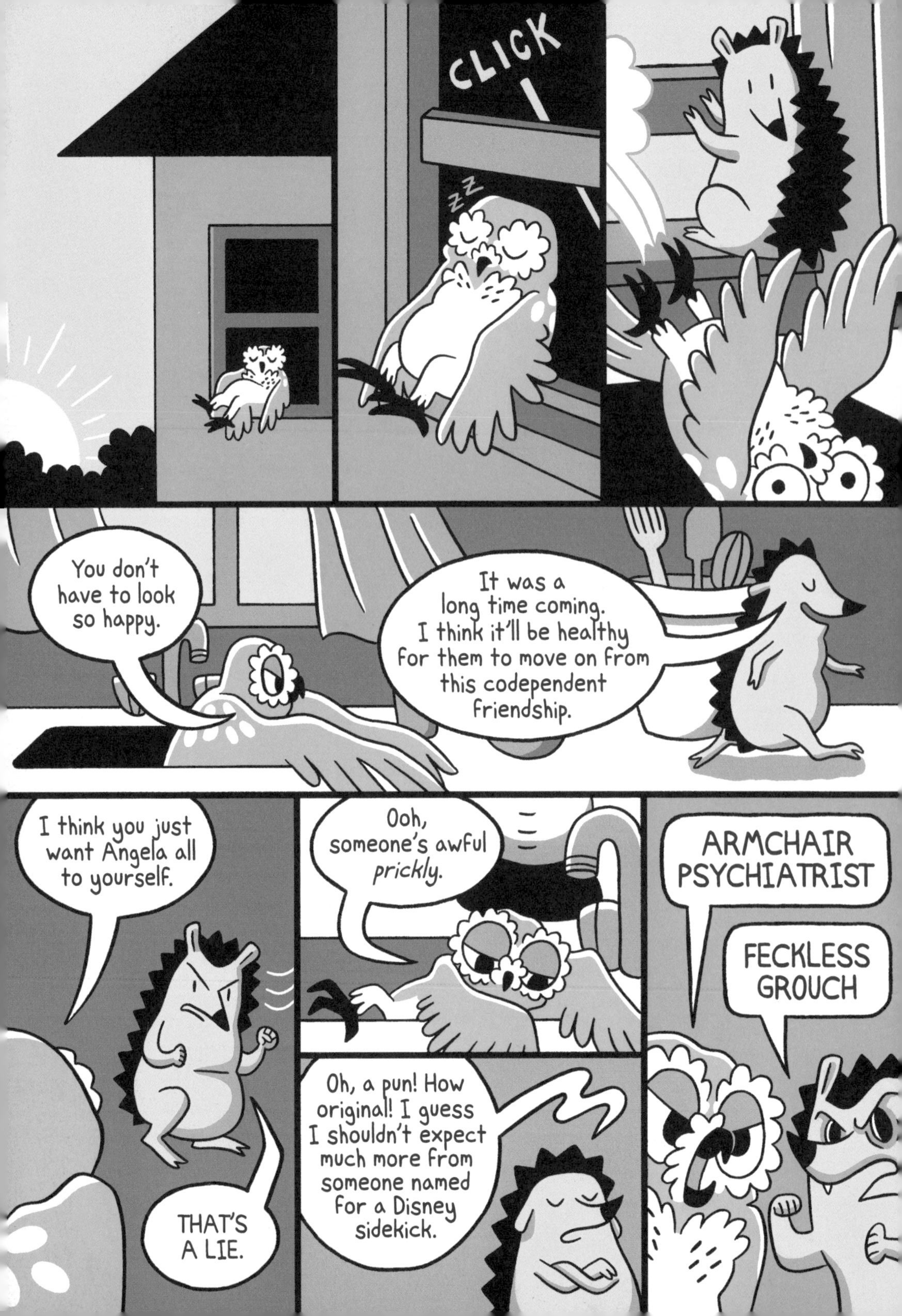
CLICK
Z Z
You don't have to look so happy.
It was a long time coming. I think it'll be healthy for them to move on from this codependent friendship.
I think you just want Angela all to yourself.
THAT'S A LIE.
Ooh, someone's awful *prickly*.
Oh, a pun! How original! I guess I shouldn't expect much more from someone named for a Disney sidekick.
ARMCHAIR PSYCHIATRIST
FECKLESS GROUCH

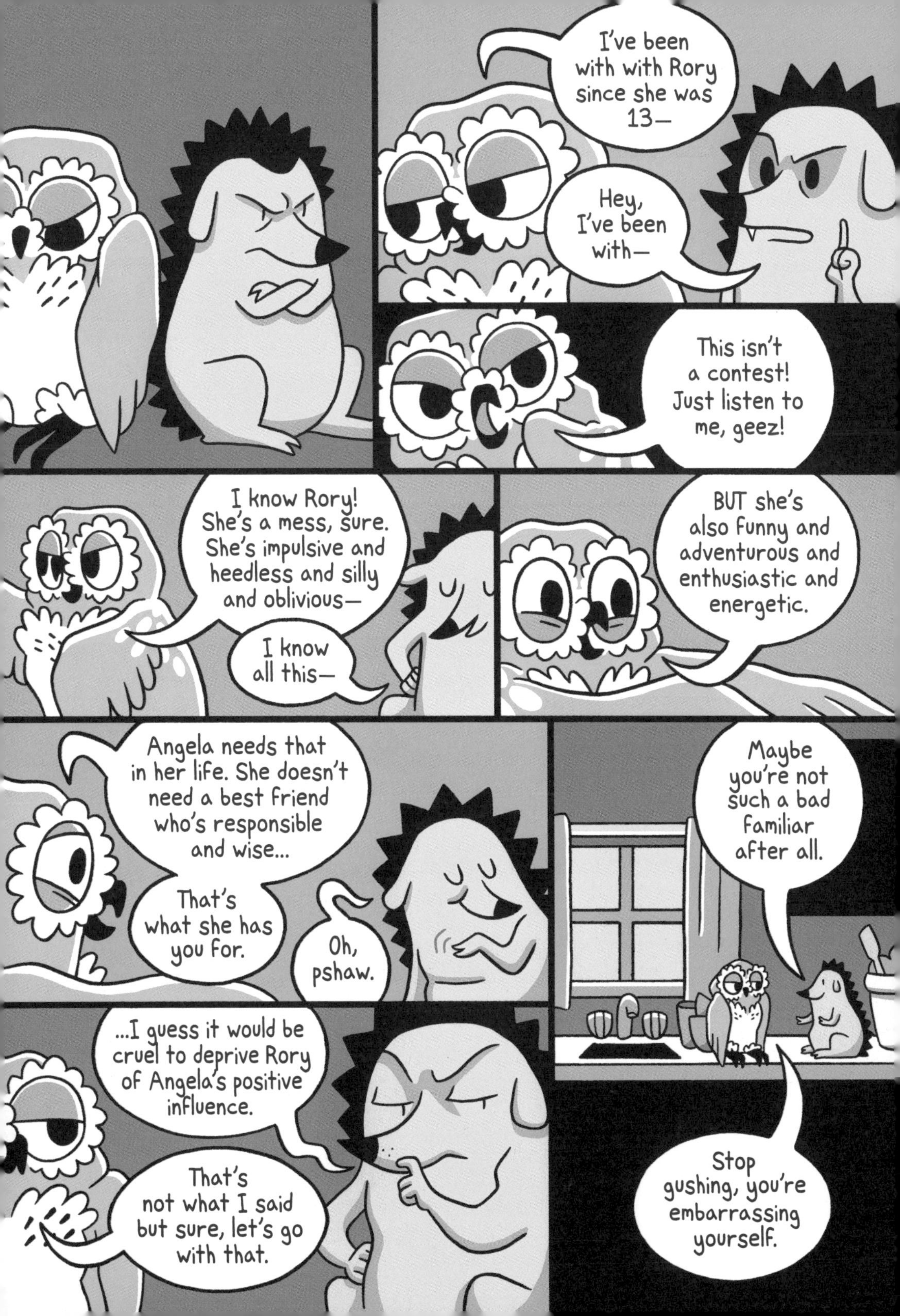
I've been with with Rory since she was 13—
Hey, I've been with—
This isn't a contest! Just listen to me, geez!
I know Rory! She's a mess, sure. She's impulsive and heedless and silly and oblivious—
I know all this—
BUT she's also funny and adventurous and enthusiastic and energetic.
Angela needs that in her life. She doesn't need a best friend who's responsible and wise...
That's what she has you for.
Oh, pshaw.
...I guess it would be cruel to deprive Rory of Angela's positive influence.
That's not what I said but sure, let's go with that.
Maybe you're not such a bad familiar after all.
Stop gushing, you're embarrassing yourself.

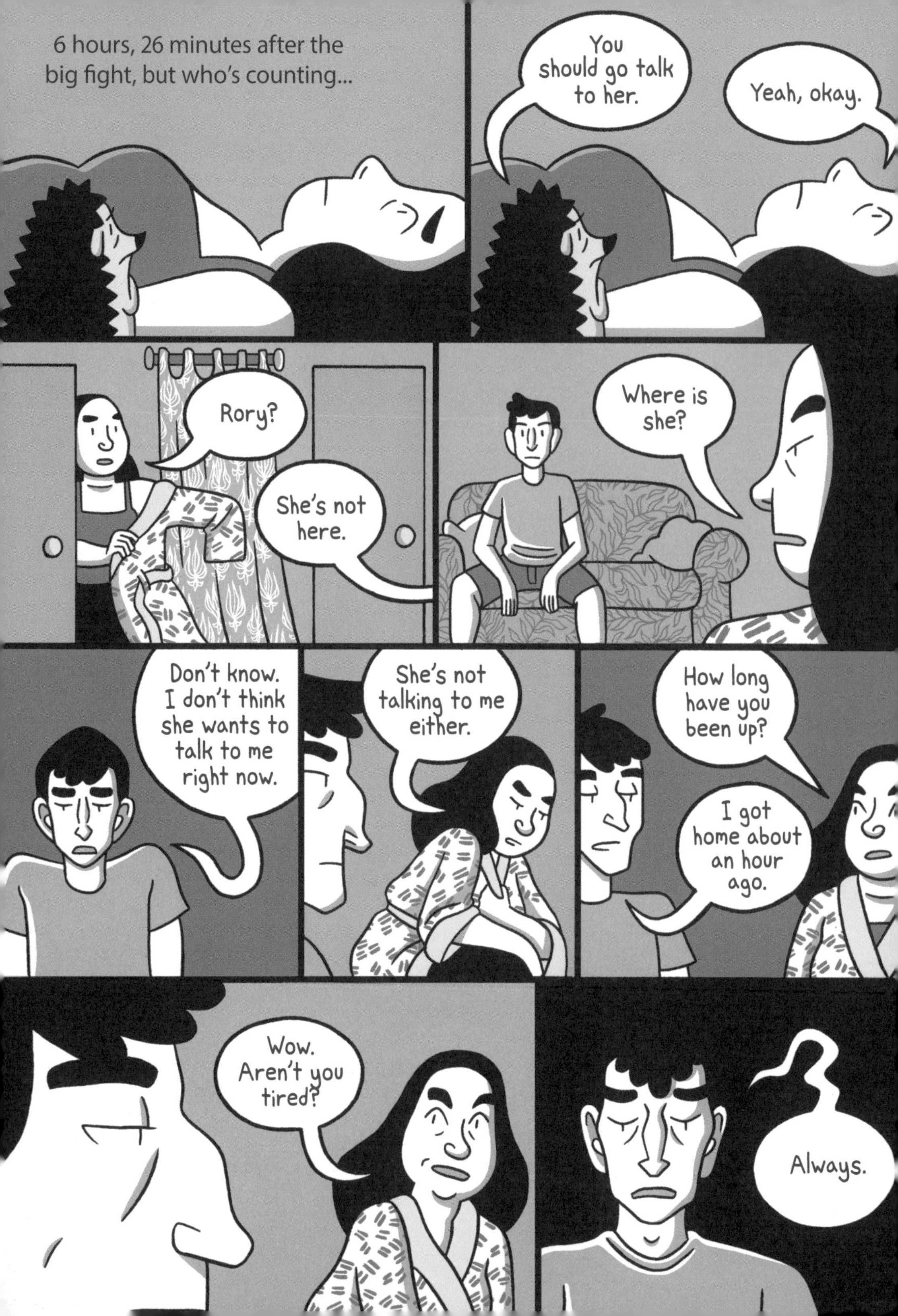

6 hours, 26 minutes after the big fight, but who's counting...
You should go talk to her.
Yeah, okay.
Rory?
She's not here.
Where is she?
Don't know. I don't think she wants to talk to me right now.
She's not talking to me either.
How long have you been up?
I got home about an hour ago.
Wow. Aren't you tired?
Always.

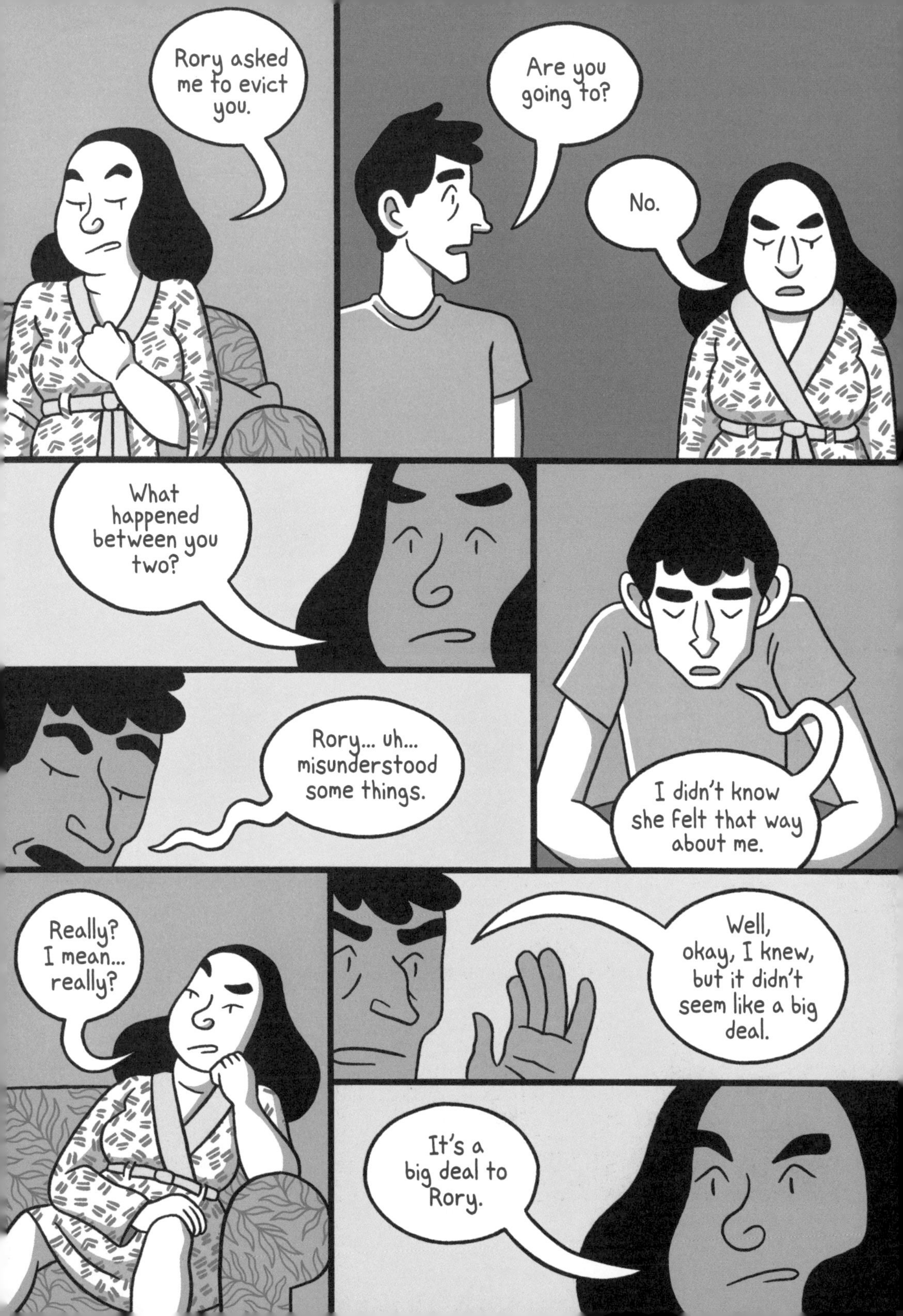
Rory asked me to evict you.
Are you going to?
No.
What happened between you two?
I didn't know she felt that way about me.
Rory... uh... misunderstood some things.
Really? I mean... really?
Well, okay, I knew, but it didn't seem like a big deal.
It's a big deal to Rory.

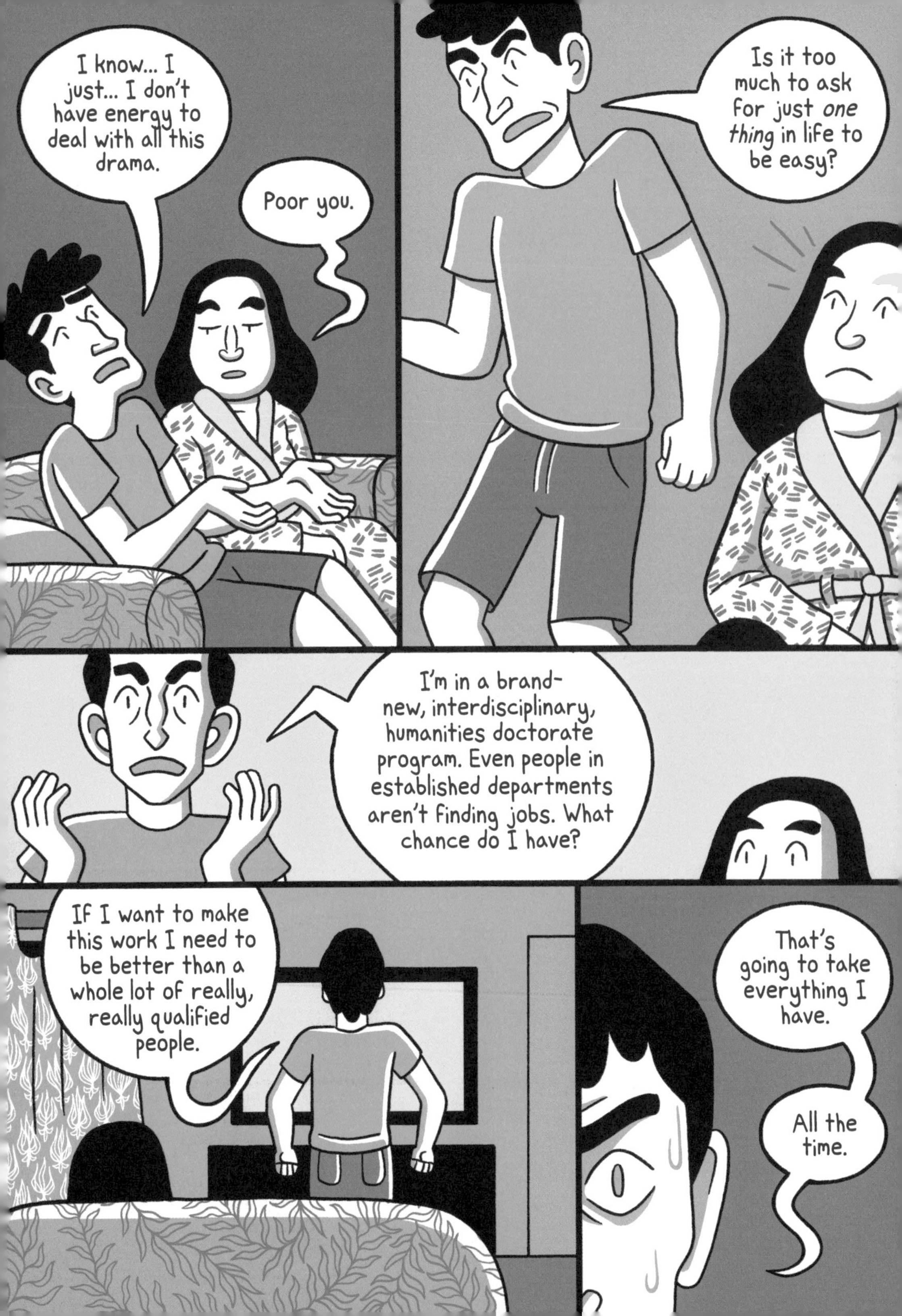
I know... I just... I don't have energy to deal with all this drama.
Poor you.
Is it too much to ask for just *one thing* in life to be easy?
I'm in a brand-new, interdisciplinary, humanities doctorate program. Even people in established departments aren't finding jobs. What chance do I have?
If I want to make this work I need to be better than a whole lot of really, really qualified people.
That's going to take everything I have.
All the time.

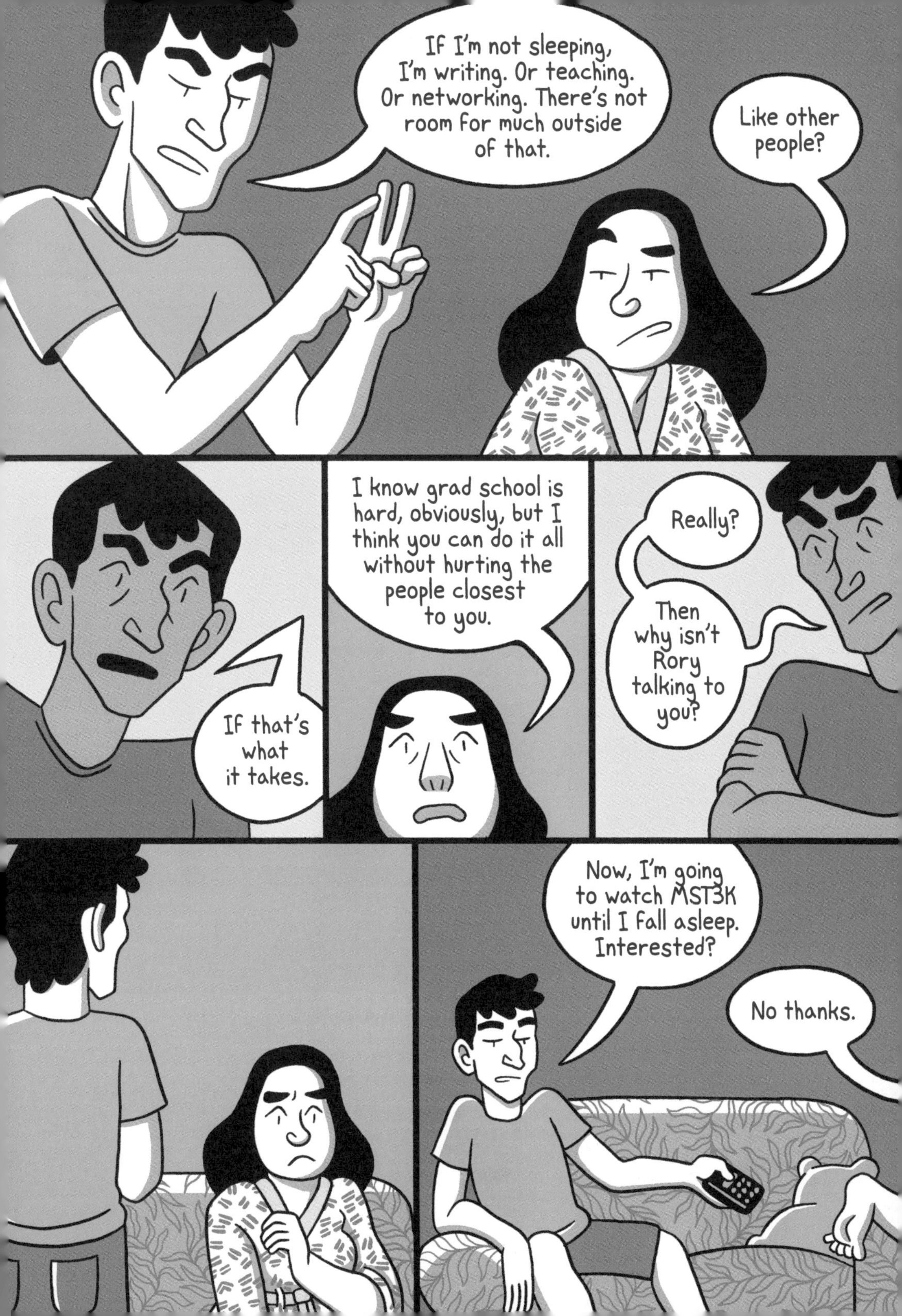

If I'm not sleeping, I'm writing. Or teaching. Or networking. There's not room for much outside of that.
Like other people?
If that's what it takes.
I know grad school is hard, obviously, but I think you can do it all without hurting the people closest to you.
Really?
Then why isn't Rory talking to you?
Now, I'm going to watch MST3K until I fall asleep. Interested?
No thanks.

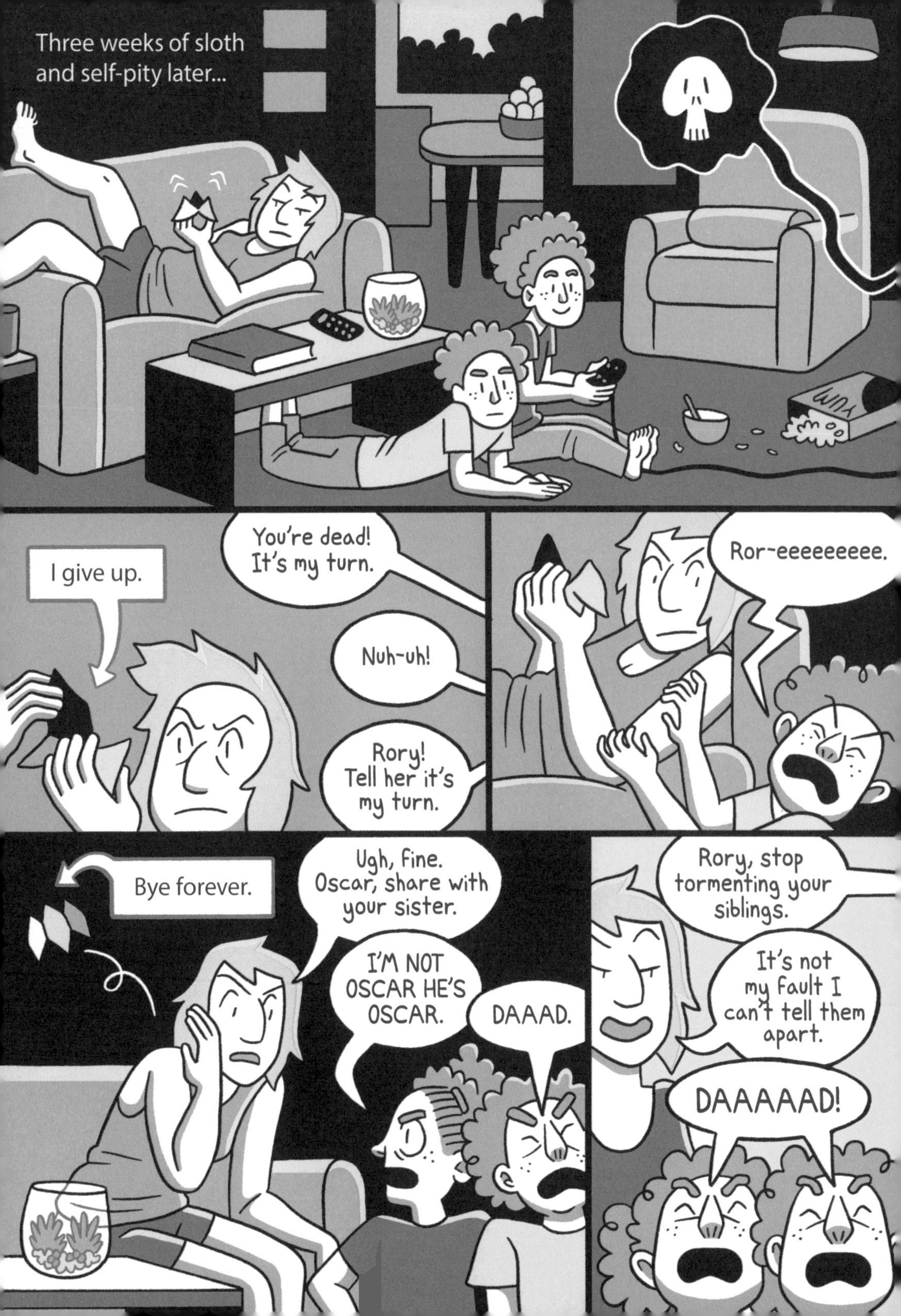

Three weeks of sloth and self-pity later...
YUM
I give up.
You're dead! It's my turn.
Nuh-uh!
Rory! Tell her it's my turn.
Ror-eeeeeeeee.
Bye forever.
Ugh, fine. Oscar, share with your sister.
I'M NOT OSCAR HE'S OSCAR.
DAAAD.
Rory, stop tormenting your siblings.
It's not my fault I can't tell them apart.
DAAAAAD!

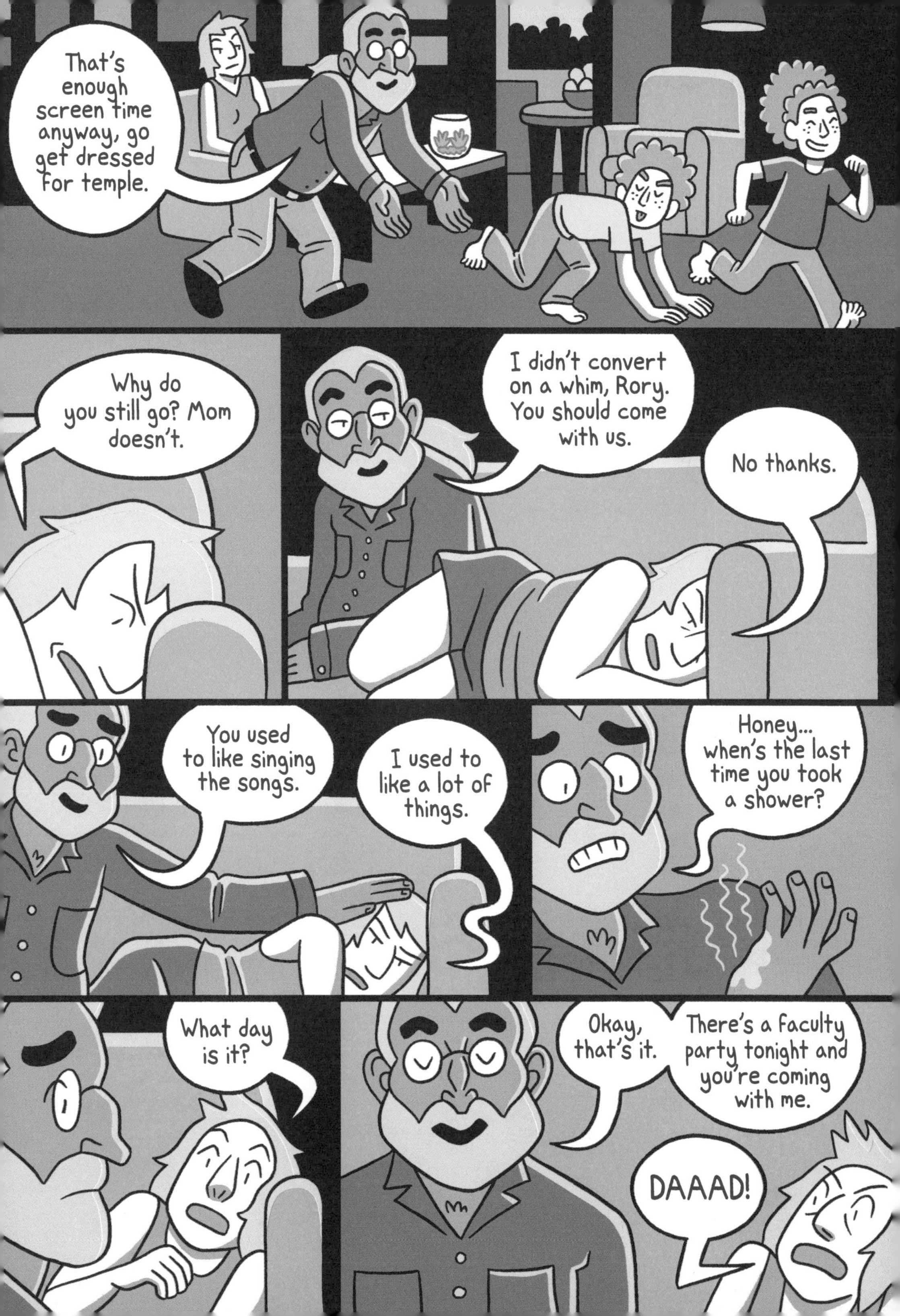
That's enough screen time anyway, go get dressed for temple.
Why do you still go? Mom doesn't.
I didn't convert on a whim, Rory. You should come with us.
No thanks.
You used to like singing the songs.
I used to like a lot of things.
Honey... when's the last time you took a shower?
What day is it?
Okay, that's it.
There's a faculty party tonight and you're coming with me.
DAAAD!

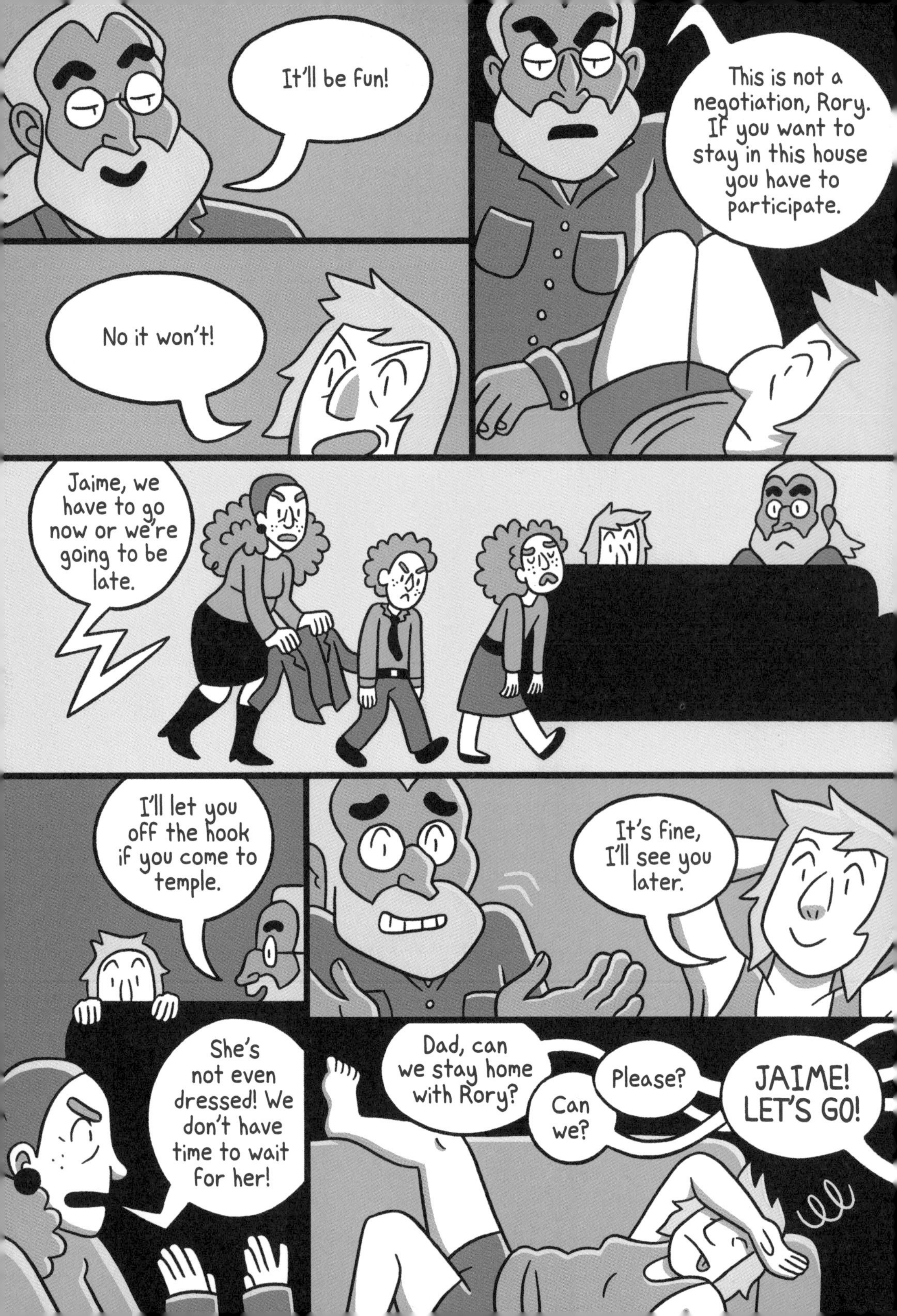
It'll be fun!
This is not a negotiation, Rory. If you want to stay in this house you have to participate.
No it won't!
Jaime, we have to go now or we're going to be late.
I'll let you off the hook if you come to temple.
It's fine, I'll see you later.
She's not even dressed! We don't have time to wait for her!
Dad, can we stay home with Rory?
Can we?
Please?
JAIME! LET'S GO!

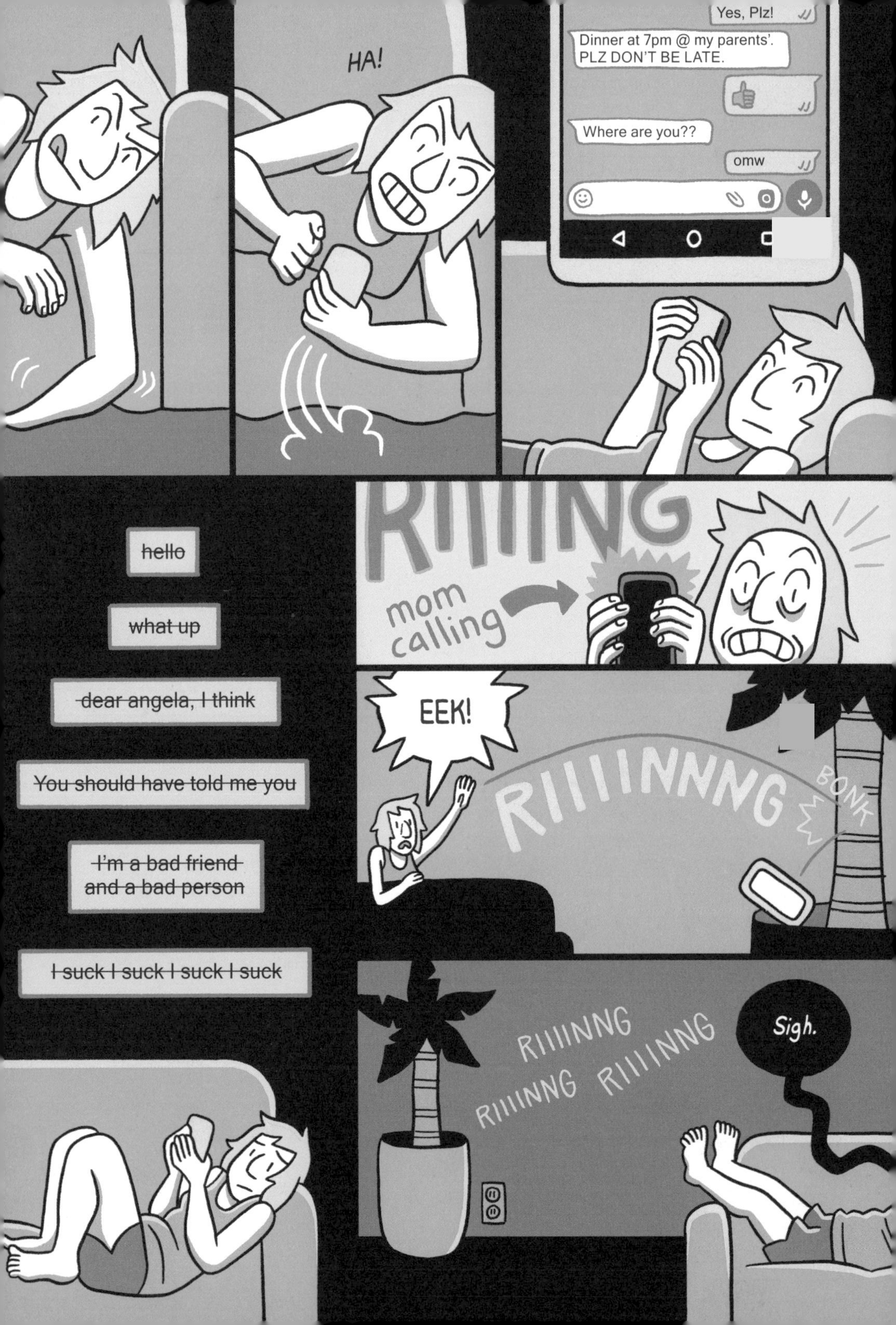

HA!
Yes, Plz!
Dinner at 7pm @ my parents'. PLZ DON'T BE LATE.
Where are you??
omw
hello
what up
dear angela, I think
You should have told me you
I'm a bad friend and a bad person
I suck I suck I suck I suck
RIIIING
mom calling
EEK!
RIIIINNNG
BONK
RIIIINNG
RIIIINNG RIIIINNG
Sigh.

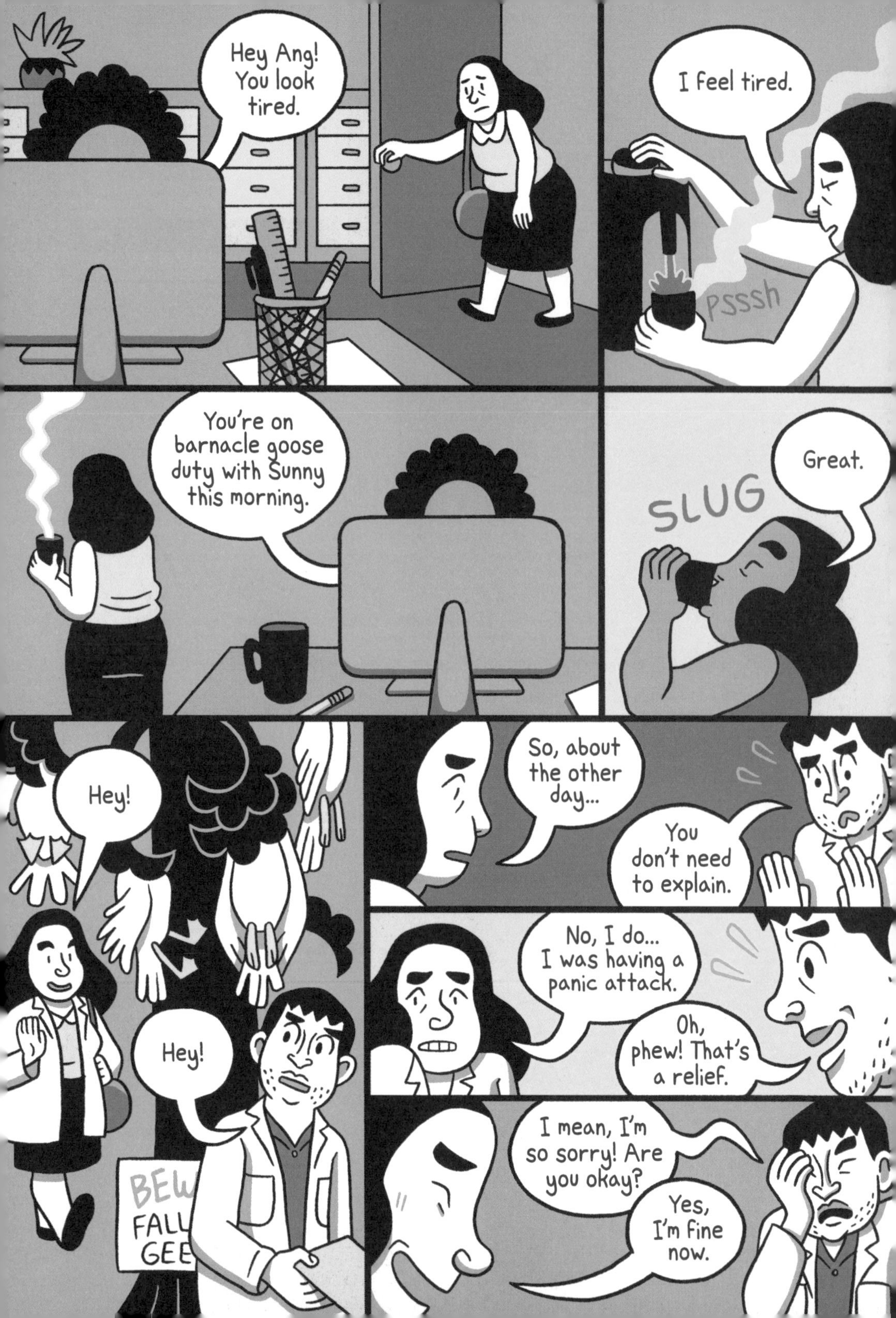
Hey Ang! You look tired.
I feel tired.
PSSSH
You're on barnacle goose duty with Sunny this morning.
SLUG
Great.
Hey!
Hey!
BEW
FALL
GEE
So, about the other day...
You don't need to explain.
No, I do... I was having a panic attack.
Oh, phew! That's a relief.
I mean, I'm so sorry! Are you okay?
Yes, I'm fine now.

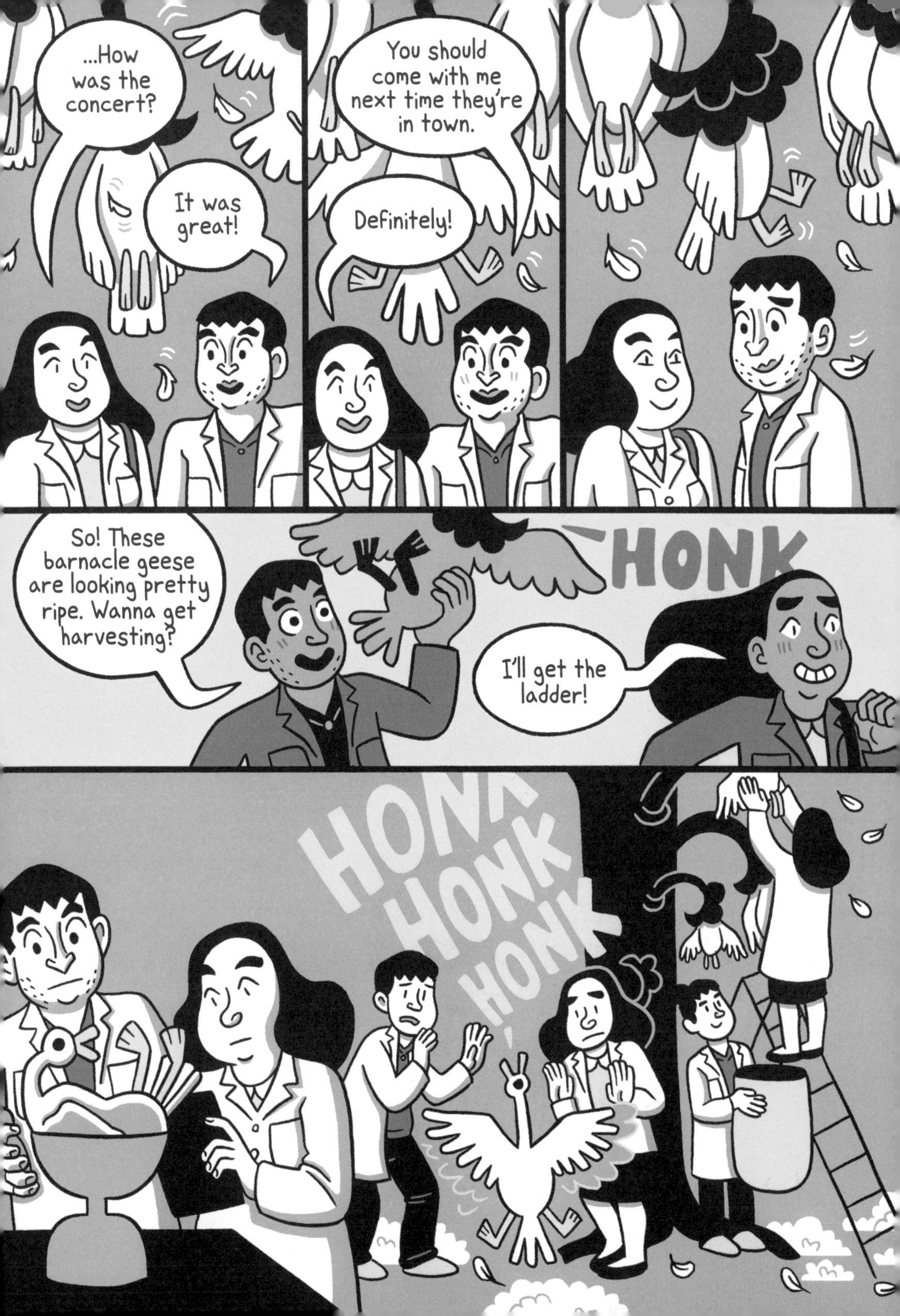
...How was the concert?
It was great!
You should come with me next time they're in town.
Definitely!
So! These barnacle geese are looking pretty ripe. Wanna get harvesting?
HONK
I'll get the ladder!
HONK
HONK
HONK

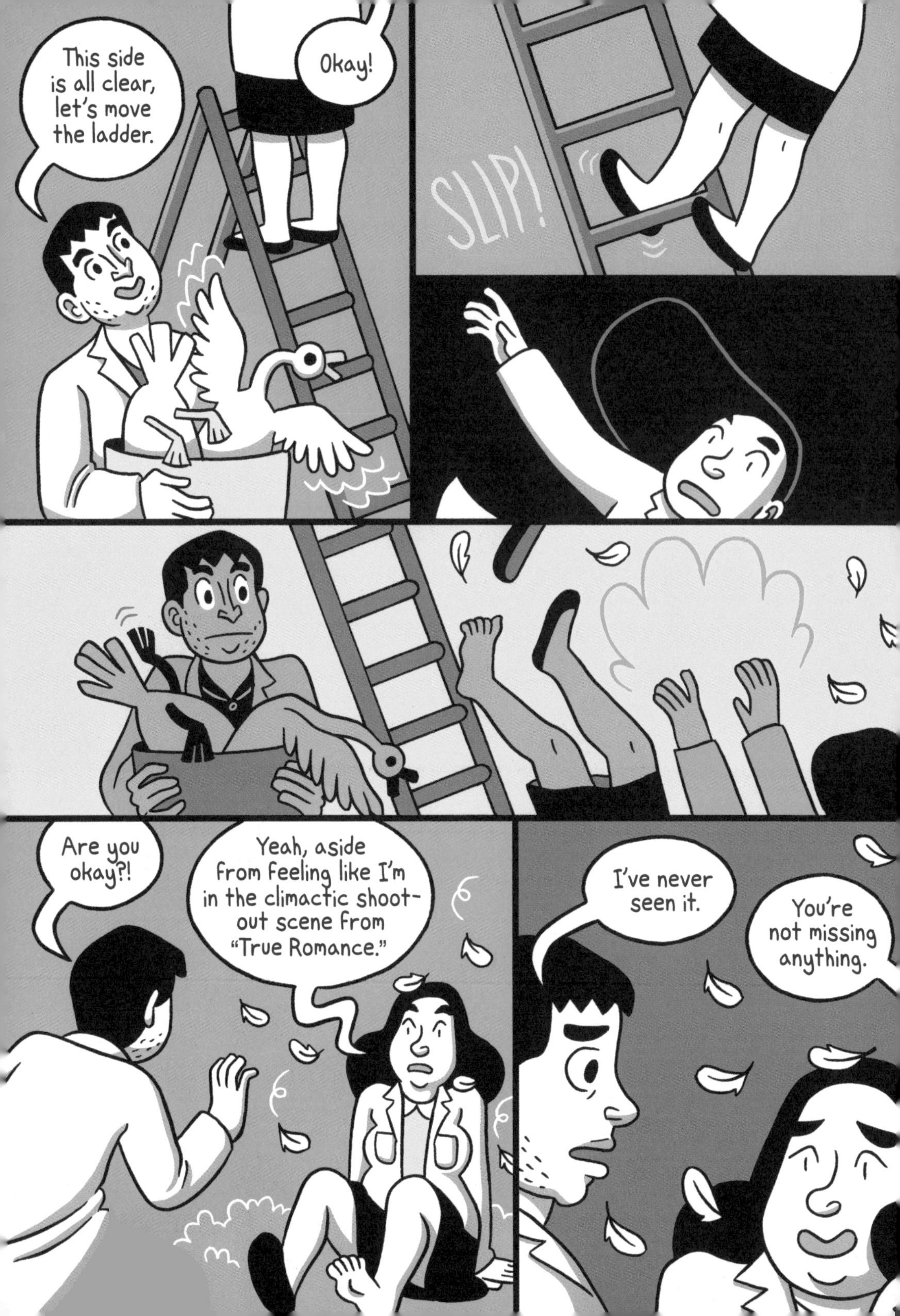
This side is all clear, let's move the ladder.
Okay!
SLIP!
Are you okay?!
Yeah, aside from feeling like I'm in the climactic shoot-out scene from "True Romance."
I've never seen it.
You're not missing anything.

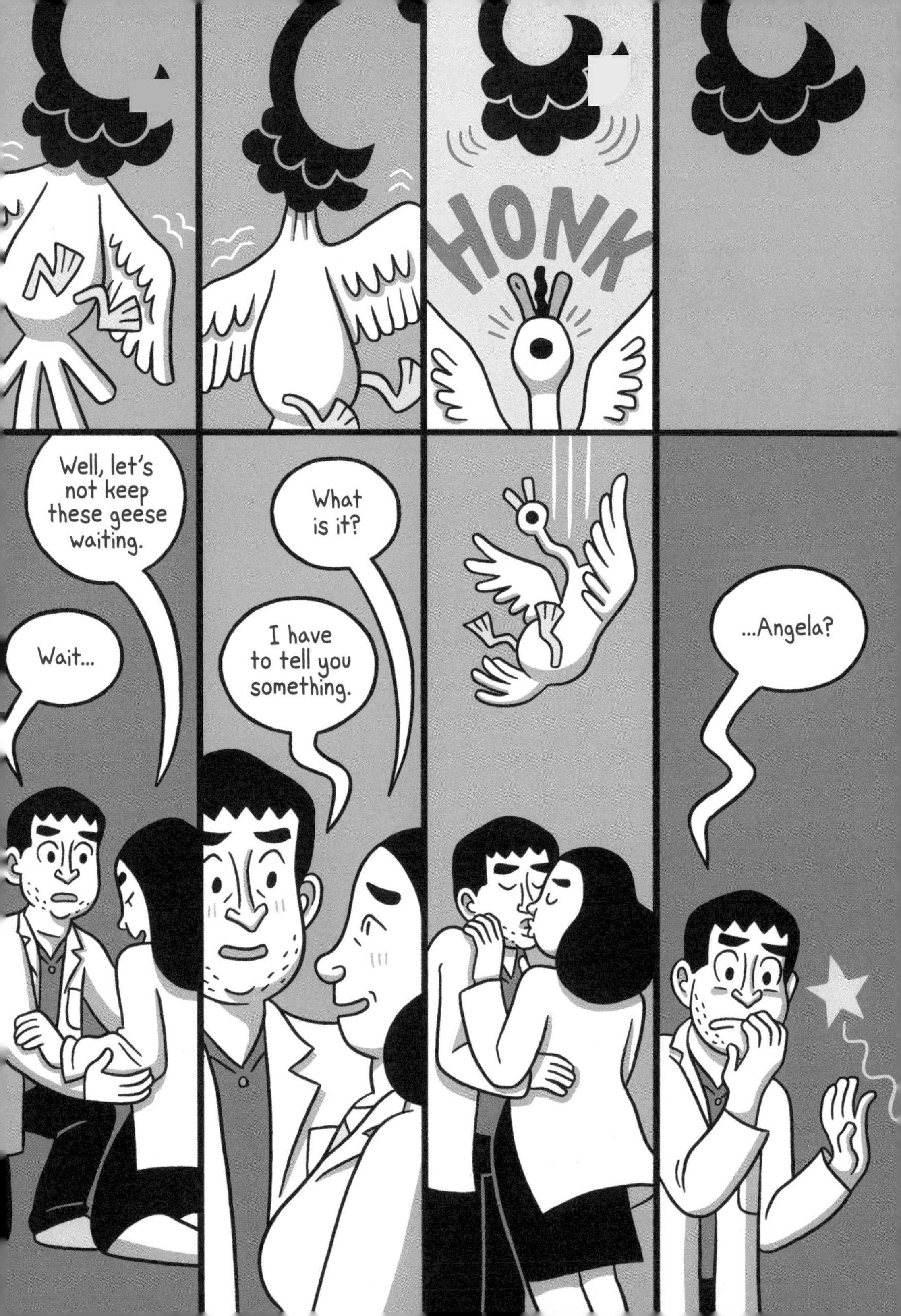
HONK
Well, let's not keep these geese waiting.
Wait...
What is it?
I have to tell you something.
...Angela?

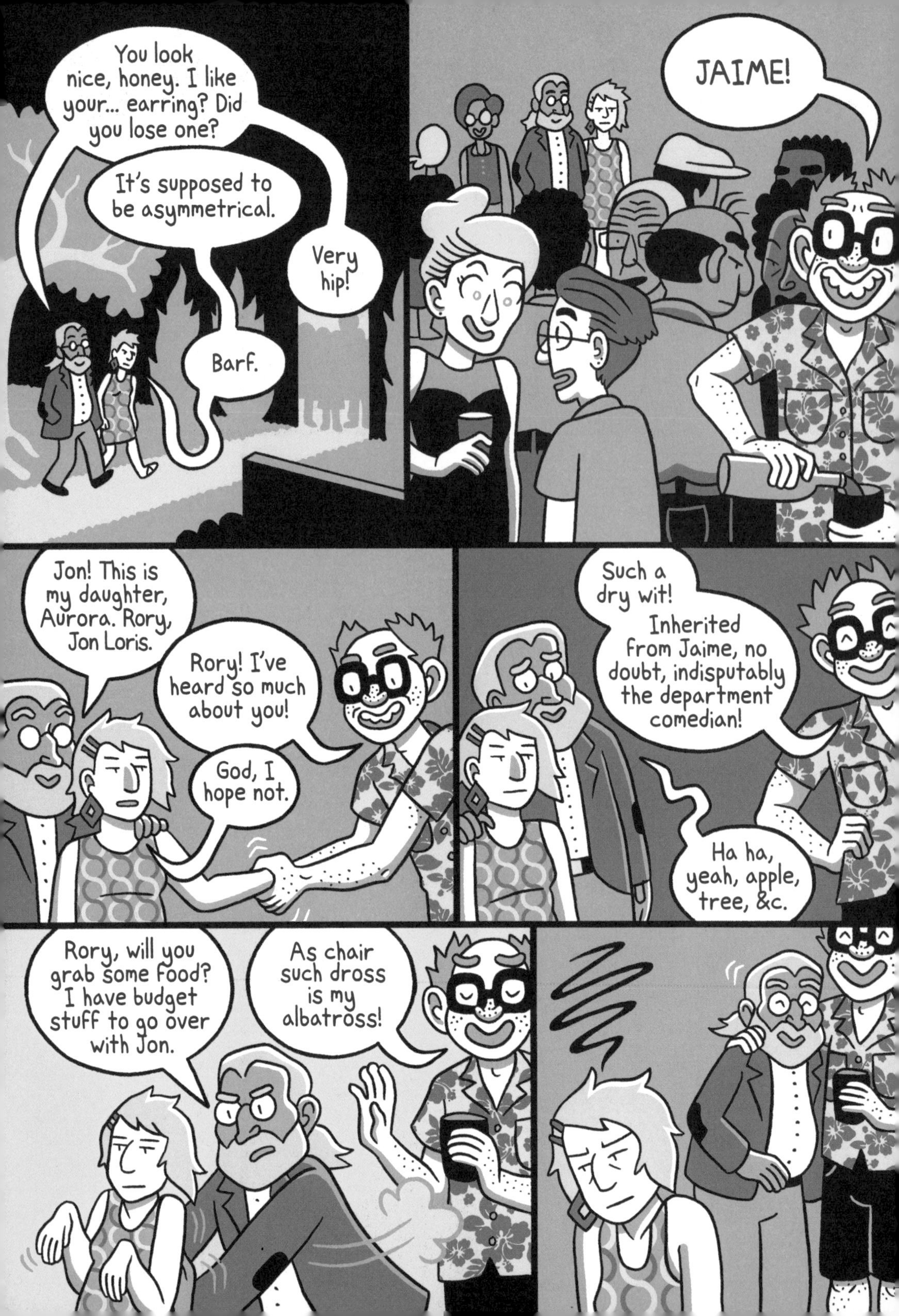
You look nice, honey. I like your... earring? Did you lose one?
It's supposed to be asymmetrical.
Very hip!
Barf.
JAIME!
Jon! This is my daughter, Aurora. Rory, Jon Loris.
Rory! I've heard so much about you!
God, I hope not.
Such a dry wit!
Inherited from Jaime, no doubt, indisputably the department comedian!
Ha ha, yeah, apple, tree, &c.
Rory, will you grab some food? I have budget stuff to go over with Jon.
As chair such dross is my albatross!

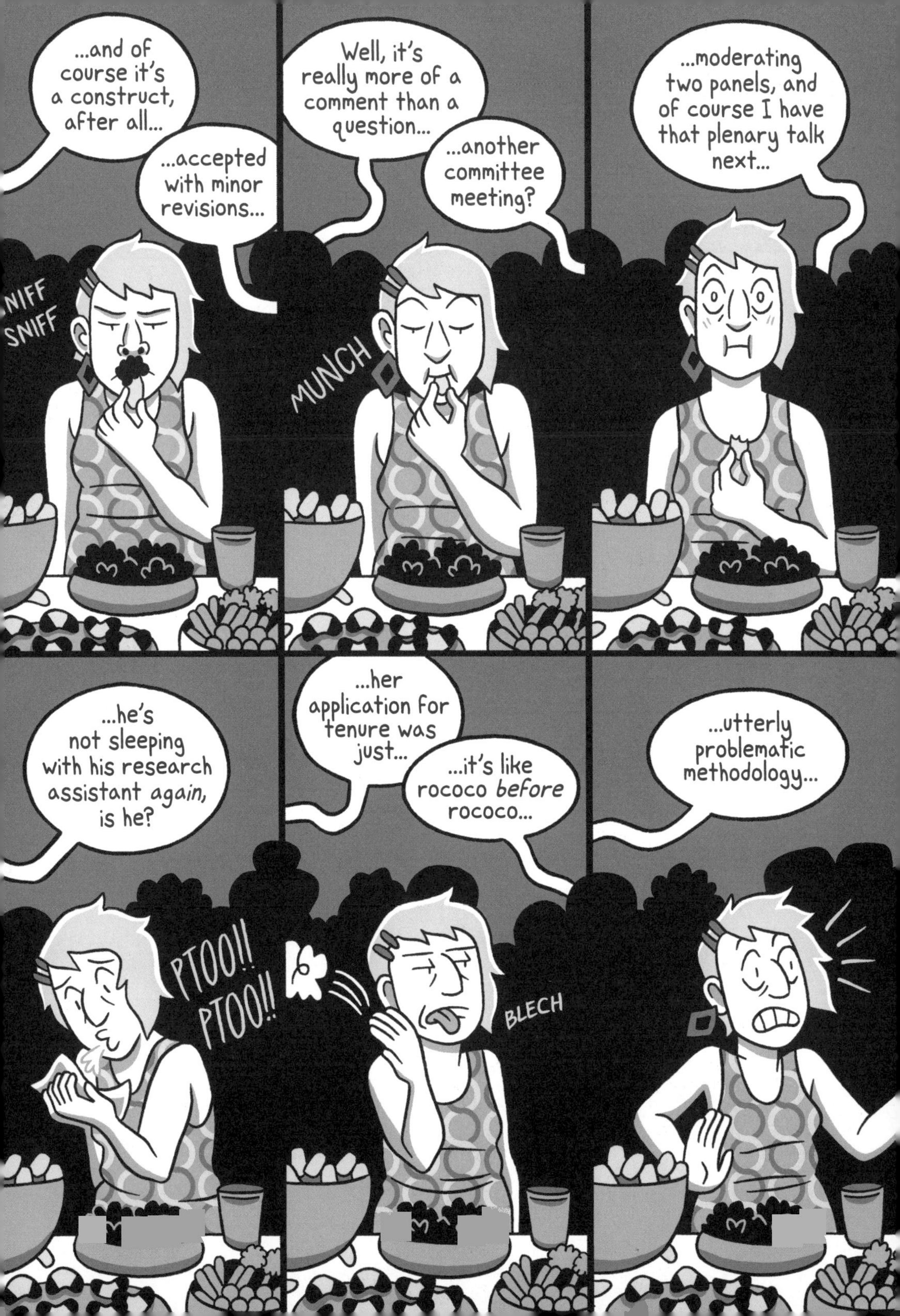
...and of course it's a construct, after all...
...accepted with minor revisions...
NIFF SNIFF
Well, it's really more of a comment than a question...
...another committee meeting?
MUNCH
...moderating two panels, and of course I have that plenary talk next...
...he's not sleeping with his research assistant *again*, is he?
PTOO!! PTOO!!
...her application for tenure was just...
...it's like rococo *before* rococo...
BLECH
...utterly problematic methodology...

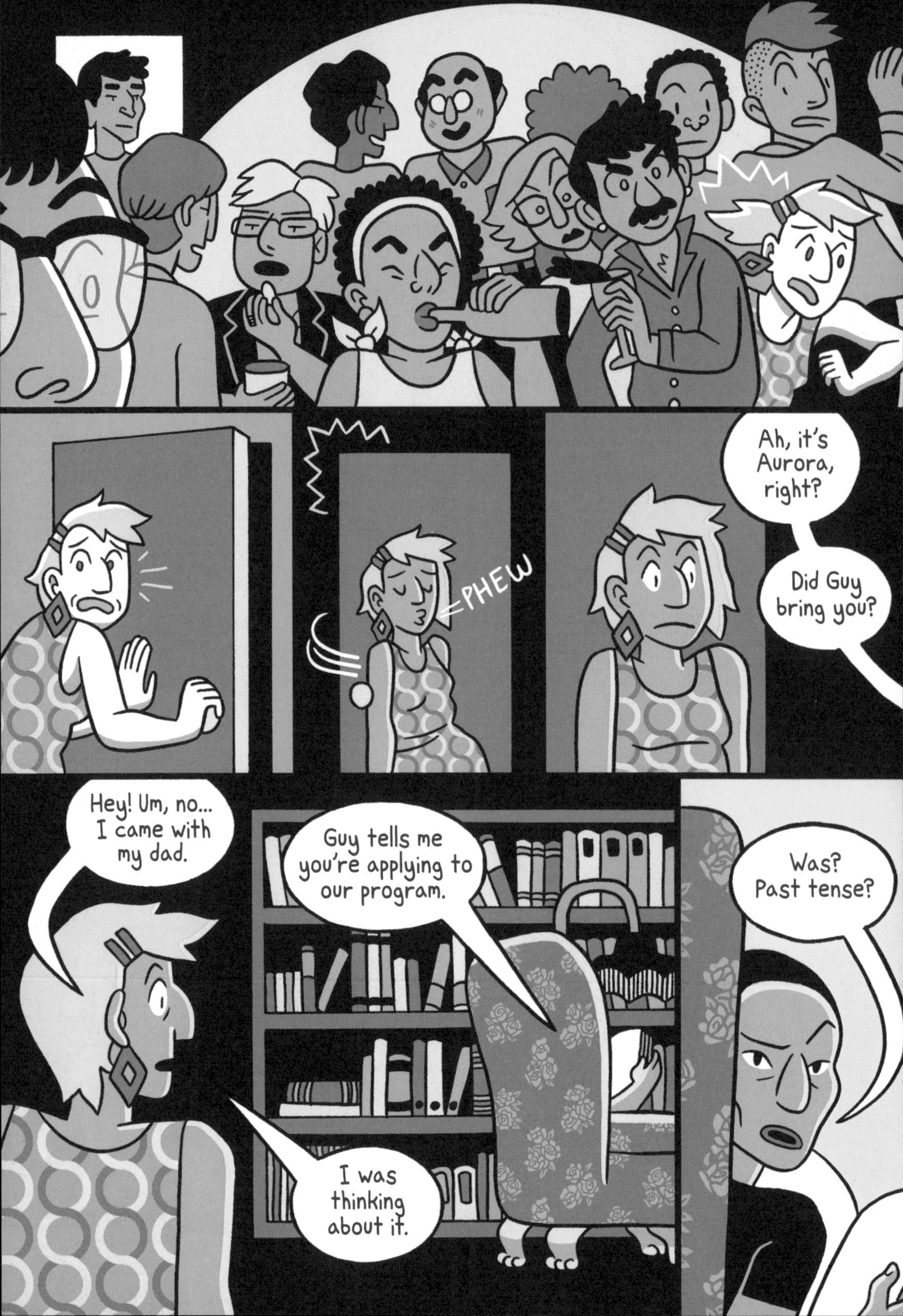

PHEW
Ah, it's Aurora, right?
Did Guy bring you?
Hey! Um, no... I came with my dad.
Guy tells me you're applying to our program.
I was thinking about it.
Was? Past tense?

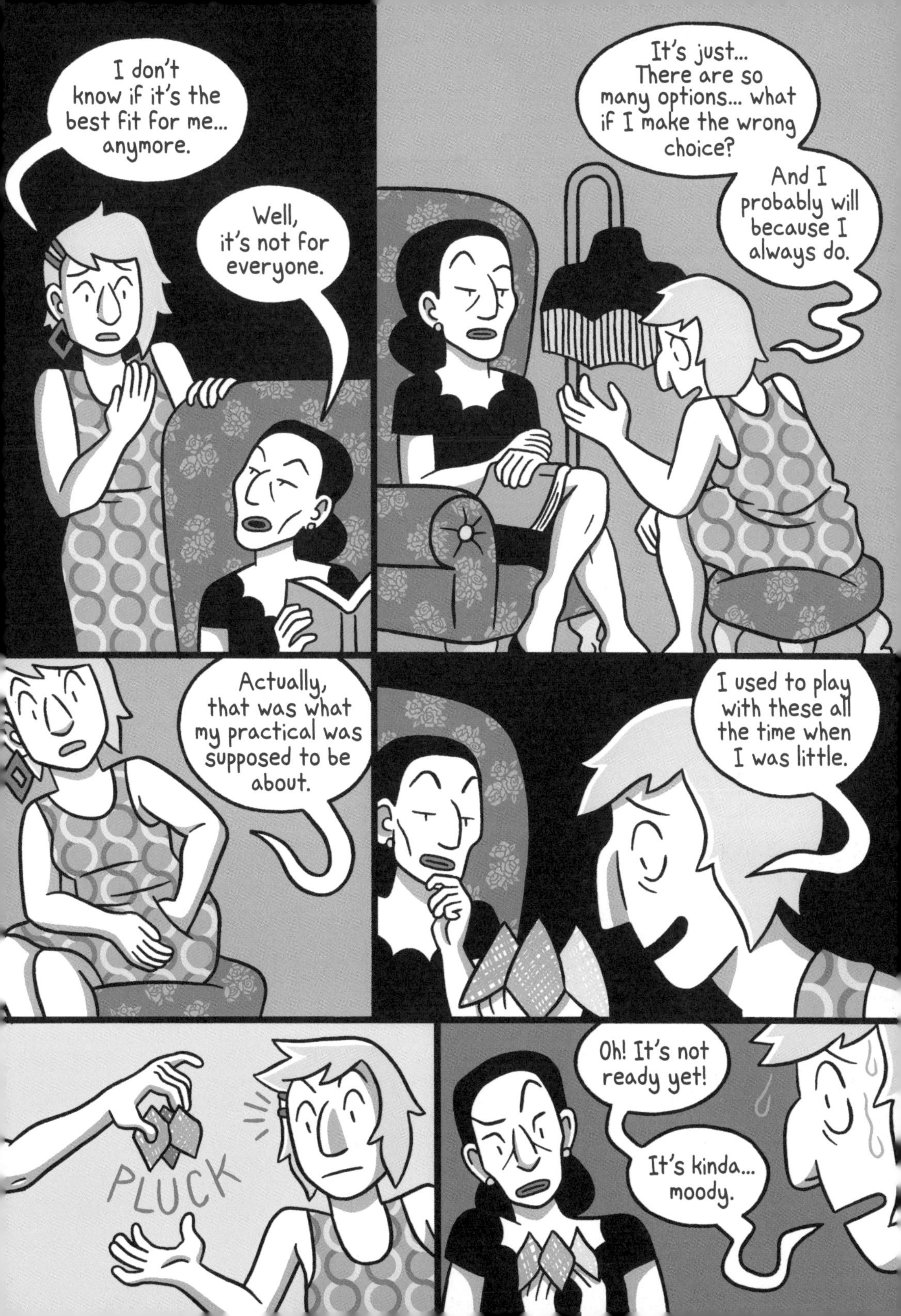
I don't know if it's the best fit for me... anymore.
Well, it's not for everyone.
It's just... There are so many options... what if I make the wrong choice?
And I probably will because I always do.
Actually, that was what my practical was supposed to be about.
I used to play with these all the time when I was little.
PLUCK
Oh! It's not ready yet!
It's kinda... moody.

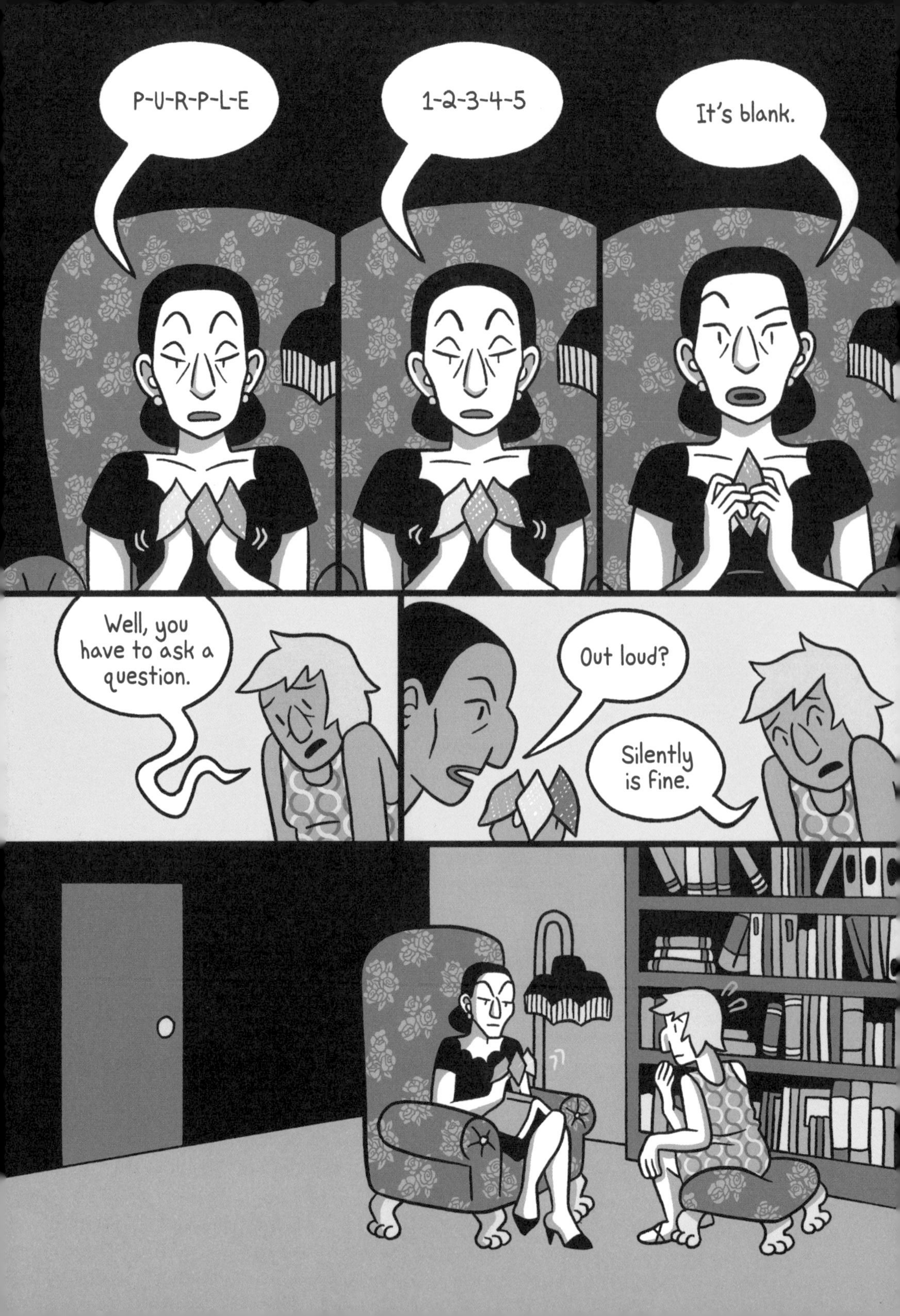
P-U-R-P-L-E
1-2-3-4-5
It's blank.
Well, you have to ask a question.
Out loud?
Silently is fine.

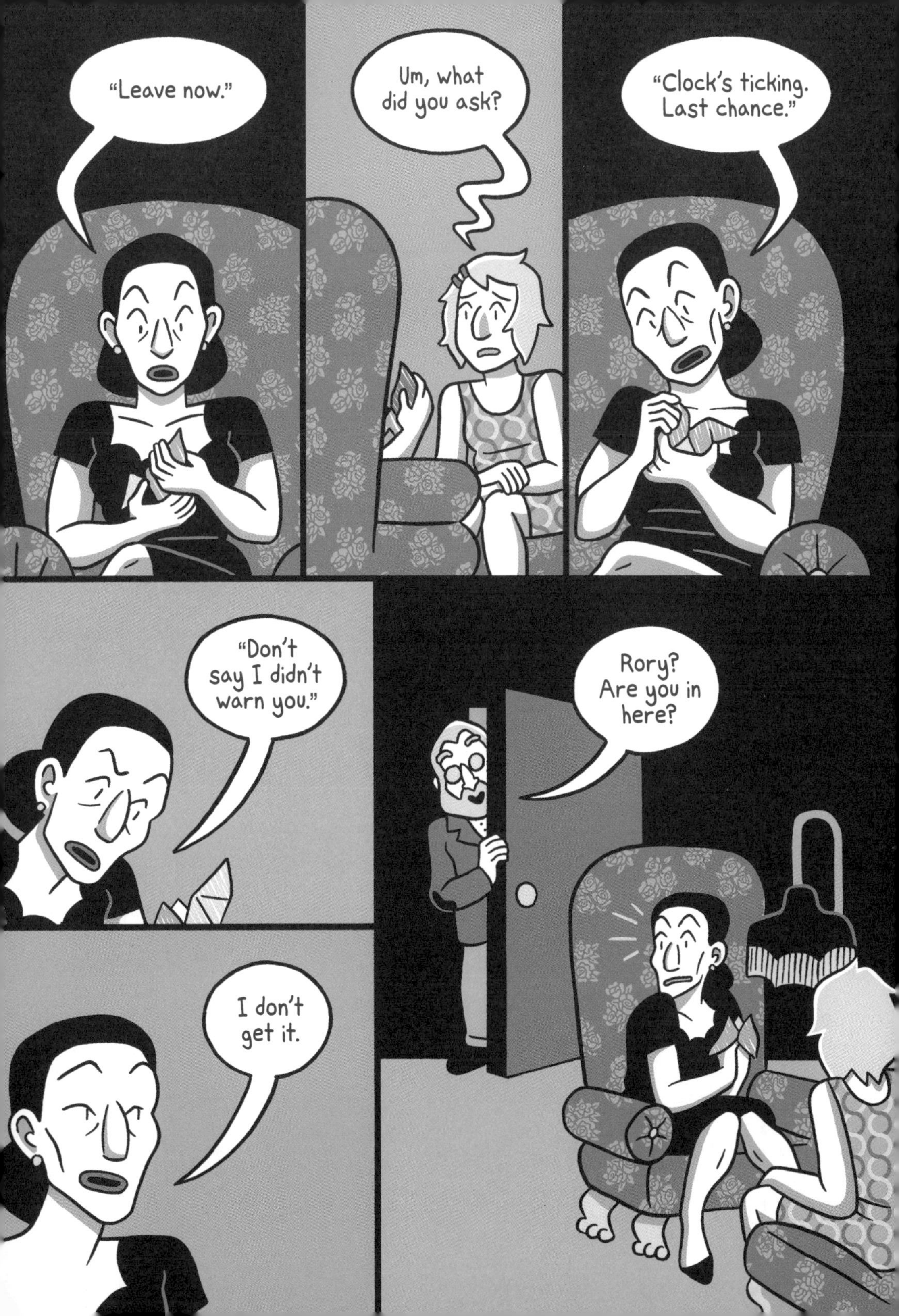
"Leave now."
Um, what did you ask?
"Clock's ticking. Last chance."
"Don't say I didn't warn you."
I don't get it.
Rory? Are you in here?

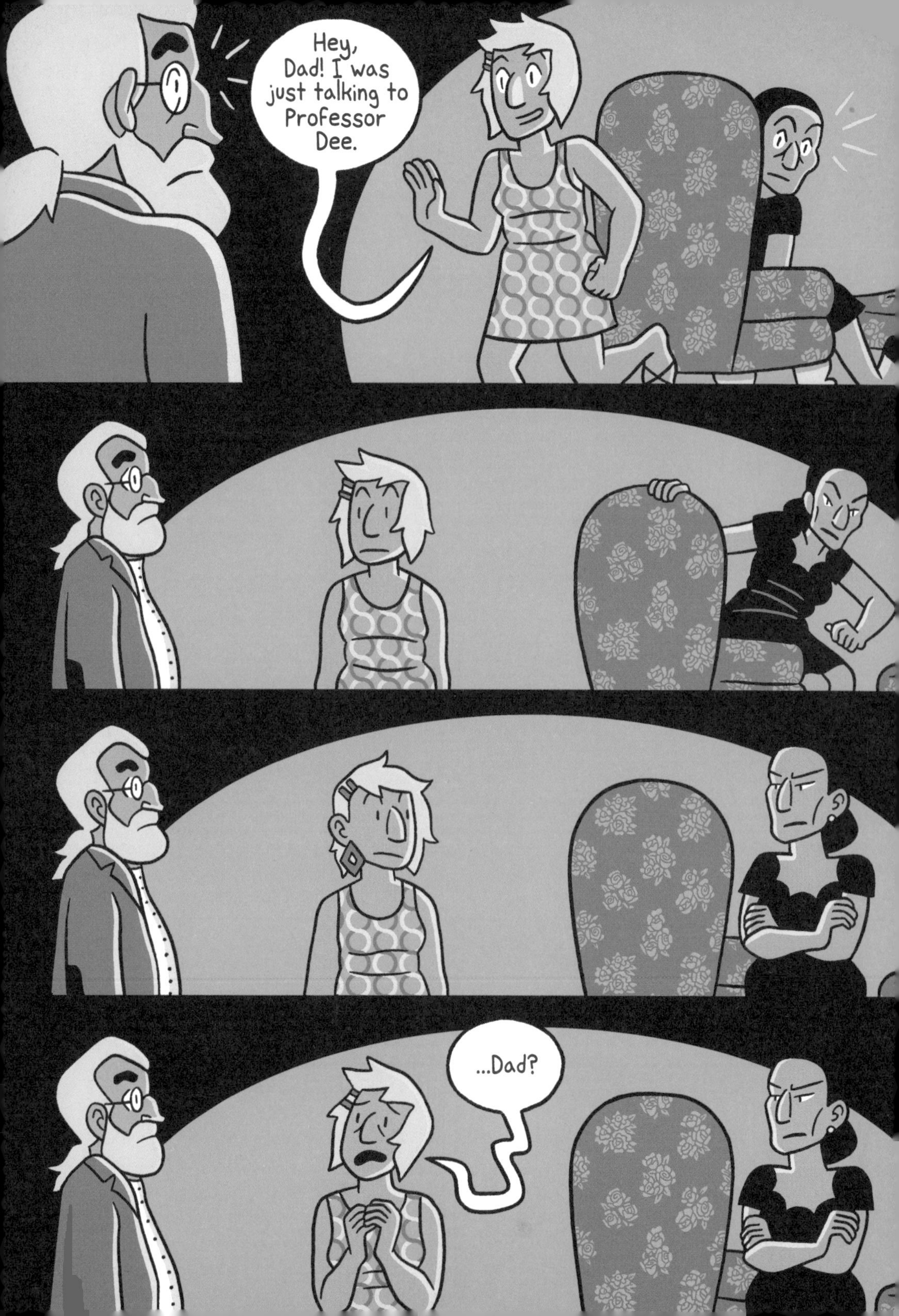
Hey, Dad! I was just talking to Professor Dee.
...Dad?

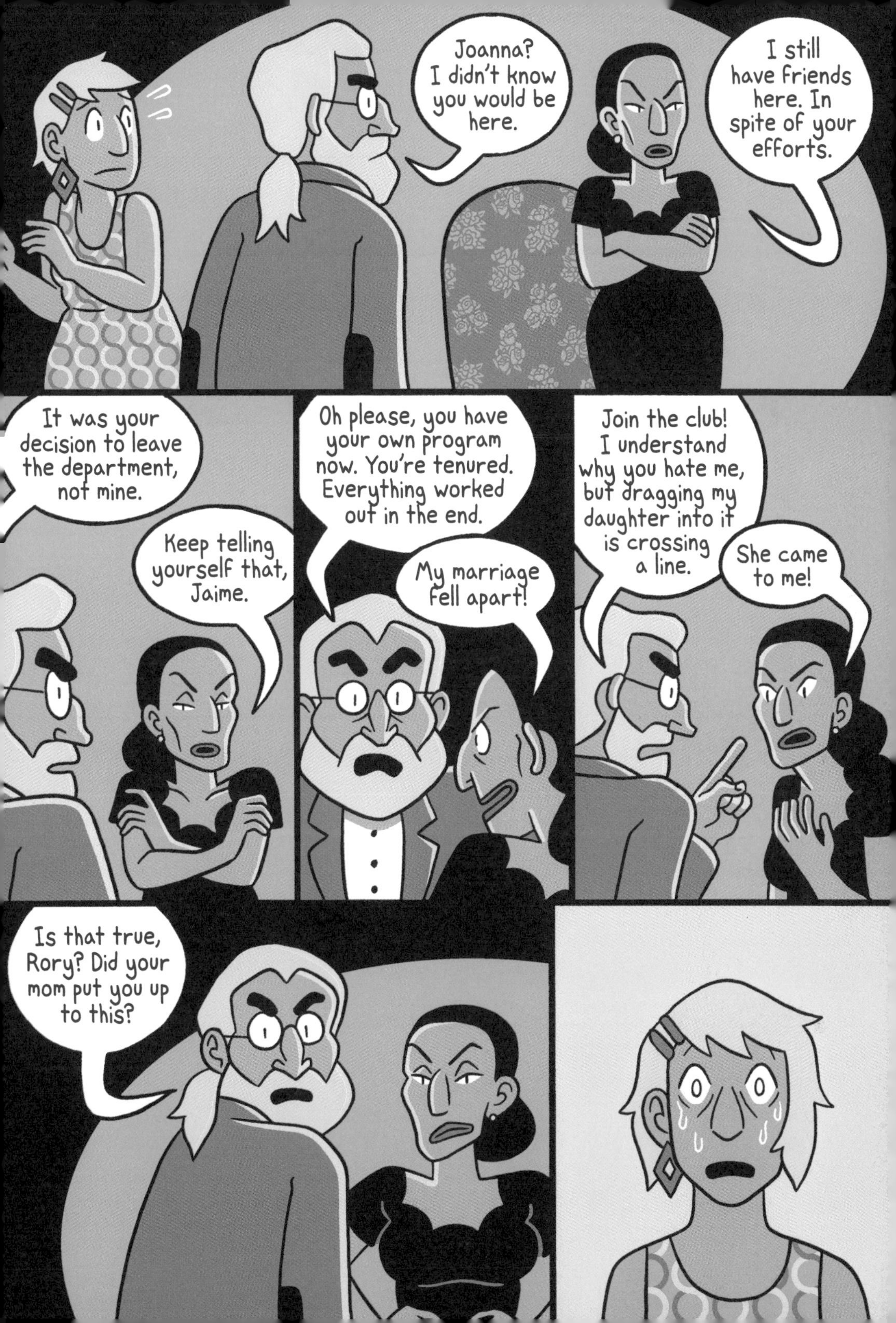
Joanna? I didn't know you would be here.
I still have friends here. In spite of your efforts.
It was your decision to leave the department, not mine.
Keep telling yourself that, Jaime.
Oh please, you have your own program now. You're tenured. Everything worked out in the end.
My marriage fell apart!
Join the club! I understand why you hate me, but dragging my daughter into it is crossing a line.
She came to me!
Is that true, Rory? Did your mom put you up to this?

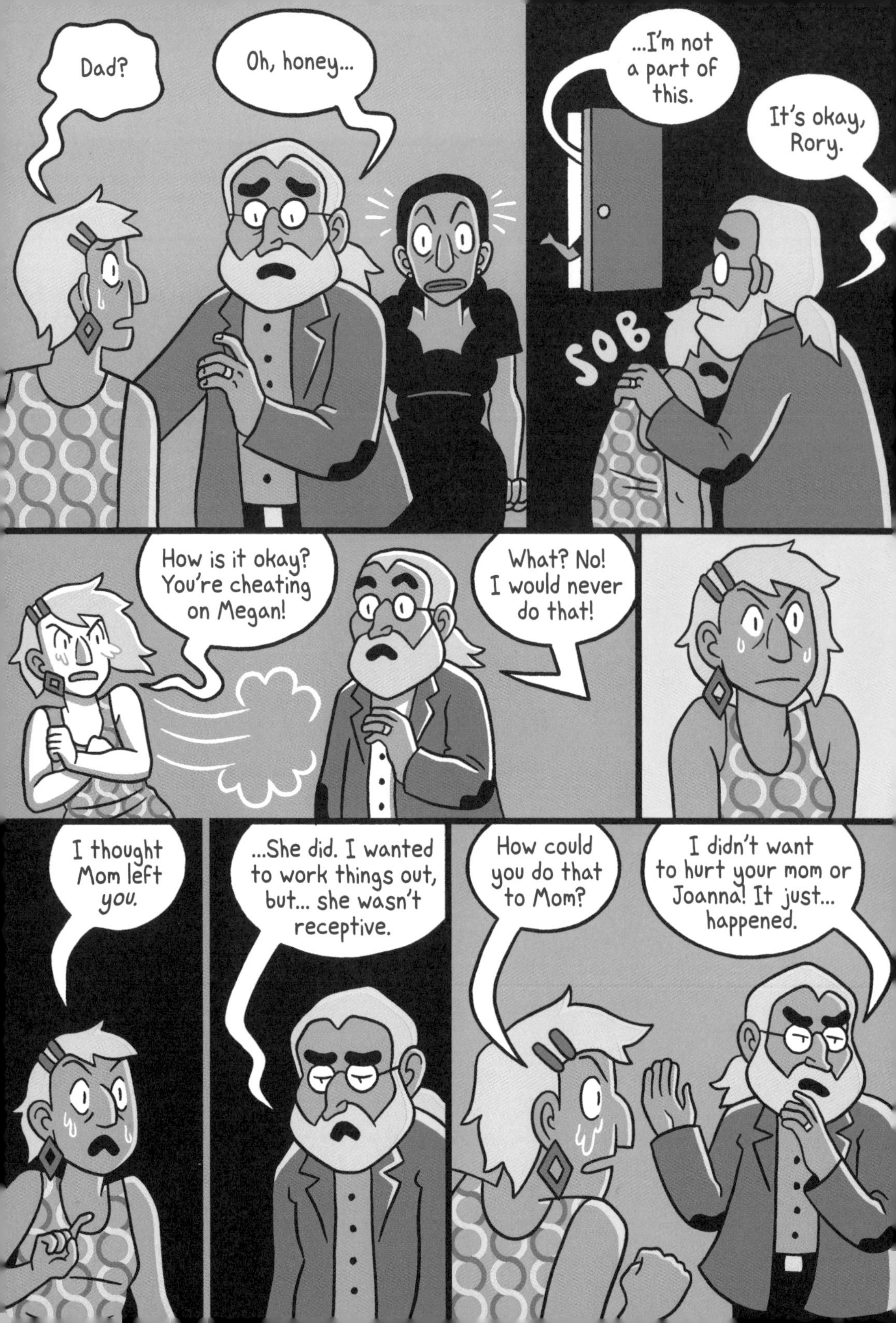
Dad?
Oh, honey...
...I'm not a part of this.
It's okay, Rory.
SOB
How is it okay? You're cheating on Megan!
What? No! I would never do that!
I thought Mom left *you.*
...She did. I wanted to work things out, but... she wasn't receptive.
How could you do that to Mom?
I didn't want to hurt your mom or Joanna! It just... happened.

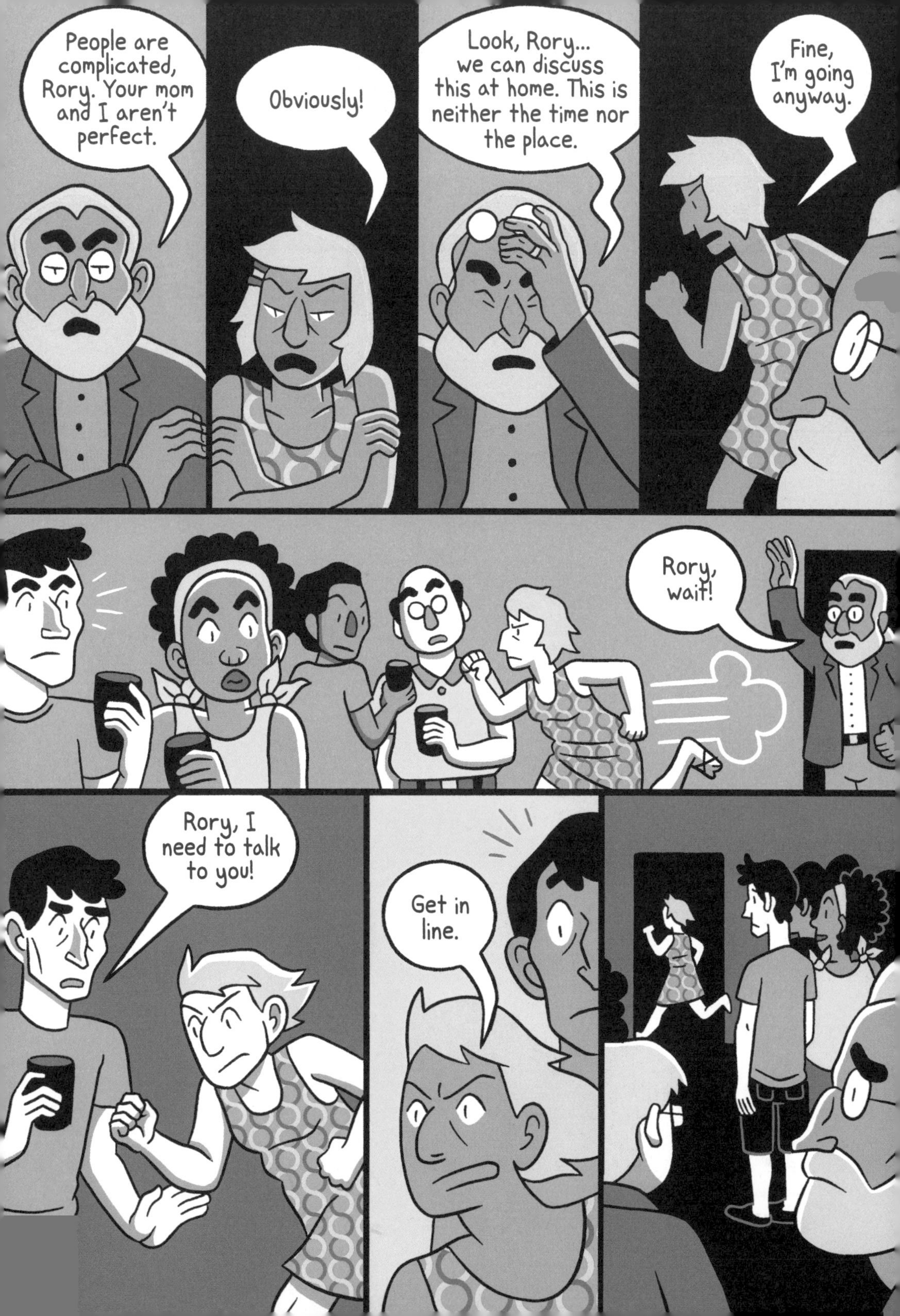
People are complicated, Rory. Your mom and I aren't perfect.
Obviously!
Look, Rory... we can discuss this at home. This is neither the time nor the place.
Fine, I'm going anyway.
Rory, wait!
Rory, I need to talk to you!
Get in line.

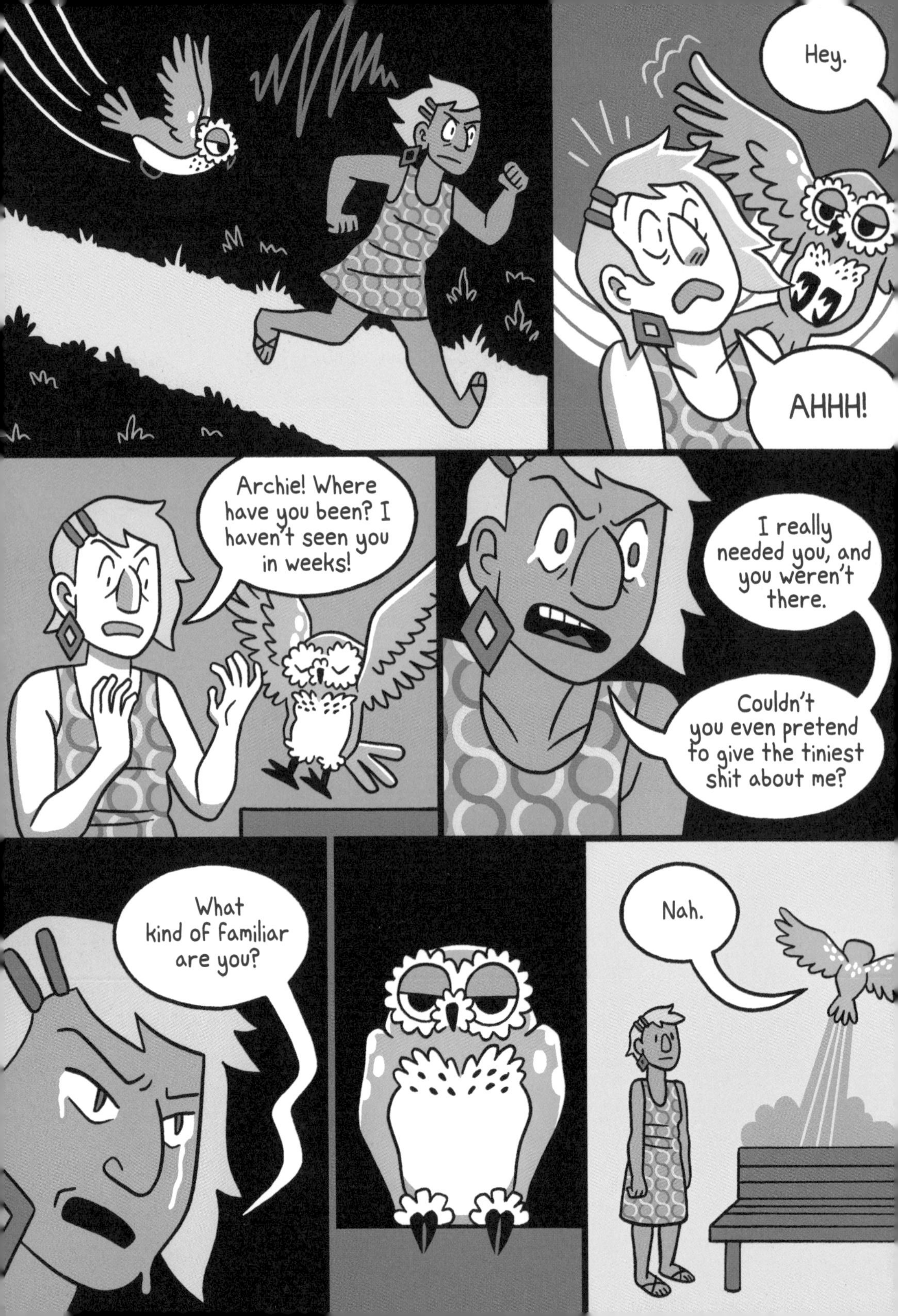
Hey.
AHHH!
Archie! Where have you been? I haven't seen you in weeks!
I really needed you, and you weren't there.
Couldn't you even pretend to give the tiniest shit about me?
What kind of familiar are you?
Nah.

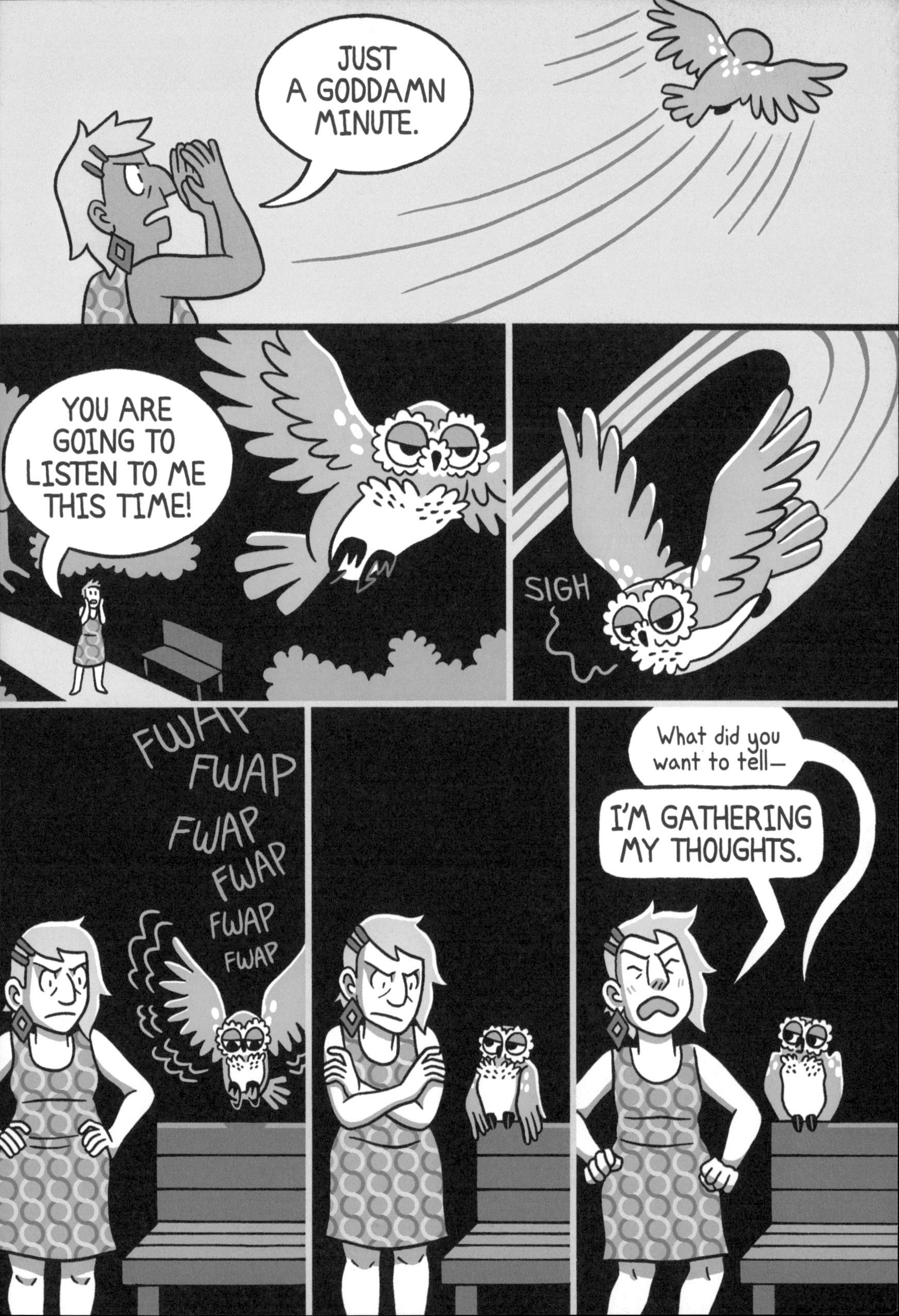
JUST A GODDAMN MINUTE.
YOU ARE GOING TO LISTEN TO ME THIS TIME!
SIGH
FWAP
FWAP
FWAP
FWAP
FWAP
FWAP
What did you want to tell—
I'M GATHERING MY THOUGHTS.

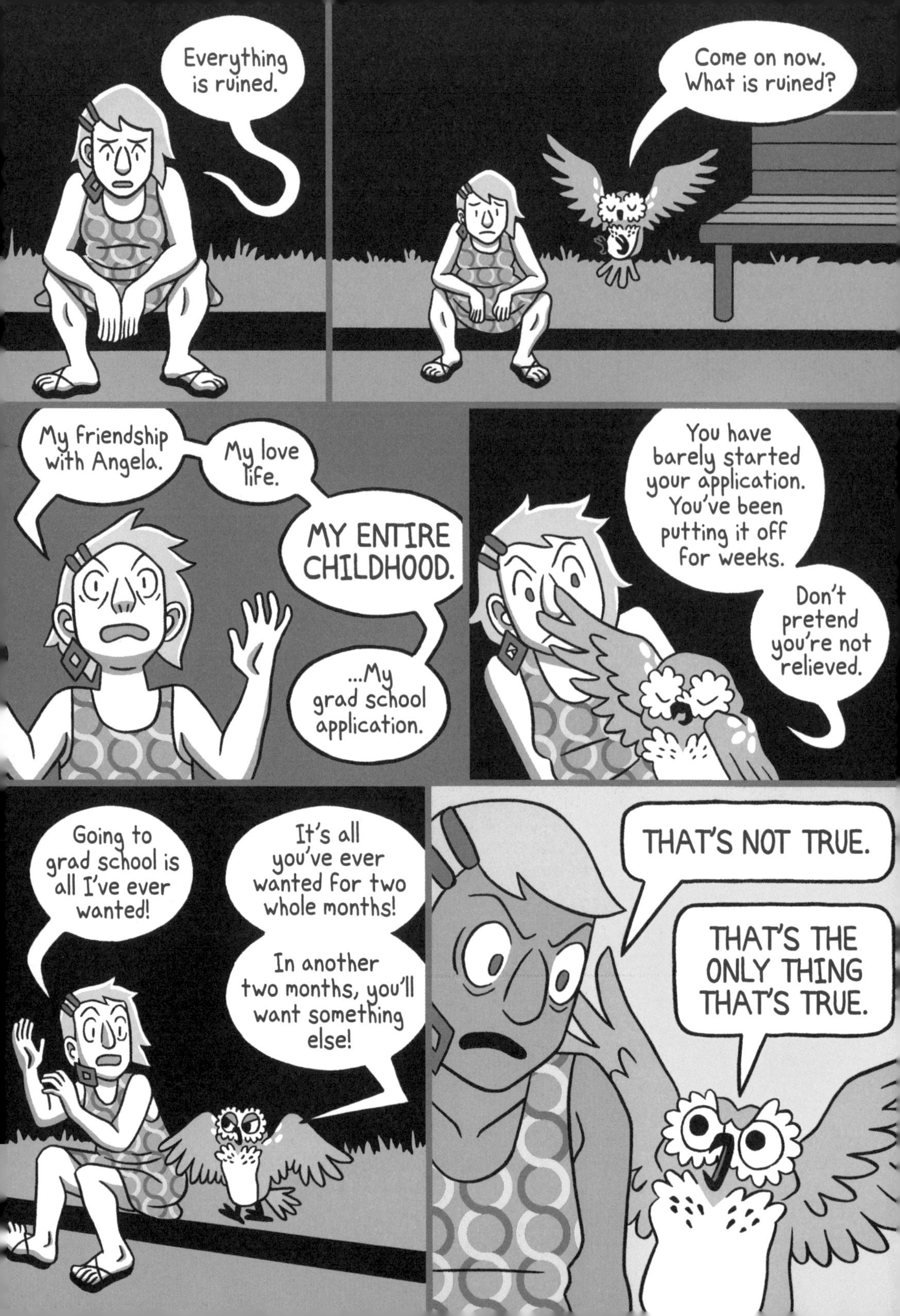
Everything is ruined.
Come on now. What is ruined?
My friendship with Angela.
My love life.
MY ENTIRE CHILDHOOD.
...My grad school application.
You have barely started your application. You've been putting it off for weeks.
Don't pretend you're not relieved.
Going to grad school is all I've ever wanted!
It's all you've ever wanted for two whole months!
In another two months, you'll want something else!
THAT'S NOT TRUE.
THAT'S THE ONLY THING THAT'S TRUE.

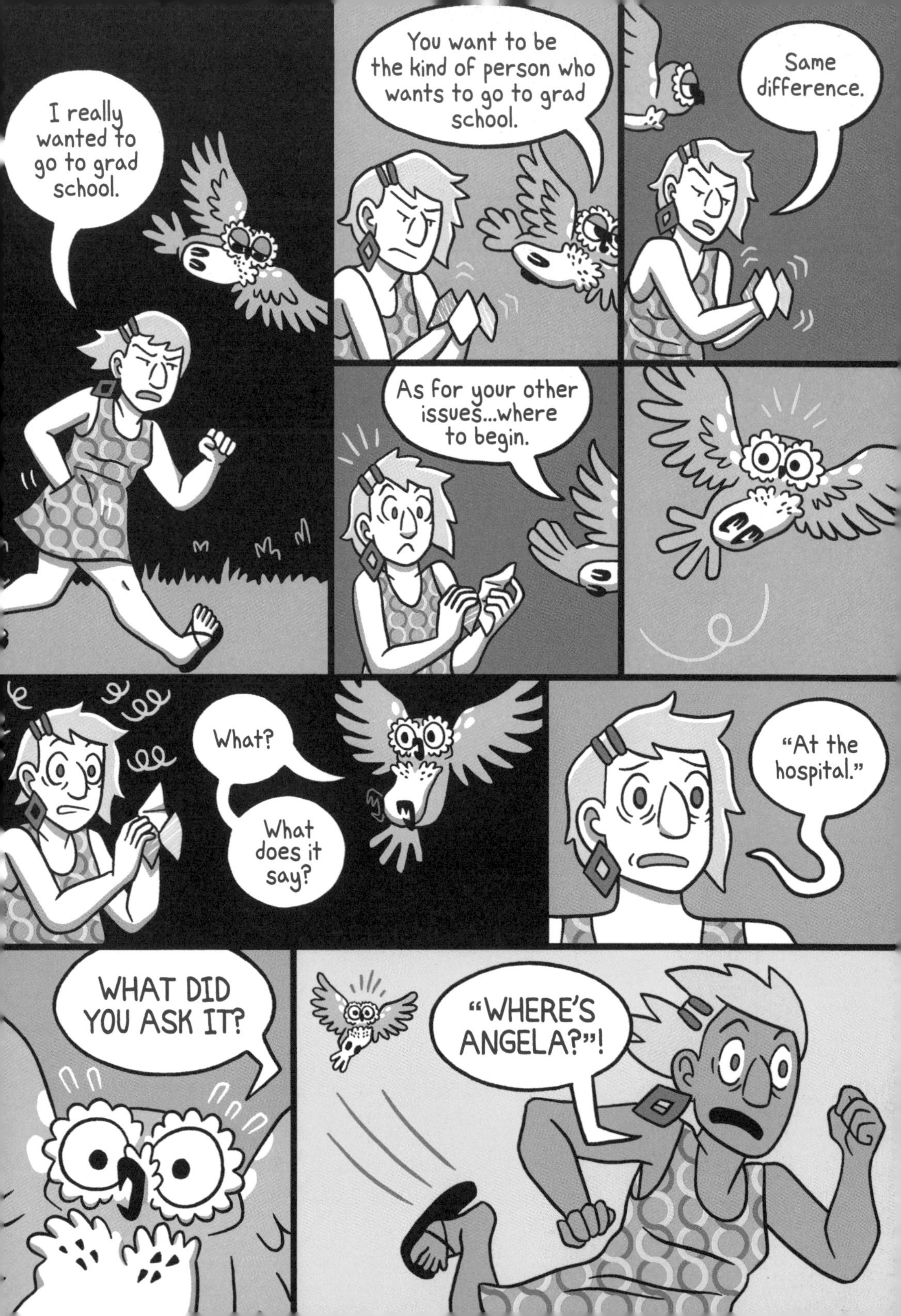
I really wanted to go to grad school.
You want to be the kind of person who wants to go to grad school.
Same difference.
As for your other issues...where to begin.
What?
What does it say?
"At the hospital."
WHAT DID YOU ASK IT?
"WHERE'S ANGELA?"!

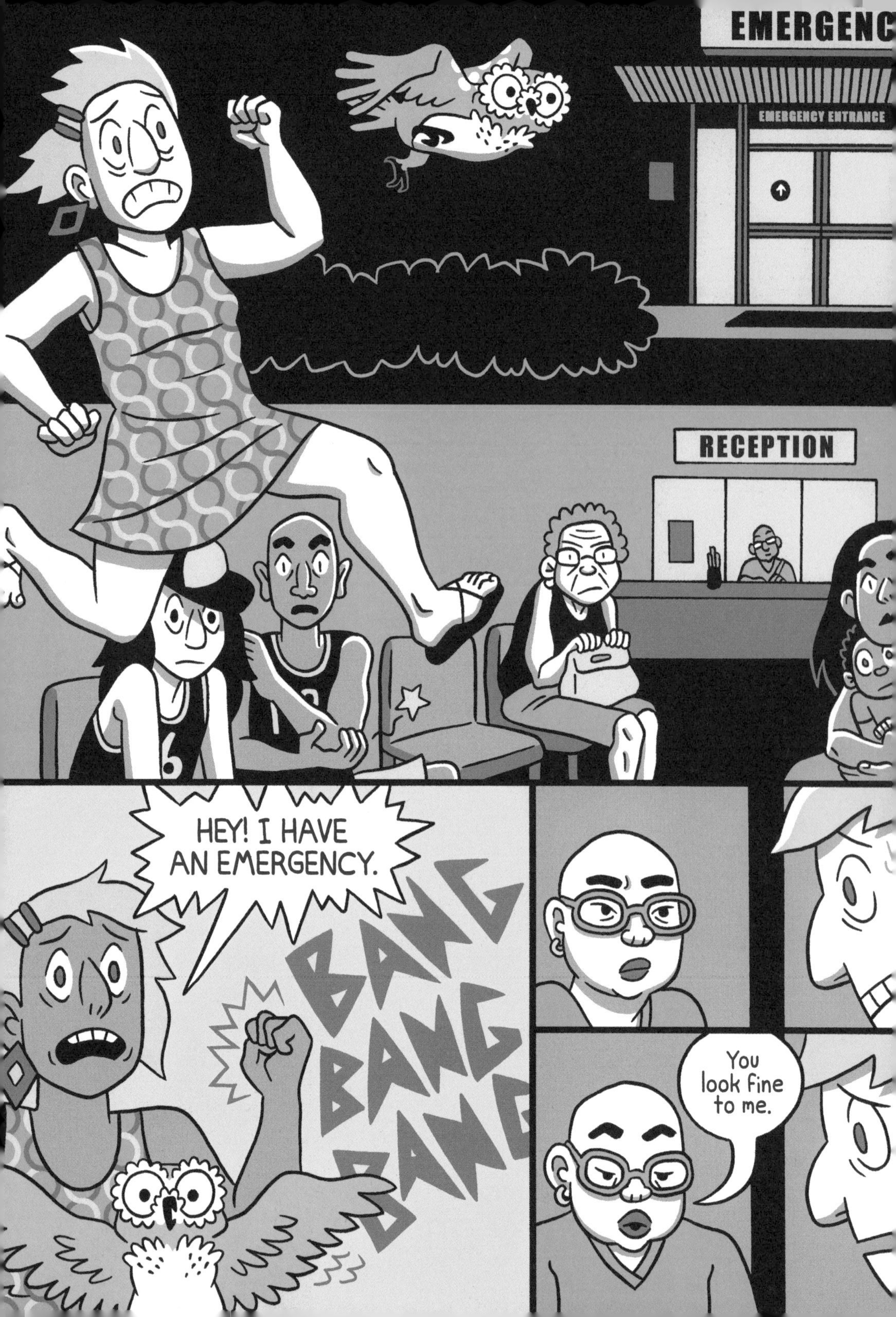
EMERGENC
EMERGENCY ENTRANCE
RECEPTION
HEY! I HAVE AN EMERGENCY.
BANG BANG BANG
You look fine to me.

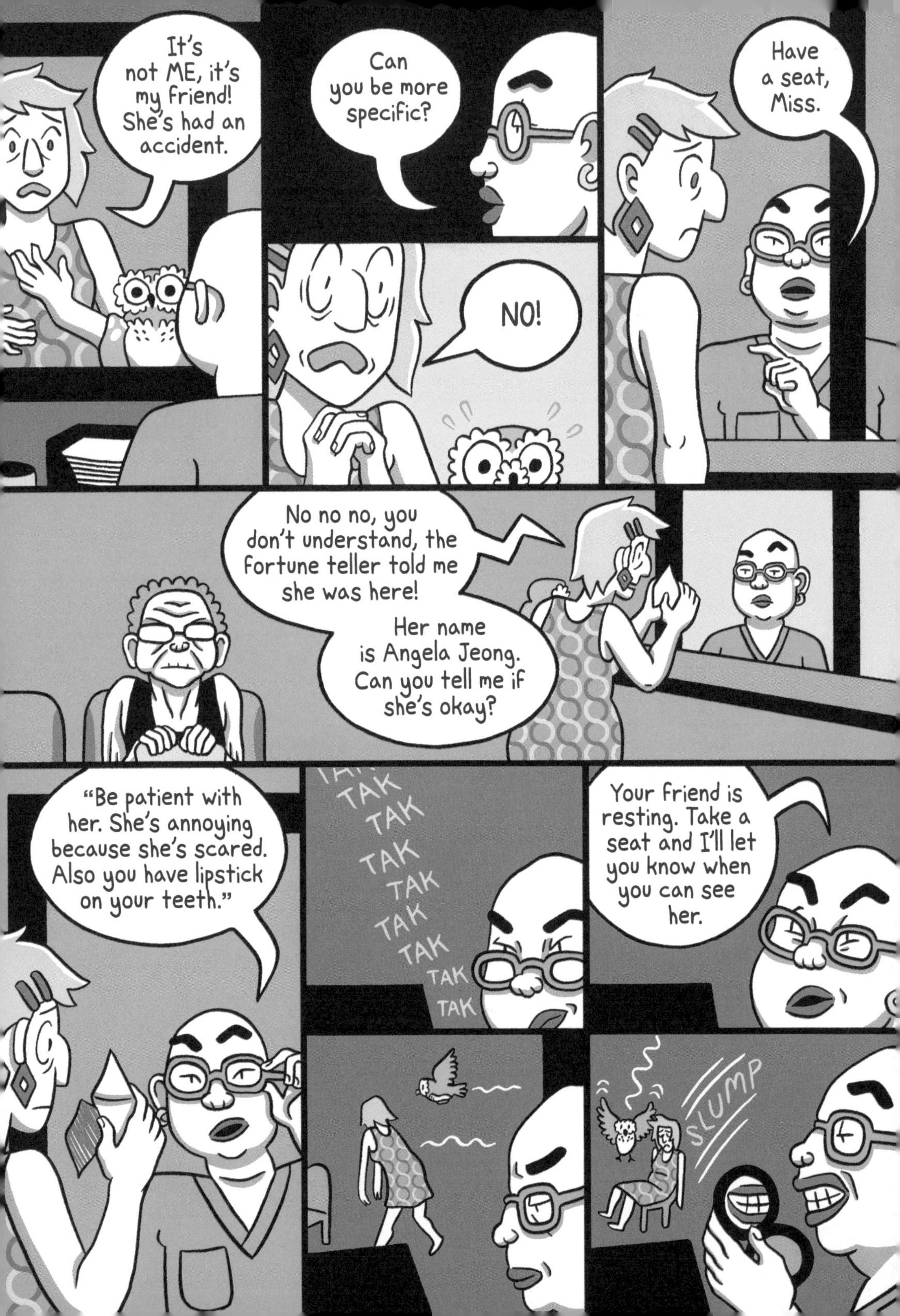

It's not ME, it's my friend! She's had an accident.
Can you be more specific?
NO!
Have a seat, Miss.
No no no, you don't understand, the fortune teller told me she was here!
Her name is Angela Jeong. Can you tell me if she's okay?
"Be patient with her. She's annoying because she's scared. Also you have lipstick on your teeth."
TAK TAK TAK TAK TAK TAK TAK TAK TAK
Your friend is resting. Take a seat and I'll let you know when you can see her.
SLUMP

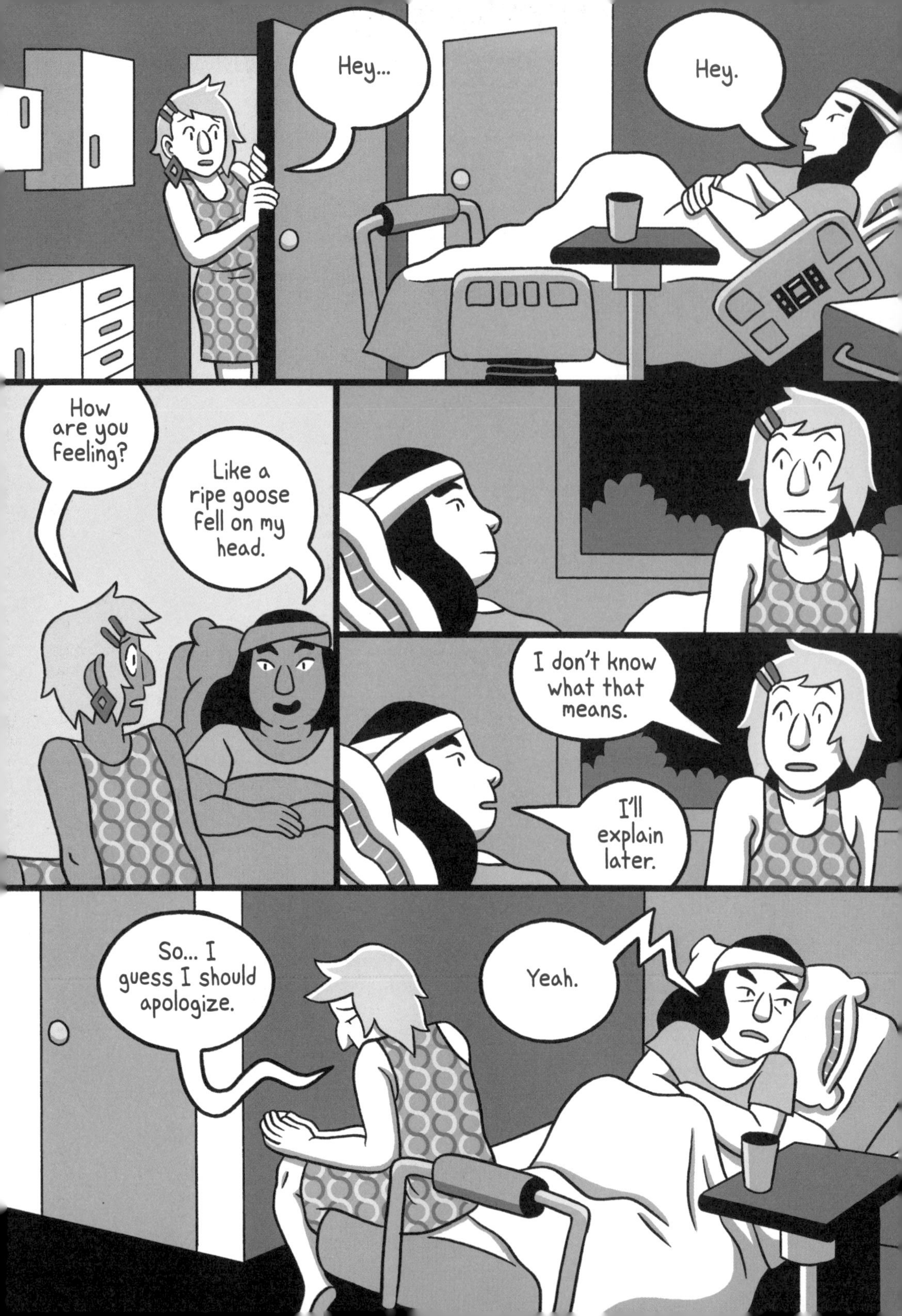
Hey...
Hey.
How are you feeling?
Like a ripe goose fell on my head.
I don't know what that means.
I'll explain later.
So... I guess I should apologize.
Yeah.

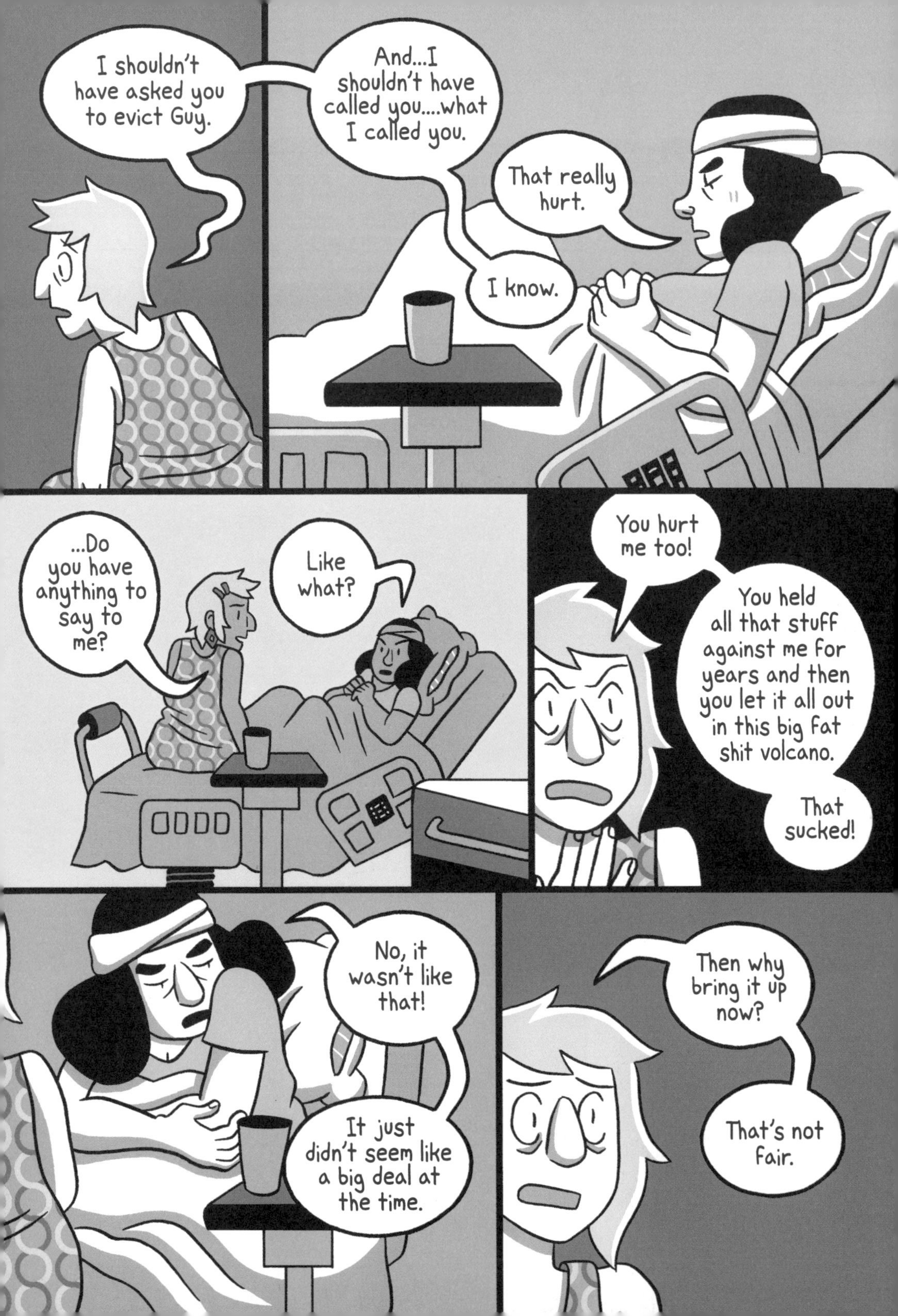
I shouldn't have asked you to evict Guy.
And...I shouldn't have called you....what I called you.
That really hurt.
I know.
...Do you have anything to say to me?
Like what?
You hurt me too!
You held all that stuff against me for years and then you let it all out in this big fat shit volcano.
That sucked!
No, it wasn't like that!
It just didn't seem like a big deal at the time.
Then why bring it up now?
That's not fair.

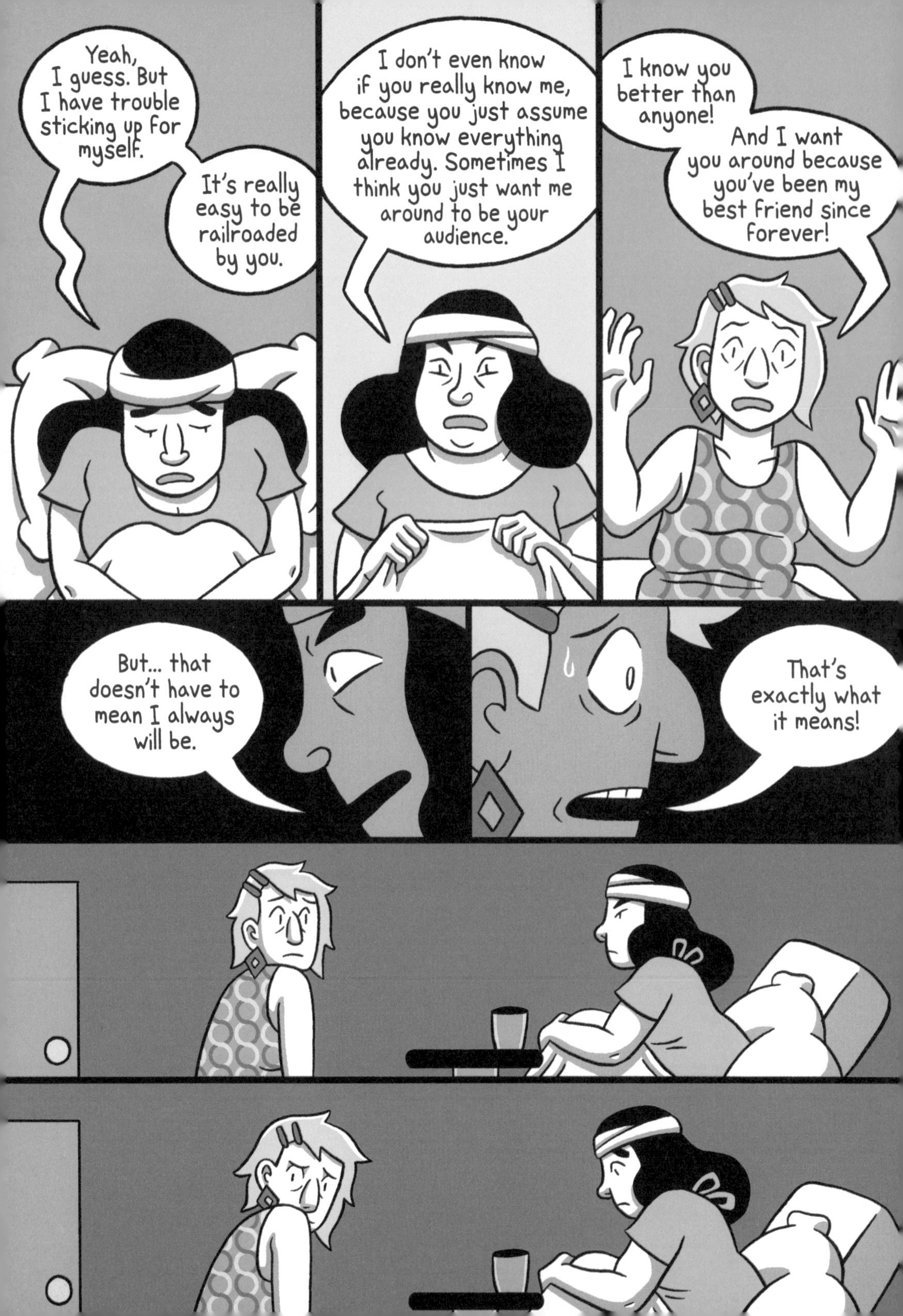
Yeah, I guess. But I have trouble sticking up for myself.
It's really easy to be railroaded by you.
I don't even know if you really know me, because you just assume you know everything already. Sometimes I think you just want me around to be your audience.
I know you better than anyone!
And I want you around because you've been my best friend since forever!
But... that doesn't have to mean I always will be.
That's exactly what it means!

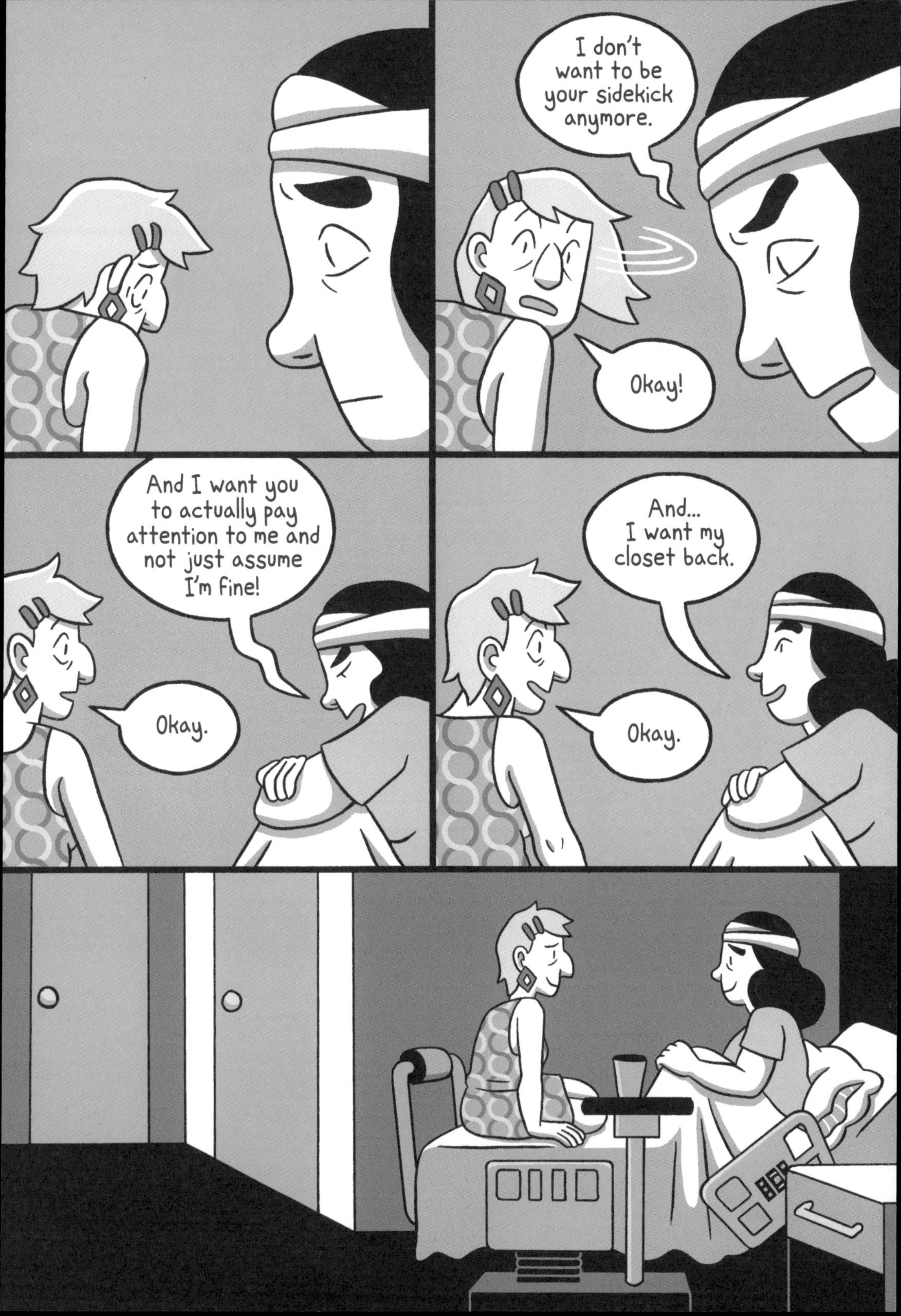
I don't want to be your sidekick anymore.
Okay!
And I want you to actually pay attention to me and not just assume I'm fine!
Okay.
And... I want my closet back.
Okay.

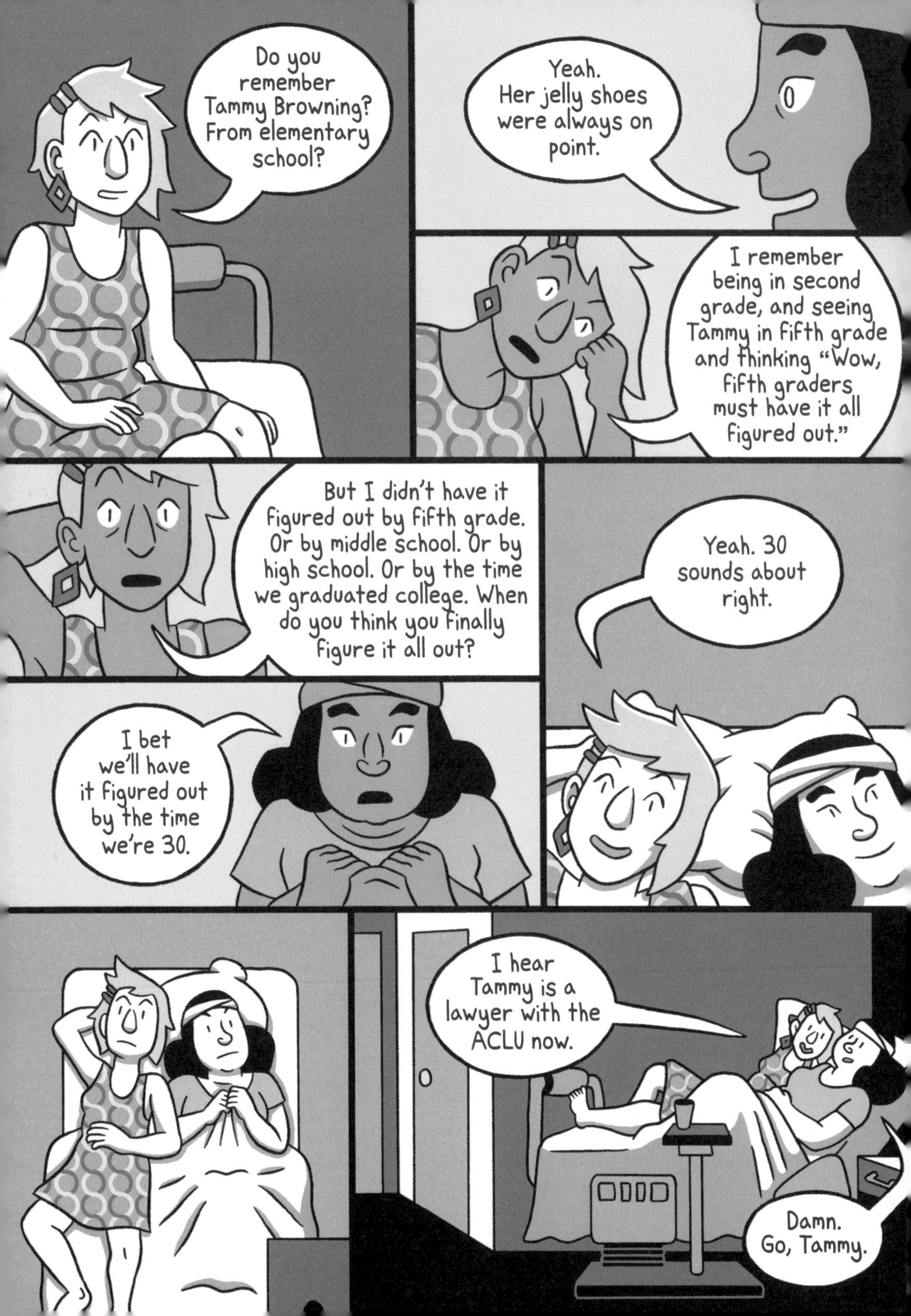
Do you remember Tammy Browning? From elementary school?
Yeah. Her jelly shoes were always on point.
I remember being in second grade, and seeing Tammy in fifth grade and thinking "Wow, fifth graders must have it all figured out."
But I didn't have it figured out by fifth grade. Or by middle school. Or by high school. Or by the time we graduated college. When do you think you finally figure it all out?
Yeah. 30 sounds about right.
I bet we'll have it figured out by the time we're 30.
I hear Tammy is a lawyer with the ACLU now.
Damn. Go, Tammy.

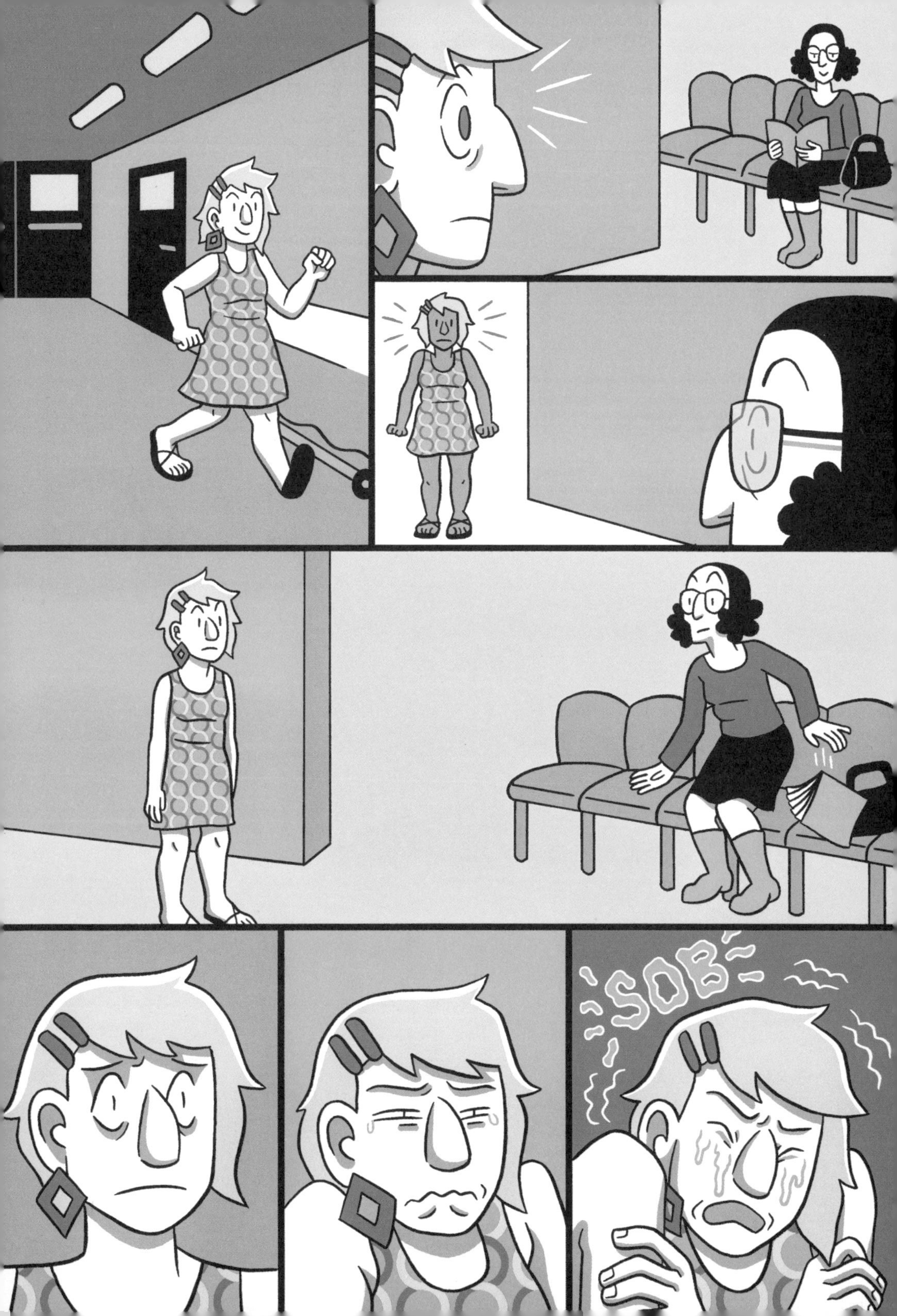
SOB

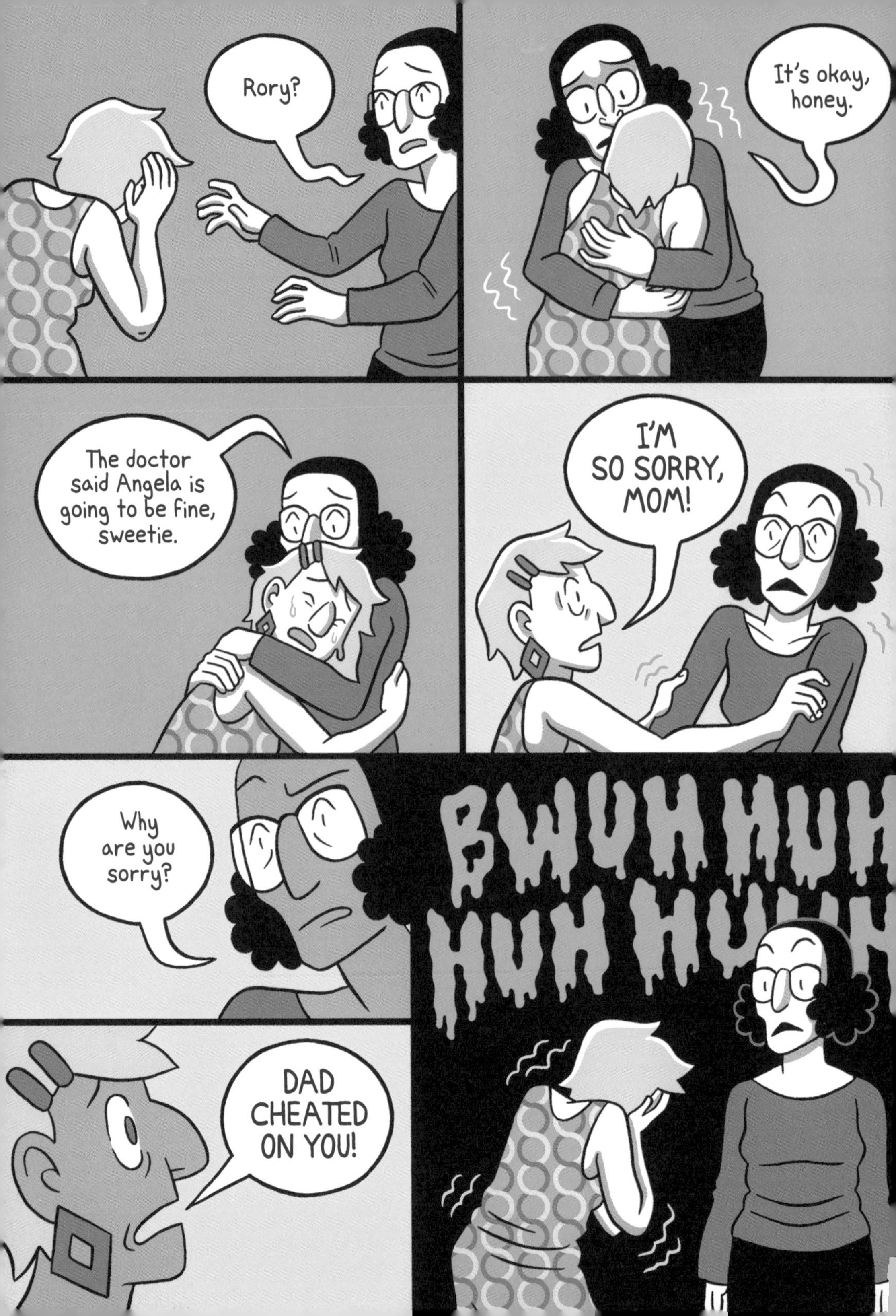
Rory?
It's okay, honey.
The doctor said Angela is going to be fine, sweetie.
I'M SO SORRY, MOM!
Why are you sorry?
DAD CHEATED ON YOU!
BWUH HUH HUH

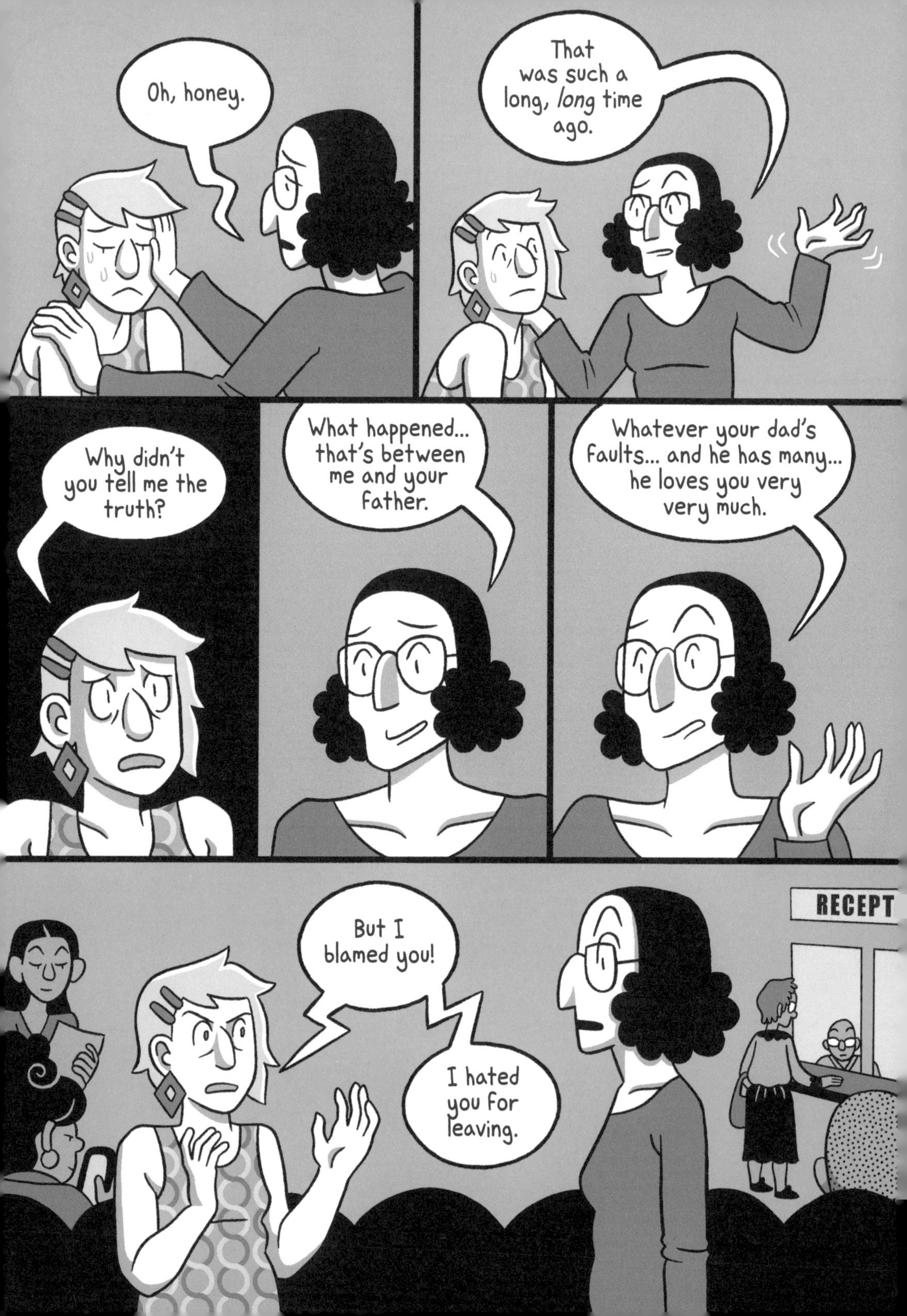
Oh, honey.
That was such a long, *long* time ago.
Why didn't you tell me the truth?
What happened... that's between me and your father.
Whatever your dad's faults... and he has many... he loves you very very much.
But I blamed you!
I hated you for leaving.
RECEPT

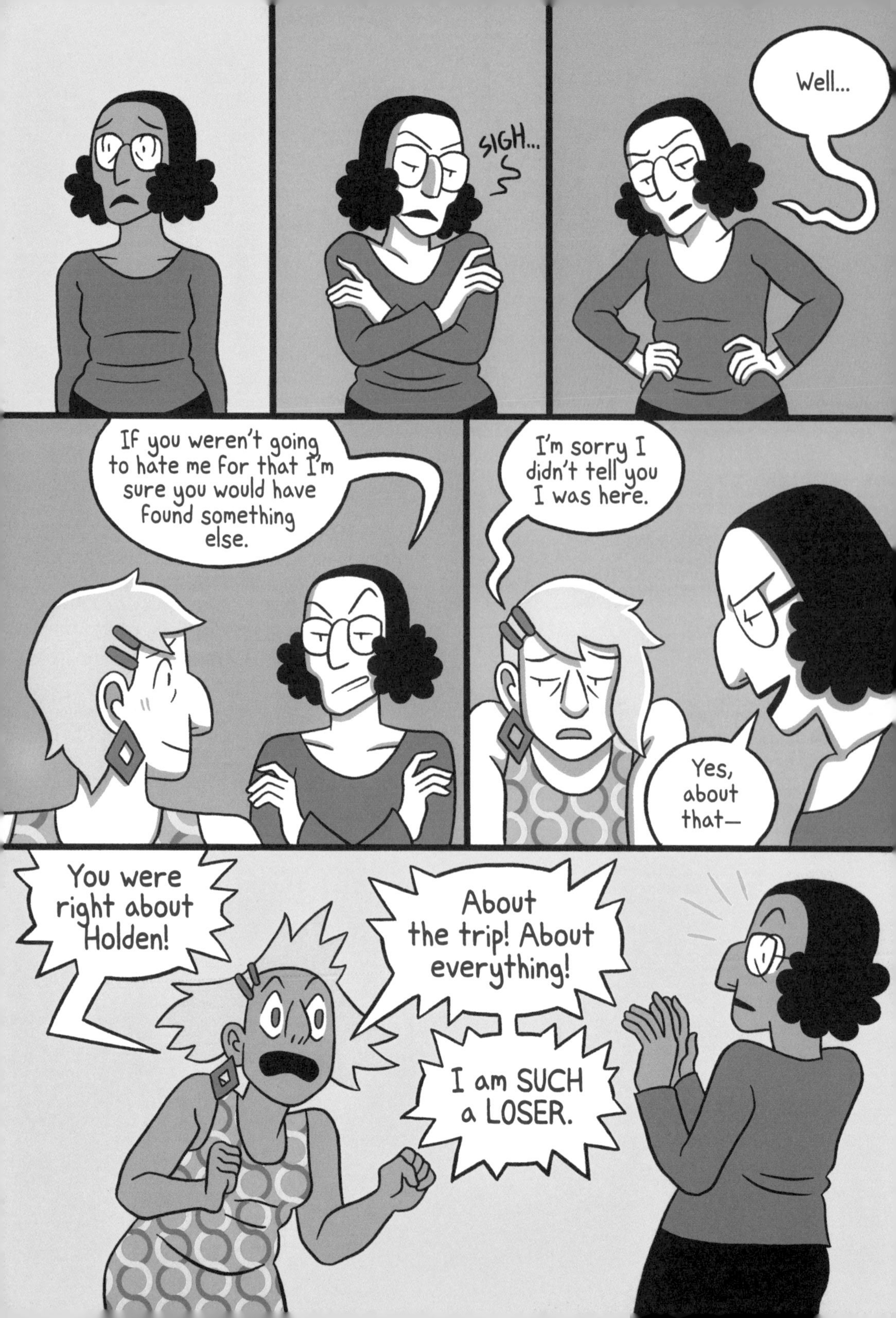
SIGH...
Well...
If you weren't going to hate me for that I'm sure you would have found something else.
I'm sorry I didn't tell you I was here.
Yes, about that—
You were right about Holden!
About the trip! About everything!
I am SUCH a LOSER.

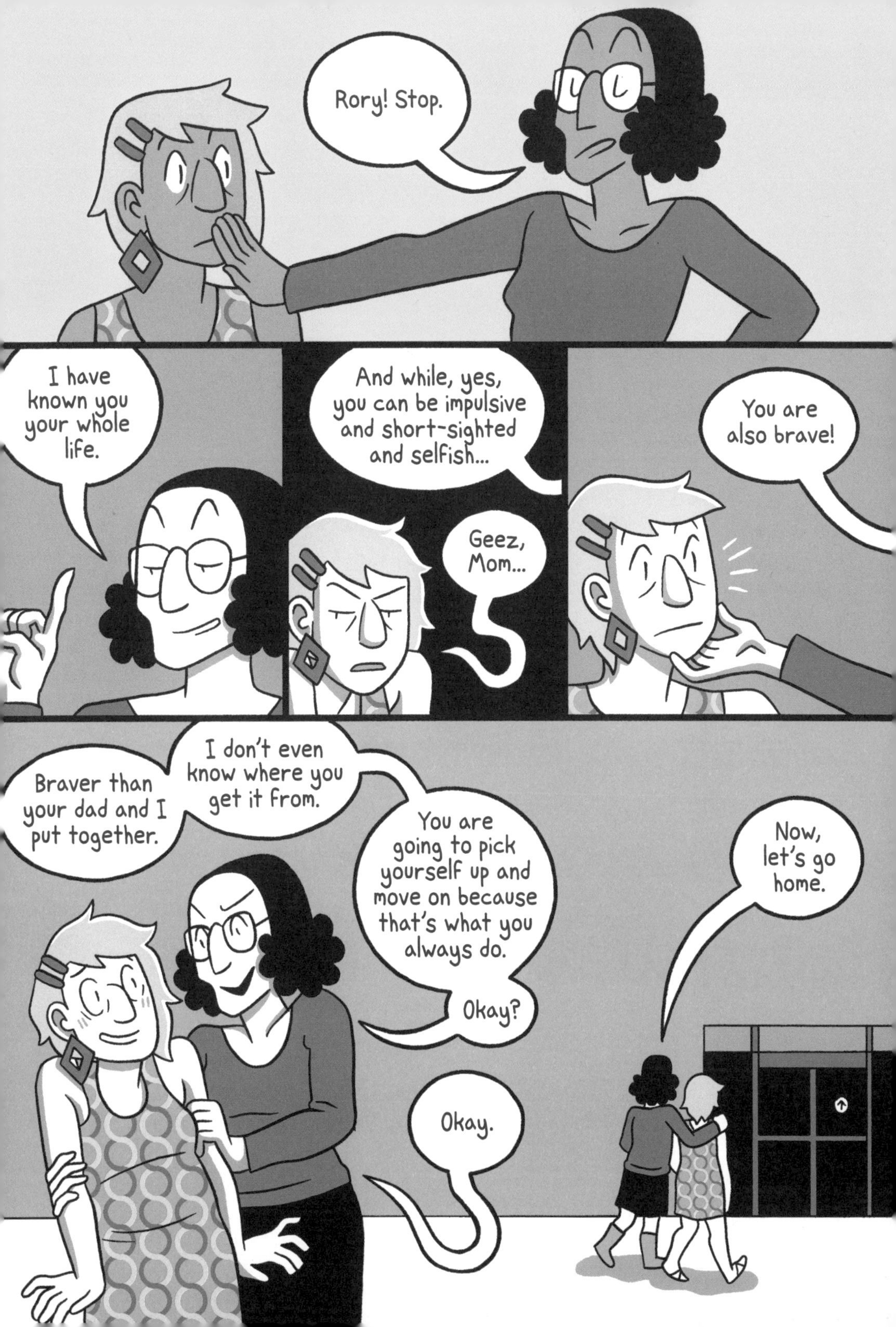

Rory! Stop.
I have known you your whole life.
And while, yes, you can be impulsive and short-sighted and selfish...
Geez, Mom...
You are also brave!
Braver than your dad and I put together.
I don't even know where you get it from.
You are going to pick yourself up and move on because that's what you always do.
Okay?
Okay.
Now, let's go home.

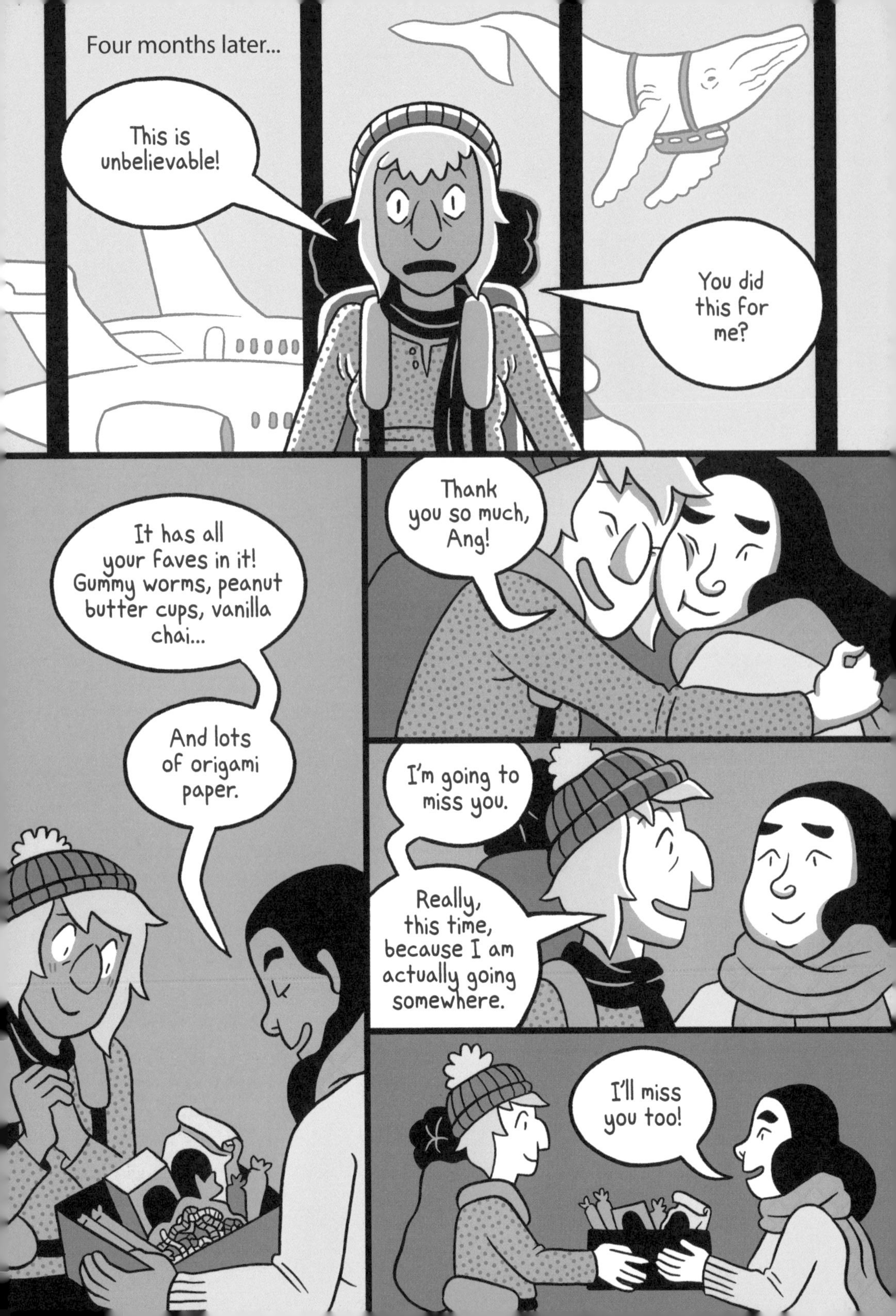
Four months later...
This is unbelievable!
You did this for me?
It has all your faves in it! Gummy worms, peanut butter cups, vanilla chai...
And lots of origami paper.
Thank you so much, Ang!
I'm going to miss you.
Really, this time, because I am actually going somewhere.
I'll miss you too!

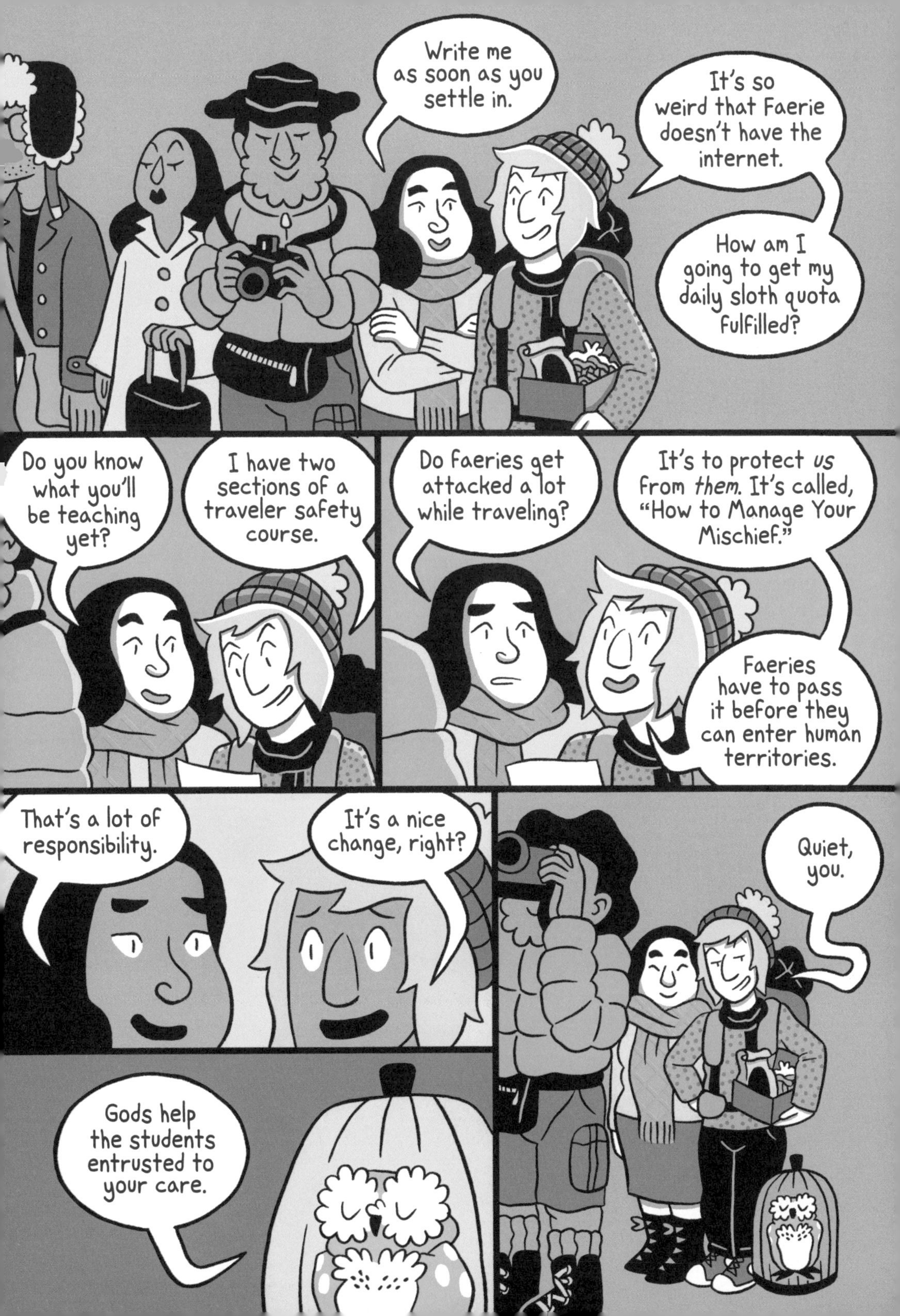
Write me as soon as you settle in.
It's so weird that Faerie doesn't have the internet.
How am I going to get my daily sloth quota fulfilled?
Do you know what you'll be teaching yet?
I have two sections of a traveler safety course.
Do faeries get attacked a lot while traveling?
It's to protect *us* from *them*. It's called, "How to Manage Your Mischief."
Faeries have to pass it before they can enter human territories.
That's a lot of responsibility.
It's a nice change, right?
Gods help the students entrusted to your care.
Quiet, you.

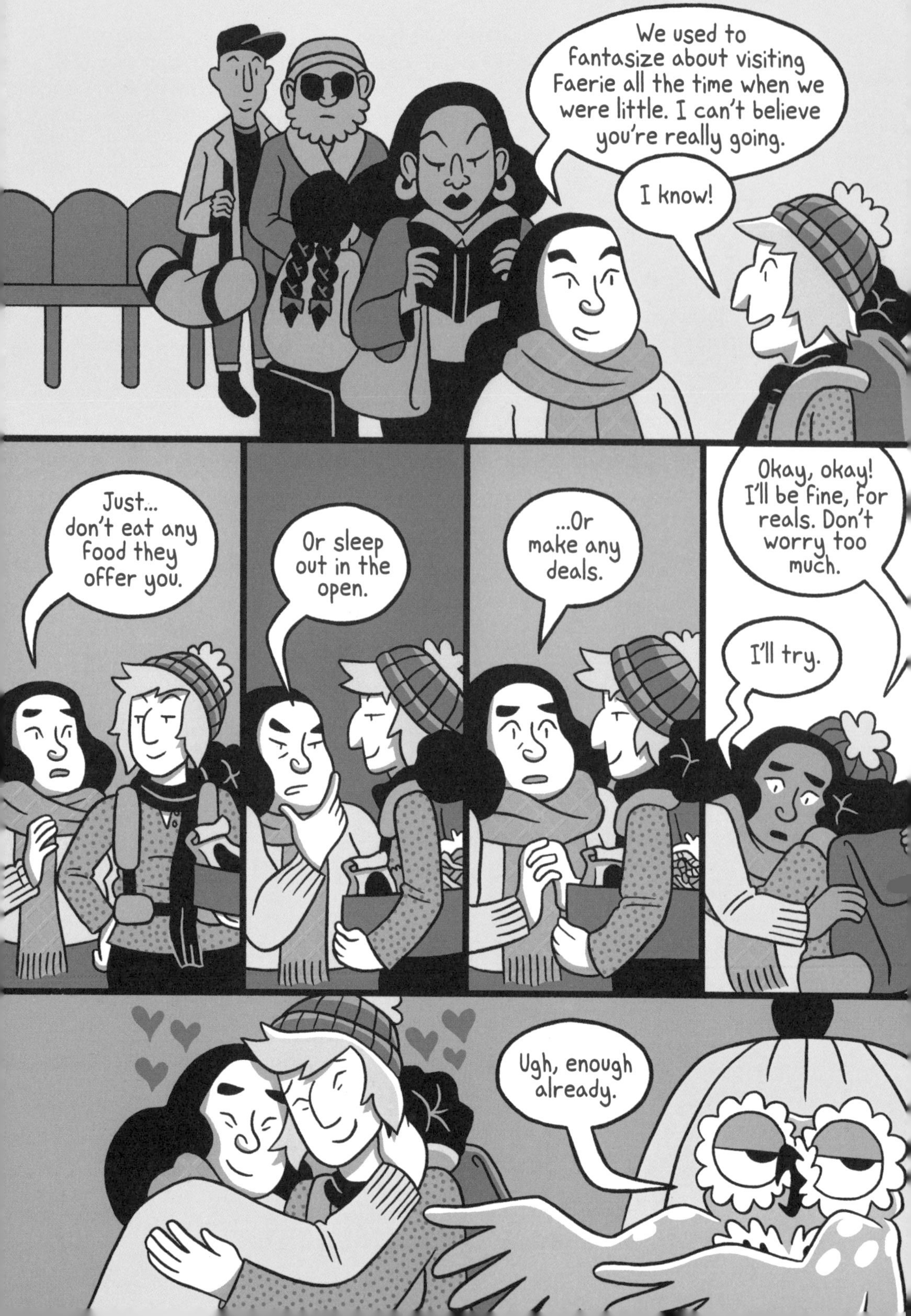
We used to fantasize about visiting Faerie all the time when we were little. I can't believe you're really going.
I know!
Just... don't eat any food they offer you.
Or sleep out in the open.
...Or make any deals.
Okay, okay! I'll be fine, for reals. Don't worry too much.
I'll try.
Ugh, enough already.

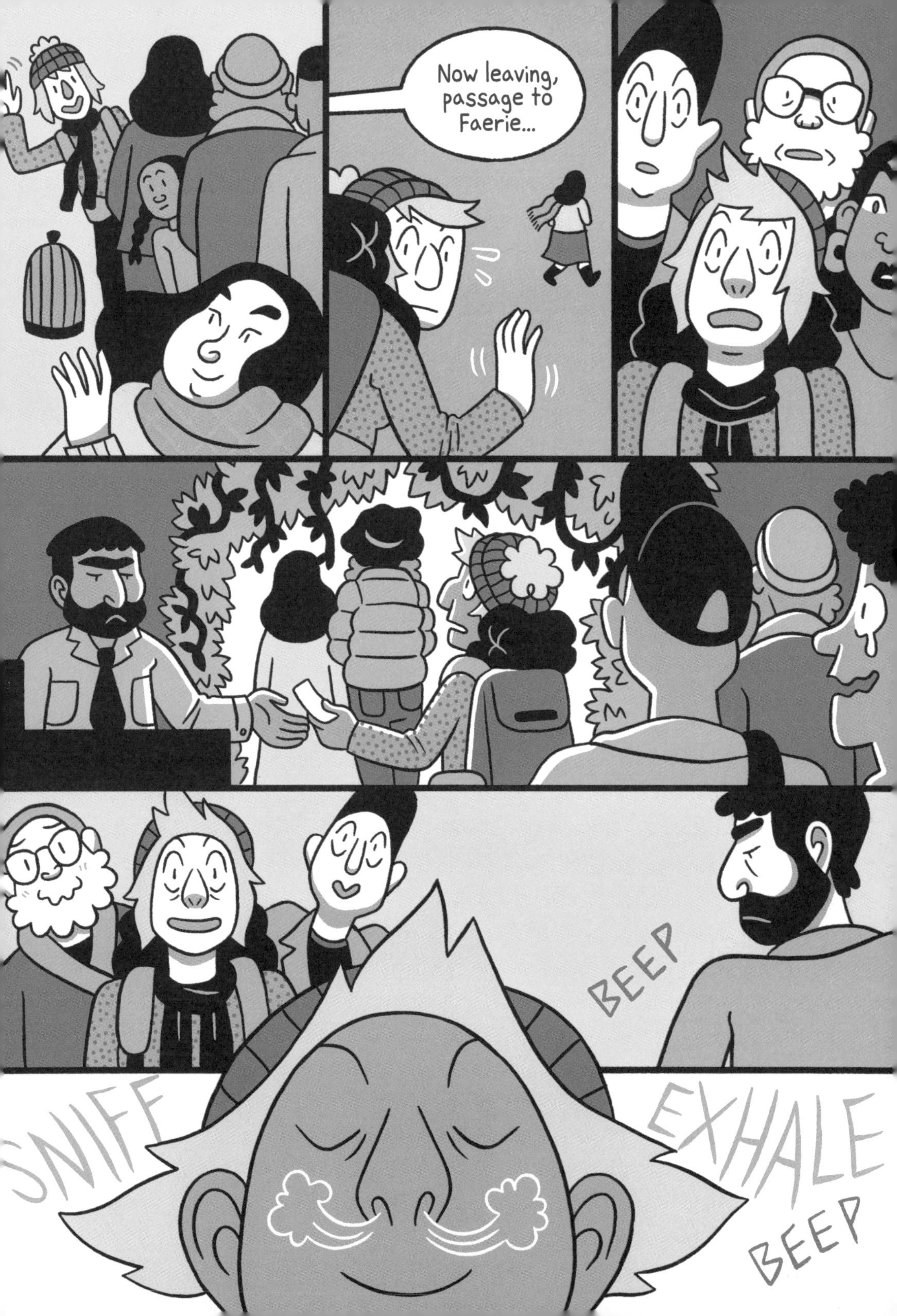
Now leaving, passage to Faerie...
BEEP
SNIFF
EXHALE
BEEP

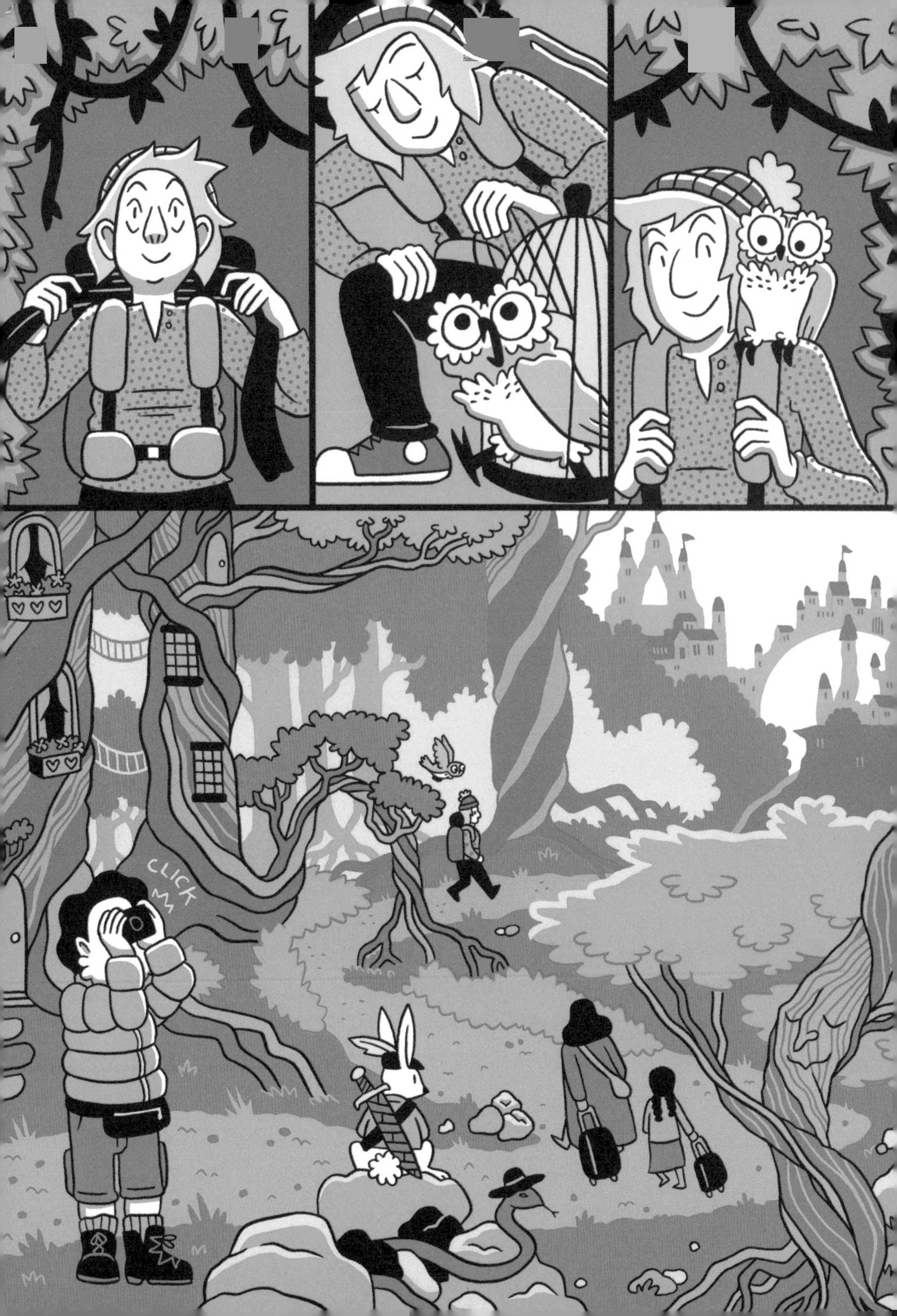
CLICK

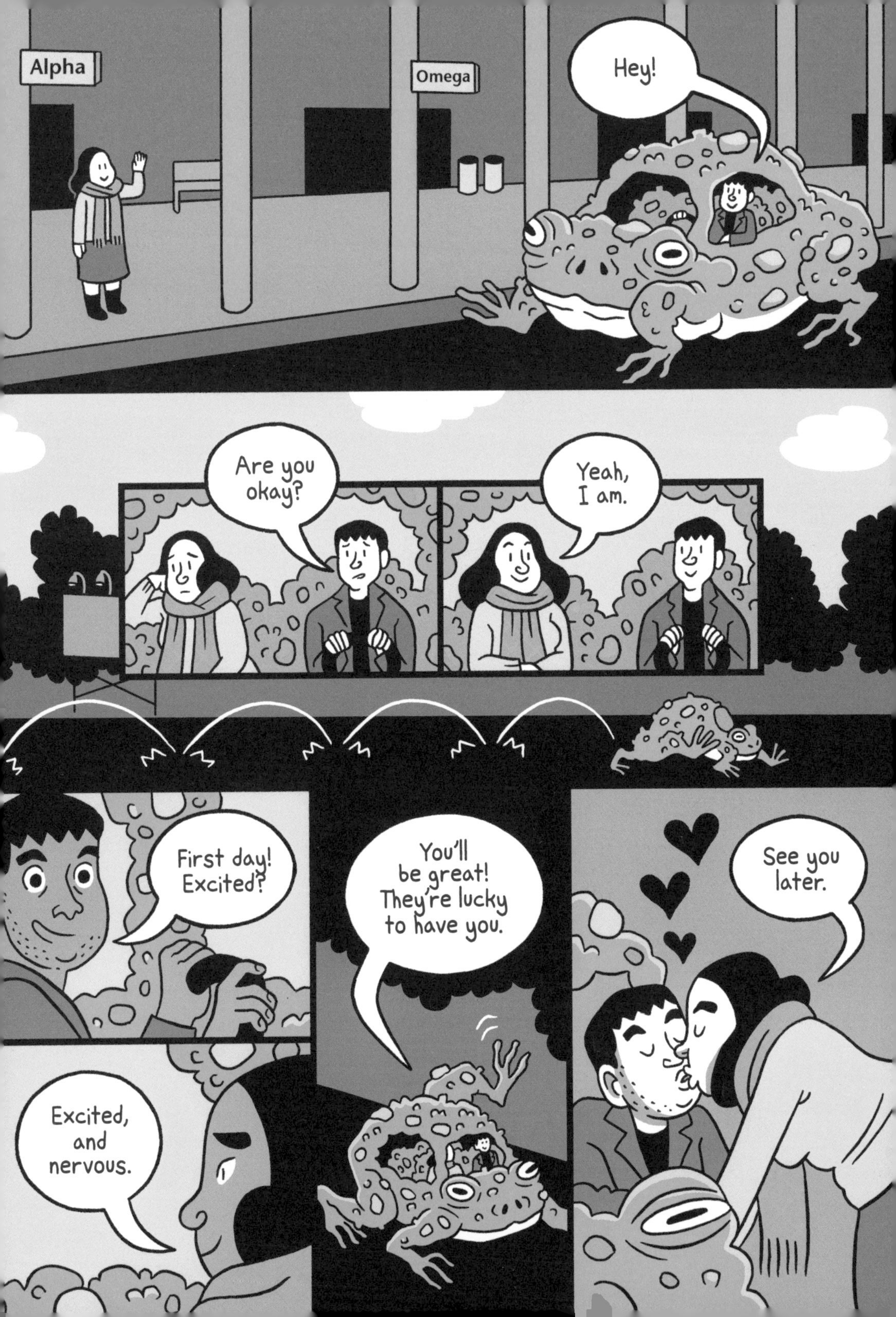
Alpha
Omega
Hey!
Are you okay?
Yeah, I am.
First day! Excited?
Excited, and nervous.
You'll be great! They're lucky to have you.
See you later.

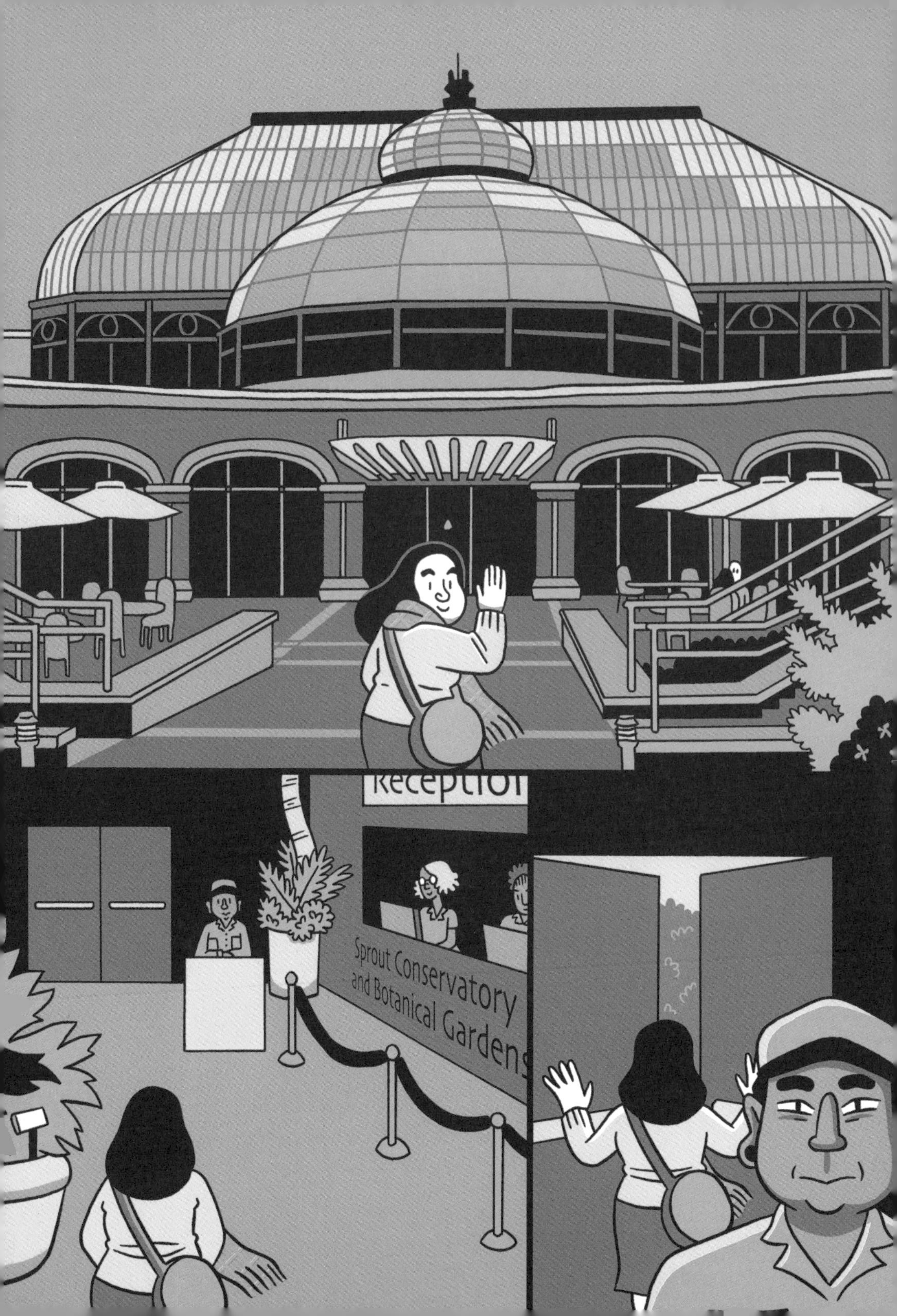
Sprout Conservatory
and Botanical Gardens

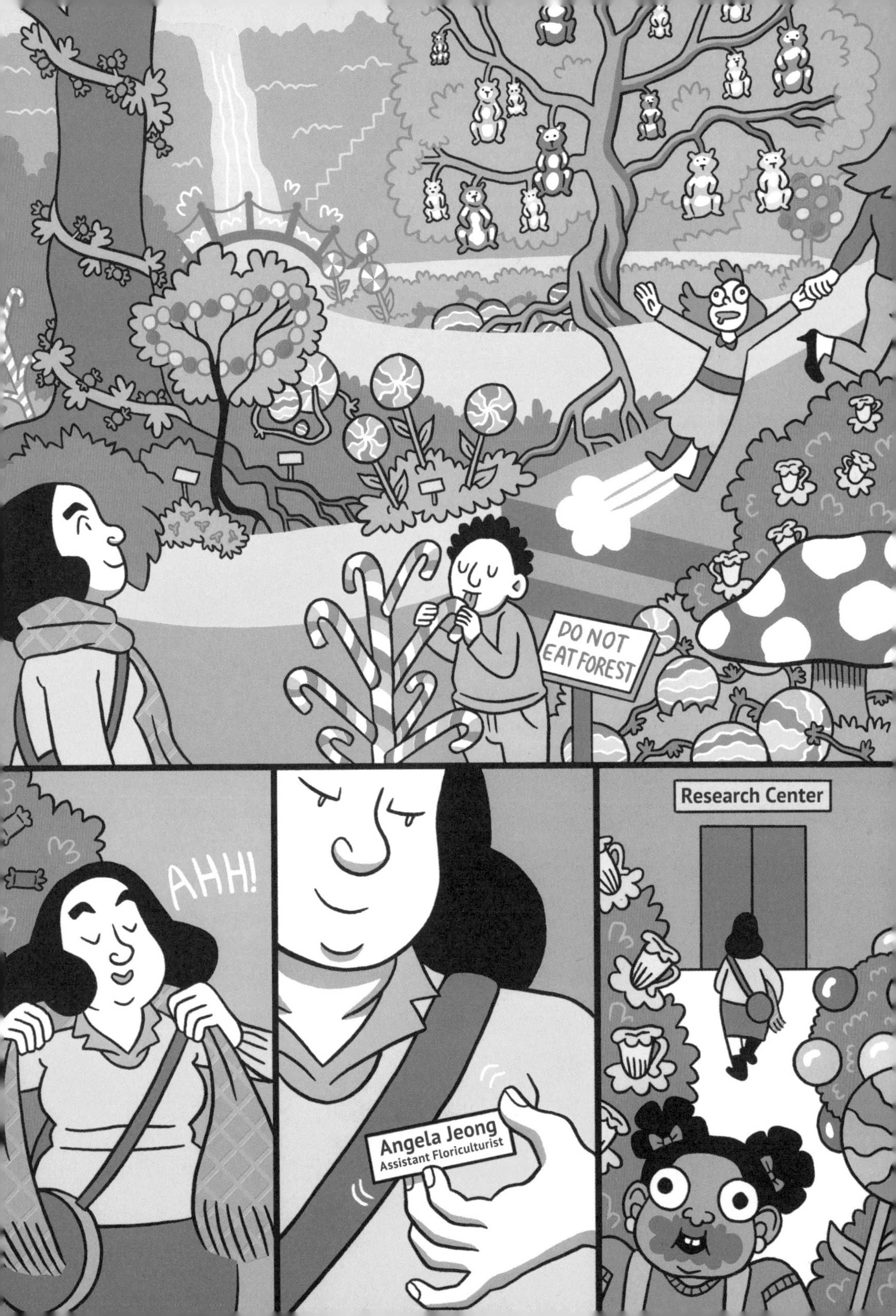
DO NOT EAT FOREST
AHH!
Angela Jeong
Assistant Floriculturist
Research Center

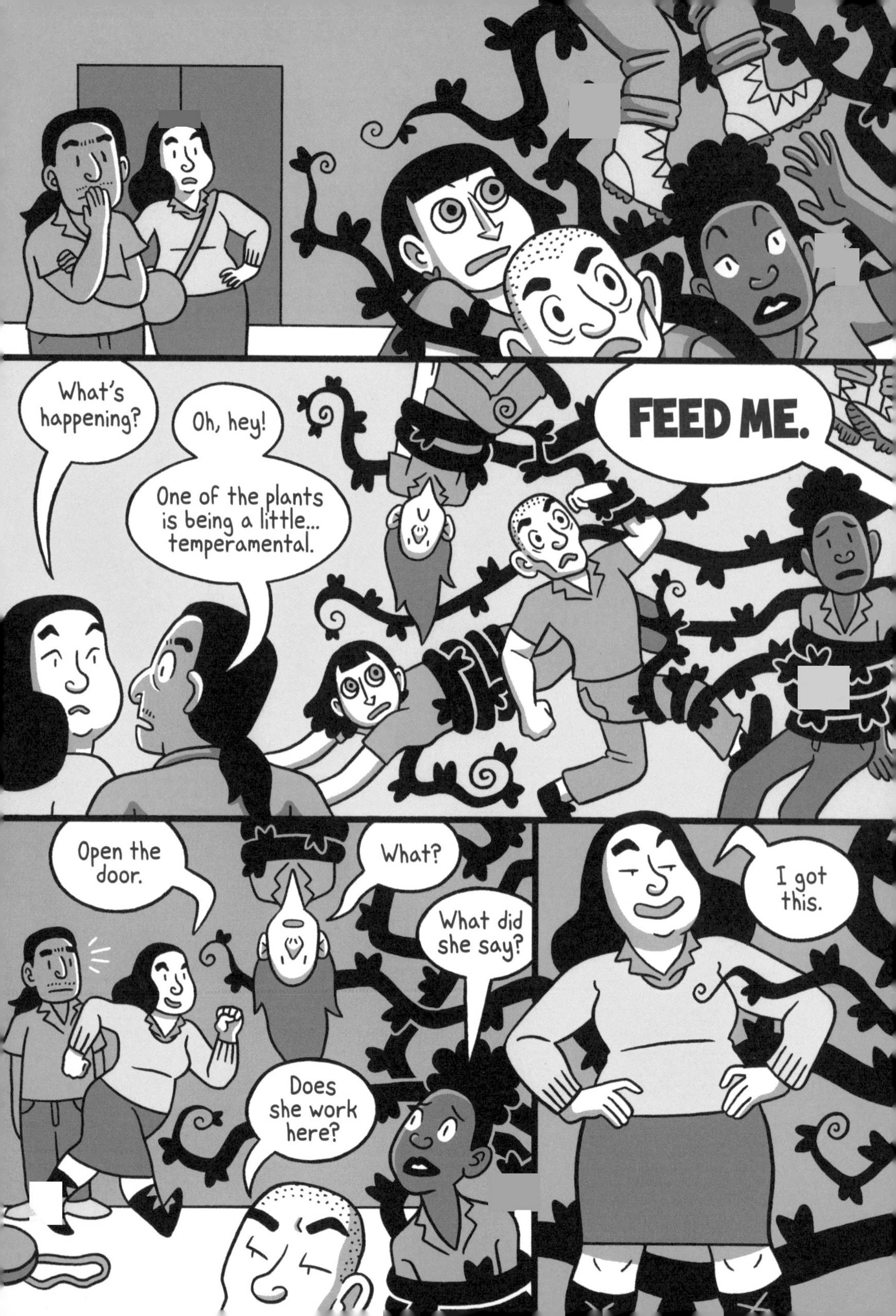

What's happening?
Oh, hey!
One of the plants is being a little... temperamental.
FEED ME.
Open the door.
What?
What did she say?
Does she work here?
I got this.

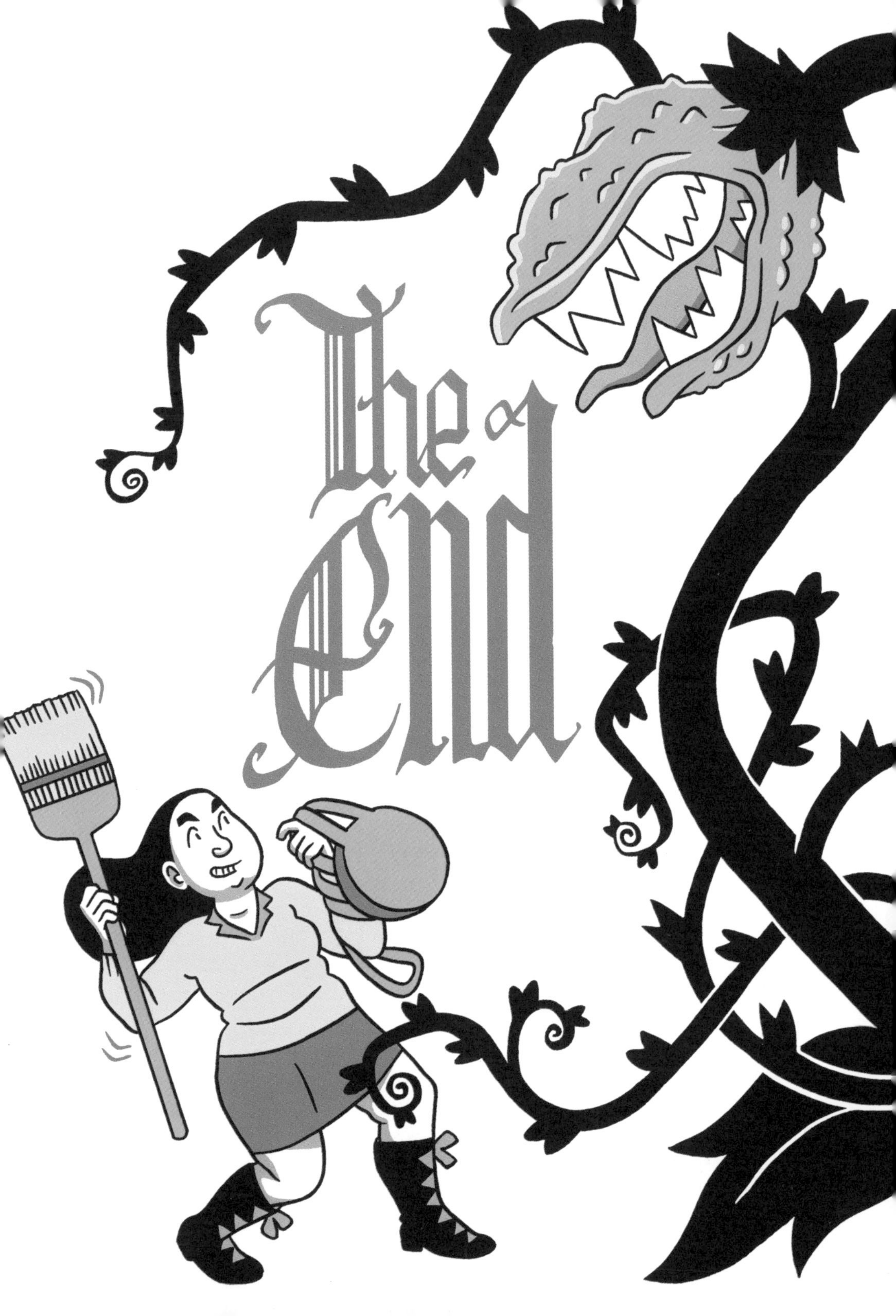
The End

Thank You

Jenn would like to thank her husband, Steve, and all of the friends and family members who hold her up and help her grow. She is particularly indebted to Stephanie Jordan-Rensing, her blood sister, and Dee Kanay, her fake sister. She would also like to thank mint chocolate chip ice cream and *Star Trek: Deep Space Nine.*

Sophie would like to thank her family and Patreon supporters for their encouragement throughout the making of this book, especially her husband, Carl. She is also grateful to the Tulsa Artist Fellowship for their support, without which this book would probably be coming out sometime in the 2030s. She would also like to add the disclaimer that all similarities to any current family members or former boyfriends is purely coincidental.

Jenn and Sophie would like to thank Chris and all those who helped bring this book to life at Top Shelf. They would also like to thank each other for their amazing aptitude for friendship, creative problem solving and puns. No, seriously, they are trapped in an endless feedback loop of mutual love and appreciation. Send snacks.

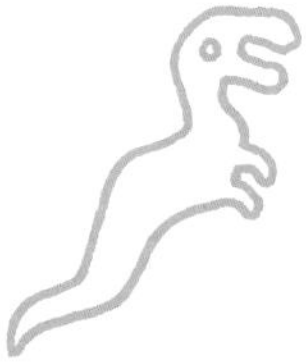

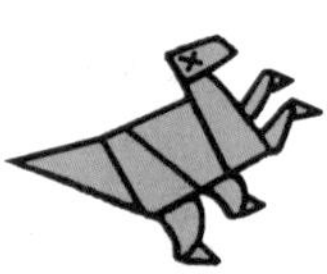